Pioneers in Canadian Criminology

Recent Books by John Winterdyk

Crime Prevention: International Perspectives, Issues and Trends (2017)

Canadian Criminology (third edition, 2016)

Youth at Risk and Youth Justice: A Canadian Overview (second edition, 2016)

Juvenile Justice: International Perspectives, Models and Trends (2015)

Adult Corrections in Canada (2013)

Human Trafficking:
Exploring the International Nature, Concerns, and Complexities (2012)

Pioneers in Canadian Criminology

Edited by

John Winterdyk

Rock's Mills Press
Oakville, Ontario
2017

Published by
ROCK'S MILLS PRESS
www.rocksmillspress.com

ISBN-13 (paperback): 978-1-77244-059-1
ISBN-13 (casebound): 978-1-77244-061-4

Unless otherwise indicated, photographs included in the text are provided by and with the permission of the authors and editor.
Cover image: www.freeimages.co.uk.

Library and Archives Cataloguing in Publication (CIP) data is available from the publisher. Contact us at customer.service@rocksmillspress.com.

Acknowledgements

In high school, I was fascinated with geography and history. For a while I thought I might end up studying one of these subjects when I went to university. However, some of the experiences and encounters I'd had as a young person resonated deep in my (sub)consciousness, pulling me instead to psychology and then criminology.

I share this brief personal anecdote because in many respects this book blends my past fascination with history with my eventual choice of criminology.

While completing some of my undergraduate courses in criminology, I became fascinated with Mannheim's 1971 book *Pioneers in Criminology*. I still have the book and it is clear from all the highlighting and notations that I spent a lot of time reading every entry, in some cases a number of times. Since Mannheim's book was published there has been no shortage of criminology and criminal justice texts gathering together classic articles by many of the leaders in the field. Yet, aside from the odd Festschrift or memorial volume devoted to the life and times of some recently deceased scholar or criminal justice "giant," no Canadian publication devoted to pioneers of Canadian criminology and criminal justice has yet emerged—until now.

I am extremely grateful that David Stover, the publisher of Rock's Mills Press, almost instantly embraced the idea of a book on the pioneers of Canadian criminology and criminal justice. I am also indebted to the numerous colleagues across the country who so kindly and willingly offered up names of those they thought I should consider including. Amongst the biggest supporters was Irvin Waller. In addition to agreeing to contribute to this volume, he offered up a bevy of names—some of which I realized after some research that I really should have thought of myself! I am also very appreciative of those pioneers still living who were willing to contribute to the book and who in fact encouraged me to follow through with this project. Their encouragement wasn't from a desire for personal acclaim or recognition but from an appreciation of the contribution the project would make to our field and the importance of carrying it out before the living memories forever fade. I am also touched and beholden to the fine scholars who agreed to prepare entries on their former mentors who are recognized pioneers in the field, and to others who agreed to prepare entries on pioneers within the legal, law enforcement, and correctional fields.

I give very special thanks to Nancy Wright (who also serves as an editor with the Canadian Criminal Justice Association, or CCJA) for her kind help with various editorial duties and for providing some suggestions that helped to further enrich this book. Although we have yet to meet in person, she has become a dear friend, and I have enjoyed following her journey into undertaking work on her Ph.D. during the preparation of this book.

I would be remiss if I did not mention my family and all who are dear to me. My life partner, Rose, has stood by through all the trials and tribulations that an author/editor goes through in trying to fulfill one's "role" as an academic. She has taken in stride the late nights, lost weekends, and other demands, which together add up to an incalculable number of hours that we could have—should have—shared. Her support and strength of character always find a way to ground me.

Finally, it is somewhat fitting that during the early stages of this book, Rose and I became an embodiment of this book's message—without the past there is no future—when we became first-time grandparents. We too are happy in the knowledge that something from our past will be carried forward into the future.

JOHN WINTERDYK

A Note on the Text

The contributors to this volume hail from a wide range of academic backgrounds and work in both of Canada's official languages. We have deferred to them in their choice of documentation styles and their preferred spellings of the names of academic institutions and certain other locations.

THE PUBLISHER

Contents

Foreword

John Winterdyk brought his vision to life with this genius collection—one which I wish I could have read much earlier in my own criminological journey! He has brilliantly compiled profiles of some of the key pioneers in Canadian criminology in this innovative book. In speaking of the significance of such a collection, he emphasizes the importance of history: "Knowing about our past," he writes, "is important if we are to understand the present and such knowledge may even provide a sign-post toward the future" (p. 4 of this book). In this sentiment he echoes a teaching expressed by Mohawk scholar and law professor Patricia Monture-Angus (1995:86): "You must know where you have been in order to know where you are going."

This book is first and foremost about "stories." As Winterdyk states, "My goal was to simply let [pioneers] tell 'their story' rather than try to ensure they followed a template" (p. 7). As such, it provides a historical timeline of Canadian criminology through the medium of those stories. This for me was so refreshing—learning through stories has always been one of the ways I've learned from my dad, who is a brilliant (and funny) storyteller. What is unique to this collection is the way the personal stories and histories complement the timeline of criminological development. Context helps us understand why these pioneers did what they did, studied what they studied, and also how criminology as a discipline in Canada came to be.

Learning these stories is an approach that one typically doesn't see within criminology. In many ways, this approach and the book itself serve to personify and situate the discipline. We hear of marriages, honeymoons, children, divorces, and other, sometimes unusual, life experiences: in their years before criminology, Gwynne Nettler worked as a Hollywood stuntman (p. 134), Patricia Brantingham played on her intercollegiate basketball team at Columbia University (p. 192), and Jim Hackler served as an assistant battalion surgeon in the U.S Army (p. 138). These personal aspects of peoples' lives are interwoven with their journeys to and within criminology, as well as their criminological research agendas, findings, and writings.

We sometimes glimpse the circumstances that led people to move great distances in order to pursue their studies or careers. Ezzat A.

Fattah, dissatisfied with the political and legal system in his native Egypt but unable to leave without an exit visa, yet found a way to do so by obtaining a scholarship at the University of Vienna. He boarded a plane with one suitcase, not to return to Egypt for 11 years. We also learn how confronting and overcoming challenges shaped the directions scholars took in their criminological journeys. François Fenchel shares with us insights into how Denis Szabo's years in the military, including becoming a cadet at age ten, influenced the direction of his later life, including developing "a contempt for authority and a rebelliousness against regulations" (p. 31). Or consider the case of Jo-Anne Wemmers, who took on the challenge of teaching a course not in her first language and had to write out her lecture notes in response to student complaints, only to turn those notes into a best-selling book (p. 124)! And so we glimpse people's aspirations and the drives behind those aspirations—how their lives shaped their work and their work shaped their lives.

Some pioneers contributed to many different areas of criminology, including various subfields or complementary disciplines such as victimology, while others were more "area-specific," making their contributions in defined areas such as policing or corrections. Reading pioneers' stories reveals the many approaches—applied and theoretical—that one can take to criminology. Thus this book reflects how there is room for various ways of carrying out criminological research, all contributing in their own ways to the path criminology has taken in Canada.

Another theme present throughout this collection is the trajectory of influence of mentors and teachers. Many of the contributors note how they were inspired by those who came before. Marc Le Blanc notes how Denis Szabo grabbed his attention "with his enthusiastic presentation" and "unconventional dress" (pp. 84–85). François Fenchel also reflects on his experience learning from Denis Szabo, and describes how he remembers the way Szabo presented his ideas even more than "what was actually presented": "It was his personality that fascinated me" (p. 30). Fenchel describes the collection of photographs in Szabo's office that captured not only his travels around the world but what he "had undertaken in the name of the discipline"—"a reflection and the story of his life" (p. 30). Fenchel's words brought to mind the first time I walked into Dr. Irvin Waller's office, with Waller explaining the trajectory of crime prevention through Canadian history, beginning with a pamphlet on crime prevention through social development and leading all the way to the real-world policy changes over which he had such a major influence (covered in Chapter 13 of this book). Waller's office also featured pictures of him around the world in various locations where he has given presentations on smart crime policy—and influenced government leaders to make change.

I've had the honour of working with three pioneers whose work is reflected in this collection: Rick Linden, who was a member of my thesis committee; John Winterdyk, who was a reader on my thesis; and, of course, Irvin Waller, head supervisor of my Ph.D. work, who had and continues to have a major impact on my life. In reading this book, I came to learn more about those I have worked with, including the story of what brought my thesis advisor to criminology and what motivates him to change the world. I was also astonished to read that it is his way of measuring incarceration rates that is now the international standard—rates and figures that I show every year to my criminal justice students! This fact also triggered me to reflect on the great humility of many of these pioneers.

We don't always hear about how many times teachers go out of their way to help students, or the sheer amount of compassion many have had for students and others. In this collection, Haggerty, Doyle, and Chan note how Richard V. Ericson "was known among friends as a person of great human compassion as well as possessor of a sharp sense of humor" (pp. 167–68). He was someone who went "above and beyond" for students, including helping a student who found himself temporarily homeless (p. 168).

I remember countless times when Irvin went above and beyond the call of duty as my thesis supervisor, helping me to get my first publications, guiding me step-by-step through the process of publishing, and recommending me as a speaker for conferences or other events. In particular, I remember walking into his office for one thesis meeting. When he saw the stressed look in my eyes, he asked, "Have you been jogging?" I replied, "I've been so busy reading and writing I haven't had time." In the end, his only recommendation that day was "to go jogging." Irvin knew how important athletics was for me, and he also believes in the importance of balancing intellect and exercise. He would also remind me to go jogging before presentations when I was travelling. I still follow this invaluable advice today, and now I find myself giving the same advice to my students!

Marc Le Blanc tells us that he "had enormous fun" during his career and still does, and wishes "the same to future generations of criminologists" (p. 103). His reflection reminds me of something I have recognized in my own evolving career, still as a junior criminologist: the importance of encouraging and supporting those next generations—our students! This was something that was embodied in every single meeting and class I had with my Ph.D. supervisor. He has always been an advocate for students, recognizing that they will carry on the important work of reducing harm in this world. While honouring those who came before, we must also remember the importance of supporting students on their journey. We must motivate them, encourage them to follow their passions, let them know that they "can do it"—that they can make a difference in this world. This was the best thing that Irvin did for me, and it is something I will continue to pass on to my students. As Irvin writes in this collection—this is something he also modelled and relayed to me—"Use your power, of which you may not yet be aware" (p. 188).

Finally, through reading this collection you will also come to see the interconnectedness of people's stories—the interwoven paths of many of the pioneers, be it through mentoring, researching or publishing together, having neighbouring offices, or crossing paths in their universities' shared spaces or computer labs. As Winterdyk observes, "The criminology/criminal justice community is not only small but closely linked and intertwined" (p. 288). While the stories in this book are those of individuals, they also represent a collective story—one of triumphs, passions, hardships, and success—a story which will continue, with its roots traced back to these original pioneers. We must remember that it is the criminology students of today who will continue that story. How do you want them to carry that legacy forward? To that end, this book should serve as a true inspiration.

LISA MONCHALIN

References

Monture-Angus, P. (1995). *Thunder in My Soul: A Mohawk Woman Speaks*. Halifax: Fernwood Publishing.

Pioneers in Canadian Criminology

Introduction

As academic disciplines, Canadian criminology and criminal justice have a rich and varied albeit comparatively short history. It was just over 50 years ago that the first criminology program was established at the Université de Montréal. Aside from a growing number of tributes occasioned by the passing of key academics and practitioners in the field and the odd *Festschrift* (a publication honouring an academic scholar, presented during his or her lifetime), we have no consolidated account of the legacy of the pioneers who have helped forge these disciplines.

One of the key challenges in conceptualizing this book was to decide on a precise meaning to the term *pioneer*. In the end, the selection criteria for this book encompass individuals who are recognized by their peers as having been among the first important players in the development of Canadian criminology or criminal justice as a field of inquiry.

Even as a high school student I was intrigued by history and in retrospect am somewhat surprised that I did not end up studying the subject upon entering university. However, my practicum placement as director of Project D.A.R.E. ("Developing through Adventure, Recreation, and Education") while studying psychology is what made the difference for me. I became fascinated with the topic of youth-at-risk and, upon the advice of one of my professors, ventured off to Simon Fraser University (SFU) to further my studies in the then-fledgling discipline of Canadian criminology.

At the time, SFU offered one of the only criminology programs in the country. I was fortunate to study not only under many of the field's trailblazers (some of whom are profiled in this book) but also to attend various international meetings that afforded me the distinct honour of meeting other "Canadian" pioneers, such as Denis Szabo, Irvin Waller, and Curt Griffiths, among others.

The word "Canadian" appears in quotation marks in the previous sentence because many of the early pioneers were and are first-generation Canadians, such as Szabo, or visiting professionals like Gwynne Nettler.[1] Their varied international experience has had a noticeable impact on forging Canadian criminological and criminal justice thought and practice. In fact, it was precisely their wide-ranging backgrounds that made Canadian criminology slow to forge its own identity. For example, even though the first criminology program was established in 1960, it was not until 1987 that the first edition of **Rick Linden**'s *Criminology: A Canadian Perspective* would appear (it is now in

[1] Nettler worked at the University of Alberta for about 25 years before returning to the United States.

its eighth edition). It was 1994 when **Jim Hackler** (whose profile is included in this collection) published a thematic introduction to crime and criminality within the Canadian context, his *Crime and Canadian Public Policy.*[2] These and subsequent textbooks on juvenile justice, law enforcement, criminal justice, and related topics began to mark a movement away from over-reliance on American materials. However, even before the emergence of Canadian-authored or -edited texts specific to the field of criminology, a number of notable titles appeared in the 1970s and early 1980s that were authored or edited mainly by Canadian sociologists (as opposed to criminologists) and focused more on the practical issues of criminal justice. Several of the more noteworthy books and articles in this group include the following:

- **William Thomas McGrath** (ed.) (1965; 1976). *Crime and Its Treatment in Canada.* Toronto: Macmillan. McGrath was the former executive director of the Canadian Criminology and Corrections Association and produced a number of original books that helped to forge a Canadian "identity" for the discipline. For example, in 1964 he published *Youth and the Law,* and in 1956 he wrote a controversial book which today is largely forgotten—*Should Canada Abolish the Gallows and the Lash?* — but which still makes for an interesting read.
- **Craig Boydell, Carl Grindstaff, and Paul Whitehead** (1972). *Deviant Behavior and Social Reaction.* Toronto: Holt, Rinehart and Winston. The edited collection included a compilation of addresses, lectures and essays on Canadian social problems, deviance, crime and corrections, and criminology (see Box 0.1).
- **Craig Boydell and Carl Grindstaff** (1974). Public opinion towards legal sanctions for crimes of violence. *Journal of Criminal Law and Criminology,* 65(1): 113–115. One of the first articles to study Canadian public opinion on crime severity.
- **Craig Boydell, Carl Grindstaff, and Paul Whitehead** (1974). *The Administration of Criminal Justice in Canada.* Toronto: Holt, Rinehart and Winston. An early overview of the administration of criminal justice in Canada.
- **Ingrid Connidas** (1979). Problems in the use of official statistics for Canadian Justice System research. *Canadian Journal of Criminology,* 21(4): 397–415. This article represents one of the first pieces to critically evaluate the use of official statistics when studying the Canadian criminal justice system.
- **Maurice Cusson** (1983). *Why Delinquency?* (translation by Dorothy R. Crelinsten of *Delinquants pourquoi?*). Toronto: University of Toronto

[2] In 1958 the then *Canadian Journal of Corrections* (later to become the *Canadian Journal of Criminology and Criminal Justice*) published an article with a similar theme, but the journal was not as widely read and the discipline had not yet truly established itself.

Press. This novel book was one of the first (if not *the* first) to deal with juvenile delinquency in Canada. However, the focus is more on explaining delinquency than discussing specific issues relating to juveniles in this country. Using a social structural and rationalist approach, Cusson argues that juvenile delinquents are not cold and calculating, but, rather, relatively confused and naïve individuals struggling to find their way in life and ending up for a variety of reasons engaged in delinquency to meet their need for excitement, defense of self-interests, identity formation, and to obtain certain goods.

- **Craig Boydell and Ingrid Connidas** (eds.) (1982). *The Canadian Criminal Justice System.* Toronto: Holt, Rinehart and Winston. This collection, edited by husband and wife, applied a social systems approach (i.e., such systems are open, interdependent, and have formal and informal goals as well as conflicting goals) to its coverage of the Canadian criminal justice system.
- **Augustine Brannigan** (1984). *Crimes, Courts and Corrections: An Introduction to Crime and Social Control in Canada.* Toronto: Holt, Rinehart and Winston. As the title indicates, a sociological perspective and range of excellent examples ground the Canadian content and demonstrate the overlap between the more scientific study of crime and the more practical study of the administration of criminal justice. The five sections offer a rich introductory overview of the main elements of the Canadian criminal justice system.

Shortly after I began my teaching career at a post-secondary institution, I was somewhat surprised to learn that most of my students knew more about the general history and evolution of criminology and criminal justice than they did about *Canadian* criminology and criminal justice, including key contributors to the Canadian discipline. Yet, as the reader will learn, criminology and criminal justice in Canada have a unique heritage that deserves to be captured for the benefit of current and future students of these fields.

Even though we now live in a fast-paced world in which history often takes a back seat, it is generally recognized that history still plays an important and relevant social role. Yet, unfortunately, we appear to define ourselves more by where we are going rather than where we came from. Who today knows, for example, which Canadian prime minister proposed the creation of the Supreme Court or established the Royal Military College of Canada (one of Canada's first post-secondary institutions), or the name of Canada's oldest university?[3]

It has been said that whoever controls the past controls the future. To deny

[3] Alexander Mackenzie, Canada's second prime minister between 1873 and 1878, proposed the creation both of a Canadian Supreme Court and of the Royal Military College. Saint Mary's University in Halifax is Canada's oldest university. It was established in 1802.

the wisdom of our past is to risk repeating our mistakes. Or, as George Orwell put it: "The most effective way to destroy people is to deny and obliterate their own understanding of their history." Knowing about our past is important if we are to understand the present and such knowledge may even provide a sign-post toward the future.

My interest in this project was further inspired by an earlier effort that saw the inclusion of eight short autobiographical sketches in the first edition of my

Box 0.1. Craig Boydell, Trailblazer

According to a profile of Professor **Craig Boydell** on the Western University website, Boydell was born and raised just outside New York City in Fair Lawn, New Jersey. He graduated with honours from Rutgers University and the University of Massachusetts, where he earned his M.A. and Ph.D. in sociology, specializing in criminology and demography.

He joined Western in 1969 and during his more than 30 years there was not only an active academic but also for 15 years the head coach of the Western Mustangs men's basketball team, during which time he led the team to one national championship, five conference championships, and four Ontario championships.

Like most foreign academics recruited by Canadian universities, he was hired by Western with a mandate to develop courses and programs with Canadian content during a period of major growth in the university's Faculty of Social Science. Throughout his academic tenure, Boydell established over a dozen new courses and also co-edited five textbooks.

Although he remained in the sociology department throughout his academic career, he played an instrumental role in developing Canadian-oriented criminal justice textbooks for rapidly growing criminology and criminal justice programs across the country.

textbook, *Canadian Criminology* (Toronto: Prentice Hall, 2000). Although the appendix was dropped in the second edition (2004), the significance of the initiative never left me. Liqun Cao (now teaching at the University of Ontario Institute of Technology [UOIT] in Oshawa) and I then compiled a 2004 collection featuring eight of the leading pioneers in comparative criminology and criminal justice. The resulting book, although perhaps not widely adopted, was a true labour of love. I learned a great deal from those who were included in the book. These two experiences reinforced my interest in one day repeating the exercise but with a focus this time on criminology and criminal justice pioneers who had spent most of their professional and/or academic careers living and working in Canada.

It has taken a few years for me to get around to this project—as my wife will attest, I was rather busy with other matters!—but now as my career is entering its twilight years I thought I should revisit and build on the initiative I started almost 20 years ago.

In order to create the framework for the book, I consulted with numerous colleagues across the country and invited them to provide me with a list of people they thought I should include. The call was well-received, but the resulting list was far more extensive than even I had imagined. Therefore, I used a slightly modified frequency count to identify who "absolutely" had to be included. After narrowing down the list in this way, I began to invite individual pioneers to contribute to the collection. Unfortunately, but understandably, not everyone approached was able to participate. Those few who were not able to participate cited such reasons as other pressing deadlines and competing academic and professional commitments that did not allow them the time necessary to prepare a chapter. Aside from those who had to beg off, some readers might wonder why certain other individuals are missing from the book. In some cases their names did not appear frequently enough in the survey; or, in other instances, I was unable to find anyone who could prepare the entry and could not locate sufficient information to prepare an entry on their behalf. Given the risk of inaccuracy in such cases, or of only providing cursory information about an individual, I chose instead to not to include them. While I would have liked to pay homage to each and every pioneer, certain decisions had to be made.

Once I was able to finalize the list of persons that I wanted and was able to include in the book, I decided—to compensate for not being able to prepare a richer accounting of certain pioneers—to include three chapters touching on pioneers in the Canadian criminal justice system as a collective group. Therefore, the book includes chapters on pioneers in Canadian law enforcement, in the legal/judicial system, and in corrections. Each of these chapters was prepared by an expert in that field.

As already noted, I could not include everyone who was mentioned and for various reasons I may have missed others who would justifiably qualify as pioneers. At the risk of overlooking someone, I will simply mention a few people who arguably should be included but who moved to institutions outside Canada and so, while occasionally still contributing to the Canadian criminology and/or criminal justice literature, are no longer as actively involved. Several names that might resonate with the reader include: **Julian Roberts,** formerly at the University of Ottawa but now at Oxford University; **Philip Stenning,** formerly at the University of Toronto but now at Griffiths University in Australia (see chapter 18); **John Hagan,** formerly at the University of Toronto and now at Northwestern University in the United States; **Ian Gomme,** formerly at Memorial University and several other Canadian universities, before moving to Colorado State University; and **Walter Dekeseredy,** most recently at UOIT but now at West Virginia University. They, among others, have gone on to distinguished academic careers outside Canada. John Hagan, for example, was the 2009 recipient of the prestigious Stockholm Award in Criminology.

Then there are those who might not have been quite so immersed in criminology or criminal justice, but who made some notable contributions to the field. Again, at the risk of overlooking some individuals, several names that readers might recognize include: **William Gordon West** (recognized for his work in the area of juvenile justice and the notion that what differentiates "hard-core" delinquents from non-delinquents is their marked need for stimulation); **Paul Gendreau** (a correctional psychologist who in addition to establishing the Centre for Criminal Justice Studies at the University of New Brunswick in 1995 also received international recognition for his studies of the criminal justice system); **Robert R. Ross** (an international authority on offender rehabilitation and the prevention of antisocial behavior); **Robert Ratner** (one of Canada's pioneers in critical criminology);[4] **Maurice Cusson** (like Gordon West, another Canadian academic pioneer in the area of juvenile justice); **Elizabeth (Liz) Elliott** (who, although not the first to formally introduce the practice of restorative justice within a criminal justice context in Canada, was the founding co-director of the Centre for Restorative Justice in the School of Criminology at Simon Fraser University and actively involved in prisons and restorative justice from 1981 until her passing in 2011);[5] **Holly Johnson** from the University of Ottawa;[6] **Carol LaPrairie** (one of Canada's best-known and best-loved Aboriginal justice scholars, who died in December 2010);[7] **Ross Hastings** (one of Canada's leading pioneers in crime prevention);[8] and **Mark Yantzi** (a probation officer from Elmira, Ontario) and **Dave Worth** (a Mennonite prison support worker), who in 1974 asked a judge for permission to arrange for two offenders to meet with victims of vandalism in order to see if reparations could be made—the first victim-offender reconciliation initiative in Canada.[9] The news of the success of their initiative quickly spread and garnered international attention.

[4] See *Canadian Journal of Criminology and Criminal Justice,* 2006, 48(5): 647–662.

[5] It is noted that the principles of restorative justice had long been practiced by Canada's Aboriginal peoples but social and cultural history along with politics delayed the acknowledgment of these principles within the purview of the formal Canadian criminal justice system. For a more detailed accounting see Curt Griffiths (1996), Sanctioning and healing: Restorative justice in Canadian aboriginal communities, *International Journal of Comparative and Applied Criminal Justice,* 20(2): 195–208.

[6] She was principal investigator of Statistics Canada's first national survey on violence against women and serves as a coordinator of the International Violence against Women Survey and as a member of the UNECE Task Force on Violence against Women Surveys.

[7] See Christopher Murphy and Philip Stenning (2014), *Canadian Journal of Criminology and Criminal Justice,* 56(4): 383–389.

[8] On February 16, 2016 Canada lost a pioneer of evidence-based and compassionate crime prevention. As Irvin Waller commented, Ross Hastings was "an active and respected voice in local, national, and international crime prevention efforts. He was the inaugural Chair of the National Crime Prevention Council and the founding co-director of the University of Ottawa Institute for the Prevention of Crime. He was a committed advocate for community-based crime prevention and at-risk youth, advising a range of agencies including the European Commission, the RCMP, the Ontario Provincial Police, and the International Centre for the Prevention of Crime."

[9] Unfortunately, after operating for some 20 years, in 2004 the program ceased to operate due to a lack of funding. Until then it had been the longest running program of its type in North America.

Although I provided basic guidelines for those contributors who were able and willing to prepare their own entries, my goal was to simply let them tell "their story" rather than try to ensure they followed a template. In this way, I think each has created a nuanced account of their career which could not otherwise have been captured. In my "Closing Thoughts," I offer some reflective comments.

One can sense a certain level of pride but also humility about the work that they've done among those who prepared their own entries. I think the reader will also become attuned to the personal pleasure and satisfaction that the contributors reflect in their chapters. In learning how active they've been, I am deeply honoured by their willingness to make the time to contribute to this project.

Students who are still in the early phases of their academic careers may not fully appreciate what it takes to attain the status enjoyed by the people represented in this volume. Yet, upon reading the entries, the reader will quickly come to recognize the level of commitment every pioneer has given to his or her career. But none of the profiles dwell on that level of commitment and dedication. The omission is not intentional but if I reflect on my own academic career, it is perhaps a by-product of the unique, if not extraordinary, environment in which we work. While we might admire or even be in awe of what those represented here have accomplished, there is no doubt that it has come at some personal cost, including family sacrifices. Yet, as one might expect, none of them has ever complained about how tirelessly they work(ed).

Although I did not ask the contributors to provide a complete elaboration of their CVs, the reader will quickly appreciate the volume of work they have all engaged in. Where possible, I have selectively noted key publications.

Canada is a socially and culturally diverse nation made up of settlers and Aboriginal peoples. Most of the founding pioneers in Canadian criminology and criminal justice came to this country from somewhere else. Their eclectic backgrounds fueled the development of a unique identity for Canadian criminology and criminal justice, one that is increasingly recognized internationally and that contrasts to the historically more provincial approach in the United States. The work of the pioneers embodies an overarching degree of optimism that Canadian criminology and criminal justice have already "come a long way" and, by extrapolation, hint at considerable opportunity for those interested in pursuing a career in either field (see, for example, the closing comments of Paul and Patricia Brantingham in chapter 14). What is perhaps most heartening is the sense that students no longer need to venture far afield to obtain a quality education in criminology or criminal justice.

Something else that shines through while reading the stories of the people represented in this book is the fact that they are eclectic, global, and multicultural in their viewpoints. These are qualities not all countries can lay claim to, but which are part-and-parcel of a Canadian identity that is still being forged through a commitment to the multicultural reality of this country.

I would be remiss in not acknowledging the efforts of those contributors to this anthology who assisted in preparing entries for those pioneers who for one reason or another were themselves unable to participate, as well as those who helped write the chapters on some of the key pioneers within law enforcement, the legal and judiciary system, and in corrections. And, finally, an expression of deep appreciation is certainly owing to authors Michael Weinrath and Steve Kohm, who have provided an overview on the discipline itself. It is clear from their first chapter that criminology and criminal justice programs have flourished over the past half-century.

It bears noting that while I considered organizing the book alphabetically, regionally, or chronologically, in the end (the opening chapter and three final chapters aside), the (auto)biographies are presented in a somewhat randomized order with the hope that no one will feel slighted in any way. That said, the early chapters include pioneers primarily from eastern Canada and in particular Quebec, while the remaining entries cover the rest of Canada. The book concludes with some thoughts about the project and future aspirations.

Some observers suggest that the proliferation of criminology and criminal justice programs across the country speaks to changed priorities in Canadian society, with concerns over public safety, crime prevention, and transnational crimes such as terrorism, human trafficking, and identity theft figuring more prominently. For example, in the past decade, public opinion surveys show that Canadians no longer feel as safe as they once did; yet, fortunately and perhaps ironically, those fears are largely misplaced. As most readers are likely aware, official crime rates in this country have been declining since the mid-1990s. Taking a more positive view, the growing number of criminal justice and criminology programs reflects the evolution of the criminal justice system. In addition to criminal justice system staff members receiving much more intensive academic and professional training, we've also seen a diversification of roles across the criminal justice continuum. For instance, there has been growth in the number of people employed by private security firms, expansion of specialized policing units (e.g., domestic violence, hate crime, cybercrime, human trafficking, etc.), and diversification of the judicial system (e.g., drug courts, domestic violence courts, alternative dispute resolution models, sentencing circles, mental health courts, etc.). And within the field of corrections there have also been major changes, including the introduction of youth justice programs, electronic monitoring, specialized programs for Aboriginal offenders, adult alternatives measures programs, and so on.

While no criminal justice system is perfect, a review of relevant research shows that not only are Canadian criminology and criminal justice students recognized as well-trained, but our criminal justice system itself is the envy of many countries. For example, Canada pioneered the use of restorative justice within a criminal justice context; the Royal Canadian Mounted Police have often been sought out by other countries for their expertise; numerous current and former correctional officials have provided their knowledge and expertise internationally; and we have had former lawyers serve in very high positions, including Louise Arbour, who served as the first chief prosecutor of the International Criminal Tribunals for the former Yugoslavia and Rwanda.

Finally, to borrow a phrase from my *Lessons from International/Comparative Criminology/Criminal Justice* (2004), "this anthology should not be viewed as an exercise in narcissism or egotism" (p. 4). Rather, it offers some of the leading experts and pioneers in the field the opportunity of sharing their stories in the hope of providing current and, perhaps more importantly, aspiring scholars with the motivation to engage in similar work.

JOHN WINTERDYK

ONE
A History of Criminology and Criminal Justice Programs in Canada

Steven Kohm and Michael Weinrath

Introduction

According to one recent study, there are 75 clearly discernible criminology and criminal justice B.A., Honours, Masters and Ph.D. degree-granting programs across Canada (Gorkoff 2013). This total does not include the numerous one- and two-year college level programs that provide transfer credit, technical training, or both to Canadian students. Majors are abundant, and it is not an understatement to say that criminology/criminal justice programs are among the most popular degree programs on Canadian campuses today (Kohm, Gorkoff, Jochelson and Walby 2014). Surprisingly, this phenomenal growth and popularity has a relatively short history. Some 65 years ago, there were no standalone programs in criminology or criminal justice to be found in Canada's universities. While the roots of Canadian criminology could be found scattered among departments of law, sociology and social work, concerted efforts to establish coherent standalone programs did not gain momentum until the early 1960s. Since that time, the growth of the discipline has been nothing short of remarkable.

In this chapter we outline the beginnings, rise and recent rapid expansion of Canadian postsecondary criminology and criminal justice programs. We begin with a brief history of Canadian university programs in criminology and criminal justice studies before moving to some of the larger challenges currently facing the discipline and its future. The discipline, long subject to debate over whether its base should be more theoretical or applied, is now experiencing pressure to move away from scholarship toward a more practical, corporate model of education that aligns with broader shifts in Canadian postsecondary education (Chunn and Menzies 2006; Huey 2011). We assess the problems and prospects brought on by pressures internal and external to the discipline and conclude the chapter by speculating about the future of Canadian university criminal justice and criminology programs.

Before moving to our historical overview of university programs in criminology and criminal justice it is worthwhile emphasizing the challenges inherent in this undertaking. While it might seem an obvious and straightforward task, in reality, there are important conceptual difficulties in even delineating the object of our historical inquiry. Certainly, we include in our discussion university departments and academic units that are named "criminology" and/or "criminal justice." Some of these academic units are administratively designated departments while others are centres, schools, or institutes with both teaching and research functions. However, there are several other academic units in Canadian universities with different names that are engaged in the study of crime and criminal justice. For example, there are programs in Police Studies, Legal Studies, Law and Society, and Justice Studies, to name but a few examples of the range of academic units that make up what we refer to more broadly as the "justice disciplines" (Kohm et al. 2014). While it can sometimes be difficult to discern which of these differently-named programs is centrally engaged in the work of criminology and criminal justice studies, our object of inquiry becomes even murkier when we consider the many distributed, interdisciplinary programs that exist across and between several different departments or academic units. We can find many examples of distributed interdisciplinary programs leading to certificates and degrees in criminology, justice studies, policing, and so on. Moreover, how do we count the many sociology departments that offer "streams" or "concentrations" in areas with names such as crime and community, deviance, and/or socio-legal studies? By way of example, and by no means an exhaustive list, some of the Canadian sociology programs which have such streams include the University of Brandon (Crime and Community), University of Waterloo (Legal Studies), and University of Saskatchewan (Aboriginal Justice). Add to this the many college-level programs in Policing and Justice that provide students with their first encounter with criminology and criminal justice studies, including two-year diploma programs found at numerous Ontario colleges, such as Community and Justice Services (e.g., Algonquin, Cambrian, Canadore, Centennial, Conestoga, Fleming, Georgian, Humber, Loyalist, Niagara, St. Clair, Sheridan, Mohawk, and St. Lawrence Colleges) and Police Foundations (e.g., Algonquin, Canadore, Centennial, Confederation, Georgian, Durham, Loyalist, Mohawk, Northern, Sault, St. Clair, Sheridan, and Seneca Colleges). Many of these programs facilitate university transfer credits and some have articulation agreements with university programs in criminology.[10] Furthermore, in recent years, a number of college programs in criminology and criminal justice have evolved into university programs (e.g., Mount Royal University in 2009;

[10] The Western Regional Criminology Articulation Committee (WRCAC) meets annually to discuss criminology and criminal justice programs in the four western provinces and to ensure consistency between college and university courses in the region and to facilitate transfer between institutions.

Vancouver Island University in 2009; University of the Fraser Valley in 2008; Algoma University in 2008) and others may soon follow. So, should college programs also be considered in our historical overview?

We contend that the history of criminology and criminal justice in Canada must consider these varied examples of programs emanating from diverse quarters in postsecondary education. In fact, the history of Canadian criminology and criminal justice can be read as a struggle over where best to place the study of crime and justice in our advanced education system. As noted above, our discipline has been characterized by intense debate about how best to balance the need for practical, applied education that can serve the needs of state agencies of justice while also accommodating scholarly aspirations for theoretical and methodological rigour and healthy critique of criminal justice policy (Chunn and Menzies 2006; Huey 2011). The result of this longstanding tension has been a tendency for the postsecondary study of crime and justice to become sometimes fractured and often contested among academics and practitioners in a variety of institutional locations. While we cannot point to a single watershed moment to exemplify this tension, such as the well-known demise of the Berkeley School of Criminology and the concomitant rise of the criminal justice education movement in the United States (see, for example, Morn 1995), we return to this theme of tension and fragmentation in our discussion of the history of the discipline in Canada and the broader issues facing postsecondary education in the twenty-first century.

Beginnings: 1950s, 1960s and 1970s

For students studying justice in Canada, *de rigueur* topics in first year include reference to two seminal federal government inquiries into Canadian corrections, the *Archambault Report* (1938) and the *Fauteux Report* (1956). Both are inextricably linked to the establishment of standalone Canadian university criminology and criminal justice programs (Parkinson 2008). Both recommended the development of programs in higher education that might better inform correctional policies through scientific research (Gorkoff 2013). The first innovative but ultimately failed attempt at such a department was initiated at the University of British Columbia (UBC) between 1951 and 1959 (Parkinson 2008). The creation of the program arose out of the B.C. Prison Commission report in 1950 which called for UBC to begin to offer training in criminology. Initially placed in the Department of Economics, Political Science and Sociology in the Faculty of Arts and Science, the reformist program had links to a new correctional institution and was focused on providing university education for criminal justice workers and research supporting policy development. The UBC criminology program was comprised of nine criminology courses, a B.A. and M.A. in criminology, a post-graduate diploma and several non-credit options for correctional staff

(Parkinson 2008:599). However, the UBC criminology program could not survive intra-departmental tensions between scholars advocating for a more academic approach, territoriality asserted by the School of Social Work and turnover of key advocates from the department's early days such as Elmer "Kim" Nelson, who had come from California and was a driving force in the development of the UBC program (Parkinson 2008:598). Also, playing a role in the demise of UBC Criminology was the fact that, fundamentally, there was little agreement among academics and professionals about the nature of the discipline of criminology: "Should the program be in the School of Social Work or the Faculty of Arts? Was criminology an academic field or an applied field?" (Parkinson 2008:604). Ultimately, a satisfactory compromise could not be negotiated at UBC and despite interest on the part of university administration and some faculty in developing a centre of criminology as envisioned by the *Fauteux Report*, the criminology program was shuttered and all but one course transferred to the School of Social Work (Parkinson 2008:605).

Gary Parkinson (2008) points out the irony of the timing of the demise of the UBC criminology program. The UBC program was discontinued just as developments in the field were gaining strength across Canada. For instance, what would eventually become Canada's flagship scholarly journal in the field, *The Canadian Journal of Criminology and Criminal Justice*, was launched in October 1958 as *The Canadian Journal of Corrections* (Parys 2014:48). Like the UBC program, the journal exemplified the tension between theory and practice. Articles appearing in the early volumes were primarily authored by practitioners drawn from agencies directly connected to government, social workers, clergy, and medical/psychiatric professionals. However, by the early 1960s, the journal became a venue in which to debate the formation of a more coherent scientific discipline of criminology (Szabo 1963:29). Following closely on the heels of the establishment of University of Montreal's Department of Criminology in 1960, the journal devoted a special issue in 1963 to a discussion of the new discipline and the possible establishment of a national institute of criminology (Parys 2014:49). Given the urgency with which the discipline of criminology developed in the years immediately following the closure of the UBC program, one can't help but consider this as a lost opportunity for that university. According to Robert Ratner (2006), a UBC critical criminologist who worked in the Department of Sociology, the failure of criminology at UBC to persist as a degree program was the result of a university that was "a conservative bastion, loathe to accommodate a new and potentially troublesome discipline" (p. 649). However, UBC established a certificate program in criminology—"a certain moneymaker for Continuing Studies" (Ratner 2006:649). The Criminology Certificate Program which ran between 1969 and 1982 "for the benefit of service personnel in law enforcement, corrections, and related occupational fields" was to be "less technical and more 'liberal' in intent, and inter-disciplinary in content" (Ratner 2014:149–150). Nevertheless, beyond briefly flirting with non-university credit for criminal justice professionals, UBC effectively ceased to offer postsecondary education in criminology on the eve of the great expansion of the discipline across Canada. According to the university's website, as of 2017 there were only a couple of faculty members in the Peter A. Allard School of Law at UBC who teach the occasional course in criminology and/or criminal justice.

In the two decades following the demise of the UBC criminology program, government pressure continued on universities to provide more academic training for those who might work in law enforcement and corrections, as well as to build the capacity for the development of rational public policy based on social science research in the newly imagined discipline of criminology. This culminated in federal funding in the 1960s and 1970s to establish several Canadian university centres of criminology. According to Gorkoff (2013:65), "it is safe to say that within these centres, modern Canadian criminology was born."

The interdisciplinary centres of criminology at the Universities of Montreal, Toronto and Ottawa were developed in the 1960s (Gorkoff 2013; Hackler 1994). Montreal (established in 1960) integrated several disciplines and was the first Canadian university to offer a B.A., M.A. and Ph.D. in criminology. Writing in 1963, founder **Denis Szabo** argued that criminology was in fact an autonomous science that should not be "subordinated to one of the traditional disciplines" (p. 30). **James Hackler** (1994) suggests that the early work of the Montreal criminologists was influential in progressive public policy in Quebec, including the promotion of more youth intervention. The approach of the Montreal centre was interdisciplinary and primarily theoretical, although Hackler (2006) notes that there were some more practical elements to the program, including training for correctional workers in the field. Szabo (1963:31) argued that criminological education at the university level "should be clearly interdisciplinary, closely interrelated with criminology practice and, finally, connected to fundamental and applied research." However, while Szabo (1963:37) believed that theory and practice should be integrated in a university criminology program, he believed that "criminological teaching, designed to train technicians within the scope of our discipline, must be organized outside of universities."

The University of Toronto Centre of Criminology (established in 1963) began as a research unit before establishing an M.A. program in 1971 (Doob 1983:256). An undergraduate program was established in 1981 and a Ph.D. program in 1989 (http://criminology.utoronto.ca/about-us-2/history). The early scholarly work emanating from the Centre of Criminology at the University of Toronto might be typified as less aligned with government departments and more critical of police and social institutions of control (Hackler 1994). It is also noteworthy that the University of Toronto's Centre of Criminology was founded by a legal scholar rather than a social scientist with sociological training (as was the case at the University of Montreal). Founding director **John Edwards** explained that the idea for the centre emerged out of a proposal he developed while teaching a course in criminology within the Faculty of Law at Dalhousie University in 1958–59 (Edwards 1982:850). He advocated "the establishment of regional institutes of criminology in selected Canadian universities" (Edwards 1982:850). Furthermore, Edwards' vision of criminology

> emphasised the need for such institutes to adopt a broad interpretation of criminology, not limited just to the study of penal institutions and correctional practices, but including the study of crime, the criminal law, the administration of criminal justice, deviant behaviour, sentencing and the treatment of offenders, as well as the contributions of the forensic and medical sciences to an understanding of the phenomenon of crime. (Edwards 1982:850)

Edwards was insistent that the Toronto Centre of Criminology be an independent academic unit "outside such divisions as the Faculty of Law, the Faculty of Arts and Science, and the departments of Sociology and Psychology, any one of which might rightfully claim to have a special responsibility for the development of criminology as an offshoot from its particular discipline" (Edwards 1982:852). Edwards's interdisciplinary vision ensured that a broad range of academic disciplines contributed to the work of the centre in the first two decades of its operation including "history, economics, law, sociology, psychology, philosophy, medicine, biology, anthropology, political science, computer science, religious studies, pharmacology, and clinical biochemistry" (Edwards 1982:852–853). In time, the Centre of Criminology would offer B.A., M.A., and Ph.D. programs in criminology and boast an impressive record of research from internationally respected criminologists such as **Anthony Doob**, who was recently honored by the *Canadian Journal of Criminology and Criminal Justice* for his decades-long and highly influential body of criminological research with a special issue titled "A Festschrift in Honour of Anthony N. Doob" (Sprott and Roberts 2013).

Not surprisingly, given the disciplinarily background of its founder, Hackler (2006) notes that the early research at the University of Toronto Centre of Criminology was largely directed toward law. However, "the centre later reflected the influence of informal links with the Clarke Institute of Psychiatry and has conducted research on the police, the courts and other agencies of control in Canada" (Hackler 2006). Moreover, a number of criminologists forged links with the University of Toronto Centre for Addiction and Mental Health and the Centre of Criminology soon developed an international reputation for its research on issues of social policy and drugs (Hackler 2006). In 2011, the University of Toronto renamed its criminology unit The Centre of Criminology and Sociolegal Studies "to better reflect the scope of its research and focus" (http://criminology.utoronto.ca/about-us-2/history).

A department of criminology was established at the University of Ottawa in 1967 by Dr. **Tadeusz Grygier**, a Polish-born psychologist who obtained his Ph.D. from the London School of Economics in 1950. When the idea of a new discipline of criminology was debated in the pages of the *Canadian Journal of Corrections* in 1963, Grygier contributed to the debate from his position at the University of Toronto within the School of Social Work and Department of Psychology. He argued for an empirical and scientific approach to criminology that followed "the inductive-deductive methods of modern science" (Grygier 1963:42). Such an approach would be focused on the "scientific control of criminal behavior" and rely upon "prediction methodology, careful experimentation, and statistical analysis" (Grygier 1963:43).

According to Grygier's biography, he was initially hired by the University of Toronto in 1960 to establish a criminology centre. However, despite obtaining funding from the government of Ontario and writing a lengthy proposal "the university arranged a committee chaired by the Dean of Law, and appointed as the new Centre's director a distinguished professor of law, who had no interest in empirical criminological research" ("Dr. Tadeusz Grygier" 2014). Nevertheless, by 1967 Grygier was able to realize his lifelong dream of establishing what he believed was the world's first department of *applied* criminology at the University of Ottawa instead of Toronto ("Dr. Tadeusz Grygier" 2014). Rather than taking the form of a centre or institute, the University of Ottawa established a program in criminology with a master's degree in 1967. The program initially focused on applied work, at one time offering a master's degree in correctional practice. At the outset, Ottawa was noted for having a truly international faculty, recruiting faculty members from places such as Sri Lanka, Poland, and the United Kingdom (Hackler 1994).

In the 1970s, Simon Fraser University (SFU) in suburban Vancouver became the next major criminology centre, seizing the opportunity when UBC hesitated to restart their program (Griffiths and Palys 2014). The proposal for a criminology program was developed in 1972 by Dr. **Ezzat Fattah**, then an Associate Professor of Criminology at the University of Montreal who was a one-time Cairo prosecutor (Griffiths and Palys 2014). Fattah envisioned the new criminology program as both interdisciplinary and practical in its focus. Griffiths and Palys (2014:19) describe the vision as one that "required both horizontal and vertical integration; the horizontal integration would come from a balanced attention to the partial knowledge emerging from criminology's contributing disciplines (psychology, sociology, psychiatry, law, and so on) while vertical integration would come from the mixture of theory and practice."

The criminology program at SFU was approved in 1975 and initially only offered an undergraduate degree because, in Fattah's view, this better suited the needs of the local criminal justice workforce and prospective practitioners of justice (Griffiths and Palys 2014:20). The proposed curriculum was ambitious and included 44 courses that provided undergraduate students with the ability to choose areas of concentration or interest while still receiving a basic overview of all aspects of crime and the criminal justice system (Griffiths and Palys 2014:22). Notably, there were some internal objections to the development of criminology at SFU. The Department of Sociology and Anthropology objected to what it saw as significant overlap with its own course offerings in the area of deviance and socialization (Griffiths and Palys 2014:23). Despite these concerns, as well as other concerns expressed in the SFU student newspaper, the School of Criminology at SFU became established as one of the largest undergraduate and graduate criminology programs in the country with 27 full-time faculty drawn from a range of disciplines including psychology, sociology, law, biology, political science, geography, and anthropology (Griffiths and Palys 2014:16). Arguably unique to the Canadian postsecondary environment, Canadian criminology and criminal justice programs were among the first to be interdisciplinary in nature. This was in part due to the diversity of early staff (e.g., Szabo, Grygier, and Fattah), who were attracted and hired by the various universities offering criminology/criminal justice programs at the time.

While Quebec, Ontario and British Columbia saw the development of interdisciplinary centres of criminology, in both Alberta and Manitoba it was sociology departments that led the charge in developing regional centres of criminological research and teaching in the 1970s. At both Prairie institutions, undergraduate criminology degree programs found an institutional home within sociology departments. At the University of Alberta, an applied M.A. degree in criminal justice was established in 1975, which Hackler (2006) notes "is the only applied program in the Faculty of Arts." In 1973, a School of Human Justice was established at what was then the Regina campus of the University of Saskatchewan (Greenberg 2014:121). Hackler (2006) describes the research and teaching within the Regina school as focused on criminal justice. Greenberg's (2014) overview of the development of the program suggests it was broad and interdisciplinary but with significant roots in social work, as well as the social sciences. Additionally, through this time period, courses related to crime, deviance and social control were offered through many sociology departments across Canada although none offered a major or degree called criminology.

The 1980s: Community Colleges and Stability

The 1980s saw few new university programs developed in criminology and criminal justice. At this time, Simon Fraser, Toronto and Montreal were generally regarded as the three top centres for criminological research and education (Hackler 1994). Nevertheless, criminology programs based in sociology departments outside these three urban centres thrived. The University of Alberta launched a B.A. in criminology in 1982 (Hackler 2006). The Alberta B.A. was notable in that it was administratively located in the Department of Sociology and was comprised of courses in that department, yet it also required a significant number of courses drawn from other departments such as Psychology. The program also included a field practicum component giving the degree a more applied focus than the comparable B.A. in sociology. Similarly, at the University of Winnipeg, an interdisciplinary distributed major named Studies in Justice and Law Enforcement was established in 1979 and drew from courses primarily in the Departments of Psychology, Sociology and Political Science that were related to criminal behavior, deviance and law. In 1980, the newly established University of Regina relocated the Human Justice program to the Faculty of Social Work (Greenberg 2014:122). As well, through this period, various community colleges (e.g., Douglas, Capilano, Langara, and BCIT [British Columbia Institute of Technology]), as well as the Justice Institute of British Columbia (JIBC) throughout British Columbia, provided students with opportunities to obtain certificates or diplomas in criminology or in some cases to complete university transfer credits toward a criminology B.A. degree at Simon Fraser.

Postsecondary studies in criminal justice, on the other hand, appeared to be more centred in community colleges in this period (Gorkoff 2013). Mount Royal College in Calgary was not yet a full degree-granting university in this period but it did offer diplomas and certificates in policing and corrections as well as transfer credits in criminology (King and Winterdyk 2014: 137). Similar justice-related programming was offered through Grant McEwan College and Medicine Hat College in Alberta at this time (King and Winterdyk 2014:137). Likewise, in Ontario and Quebec, community colleges offered diplomas and certificate programs in a variety of policing, criminal justice and social services fields and many developed articulation agreements with universities in the region.

So, while the 1980s was marked by little growth in criminology and the entrenchment of criminal justice studies within community colleges in many regions of Canada, changes and expansion of the discipline were just over the horizon in the 1990s.

1990s and 2000s: Explosion in Programs

In the 1990s and continuing into the 2000s there was significant growth in Canadian university criminal justice and criminology programs. This was driven by two apparent movements in the field. The first was an upgrade in accreditation to many Canadian community colleges that became degree-granting institutions (Gorkoff 2013). Many of British Columbia's "university colleges" became designated universities including Fraser Valley, Vancouver Island, Royal Roads, Thompson Rivers, and Kwantlen Polytechnic. Elsewhere, Mount Royal University in Calgary emerged from its previous college structure to offer a B.A. program in justice studies. In Toronto, Ryerson Polytechnic Institute became a full-fledged degree granting university in 1990 and faculty in the Psychology Department quickly established a part-time justice studies B.A. program directed toward criminal justice practitioners in 1996 (Landau and Varma 2014:96). Secondly, during this time period a notable number of Canadian universities established criminology and criminal justice departments and/or programs. Motivated in part by large student enrolments, university administrators by and large supported faculty efforts to establish standalone programs such as the one at University of Winnipeg, renamed Criminal Justice in 2004 and reconfigured as a standalone department instead of a distributed major (Weinrath 2014). In 2002, the University of Ontario Institute of Technology (UOIT) became what was at the time Ontario's newest university, accepting its first students in 2003. UOIT established a B.A. degree in criminology and justice and an M.A. degree in criminology within its interdisciplinary Faculty of Social Science.[11] Similarly, York University's Department of Social Science began offering a B.A. degree in interdisciplinary criminology in 2003 while Wilfrid Laurier University at its Brantford campus began offering an interdisciplinary criminology B.A. in 2004 and an M.A. degree in 2011. Criminology and criminal justice programs quickly became among the most popular majors in Canadian universities (Kohm et al. 2014). While Montreal, Toronto and Simon Fraser continue to be the most prolific research centres, diverse scholarly work is being done throughout the country, and a greater number of graduate programs now provides a range of opportunities for students to continue to develop and grow.

Because of their interdisciplinary nature, criminology and criminal justice lend themselves to a number of configurations and inventions in different university settings. In particular, the degree of interdisciplinarity varies considerably. Many of these manifestations have evolved over time, while

[11] In 2008 Algoma University in Sault Ste. Marie, Ontario became Canada's newest university. It offers several criminology and criminal justice classes at the undergraduate level in its Department of Sociology. However, Algoma does not offer a standalone B.A. degree in criminology or criminal justice at this point in time.

others have shown more stable features. For example, Simon Fraser's undergraduate program has always provided a tremendous diversity of criminology courses for undergraduates but requires interdisciplinary electives from other departments (e.g. sociology, psychology, and political science). The University of Alberta's criminology B.A. is comprised mostly of sociology courses but also requires significant interdisciplinary offerings from a variety of departments. In contrast, the University of Manitoba does not focus on interdisciplinarity: its criminology degree courses are all from sociology except for an undergraduate criminal law course taught by faculty members from the law school.

Having so far provided a broad overview of the general development of criminology and criminal justice programs over the past 65 years by focusing most of our attention on the development of the major centres in Toronto, Ottawa, Montreal and Vancouver, we now turn to several brief sketches of lesser-known criminology and criminal justice programs to demonstrate the diversity of the justice disciplines today in Canada. The three programs discussed below were selected based upon our familiarity with them and the availability of published scholarly sources of information about their history and development. We concede that there are other Canadian university programs that could equally provide rich case studies of the diversity of post-secondary education in criminology and criminal justice studies. We offer the three sample programs below as simply suggestive of the diversity of today's criminology and criminal justice programs.

Programs in Canada Today

Criminal Justice, University of Winnipeg: In 1979 the University of Winnipeg established a distributed interdisciplinary major program titled "Studies in Justice and Law Enforcement" (JLE) that relied totally on existing course offerings from several departments, most notably Political Science, Psychology and Sociology. The program was coordinated in turn by a faculty member based in the Psychology Department and later a sociologist. In the 1990s, the first designated faculty members were appointed to Justice and Law Enforcement and the first JLE designated courses were developed. In this transitional phase through the late 1990s and early 2000s, students were required to select justice-themed courses from more than a dozen departments while also taking a handful of required courses and electives delivered by faculty attached to the JLE program. In 2004 the program was renamed "Criminal Justice Studies" and in 2006 full departmental status was obtained after considerable lobbying and internal struggles (Weinrath 2014). Soon after achieving this new status, the department developed a more coherent criminal justice curriculum that included: 1) required core courses in interdisciplinary theory, research methods, and criminal law; 2) elective courses offered from within the CJ department; and 3) a requirement that students take several justice-themed interdisciplinary elective courses taught by more than a dozen departments across the university. The program was designed to provide a clear criminal justice focus while maintaining its interdisciplinary roots (Jochelson et al. 2013). The program has grown from a small thematic distributed major with no designated faculty to one that now attracts more majors than any other program in the Faculty of Arts. In 2009, an Honours program was established largely to appeal to students interested in pursuing further academic studies at the graduate level. In 2015, the University of Winnipeg Senate approved a new M.A. degree program in Criminal Justice and the proposal is awaiting formal government approval.

Justice Studies, University of Regina: This program, housed at the University of Saskatchewan's Regina campus, began as the School of Human Justice in 1973, providing a degree equivalent to the social work designation. In 1980 the program was moved to the newly formed University of Regina Faculty of Social Work (Greenberg 2014). While always incorporating a multidisciplinary curriculum, in 1997 the department moved away from its social work emphasis towards a greater concentration of justice courses, and was relocated to the Faculty of Arts. The Justice Studies Department used to offer two undergraduate degree programs, a Bachelor in Human Justice (BHJ),[12] the other in Police Studies (BPS), and two M.A.'s, one in Justice and the other in Policing. The two undergraduate degree programs share 10 overlapping courses and course content spans a variety of interdisciplinary subject areas such as "criminological and social justice theory courses; methods; legal and restorative justice courses; and themed courses such as mental health and substance abuse in a justice context; advocacy strategies, environmental justice, and food, hunger and justice" (Greenberg 2014:126). The program also offers the students an opportunity to obtain three different types of advanced certificates in Police Studies, Justice Studies, and in Criminal and Restorative Justice.

The program has traditionally provided a considerable applied or practical focus by offering extensive student practica opportunities in local criminal and social justice field placements.

Criminology, Ryerson: In 1996, Justice Studies began as a part-time degree completion program developed by faculty in the Psychology Department. The program was originally aimed at criminal justice practitioners, and transfer credits for college courses and practitioner experience were generous. The program became moderately popular with students despite limited accessibility in the evenings (Landau and Varma 2014). In 2004, the School of Justice Studies partnered with other departments to offer a four-year B.A. degree in criminal justice. The school became the Department of Criminal Justice and

[12] This program was to be phased out by 2017.

Criminology in 2006 and hired four new faculty members. Student enrolments burgeoned, and the type of students applying (strong high school succession with good credentials) resulted in a shift in the program from "job readiness" to a "critical, theoretical and substantively interdisciplinary program" (Landau and Varma 2014:99). The department distinguishes its "applied" or "practice" approach by emphasizing practice in advocacy and social justice action by its students, in addition to more traditional student placements in criminal justice agencies. The interdisciplinary roots of criminology are reflected within the scholarly training of their faculty members who possess doctoral training in "Criminology, Social Anthropology, Women's Studies, Law, Sociology and History" (Landau and Varma 2014:101). In 2013, the department changed its name again, to simply "Criminology," believing that the broader scope of the term better reflected the research approaches of the faculty and was less confusing to prospective students (Landau and Varma 2014). The department has recently announced that it is launching an M.A. degree program in criminology.

Current Trends

While there is considerable diversity in the structure of criminology and criminal justice programs in Canadian universities, expansion and proliferation of new programs is clearly the current trend. Growth appears to be taking place in three general ways:

1) Established interdisciplinary university departments of criminology and criminal justice are expanding into graduate level training. For example, both Ryerson and Wilfrid Laurier (Brantford) have recently announced new M.A. degrees in criminology. In the fall of 2016 the University of Windsor in Windsor, Ontario launched its new Master's of Arts in Criminology degree. And as noted earlier, the University of Winnipeg has internally approved the development of an M.A. degree in criminal justice. It is likely that more new graduate programs in criminology and criminal justice will be launched as traditional undergraduate student enrolments begin to decline at many Canadian universities and as demand for graduate education increases within a broader context of degree-inflation in Canadian society.

2) New standalone interdisciplinary programs in criminology and/or criminal justice are emerging particularly at smaller, newer and/or less established universities. For example, Vancouver Island University (VIU) in Nanaimo, B.C. now houses a B.A. degree program in interdisciplinary criminology as does Kwantlen Polytechnic University (KPU), located in the Lower Mainland of British Columbia. In both cases, these new universities have emerged from existing community colleges in the province. Institutions that once provided certificates, diplomas and university transfer credits in criminology and criminal justice are being transformed into full-fledged university degree-granting

institutions. It is noteworthy that Canada's newest universities appear to be eschewing more traditional disciplines and programs for interdisciplinary programs like criminology and criminal justice. For example, University of Ontario Institute of Technology (UOIT) established a new undergraduate major in criminology and justice within its Faculty of Social Sciences and Humanities. Established in 2002, UOIT does not offer a more traditional sociology degree. Degree programs in justice studies and criminal justice can also be found in Canada's new online and hybrid universities such as Royal Roads[13] on Vancouver Island in British Columbia and Alberta's Athabasca University, which is acknowledged as one of Canada's leading online universities. Meanwhile, in eastern Canada, the University of Fredericton in New Brunswick offers what it calls a diploma-to-degree program in criminal justice that is delivered entirely online in partnership with Husson University in Maine. Upon completing the two-year diploma at the University of Fredericton, students may transfer their credits to Husson University and complete a four-year bachelor's degree in criminal justice. In general, newer online and hybrid universities seem less constrained by disciplinary traditions that tend to dominate in Canada's more established institutions. It therefore seems logical to assume that the emergence of new degree-granting institutions and online programs will be a significant driver of the growth of university criminology and criminal justice enrolments.

3) Sociology departments are expanding and rebranding their course offerings in crime, deviance and social control as criminology and/or socio-legal studies degree programs. This move seems to be largely the result of the growing popularity of criminology and the concomitant waning of student interest in traditional sociological areas of study. These embedded programs take a variety of forms and rely to a greater or lesser extent on interdisciplinary courses from outside of sociology. Examples of such programs include the recently inaugurated Western University criminology major and the University of Toronto Scarborough and University of Toronto Mississauga criminology and socio-legal studies major. The growth of embedded programs in sociology departments tends to be most common in established Canadian universities where standalone programs do not exist. For example, while the criminology major at the St. George campus of University of Toronto is firmly established within the standalone interdisciplinary centre, the suburban campuses did not house interdisciplinary centres and thus the Sociology Department provided an institutional base for the development of new competing undergraduate criminological and socio-legal studies programs. At

[13] According to its official website, from 1940 until 1995 the school was Royal Roads Military College. In 1995 it was decommissioned and became Royal Roads University with a unique applied and professional degree-granting focus.

our own institution (the University of Winnipeg), the Sociology Department recently discussed rebranding itself as the Department of Sociology and Criminology. It therefore seems likely that the growth of new degree programs in criminology in Canada will continue as established sociology departments reposition themselves for an uncertain future within an evolving post-secondary landscape that is becoming increasingly commodified, corporatized and linked to job training (see, for example, Huey 2011).

Challenges

Going forward, criminology and criminal justice—or more broadly the justice disciplines—face a number of challenges. Some of these challenges relate to the longstanding questions and tensions that have surrounded the establishment of the discipline since the 1950s and 1960s. Is criminology an academic discipline or an applied professional field? Is criminology properly located in standalone interdisciplinary departments, centres or institutes, or should criminology be located administratively within established disciplines such as law, sociology or even social work? More recently, questions have arisen related to the putative distinction between criminology and criminal justice. Because criminal justice is a relatively new university program in Canada, some have suggested that this creates confusion for students who would prefer a criminology degree (e.g., Landau and Varma 2014) but, as noted above, it may also reflect the historical legacy of the establishment of some of the early criminology and criminal justice programs. For example, some of the early programs were "inspired" by various federal criminal justice commissions. Others have argued that criminal justice implies a focus on the protective services rather than critical social science (e.g., Frauley 2009), and leaves open many questions about what, if anything, distinguishes criminology from criminal justice at a theoretical and substantive level (e.g., Kraska 2006; Crank 2003). Some have suggested that criminal justice is just a rebranding of mainstream "administrative" criminology, which is seen as the uncritical second cousin of a more enlightened critical criminology that is sociologically rooted (e.g., Chunn and Menzies 2006; Huey 2011). Criminal justice, according to this perspective, is a result of the forces of neo-liberalism and neo-conservativism and the drive by "university administrators to relentlessly adopt the policies and discourses of the marketplace" (Chunn and Menzies 2006: 666). Moreover, as Chunn and Menzies (2006:671) argue, the "resurgence of criminal-justice paradigms is just the latest manifestation of criminology's long-standing, and seemingly intrinsic, allegiance to constituted authority, tradition, the 'empirical' world, and the past." Thus, at a deeper level, criminology and criminal justice, based on this perspective, have longstanding and inextricable links to the state that have only become amplified in recent years as Canadian society moves toward greater emphasis on security, the management of risk and the drive toward the corporatization of the university.[14]

To be sure, students are attracted to programs in criminology in part because of an intrinsic fascination with the subject matter, but more importantly because they see the justice disciplines (e.g., criminology, criminal justice, police studies, etc.) as leading to a viable career in the justice system. In recent years a handful of criminologists have lamented the expectations of students in somewhat personal reflections of their experience teaching in liberal arts programs in criminology and criminal justice. In a widely cited American example, Mathieu Deflem (2002) reported student "resentment" at his sociological approach to teaching criminal justice while in Canada Laura Huey (2011) explains that some of the students in her policing course did not appreciate the fact that she was not an experienced police officer. By giving in to the demands of the corporate university and the desire to market programs in criminology and criminal justice to students seeking practical job-related skills, Huey (2011: 88) argues "we risk dumbing down the discipline and scaring away those students we hope to attract—the best and the brightest who are attracted to the discipline's promise but prefer to develop their knowledge and critical skills rather than becoming cop wannabes."

While a number of critical criminologists share the concerns of the scholars noted above, others see criminal justice and criminology as being uniquely positioned to weather the currents of the new corporate university while maintaining disciplinary and academic integrity. Jochelson and his colleagues (2013) argue that the criminal justice program at the University of Winnipeg, for example, has been able to navigate the narrow waters between student demands for practical knowledge and job-related skills and the need to maintain a commitment to the principles of a liberal arts university education that emphasizes critical thinking and the development of a breadth of knowledge about the physical and social worlds. With a curriculum that balances critical and theoretical coursework in interdisciplinary criminal justice and criminology while also providing opportunities for optional field placements, research practica and more applied courses taught by criminal justice professionals, the Criminal Justice Department at the University of Winnipeg provides a solid foundation for further graduate training in the social sciences while also allowing opportunities for career-minded students to receive more practical experience and training in the justice professions.[15] A similar experience has been noted by Landau and Varma (2014) at Ryerson University where the criminology program maintains a commitment to the institution's mandate of

[14] Although well beyond the scope of this chapter, for further discussion around this issue see Westheimer (2010) and/or Polster and Newson's (2015) new book *A Penny for Your Thoughts*.

[15] A similar ethos may characterize other criminal justice and criminology programs across Canada to varying degrees. Conversely, some criminal justice and criminology programs are more committed to a singular approach be it applied or academic.

providing practical and applied education by rethinking what it means to engage students in practice: "So, in addition to more traditional work with policing and community organizations, restorative justice and youth justice forums, both faculty and students are involved in social advocacy, literacy, human and civil rights, the Law Practice Program [the newly instituted alternative in Ontario to articling for law students], and immigration and settlement services" (Landau and Varma 2014:100).

It seems unlikely that the tensions and questions that have long surrounded university programs in criminology will be resolved in the immediate future. However, the diversity of programs across Canada suggests that the adaptability and flexibility of the subject is a key strength that will ensure criminology and criminal justice continue to persist and thrive even in a rapidly changing and evolving postsecondary landscape.

Conclusion

In this chapter, we have outlined the relatively short history of criminology and criminal justice in Canada. From its earliest origins within the UBC criminology program in the 1950s, through the establishment of the four founding interdisciplinary centres of criminology at Toronto, Montreal, Simon Fraser and Ottawa, through to the more recent expansion and diversification of programs in the justice disciplines in the 1990s and beyond, we have argued that the history of criminology and criminal justice is one that is characterized by the struggle to find a proper institutional place for these programs and an ongoing debate about the nature of the discipline itself as applied or scholarly. These themes continue to echo in recent debates about the rise of criminal justice programs and applied criminology within a broader context of shifts in postsecondary education in Canada that seem to favor applied and professional programs. We believe that criminology and criminal justice can continue to thrive in these uncertain times, but only by maintaining a balance between theory and practice, and a dual focus on ameliorating social problems and engagement in critical social science (e.g., Frauley 2005).

References

Archambault, J. (1938). *Report of the Royal Commission to Investigate the Penal System of Canada*. Ottawa: Queen's Printer.

Chunn, D., and Menzies, R. (2006). "So what does all of this have to do with Criminology?": Surviving the restructuring of the discipline in the twenty-first century. *Canadian Journal of Criminology and Criminal Justice*, 48(5): 663–680.

Crank, J. (2003). *Imagining Justice*. Cincinnati, OH: Anderson.

Deflem, M. (2002). Teaching criminal justice in liberal arts education: A sociologist's confessions. *ACJS Today*, 22(2): 1–5.

Doob, A. (1983). Criminological research in Canada. *Crime and Justice*, 5: 253–263.

Dr. Tadeusz Grygier, 1915–2012. (2014). Retrieved from http://socialsciences.uottawa.ca/sites/default/files/public/crm/eng/documents/OU_Biography_English_Dec 14.pdf.

Edwards, J. (1982). Directing the development of a university centre of criminology. *Dalhousie Law Journal*, 7(3): 850–886.

Fauteux, G. (1956). *Report of a Committee Appointed to Inquire into the Principles and Procedures followed in the Remission Service of the Department of Justice of Canada*. Ottawa: Queen's Printer.

Gorkoff, K. S. (2013). From plan to market ... marketizing the non-economic: The economy of higher education: markets and marketization of Canadian postsecondary education. Ph.D. Dissertation. Carleton University: Ottawa, ON.

Greenberg, H. (2014). A justice experience at the University of Regina. *The Annual Review of Interdisciplinary Justice Research*, 4: 120–134.

Griffiths, G., and Palys, T. (2014). Of big tents and handmaidens: The origins and evolution of criminology at Simon Fraser University. *The Annual Review of Interdisciplinary Justice Research*, 4: 15–42.

Grygier, T. (1963). Dimensions of criminology. *Canadian Journal of Corrections*, 5(1): 40–46.

Frauley, J. (2005). Representing theory and theorizing in criminal justice studies: Practicing theory considered. *Critical Criminology*, 13(3): 245–265.

Hackler, J. C. (2006). Criminology. The Canadian Encyclopedia Online. Retrieved from http://www.thecanadianencyclopedia.ca/en/article/criminology/.

Hackler, J. C. (1994). *Crime and Canadian Public Policy.* Scarborough, ON: Prentice Hall Canada.

Huey, L. (2011) "Commodifying Canadian criminology: Applied criminology programs and the future of the discipline" in A. Doyle and D. Moore (eds.), *Critical Criminology in Canada.* Vancouver: UBC Press, pp. 75–98.

Jochelson, R., Kohm, S. and Weinrath, M. (2013). Mitigating the protective services orientation in criminal justice: An opening salvo at the University of Winnipeg. *Canadian Journal of Criminology and Criminal Justice*, 55(1): 1–32.

King, D., and Winterdyk, J. (2014). Personal reflections on justice education at Mount Royal University. *The Annual Review of Interdisciplinary Justice Research,* 4: 135–147.

Kohm, S., Gorkoff, K., Jochelson, R., and Walby, K. (2014). Educating justice: Postsecondary education in the justice disciplines. *The Annual Review of Interdisciplinary Justice Research,* 4: 5–14.

Kraska, P. (2006). Criminal justice theory: Toward legitimacy and an infrastructure. *Justice Quarterly*, 23(2): 167–185.

Landau, T., and Varma, K. (2014). A tale of three programs: Reflections on criminological studies at Ryerson University. *The Annual Review of Interdisciplinary Justice Research,* 4: 95–102.

Morn, F. (1995). *Academic politics and the history of criminal justice education*. Westport, CT: Greenwood.

Parkinson, G. (2008). Recovering the early history of Canadian criminology: Criminology at the University of British Columbia, 1951–1959. *Canadian Journal of Criminology and Criminal Justice*, 50(5): 589–620.

Parys, S. (2014). From correction to prevention: An analysis of the *Canadian Journal of Criminology and Criminal Justice*, 1958–1983. *The Annual Review of Interdisciplinary Justice Research,* 4: 43–71.

Ratner, R.S. (2014). Educating the criminology vanguard. *The Annual Review of Interdisciplinary Justice Research,* 4: 148–56.

Ratner, R.S. (2006) Pioneering critical criminology in Canada. *Canadian Journal of Criminology and Criminal Justice*, 48(5): 647–662.

Sprott, J., and Roberts, J. (2013). A festschrift in honour of Anthony N. Doob. *Canadian Journal of Criminology and Criminal Justice,* 55(4): 457–460.

Szabo, D. (1963). Criminology and criminologist: A new discipline and a new profession. *Canadian Journal of Corrections*, 5(1): 28–39.

Weinrath, M. (2014). From studies in justice and law enforcement to the Department of Criminal Justice: A reflection from the University of Winnipeg. *The Annual Review of Interdisciplinary Justice Research,* 4: 103–119.

TWO
Denis Szabo: The Founder of Criminology in Québec

François Fenchel

Rien n'est possible sans les hommes, rien n'est durable sans les institutions.
Nothing is possible without men, nothing lasts without institutions.
JEAN MONET

Introduction

I first met Denis Szabo (born 1929) in 1998. I had just started my master's degree in criminology and was in a one-year seminar intended to "criminologize" graduates coming from other disciplines. One of the strong points of the course was the procession of prominent people in francophone criminology who came to speak to the class. Maurice Cusson, Jean-Paul Brodeur, Pierre Landreville, Serge Brochu, and several others came to talk to us about their field and stimulate our interest in working with them. The seminar was given by André Normandeau, who himself was already well known at the time as the public face of criminology. My background was in psychology, a discipline whose pioneers hailed from a far-off time, and this parade of living founders astonished me and gave the impression of a living science still in the act of creation.

And then Denis Szabo arrived. He was presented as none other than the founder of criminology in Québec. When you saw him, you knew there was something different about him. Though he was old, he stood straight and tall, his eyelids drooping, but his look was piercing. Before doing or saying anything, he surveyed the class with a keen expression of interest, and in a manner that we knew we were being assessed in some capacity. His exceptionality extended to his speech. He spoke a cosmopolitan French, the timbre of his voice reminding me of the radio announcers of old, with a touch of an accent here and there that indicated an upbringing in some foreign land. His speech was erudite, full of uncompromising references that made us witnesses to a lifetime of accumulated knowledge. I took in very little from his original presentation of his life's work, of the creation of criminology at Université de Montréal, because, as I must admit, I paid more attention to the form than the content, to the way he presented things rather than what was actually presented. It was his personality that fascinated me.

During this period, Szabo had a tiny office at the School of Criminology, with a sign above the door that read "A Visual History of Criminology." Once you stepped in, you immediately understood its meaning; the walls were covered with pictures and photos that chronicled the decades he had spent developing the discipline and capturing the extensive travels around the world he had undertaken in the name of his discipline. There were pictures of important people posing for posterity, group photos immortalizing solemn participants at events, and, especially, photos of himself. Denis Szabo frequently appeared in the centre of this pictorial history, of *his* history. It was not vanity so much as it was the way of things. These photos were, to a large extent, a reflection and the story of his life.

Dennis Szabo. Photograph c. 1975, from the author's private collection (photo provided by Prof. Szabo).

Throughout my Ph.D., which covered the better part of the 2000s, I often sat in his office. There was a respectful and friendly rapport between us, and so I was asked to record the stories behind the pictures in which he so often appears. This, quite naturally, led to the recounting of his life story.

This chapter does not go into exhaustive detail of all the aspects of Denis Szabo's career, nor does it provide a comprehensive list of his achievements and various distinctions. To date, the most complete coverage of Szabo's life can be found in interviews conducted by Fournier (1998). Nor is this chapter a question of reconstructing in detail the history of Université de Montréal's School of Criminology, even though its founder is closely linked to this history. Szabo himself has told it several times (Szabo 1977, 1963, 1961), as have other participants in this history (Normandeau 2002, 1987; Bertrand and Normandeau 1984). I likewise avoid recounting the history of the period, where one must distinguish between individual contribution and social conditions that explain the form and outcome of institutions. One needs only to consult Poupart (2004) on this topic for a detailed analysis of the intellectual, academic, and administrative determinants that influenced the institutionalization of criminology at the Université de Montréal.

Based primarily on a series of interviews conducted with Szabo in 2010 and

2015, some of which have already been published (Fenchel 2010), what follows is above all a biographical essay intended to draw out the meaning that a man has given to his life's work. I wish to evoke the major stages in this man's journey, his roots, beginnings, choices, and ambitions, recognizing one fundamental bias, that my subject was the prime mover of his own existence.

Szabo's Youth and Schooling

Denis Szabo was born June 4, 1929 in Budapest, Hungary. The son of a gendarmery officer, young Szabo was quickly directed towards a military career. He became a cadet at 10 years of age and received an officer's education during the Second World War. From this period of his life, from this education dedicated to serving the homeland dutifully and obediently, Szabo drew opposing lessons that would guide the rest of his life. First, he rather unexpectedly developed a contempt for authority and a rebelliousness against regulations and bureaucracy. In a military order that restricted all spontaneity, where everything that was not expressly allowed was forbidden, he freed himself by adopting an obstinately undisciplined attitude. Penalties and punishment followed. As if to balance this first character trait, however, his years in the Hungarian army strongly impressed upon him the value of time. In the meticulously controlled world of military life, young Szabo acquired a deep understanding of time's limitations, its finiteness, and thus the importance of making the best use of it. This was the supreme rule that would guide his life from then on.

In 1945, Germany's defeat left its Hungarian ally under Soviet occupation, and it was in an uncertain social and political climate that Szabo continued his studies. He finished his lyceum (secondary) education two years later, and began university studies at the University of Budapest, moving towards sociology. That was where he met his first mentor, Professor **Alexandre Szalai**, chair of the sociology department, who would have a crucial influence on him. Under his guidance, the young Szabo discovered a curiosity for questions at the heart of the social sciences: the meaning of history, the nature of knowledge, the causes and consequences of social change, and so on. One book came to symbolize these questions: Szalai put in his student's hands a colossal work, *Philosophie der Geschichte als Soziologie* (*The Philosophy of History as Sociology*) by the German scholar **Paul Barth** (1858–1922), who saw sociology as a universal discipline that was the sum of all the social sciences. The complex and demanding book was grounded in an erudition that greatly surpassed that of the young Szabo. For the mentor, it was where one must start. And that, therefore, was where Szabo started. For a very curious young man who could not tolerate not understanding, it was a powerful motivation.

In the meantime, the Soviet occupation's grip on the country increased, and the creation of the Hungarian People's Republic in 1949 made it a satellite regime of the Soviet Union. The enemies identified by the regime began adding up: liberals, socialists, aristocrats, clergy members, and so forth. Szabo saw the categories of suspicious people grow, and was not inclined to exonerate himself and his roots by joining the concert of denunciators. The rebellious cadet was not far away. With some university friends, he made plans to go into exile. In February 1949, Szabo crossed the Austrian border and made it to the American occupation zone in Vienna before then travelling on to Belgium a few months later. It was thus as a political refugee that Szabo left his country, having seen and experienced the dangers of two successive totalitarian regimes. These perils were well illustrated by the personal destiny of his mentor Szalai. Having become a suspect due to his social-democratic allegiances, he was stripped of his university chair, accused of espionage, and sent to prison in 1950, where he spent several years.

While living in Belgium, Szabo enrolled at the Université of Louvain in Political and Social Sciences. One of his mentors and teachers was Professor Jacques Leclercq (1891–1971),[16] a Roman Catholic priest and specialist in natural law and moral philosophy who seemed to be worlds apart from the Marxist realism context of his mentor Szalai.

Leclercq's empiricism, namely an appreciation for the facts themselves rather than their representations, suited Szabo. At the same time, Szabo familiarized himself with the work of Vilfredo Pareto, approving of the quantitative tendencies of an "experimental" sociology at war with ideologies, as well as that of Rudolf Carnap and other members of the Vienna School, whose manifesto prescribed a positivist social science based on logical analysis and strict empiricism. Szabo was likewise impressed by American sociology, and read the *American Journal of Sociology* from cover to cover, familiarizing himself with decades' worth of research.

It was in this intellectual ferment that he began writing what would become *Crimes et villes*, his Ph.D. thesis in sociology. What is noteworthy about the subject chosen is that it came as a response to the concerns of the time. For the generation of postwar European sociologists, the question of social change focused in particular on the problems of urbanization. People were leaving behind traditional ways of life and entering into a world of accelerated change that needed to be understood. Szabo took a macro-perspective by which to examine urban society, analyzing the effect of the city on society from various perspectives and themes (e.g., impact on social life, demographics, labour market, public health, etc.). This resulted in a considerable amount of analysis and a draft with which he was not satisfied. Reacting against an armchair sociology at odds with his positivist approach, he wanted

[16] Leclercq helped to found the program and today the building that houses the department he helped to establish is named after him.

to anchor the subject in social reality by taking an empirical approach. But, first he had to choose one subject out of a multitude of topics. His research subsequently led him to Paris where he benefited from the supervision of, among others, Professor **Henry Lévy-Bruhl** (1884–1964), a lawyer and sociologist, at the École pratique des hautes études (EPHE), and **Alfred Sauvy** (1898–1990), a demographer and anthropologist, at the Institut national d'études démographiques (INED; see Box 2.1). The former influenced Szabo above and beyond his studies, but, in the meantime, it was the latter who directed him towards the theme of criminality.

Szabo's thesis took on a definitive form. At its heart was a systematic comparison of the judicial districts in France and Belgium, divided by means of an urbanization index and analyzed using a series of demographic indices (e.g., divorce, marriage, children born out of wedlock, migration, etc.). His results allowed him to break with the persistent assumption, common-sense judgment, and long-time literary theme that crime was an urban phenomenon, and the city the cemetery of the nation where moral values, family, and traditions faded away, opening the door to all sorts of deviations, including crime. His thesis demonstrated that this was not the case, but that urban zones were less criminalized than their rural counterparts, and that certain rural districts were highly criminalized. Szabo concluded that the idea that urbanization was a factor in social pathology should belong to the past: it corresponded to a bygone

Box 2.1. The Decisive Moment

At the Demographic Institute, Mr. Sauvy ... do you know who Alfred Sauvy was? He was a small, unpretentious man, very erudite, a Polytechnique alumni. He wrote three or four books per year. Like everyone else, he wrote course books and treatises, but he also wrote on social subjects, and was very precise in addition to being very productive. I show up and bring my manuscript with the table of contents, and I say, "Mr. Sauvy, I need some advice. Everything interests me and I don't know where to start." "Let's see," he says. So he takes a table of contents, two or three pages long, I can still see his finger yellowed by cigarettes or a pipe as he reviews the different chapter headings: government, religion, family. He says as he reads, "Ah that, that was done by X, that was done by my friend Y, someone has just started something on that in Grenoble." And when he gets to the end, the very last heading on the list, urban criminality, he straightens his glasses on his nose, looks at me and says, "Listen, I can't see anybody, maybe a Chinese guy who defended a thesis at the Faculty of Law in the '30s on urban criminality, but that's about it, nothing came of it. Szabo, why don't you take a look at this? Look this over and come back when you can tell me what you've found." And that, my boy, is how I stumbled onto crime.

Source: Denis Szabo, interviews, 2010, our translation.

period in Western history, to the rise in urbanization, but it was not a permanent or contemporary characteristic of urban life. And since the opposition between city and countryside was fading away with the spread of the urban environment, the explanation of criminality, in particular the disparities in crime rates, must be sought elsewhere. For Szabo, it would be in social organization and culture, themes that would later direct his research interests.

Szabo submitted his doctoral thesis in 1956. His subject and approach marked a divergence with the psychiatric criminology of Louvain—the birthplace of the Belgian school of criminology. Founded and led by **Étienne De Greeff** (1898–1961), a psychiatrist and specialist in criminal psychology, it focused mainly on the study of deviant personality. De Greeff was on Szabo's Ph.D. committee and confessed some amount of surprise that there was no discussion of the criminal as an individual. This was a further indication of the innovative aspects of Szabo's work, at least in the context of the European criminological tradition.

With his Ph.D. under his belt and, two years later, a diploma from the École Pratique des Hautes Études at the Sorbonne, Szabo began looking for an academic position.

Criminology in Montréal

In 1958, Denis Szabo arrived at a crossroads. Recently married, and waiting for his first child, his career was slowly getting underway. As a lecturer in sociology at Catholic faculties in Paris and Lyon, he commuted back and forth between the two cities while he waited for a position. A former classmate at Louvain, Father **Norbert Lacoste,** had remained in contact with him. Lacoste, who was in charge of developing the Department of Sociology at Université de Montréal, encouraged him to come to Canada and join the department. Would he pull up roots once again? Szabo hesitated. But the offer surpassed what he could expect in Europe. He accepted the invitation and in September 1958 he began teaching the history of sociological thought, urban sociology, and criminal sociology.

The newcomer's disorientation was considerable. Born in Central Europe, having started his sociology studies in Budapest during the reconstruction of his war-torn country, and having frequented lofty academic institutions at Louvain and then Paris, Montréal was a "brave new world." Québec was still dominated by a resolutely conservative, institutionalized Catholicism. And yet in terms of social history, Québec was at the dawn of a period of social and political upheaval: the Quiet Revolution was coming.

Szabo seized upon the opportunities that the move offered. In the early 1960s, with the encouragement of Dean **Philippe Garigue,** the social sciences at Université de Montréal were growing quickly. In addition to sociology, the desire to expand the field led to the creation of departments of anthropology and political science. It was in this context that Szabo established a criminology program in the fall of 1960. Initially, it was a multidisciplinary master's program in the Department of Sociology, but criminology became a separate discipline in 1962. In 1965, a doctoral program was added, and the bachelor program followed in 1967. To emphasize the applied and professional nature of criminology, the Department became a School in 1971. So, within a short ten-year span, Denis Szabo had all but ensured the legacy he would leave.

Personal motivation played a role in the creation of the criminology program. For Szabo, the possibilities inherent in establishing a new field would take him well beyond his own training. Crime is a subject of legitimate sociological concern, but it is also a subject that can unite various approaches and types of knowledge. As Szabo saw it, criminology could involve a multidisciplinary education comprising, in particular, the etiology of delinquent behaviour, the social sources of deviancy and criminality, the evaluation of the criminal justice system, and the clinical treatment methods for psychosocial re-socialization and rehabilitation. Thus Szabo envisaged a criminology capable of influencing criminal justice policies and transforming its practices. To compensate for imperfections and weaknesses in the existing system that research might identify, criminologists working in institutions could transform them from the inside. For Szabo, the key was to create a functional alliance between criminological theory and practice.

Establishing the criminology program was an ambitious undertaking as Szabo needed to find the right people—those having the necessary knowledge to teach in areas such as medicine, psychology, and law as well as sociology. To initiate the program, Szabo identified the specialists whose knowledge and experience already constituted, before his arrival, the foundations of criminological knowledge and practice in Québec. There was, to begin with, Father **Noël Mailloux** (1909–1997), the founder of the Institute of Psychology and pioneer of the social sciences at Université de Montréal, whom Szabo convinced to support his project. Studies in juvenile psychopathology and delinquency carried out at the Institute represented first-rate expertise. Likewise, the close ties Mailloux had with Boscoville, a growing rehabilitation centre for young delinquents, ensured that criminology students had access to places where they could practice. Szabo could also count on Bruno M. Cormier (1919–1991), one of the pioneers of forensic psychiatry and clinical criminology in Canada who had been working as a psychiatrist with the Faculty of Medicine at McGill University. Working with the prison population at St-Vincent-de-Paul, Cormier was able to provide access to theoretical and practical training, and provide adult delinquents with possibilities similar to those that Father Mailloux provided to young people. In both cases, they were places where future criminologists could observe and experiment, and receive general and specialized training.

Several of the first professors at the School came from the Institute of Psychology at Université de Montréal. They included Marcel Fréchette, Pierre Morin, and Justin Ciale. Henri Ellenberger, psychiatrist and medical historian, joined the team, as did jurists such as Henri-Masson Loranger; both were recruited to teach criminal law. As the years passed, new professors were recruited who had carried out their studies in Montréal (e.g., Ezzat Fattah, Marc Le Blanc, Pierre Landreville, and Maurice Cusson) or who had obtained their Ph.D.'s abroad (e.g., Marie-Andrée Bertrand and André Normandeau). This list, albeit incomplete, reflects the composition of a team with diversified research areas and fields of expertise.

Box 2.2. The Specificity of the Profession of Criminology

Criminology cannot currently be considered a profession. It nonetheless has potential qualities which, under certain conditions, could ensure its establishment as a profession distinct from those which we traditionally encounter in the field of criminology. Certain types of activities can be identified, activities that require training in criminology: a) the personnel in charge of the re-socialization of delinquents; b) the management personnel of establishments and services in charge of the "social defence" (police, penitentiaries, etc.); c) the personnel working in criminal justice administration and associated with the development of criminal policies; and finally d) the professors and researchers whose activities support the above sectors.
Source: Denis Szabo, *Criminologie*, 1967, our translation.

Szabo, nonetheless, applied clear criteria in his choice of professors and researchers. His theoretical and intellectual conception of criminology was based on a quantitative and positivist approach. Echoing the authors who influenced his studies, Szabo considered the production and use of quantifiable data essential to rigorous and scientifically valid work. This methodological bias, which influenced the nature of the research and set obvious limitations on the variety of work conducted, also served as to distinguish the field and ensure its sustainability in Canada. Denis Szabo's wish to establish criminology as a separate discipline necessarily required that it be distinguished from established disciplines, in particular the social services, whose graduates' field of practice overlapped with that of criminologists. Without the certification of a professional organization (which would only come some fifty years later), defining and protecting criminology's specificity implied, in Szabo's opinion, a methodological rigour that he associated with quantitative methods. Decades later, the various *Traité de criminologie empirique* (1984, 1995, 2003, 2010) of the School, edited by Szabo, and later by **Marc Le Blanc**, remain a heritage of this original intention.

In the meantime, Szabo pursued his own questions about social change and the relationship between social order and change. With the publication of his Ph.D. thesis, *Crimes et villes* (1960), Szabo's work arrived on the academic scene, attracting influential patrons. There was first of all a foreword by Henri Lévy-Bruhl, a prominent French figure in criminology and sociology of law at the École des hautes études, which gave Szabo the approbation of an esteemed scholar and thinker in the sociological tradition of Durkheim. There was also an introduction by Jean Pinatel, who at the time was a high-ranking civil servant in France's Ministry of the Interior, secretary of the International Society of Criminology (ISC), and author of a criminology column in the *Revue des sciences criminelles et de droit pénal comparé* (*Review of Criminal Sciences and Comparative Criminal Law*). Pinatel had long been concerned with reforming prisons and was a strong proponent of using an applied approach when devising reforms. He too was destined to become a preeminent figure in world criminology. With these two backing him, Denis Szabo's career had the valuable international support needed to not only establish his program but to attract scholars and students to it.

In his later work, Szabo's theoretical position was inspired by that of the renowned American sociologist from Harvard University, Talcott Parsons (1902–1979). Parsons had developed a general theory for the study of society which he called "action theory." The theory involves the study of interaction between cultures and society (i.e., macro factors) and personality (i.e., micro factors). As a sociologist, Szabo saw personality as a dependent variable, the two main variables being society and culture. In *Ordre et changement* (1969) and *L'adolescent et la société* (1972), Szabo placed social integration at the heart of criminality. Adolescents faced with social constraints could be encouraged either to conform or to rebel. Rebellion may involve non-conformity and deviance sometimes punished by law. For Szabo, the concept of deviance was complementary to criminality, a form of failed adaptation to social requirements, to the pressure to conform. Consequently, he considered the culture, standards, and values transmitted to young people to have a greater impact on crime than do social origin, career, and employment.

Szabo's thoughts on the matter led him to develop a typology describing how shared values influence the extent to which social structures, culture, and personality are integrated. The typology is presented in *Criminologie et politique criminelle* (1978), where he proposed a distinction between integrated, semi-integrated, and non-integrated societies. In an integrated society, there is a relative balance between social values and the different elements of society, including the mechanics of the justice system. A society is semi-integrated when the fundamental values are similar but their interpretations differ according to age, gender, and social class, producing tension and sources of cultural conflict. This is the case, in Szabo's opinion, for most post-industrial Western societies. Even if there is a normative order, and the rule of law serves to keep the whole together, the unintegrated parts of society bring dysfunctions of which crime is an expected outcome. Non-integrated societies, according to Szabo, are composed of heterogeneous groups with divergent values that exclude harmonious coexistence. The differences are insurmountable and are permanent sources of conflict comparable to civil war. From this perspective, Szabo envisioned an analysis of the legal and judicial system's various adaptations to delinquency.

Though he could have continued in this direction, his academic work eventually took a secondary role. New opportunities opened up in the development of criminology, and he began to consider other projects.

Opening Up to the World

In 1970, Szabo finished his mandate as School director, passing on the post to André Normandeau. By 1970, the foundations of the School were well established and the time for consolidation and international influence had arrived. It was not only about creating; it was now a question of shining the spotlight on the result and ensuring it received international recognition. The creation of the review *Acta criminologica* in 1968 (renamed *Criminologie* in 1975), for which Szabo remained the editor until 1987, bore witness to his desire to disseminate Montréal's scientific production and give it an audience. But this was only a first step; Szabo was working on a new creation that would once again lead to new possibilities or, more precisely, new horizons.

With the creation of the International Centre for Comparative Criminology (ICCC) in 1969, a centre he would direct until 1983, Szabo created a window onto the world as well as a major instrument for positioning Montréal criminology at the world level. It was through his ties with the esteemed Spanish criminologist Jean Pinatel that the project took root. Pinatel wanted criminology to spread around the world through international centres that could reinforce the contacts between Europe and America, an idea that had long been held by the International Society of Criminology. The choice of a place for what was originally envisaged as an international institute nonetheless posed a problem. The members of the society were mostly European and hesitated to set up an institution in North America. But thanks in particular to the backing of American criminologist/sociologist Marvin Wolfgang, who suggested creating an international centre rather than an institute, Szabo succeeded in garnering ISC support for the creation of the ICCC in Montréal.

The "comparative" aspect of the Centre reflected the desire for dialogue between European and North American criminologists. However, Szabo's goal for the ICCC was also to reinforce the visibility of criminology in Montréal, while providing the School's researchers with a launch pad into the international community. With government funding and a substantial grant from the Ford Foundation, Szabo got down to work. With the steadfast help of **Alice Parizeau,** who was appointed secretary general of the centre, he organized several annual conferences that brought together criminologists from the four corners of the world. The ICCC also traveled outside of Montréal, and several conferences were organized abroad, including in Central Europe, the Caribbean, Africa, and in Latin America, the last thanks to the exceptional support of **Lolita Aniyar de Castro,** professor at the University of Zulia in Maracaibo, Venezuela. Szabo moved forward with a well-established plan to cover as much ground as possible, and kept track of his progress with a large map of the world hung on a wall in his office, planting little flags wherever the ICCC was present.

Through his efforts to internationalize the Centre, Szabo thus consolidated Montréal criminology. However, in an ironic twist, the ICCC soon became a target of protest, and Szabo would find himself forced to defend the integrity and continued existence of the institution he had created.

In the 1970s, universities were home to intense protests against the prevailing social order and traditional institutions. This critical current, in diverse forms and ideologies, did not spare the social sciences, least of all criminology. In the case of Montréal, the ICCC was a target of choice: it had become suspect because of its ties with people working in the criminal justice system, its activities in countries with authoritarian regimes, and its financing, which came in part from the United States. And then an interview with Szabo published in a Montréal newspaper stirred up a hornets' nest. It was reported that, after a trip to South America, Szabo had seemingly advocated the use of death squadrons and was generally in favour of repressive police methods. The situation degenerated, a student movement was organized, and the offices of the ICCC were occupied. His life's work under attack, Szabo multiplied his public appearances in defence of criminology. The police put a quick end to the occupation of the ICCC, but not to distrust of the centre and its director. For several years afterwards, Szabo would be accused of being on the CIA's payroll, the ICCC of being in the service of totalitarian regimes, and criminology as being a science for sale. Still Szabo could not be swayed. He remained an unapologetic defender of mainstream criminology, despite some sympathies for the principles of its radical offshoot (see Box 2.3). Owing much to those who had contributed to mainstream criminology, Szabo felt the need to hold fast to his vision. And as the degree of protest decreased greatly over the years, he moved on.

During and after his leadership at the ICCC, Szabo's career continued to develop at the international level. A long list could be made of the places and persons that Szabo visited and met as he trotted round the globe. As the president of the International Society of Criminology from 1978 to 1985, he was at the heart of the discipline's global development, and oversaw dozens of international conferences and colloquiums. But even then, he still harbored the desire to create and leave behind something lasting, and so, in the 1980s, he prepared his last institutional legacy. As the scientific director of the *Revue internationale de criminologie et de police technique*, he decided to make it the official mouthpiece of a new organization, the *Association internationale des criminologues de langue française* (AICLF, International Association of French-speaking Criminologists), which he founded in 1987. It met with rapid success since, for francophone criminologists, it was a forum that allowed them to reach the international stage while avoiding the hurdles that the English

Box 2.3. On Radical Criminology

The sources of radical criminology are numerous. They go from impatience and disappointment with mediocre results and failed endeavours—that were nonetheless well thought-out—to a loss of faith in the system's ability to reform and resolve its own internal contradictions. Only a complete upheaval of the system can free the human energy needed to establish a new cultural, social, economic, and political model. It is only in this new world that public interest and private interest, personal spontaneity and collective freedom, safety for all and independence for each, will finally coincide.

This right to dream, this demand of certain minds to reject the past so as to only think of the future, this perpetual outpouring of generous intentions constitutes an indispensable component for intellectual life in all free societies. These works must be on the bookshelves of all criminologists.

The lesson of these texts is found in their excessiveness. They contribute as much to the relativity of certain ideas and behaviours as they do to the universality of other values and norms. Without going so far as to say that anti-criminology constitutes the "consciousness" of other criminologies, I would not hesitate to affirm that it expresses, dramatically so, doubts and debates that each one of us entertains in our own mind. The proposals of some of its advocates do as much to confirm some of my most solidly rooted convictions as to help erode some of my "biases" that were already undermined by doubt. However, the passionate debate set off by various anti-criminology theses does not greatly affect the daily practice of criminology. And it does not absolve us from the laborious obligation to demonstrate the inconsistencies and errors in our programs, theories, and techniques that affect the daily life, happiness, and well-being of millions of citizens.

Source: Denis Szabo, *Criminologie et politique criminelle*, 1978, our translation.

language posed for some. Over the next few years, conferences were organized in Morocco, Turkey, and Central and Latin America, places where the French language still predominated. Szabo acted as president of the organization until the beginning of the 2000s, and then, as he had done before, handed it over to posterity.

When I met Denis Szabo in the 1990s, his reputation preceded him. He had been retired as professor emeritus for a few years and did not hesitate to enumerate the acknowledgments he had received for service to criminology, including numerous honours: he was named a member of the Royal Society of Canada (1973) and of the Hungarian Academy of Sciences (1975), made an Officer of the Order of Canada (1985), appointed Chevalier (Knight) de l'Ordre des Arts et des Lettres in France (1998), and Officer of the Ordre National du Québec (1998). He was likewise made doctor *honoris causa* by the Universities of Sienna (1983), Budapest (1985), Aix-Marseille (1992), Pantios-Athens (1996), and Bucharest (2004).

This list only provides a glimpse of the distinctions that Denis Szabo received. Nor do they obscure the remarkable durability of the institutions he created. With more than 5,000 graduates since its creation, the School of Criminology at Université de Montréal has made an indelible mark on knowledge about and work with the criminal justice system in Québec. Moreover, the creation of a professional corporation of criminologists in 2015 fulfilled the vision of the founder of the School back in the 1960s. As for the ICCC, it now has some 50 regular researchers coming from several Québec universities as well as 80 associates from Québec, Canada, and several other countries. It constitutes one of the largest criminology research centres in the world.

The institutions that Denis Szabo founded throughout his career represent the aspirations of a man whose choices led him well beyond what his origins would seem to have dictated for him. As such, I would like to think that he sought not only acknowledgement for criminology but also for his own path. In a reversal of perspective that might make a sociologist smile, there is in the appreciation of his work a recognition of his own life, of the value of the path he laid out for himself. Denis Szabo's career is a powerful incentive to believe in one's own capacity for self-invention.

At the end of 2010, no longer formally attached to the School of Criminology, Denis Szabo left his office at Université de Montréal for the last time; no effort was made to dissuade him. He retired to his home on the shores of Lake Memphremagog near Sherbrooke, Quebec, where I met him on the fiftieth anniversary of the School of Criminology to hear his story one more time. At the end, I asked him to share his thoughts about the future of criminology. I think that his answer should constitute the last words of this chapter dedicated to him:

François Fenchel

I have written my legacy down on one page. One page where I list the most important issues. For example, with regard to criminal policy, we really have to change our priorities. The safety of individuals and civil society have to become priorities even though diverse forms of terrorism are plaguing us. There is also organized crime, tax havens, significant tax fraud in the world of high finance. Those are the issues that must become priorities, themes that existed in my youth but only as folklore....

We must also get rid of these wretched prisons. We must transform the penal process into a triangle that also includes the victims and restorative justice, because, whatever the difficulties might be, it will always be better than this damned miserable idea of captivity. You can do whatever you want but you can never change the humiliating, disgraceful, degrading nature of confinement.

If someone wants to start somewhere, let him start there.

Major Publications of Denis Szabo

Szabo, D. (1960). *Crimes et villes: Étude statistique comparée de la criminalité urbaine et rurale en France et en Belgique*. Paris: Cujas.

Szabo, D. (1965). *Criminologie*. Montréal: Les Presses de l'Université de Montréal.

Szabo, D. (1969). *Ordre et changement: Essai d'interprétation psycho-culturelle de l'inadaptation juvénile.* Leçons inaugurales de l'Université de Montréal, Montréal: PUM.

Szabo, D., Gagné, D., et Parizeau, A. (1972). *L'adolescent et la société.* Bruxelles: Dessart et Mardaga.

Szabo, D. (1978). *Criminologie et politique criminelle.* Paris and Montréal : Vrin and Presses de l'Université de Montréal.

Szabo, D. (1986). *Science et crime.* Paris: Vrin.

Szabo, D. (1993). *De l'anthropologie à la criminologie comparée.* Paris: Vrin.

References

Bertrand, M.-A., et Normandeau, A. (1984). Les sciences humaines à l'assaut (ou au service) des appareils de justice pénale au Québec. In Lévesque, G. H., et al. (eds.), *Continuité et rupture. Les sciences sociales au Québec* (319–336). Montréal: PUM.

Fenchel, F. (2010). Engendrer une pensée criminologique. Entretien avec Denis Szabo. *Criminologie*, 43(2): 11–29.

Fournier, M. (1998). *Entretiens avec Denis Szabo.* Montréal: Éditions Liber.

Normandeau, A. (1987). La petite histoire de la criminologie au Québec (1960–1985). *Revue internationale de criminologie et de police technique*, 1: 67–71.

Normandeau, A. (2002). La criminologie au Québec. *Problèmes actuels de science criminelle*, 5: 93–126.

Poupart, J. (2004). L'institutionnalisation de la criminologie au Québec: une lecture sociohistorique. *Criminologie*, 37(1): 71–105.

Szabo, D. (1961). Un nouvel enseignement de la criminologie au Québec. *Revue internationale des sciences sociales*, 13(2): 328–231.

Szabo, D. (1963). Criminologie et criminologue: discipline et profession nouvelles. *Revue internationale de criminologie et de police technique*, 17 (1): 13–22.

Szabo, D. (1977). Histoire d'une expérience québécoise qui aurait pu mal tourner. *Criminologie*, 10 (2): 5–38.

THREE

From the Land of the Pharaohs to Lotus Land: The Life and Criminological Achievements of Ezzat A. Fattah

Ezzat A. Fattah

Introduction

Had a fortune teller told Ezzat Fattah while he was growing up in Egypt that he would become a Canadian criminologist living in Vancouver, he would have thought that person out of her or his mind. Yet this is precisely the trajectory his life took. Fattah was the middle of five siblings born in a small town in Upper Egypt called Asyut. His father, one of a handful of Egyptians who obtained an M.D. early in the twentieth century at a time when less than 5% of the population could read and/or write, was detained during World War I in a concentration camp together with a group of compatriots opposed to the British occupation of Egypt. In an attempt to break up the group once they were released at the end of the war, the British Authority forbade Ezzat's father from practicing medicine in Cairo where all his family lived and dictated that he be exiled to Asyut 320 kilometres away! As destiny had it, it was there that Ezzat's father met and married the sister of an appeal-court judge who later became a justice of the Supreme Court of Egypt and served as a role model for Ezzat's future. Once he obtained his baccalaureate, Ezzat was expected to follow in the footsteps of his eldest brother and go to medical school. But the injustices he witnessed all around him led him to naively believe that law is the primary instrument of reform and the most effective vehicle for social change. Alas, before too long this belief was shattered!

Admitted to the Faculty of Law at the University of Cairo in 1944, he obtained his law degree in 1948, at age 19 the youngest student ever to graduate from an Egyptian law school. A year later he was appointed an assistant prosecutor in Alexandria. The following 12 years brought about several promotions together with the customary rotations to different Egyptian cities and towns, including Port Said (the Mediterranean entrance to the Suez Canal) and Sohag, a small town in Upper Egypt. By the end of the 1950s he was chief prosecutor in Cairo but in 1961 at the height of a promising judicial career he made the life-changing decision to leave Egypt.

From Dogmatic Law to Empirical Social Science, From Oppressive Military Rule To Democratic Freedom

Although Fattah served as a public prosecutor for 12 years, it did not take him long to realize that the law, particularly in a non-democratic society, can be an instrument of injustice, used by the powerful to oppress the powerless and to reinforce the privileges of the ruling classes. While a prosecutor in small Egyptian towns, he was tormented by the fact that peasants and labourers who could neither read nor write were dragged before the courts and punished for violations of laws they did not understand or, if understood, did not agree with.

This disillusionment with the law combined with the vagaries of an ill-equipped, understaffed justice system were disheartening. With it came the realization that crime is a social and cultural problem that cannot be solved simply by passing a law or dispensing punishment, however severe. For example, vendetta was a widespread custom in Upper Egypt as it was in parts of southern Europe. Ezzat soon realized that no criminal law and no punishment, be it the death penalty or life imprisonment, would solve the problem or change the custom. He believed that only a major cultural change could eliminate such an entrenched barbaric tradition.

Another eye-opener, early in his career as a prosecutor, confirmed this conviction. In the early 1950s, he was a public prosecutor in Alexandria assigned to drug cases. The use of hashish and opium was endemic though understandable. Living in squalid conditions with no hope of any kind, the masses tried to escape their miserable lives. As alcohol was prohibited by their religion, they turned to other mood-modifying drugs. As a result, the use of drugs became an alarming and widespread social problem. When the military came to power after the overthrow of the Egyptian monarchy in 1952, the new government decided that something had to be done. The approach, typical of the mentality of army and police officers, was to get tough—extremely tough. The maximum penalty for drug trafficking had been three years' imprisonment with no minimum sentence. Overnight this was changed to a minimum mandatory sentence of life imprisonment with hard labor and no possibility of extenuating circumstances. The new law took away any discretion the judges had. The military officers who brought in the new law thought they could now relax: No one in his right mind would risk going to prison for life to earn a few Egyptian pounds selling or smuggling drugs. But as the prosecutor dealing with drug cases, Ezzat could observe firsthand the consequences of the new law. They were exactly the opposite of what the lawmakers anticipated. Trafficking in drugs became much worse, not better. It was not difficult for him to see why. Except when very large quantities of drugs were seized, members of drug squads were very reluctant to formally proceed with the charges. Offenders caught with small amounts or even medium-sized amounts were given a slap on the wrist, had the drugs confiscated, and were warned not to do it again or else! As the prosecutor, Ezzat was incensed that the penalty for drug trafficking was now more serious than the usual penalty for willful homicide, and tried to find some way of not proceeding with the cases to court. In the few cases where he had to go to court, the three judges presiding over felony proceedings were extremely reluctant to convict and quite often acquitted the accused, either under the pretext that the evidence was insufficient or simply on a technicality. The rules of search and seizure made such acquittals rather simple. As the new law made the sanction much less certain than was the case when the maximum sentence was three years, any deterrent effect was reduced rather than increased. But with the new though rather theoretical risk of life imprisonment, the price of drugs skyrocketed and the prospect of greater profits attracted hundreds of new traffickers. A greatly increased risk for border patrols was another side-effect of the new law. Drug smugglers who faced the prospect of being arrested were now willing to shoot to kill those trying to catch them. They had nothing to lose since the penalty for drug smuggling was now the same as for murder. As the political situation in Egypt worsened under the military regime of Colonel Nasser, following the dissolution of an unsuccessful union with Syria, Ezzat found it unbearable to live in a police state where the principle of the independence of the judiciary was in jeopardy. He felt he had no option but to leave. The decision was met with vehement objections from his mother, siblings and other family members. (His father had passed away four years earlier.) They could not believe that someone, even out of principle, would leave a secure and very promising position for an unknown future elsewhere.[17]

[17] Promotion in the Egyptian judiciary is based on seniority. As the youngest member of his cohort, Ezzat's chances of becoming the chief justice of the Supreme Court of Egypt prior to reaching retirement age were almost certain.

Egyptian citizens could not leave the country unless they obtained an "exit visa," which was never given for tourist purposes. Only medical, business and study purposes were acceptable as grounds for travelling abroad. Luckily for Ezzat, the government of Austria was offering a scholarship for studies at the University of Vienna. A competition was held and Ezzat won. In October 1961, he boarded a plane for the Austrian capital, travelling with one suitcase. He never looked back and did not return to Egypt to see his family until 11 years later, when Anwar Sadat, who succeeded Nasser as head of state in 1970, promised a more open society.

A New Life in Vienna, City Of Wine, Music And Song

At this time, the University of Vienna had neither a graduate nor undergraduate criminology program. The law faculty did have an Institute for Criminal Law and Criminology headed by Professor **Roland Grassberger** (1905–1991). In their first encounter, Ezzat made it clear to Grassberger that he was more than willing to take courses in criminal law and criminal procedures to familiarize himself with Austrian and Germanic law, but that his primary interest was to take courses in the social and behavioral sciences as well as courses in statistics and research methodology. The wonderful three years he spent in Vienna saw him carry out a combination of course work and research. As a special non-degree seeking student, he was allowed to take courses of his own choosing in any faculty. His empirical research was mainly in the new field of *victimology*, to which he was introduced by Prof. Grassberger who personally knew the founder of victimology, the German criminal psychologist and politician, **Hans von Hentig** (1887–1974).

Ezzat's love for classical music and opera, which had blossomed in Alexandria while living with an Italian family, was nurtured and broadened during his stay in Vienna, undoubtedly one of the music capitals of the world. As a university student he could spend an entire evening at the *Stats Oper* or the *Volks Oper* watching a complete opera or operetta, while standing on his feet, for one Austrian shilling, at the time the equivalent of five cents!

The original scholarship lasted one academic year, but with the support of his mentor, who later became the university's rector, it was extended for a second and then a third and final year. Fattah's next goal was to pursue a Ph.D. in criminology. At that time only a handful of universities in the world offered such a degree. The most famous was the School of Criminology in Berkeley, California. Another was the University of Pennsylvania's Sociology Department, where **Thorsten Sellin** and **Marvin Wolfgang** taught. However, a more interesting opportunity for him appeared to be the University of Montreal which, under the guidance of **Denis Szabo**, already had a master's degree program in place and was starting a Ph.D. program in criminology. An important factor in choosing Montreal was Fattah's fluency in French and his extensive background in Egyptian criminal and civil law, which were closely related to their French counterparts.

Following his successful completion of the master's degree in the record time of one year and after obtaining his doctorate in criminology in 1968, the first degree of its kind awarded in Canada—both under the supervision of psychiatrist Henri Ellenberger—Fattah was appointed an assistant professor at Montreal. Three years later he was promoted to associate professor. Invited by Simon Fraser University to found and chair the first criminology program in western Canada, he moved in 1974 with his Norwegian wife, Jenny, to Vancouver, B.C. and remains to this day professor emeritus at the same university.

Pioneering Work in Criminology

Fattah's pioneering work in Canadian criminology began in the 1960s and continues to the present. The following brief account will, it is hoped, provide the reader with an overview of a professional career that has spanned more than six decades and five continents!

Call for Decriminalization of Drugs
(Reference nos. 23, 24, 25, 28, 29, 33 and 34)

It may be fashionable today to call for the decriminalization of mood-modifying drugs. But this subject was taboo in the 1960s and 1970s. Those who dared call for drug-policy reform were considered criminological heretics, ostracized and even blacklisted by law enforcement agencies. Inspired by his experience in Egypt as a public prosecutor assigned to drug cases, Ezzat felt it was his duty to draw attention not only to the negative consequences of criminalization but also to the flagrant inconsistencies in Canadian drug policy. He argued, for example, that alcohol and tobacco, whose harmful health and social effects far exceed those of other drugs, are legal and readily available, while soft drugs such as marijuana are prohibited. He pointed to the inequalities, injustices and enormous waste in human potential caused by antiquated drug laws, publicly denouncing this misguided punitive approach in several conference lectures and numerous papers. In one of those papers, he called for a new legislative policy regarding drugs and drug addiction (references 24 and 25). Little did he foresee the consequences of this daring position. While the negative reaction of law enforcement agencies to his proposals was expected, he did not envisage that in a democratic country like Canada the opinions he expressed would be used against him. Yet, when he later solicited police cooperation for research on drugs under contract from the Government Commission on the Non-Medical Use of Drugs (the LeDain Commission), he was flatly turned down. In a meeting with an RCMP assistant commissioner in Ottawa, he was bluntly told that the police will only cooperate with, and provide data to, researchers who share their views on drugs!

The Struggle to Have the Death Penalty Abolished
(Reference nos. 3, 4, 30, 33, 34, 43, 55, 59, 60, 62, 63 and 64)

Staunch defender of human rights, sensitive to human suffering and keenly aware of the need to protect citizens against abuses of power, Fattah was troubled by Canada's retention of the death penalty. He was aware that Canadians on both sides of the issue held very emotional as well as strong philosophical and religious views, none of which could be scientifically challenged. He realized that the most important and rational justification for the death penalty was its supposedly unique deterrent effect. In the early 1970s the reformist Liberal government of Pierre Elliott Trudeau was eager to abolish the death penalty. It decided, however, to take the cautious and more acceptable course of suspending it for five years, with the intention of assessing whether such suspension had any impact on homicide rates. Under contract with the Ministry of the Solicitor-General, Fattah was asked to undertake the evaluation. He decided to take a novel approach that would allow him to come up with a reasonably reliable and believable answer to the question. The findings of the study were published in 1972 as a government report in both official languages (references 3 and 4). The English version, *A Study of the Deterrent Effect of Capital Punishment with Special Reference to the Canadian Situation,* received wide coverage in Canada and abroad. It was cited frequently during the ensuing parliamentary debates in Ottawa, during one of which Fattah was called by opposition member Eldon Woolliams "the high priest of abolition in Canada"—a derogatory reference to his being born in Egypt!

The study caught the attention of Amnesty International and led to a protracted association with the activist non-governmental organization that resulted in Fattah being invited to several international conferences to campaign for the abolition of the death penalty and for the commutation of sentences of those on death row. He was one of the rapporteurs at the historic meeting that ended with the Stockholm Declaration. He was also asked by Amnesty International to go on missions to the United States; to Libya, where he addressed that country's Legislative Assembly and had a memorable encounter with Colonel Kaddafi in which he requested (and was promised) a mass commutation of the sentences of those sitting on death row; and to Bermuda, Jamaica, Aruba/Curacao, Tunisia and Brazil.

At the Seventh UN Congress on the Prevention of Crime and the Treatment of Offenders held in Milan in August 1985, Amnesty International organized a three-member panel on the abolition of the death penalty. The international panel gave Fattah a unique opportunity to describe Canada's successful experience with the abolition of the death penalty to a truly international audience that included representatives from many retentionist countries.

Fattah's study of the deterrent effect of the death penalty led the Law Reform Commission of Canada to ask him to carry out a comprehensive review of the existing studies and literature on deterrence. His report was published in 1976 (references 7 and 8). He continued to research the thorny issue of deterrence (references 38, 39, 42, 44, and 45). When some American economists, including Isaac Ehrlich and Philip Cook, claimed their econometric models showed the death penalty to be a deterrent, Ezzat took it upon himself to highlight the shortcomings and the methodological deficiencies of those studies (reference 42).

Pioneering Explorations of the Ecological Distribution of Canadian Crime

The state of crime statistics in Canada in the first half of the twentieth century left much to be desired. Attempts were made over the years to improve their quality. Ezzat's study of the deterrent effect of the death penalty was the first systematic examination of the geographical distribution of criminal homicide and other crimes of violence across the country. It revealed some interesting patterns, and showed wide variations in homicide rates among different provinces and regions. The official statistics for the years 1962 to 1970 revealed, for example, that violent crime increases in almost a linear fashion as one moves from east to west—an observation that still holds largely true to this day.

Those previously unexamined trends provided him with a strong impetus to explore further the ecological distribution of crime in Canada by means of a series of analytical studies using statistics of reported crime. With the help of a research grant from the Ministry of the Solicitor General, Ezzat hired three of his students (Francine Bissonnet, Geral Geoffrion and Annie-Claude Sholtes) to collect and tabulate the data. The findings were gathered in several unpublished volumes. The series was titled *Essais de Criminologie Ecologique* (*Essays in Ecological Criminology*) and served as a model for later studies.

Research for the Prevost Commission

The University of Montreal's School of Criminology was influential in bringing to light glaring deficiencies in the criminal justice system. Mounting criticism led the Quebec government to set up a special commission to investigate the state of criminal justice in the province and make recommendations for reform—the Commission d'enquete sur l'adminstaration de la justice en matiere criminelle et penale au Quebec, headed by Justice Yves Prevost.

Research proposals on various aspects of the criminal justice system were submitted to the commission at its request and several projects selected and approved. A research group comprising a number of professors from the School of Criminology and the Faculty of Law was formed under the direction of Denis Szabo. In the 1960s, empirical research on criminal justice was lacking and the studies done for the commission were therefore seen as pioneering work. Subcontracting with a reputable polling company, Fattah and Andre Normandeau (see Chapter 6) carried out the first comprehensive survey of public opinion on criminal justice in the province of Quebec. In 1968, a comprehensive analysis of the findings was published (reference 1). As expected, the results were not very flattering and, in particular, not well-received by the province's lawyers. A few, like Maitre Alban Flammand, took to the air not just to criticize the findings but also to denounce the authors of the report and the entire criminology profession, describing them with the derogatory Quebec slang expression "*les touches-pipis.*" It was a classic case of shooting the messenger!

Fattah's research on public views of criminal justice in Quebec was the inspiration for a comprehensive review of public attitudes to the death penalty, a study he carried out in 1975 under contract to the Solicitor General of Canada (references 5 and 6).

Another report Fattah prepared in 1969 for the Prevost Commission dealt with the role of criminology teaching and research in the administration of criminal justice (see reference 2).

Pioneering Work in Victimology

Ezzat's interest in victimology began in the early 1960s in Vienna. He published his first article on the subject in 1966 and followed it with several others in the nascent discipline (references 17, 18, 19, 20, 21, 22, 26, 27, 31, 32, 35, 36, 41, and 47). His doctoral dissertation, an empirical study of the factors that contribute to the choice of victims in cases of murder for robbery, was published as a book by Les Presses de Université de Montreal in 1971 under the provocative and commercially attractive title (chosen by the publisher) *La Victime Est-Elle Coupable?* (*Is the Victim Guilty?*). When the title was criticized as suggesting that victims may be to blame, Fattah responded that one of the most popular adjectives used in the context of crime and justice is "innocent." Describing some victims as "innocent" implies that there are some victims who are guilty. Rather than confirming the existence of those guilty victims, the book simply poses the question.

In 1976, in the second issue of *Victimology: An International Journal*, Emilio Viano, the journal's founder and chief editor, published biographies of seven "pioneers in victimology" that included Fattah, Hans von Hentig, Benjamin Mendelsohn, Israel Drapkin, Stephen Schaffer, Margery Fry and Koichi Miyazawa. Fattah's work in victimology meriting his recognition as a pioneer was listed at the end of the biography. It comprised 18 victimological papers published over a span of 10 years from 1966 to 1976 (references 17, 18, 19, 20, 21, 22, 26, 27, 31, 32 and 36).

When Fattah published his first articles on victimology, the emerging discipline was virtually unknown, although its seminal work, Von Hentig's book

The Criminal and His Victim, had been published in 1948 by Yale University Press. Victimology was considered an esoteric subject of little significance in the family of social sciences and negligible practical significance in the realm of criminal justice. It thus became incumbent upon the pioneers not only to broaden and deepen public knowledge of what victimology was all about, but also to argue effectively for its theoretical importance, relevance, and its potentially significant practical applications, particularly in the field of crime prevention. So, in his two-part article "La Victimologie: Qu'est-elle et Quel est son Avenir?" published in 1967 in *La Revue Internationale de Criminologie et de Police Technique* (references 21 and 22), Fattah took upon himself to explain to the scientific, legal and research communities and to the general public the importance of victimology.

Then in 1991, Fattah published his ground-breaking book *Understanding Criminal Victimization* (reference 12), in which he laid down the theoretical foundations of victimology, treated topics previously little-discussed, and set the stage for future research in both theoretical and applied victimology. The book contains several novel chapters on topics hitherto under-researched or neglected, including the dynamics of criminal victimization, victim behavior as a situational variable, victim response to confrontational face-to-face victimization, victim-offender relationships, and victim/target selection. Fattah's objective was to highlight the importance of those topics and promote their study as fertile and virgin areas of research. In 2016, sadly realizing that victim advocacy has eclipsed theoretical victimology and that the important research topics he discussed in the book remained neglected, he tried to revive interest in their study in two chapters he wrote for the Festschrifts of John Dussich and Gerd Kirchhoff (references 132 and 133).

The enthusiastic reception of the book was heartening, as was the fact the book became the reference of choice for those interested in theoretical and applied victimology. The book was followed in 1997 by its criminology companion, *Criminology: Past, Present and Future—A Critical Overview* (reference 14).

As early as 1976, Fattah tackled neglected issues in victimology (e.g., "The Use of the Victim as an Agent of Self-Legitimization: Towards a Dynamic Explanation of Criminal Behavior" [references 35 and 36]). In 1979, long before terrorism became one of the most debated issues in the world, he discussed the victimology of terrorism (reference 46), followed in 1981 by another article in which he offered a typology of terrorist activities and terrorist targets (reference 52). Another paper highlighted and discussed the important role of alcohol as a victimogenic factor (reference 134).

In the 1980s, advocacy for victims of crime reached new heights and was being exploited by conservatives to make the criminal justice system more punitive. Ezzat was one of the few victimologists who were not swept away by the tide and was highly critical of right-wing attempts to politically exploit crime victims to bring about harsher sanctions and the abrogation of the rights of the accused (references 65, 72, 98, and 15). He devoted his keynote address to the thirty-third International Course in Criminology on Victims of Crime that he organized in Vancouver to the visible and hidden dangers of victim movements (references 65 and 95), and followed this by editing a book titled *Towards a Critical Victimology* (reference 13). In another edited book, he called for a switch *From Crime Policy to Victim Policy* (reference 9), yet as he explained in a chapter written for a 1997 book, the victim policy he advocates is aimed at healing, not suffering (reference 89). He made the same points in a later paper published in French and Portuguese, "From Research to Activism, From Scholarship to Partisanship, and the Resulting Impoverishment of Victimology" (references 126 and 127).

Fattah warned that well-meaning actions can have unintended consequences. For example, overly magnifying the impact of victimization can unintentionally harm victims by delaying the natural healing process (references 70, 84, 89, and 95). To counter the stereotypes propagated by the victim movement in its efforts to gain public acceptance of retributive justice, Fattah drew attention in his writings to the striking homogeneity of the victim and offender populations and to the flagrant biases in the selection of which victims are to be helped. He outlined how those biases lead to the inequalities currently prevalent in victim services, victim support and victim assistance (references 113, 114, and 122); explained how selective current victim compensation is (reference 93); and lamented governments' attempt to shift the financial burden of compensation to offenders (even those convicted of victimless crimes) through what came to be known as *victim fine surcharges*. Fattah deplored society's differential attitudes to victims and pointed to society's manifest tolerance of the victimization of those considered socially expendable due to their age, poverty, and marginality (references 112, 113, 114, and 122). In his research, he paid particular attention to victimization of the weak (the elderly), the defenceless (children), the have-nots, the deviants, the marginalized, and so on, decrying society's prejudices that result in tacit acceptance of their victimization (references 11, 51, 67, 77, 84, 87, 109 and 128). And in 1994 when he was invited to deliver the second honorary Inkeri Antilla lecture in Helsinki, he chose as the topic the interchangeable and revolving roles of victims and victimizers. Antilla, a Finnish criminologist and former minister of justice, is widely recognized for her work in professionalizing the study of victimology. In his lecture, Fattah refuted the popular stereotype of victims and offenders as two distinct, mutually exclusive populations (references 83 and 90).

In 2000, Fattah's keynote address to the tenth International Symposium in Victimology in Montreal exposed the ethical conundrums in the young discipline and offered strong arguments that victimology is in dire need of deontology (references 107 and 108).

Having highlighted throughout his criminological writings the phenomenon of the relativity of crime, Ezzat decided to prove, using numerous examples, that victimization is also relative both in time and space. He set out to show that victimization is a dynamic phenomenon and that cultural definitions of what constitute various types of victimization are undergoing constant change. Ezzat was always fascinated by the findings of ethnologists and cultural anthropologists such as Margaret Mead and others. Their studies showed beyond any doubt that there are no universal norms according to which an act can be universally defined a crime or an act of victimization. In a 1993 paper, he demonstrated the undeniable cultural relativity of victimization and insisted that it should become one of the primary research topics in comparative victimology (references 74 and 118).

That same year, Fattah received the prestigious Konrad Adenauer Prize, bestowed by the German government on a distinguished Canadian social scientist to allow him/her to spend a research year in Germany. He chose to study the changes in crime and victimization in East Germany following reunification. The study was a pioneering exploration of the changes in victimization that take place in societies in transition to democracy (reference 81). Rapid political, social and economic changes produce a number of crises, including a crisis in values and expectations. The changes also created intense feelings of frustration, relative deprivation, social alienation, insecurity and a heightened sense of victimization. All these factors have traditionally been associated with high or rising crime rates. Fattah suggested that increased crime rates lend credence to specific criminological theories, such as *opportunity theory*. Temptation, motivations and readily available opportunities were bound to produce large increases in various types of crime and victimization.

Fattah firmly believed that victimology is and should always remain an integral part of criminology. For him they were by no means parallel but complementary, or, to borrow the words of the Dutch criminologist Hoefnagels (reference 141), victimology is "the other side of criminology." To demonstrate the inseparable bond that ties both disciplines, he published in 1993 a book chapter outlining how the rational choice/opportunity perspectives can be used as a vehicle for integrating criminological and victimological theories (references 78 and 139).

Never one to watch from the sidelines, in recent years Fattah lamented the transformation of the scholarly discipline that consumed a large part of his life into a partisan, politicized and activist movement. He strongly argued for a separation of science from ideology and for drawing a line between scholarly research and political activism (references 13, 54, 66, 70, 71, 82, 85, 91, 117, 126 and 127). In later years, when punitive victimology took hold, he became highly critical of those calling for the separation of victimology from its parent discipline of criminology into a separate discipline. Invited to give the closing address to the Fifteenth International Congress of Criminology in Barcelona in 2008, he challenged the wisdom of such a misguided effort (reference 120).

To recognize Fattah's pioneering work in victimology, L'Université de Pau et des Pays de L'adour in France honored him by designating the 2002–03 "promotion" (graduation) the Ezzat Fattah Promotion. The graduating students were asked to analyze and report on his work and to present those reports at a colloquium, whose proceedings were then published in 2004 (references 117 and 137).

Calling for an End to Imprisonment

Ezzat's extensive study of the history of penal sanctions led him to the conclusion that no punishment is transcendental, permanent or immutable. A well-known and accepted axiom is that social change is inevitable and unstoppable. And so is penal change. All punishments appear only to disappear when they become incompatible with new views and attitudes. Fattah believed that imprisonment, like other outdated punishments of the past, will eventually decline and ultimately disappear. In 1978 (reference 40), he decried mounting calls for harsher sanctions after two progressive decades that witnessed a strong trend toward the mitigation of social reaction to crime and deviance. This was followed in 1982 by a paper in which he offered a devastating critique of the use of imprisonment as a retributive sanction, arguing it can never achieve the avowed goal of making the punishment fit the crime. Other papers on alternatives to imprisonment and on how to overcome public opposition to them followed (references 48, 56, 57 and 58).

In 1982, when Fattah was awarded a one-year university research professorship, one of the requirements was to deliver a public lecture on a research topic of his choosing. In the lecture, "Society without Prisons: Can Research Find a Replacement?" he traced the historical evolution of social reaction to crime and deviance, outlined examples of old, barbaric punishments that have since disappeared, and highlighted the cruel, wasteful nature of imprisonment. He predicted that, although he would not live to see the day, imprisonment will eventually be abandoned as a tragic relic from the past.

Fattah was realistic enough to know that his prediction would not be universally accepted, and that there would be a good number of skeptics in the audience and among the public. What he did not expect was criticism from a controversial B.C. judge, Les Bewley, who had not attended the lecture himself but relied on summaries in the media. Bewley attacked Fattah in the *Vancouver Sun* for being a utopian academic with no practical knowledge of the "real criminal justice system," apparently unaware of Fattah's experience working within the system.

Promoting Restorative Justice Models

At an international symposium in Helsinki in 1992 (reference 73), Fattah argued for a paradigm change in criminal justice, and a fundamental shift in penal philosophy. He urged a move away from pain-inflicting punishments rooted in metaphysical and religious beliefs to non-punitive and peaceful conflict-solving mechanisms. As well, he proposed a switch from a *guilt orientation* to a *consequence orientation*, to replace the archaic concepts underlying classical penal law with modern secular concepts resembling those that govern other branches of law (e.g., civil, commercial, labour, maritime, etc.). Unlike other areas of law that have undergone substantial evolution since the Industrial Revolution, criminal law remains frozen in time. It seems incomprehensible that medieval punishments such as imprisonment, fines, and in many countries even death have remained the sole response to violations of the law since time immemorial. How it is that in the advanced society in which we live, it has not been possible (nor acceptable) to develop positive, peaceful, non-violent methods to deal with those who violate the law? How is it that society remains fixated on pain-inflicting sanctions with their inevitable degradation and humiliation? To legal scholars attending the symposium whose careers were built under the old paradigm, the new concept sounded both radical and revolutionary, and most (except for the progressive Scandinavian criminalists present) were not amused! Far from being discouraged by the reaction, Fattah followed his original paper with others on the same theme (references 76, 86, 94, 96, 104, 105, 111, 116 and 119).

Fattah's acceptance and promotion of restorative justice was in keeping with his long-held views. It was the crystallization of the philosophy he had been proselytizing for several decades. In the paper he gave in Cape Town in 2006 (reference 119), he explained his attraction to restorative justice (RJ):

In the 1970s I was visiting the Ivory Coast as a guest professor at the University of Abidjan and decided to do a study of African homicide to gain a better understanding of the impact culture has on the rates, the nature and the types of criminal homicide.... I carefully examined the national police records on criminal homicide during the previous ten years.

Very soon I noticed that there were few, if any, cases recorded in the rural areas and the small villages of the Ivory Coast. Could it be, I thought, that the rural population in the country was much too peaceful to kill one another? Well, no! There was in fact another explanation.... [I]t did not take me long to realize that there were two, almost parallel, systems of justice operating in the Ivory Coast. One was the Western punitive system, inspired by the expiatory and retaliatory teachings of the Old and New Testaments, a system that was imposed on the Ivorian population by the colonial power, France.... The second was the indigenous, tribal system, or call it patriarchal if you want, which used customary rules and traditions to solve conflicts and to settle disputes of all kinds between the members of the community.

Getting no satisfaction from the Western system of punitive, retributive justice, and unable to comprehend why the State should steal the conflicts from their rightful owners (to use Nils Christie's idea) while doing nothing to compensate the victim's family or to achieve reconciliation between the feuding clans, those victimized simply did not report the homicides to the police, preferring instead to have the matter dealt with according to their norms and their customs. The two elements of this indigenous justice were compensation (for the death, injury or harm done) and reconciliation aimed at restoring the peace disrupted by the offence and at ensuring a future of harmonious co-existence.

And what a valuable learning experience for me that was! It brought to memory a truly remarkable case that I came across when studying the history of capital punishment in Canada. It is the story of an Indian Chief of one of Canada's First Nations tribes whose son was killed by the son of the British Garrison Commander. Intent on showing the fairness and equality of British justice, the officer insisted that his son be executed in conformity with British law. The pleas of the victim's father fell on deaf ears. He offered to adopt the killer so that he may replace his slain son. He could not, despite his personal grief, understand the rationale for the death penalty, the wisdom of doubling the loss instead of trying to minimize it. He asked himself and the commander: What purpose would be achieved by taking the life of the culprit?

But to no avail. The talion law, a life for a life, an eye for an eye, and a tooth for a tooth, had to be applied. And the so-called civilized

> Western justice had to prevail and did! The evident futility and destructiveness of such punishment was not enough to persuade a dedicated military officer to bend the rules or to listen to the wisdom of the Indigenous Chief, even if it meant sparing his own son.
>
> All this was an eye-opener. It convinced me that punishment is not and can never be the answer. It convinced me that there must be a better solution, a better response to harmful, injurious acts. I was fascinated by the tales of cultural anthropologists who studied what Western scholars denigratively called "primitive societies." Those were societies that have escaped the influence of Judaism, Christianity and Islam and thus were not inspired or affected by the religious notions of expiation and penitence.
>
> What I found remarkable was the quasi-universality of the historical evolution of social reaction to harmful and injurious acts. The reports of social and cultural anthropologists show that in every society studied there was an evolution from private vengeance to group vengeance to a system of composition, which is the earliest form of restorative justice. Moving from vengeance to compensation was a normal progression because retaliation proved detrimental to the group.
>
> But let me assure you that my favoring of Restorative Justice over punishment is not merely a humanitarian stance. It is based on a deep conviction that it is a better, viable, constructive and more effective response to harm than the deliberate infliction of pain and suffering.

In 2011 Fattah was invited to deliver the closing address at the seventh *International Conference of the European Forum for Restorative Justice* in Helsinki (reference 131). It was an unforgettable experience due to the presence of many RJ pioneers and supporters including Martin Wright, Howard Zehr, Raimo Lahti, Ivo Aertzen, the late Nils Christie, and many others.

Fattah argued that although the notion of justice is fundamental, definitions are difficult to come by. So, he invited the audience to reflect on the concept of justice and expressed his bewilderment at how punishment has become almost synonymous with justice:

> How is it that slogans such as "justice for victims" are invariably interpreted as demands for more and harsher punishments?
>
> How is it that victims who, as Nils Christie said, are the primary owners of the conflict (Christie 1977, reference 138), whose property rights were usurped, and whose rightful dues paid to them in the form of "wehrgeld" or composition were expropriated by the state, were led to believe that justice is vengeance and retaliation and that the harsher the punishment, the more just is the judgement?
>
> How is it that the theological and abstract notions of retribution,

> expiation, atonement and penitence became so entrenched in people's minds that no rational thinking, no scientific evidence, no economic crisis, no humanitarian endeavor seems to be capable of shaking such religious beliefs or lessening the incessant demands for punishment?
>
> How is it that punishment has become so universally accepted, extremely popular and so widely practiced that people and governments, even in the hardest economic times, are more than willing to waste billions and billions of dollars for no other reason but to inflict pain and suffering on those fellow citizens who have violated man-made laws?

The lecture, which received a standing ovation, was one of the most gratifying experiences of his academic life.

Founding the School Of Criminology at Simon Fraser University

Many would consider the founding of the Department (later School) of Criminology at Simon Fraser University to be Fattah's crowning criminological achievement. The obstacle-filled task of creating a new department from scratch could fill not only a book chapter but a whole volume! Space limitations do not allow even a brief relating of how it materialized in the face of formidable odds and widespread misperceptions. To singlehandedly prepare the entire curriculum and to navigate it through various university bodies all the way to the Senate and the Board of Governors in record time was held by the entire SFU community to be a remarkable achievement. Luckily, a brief but lucid history recently was published by two of Ezzat's colleagues, Curt Griffiths and Ted Palys (reference 140). They write:

> Tracing the origins and evolution of the School provides an interesting case study of a unique program that was founded on an interdisciplinary model that sought to embrace both criminal justice and criminology. Its history facilitates an examination of the potential tension between criminal justice and criminology, the potential for, and challenges of, collaboration between university-based programs, governments, and criminal justice agencies, and the professional and interpersonal dynamics that exist in a multi-disciplinary program (pp. 16–17).

Later they draw attention to

> the personal stamp placed upon the school by its founder, Dr. Ezzat Fattah, a Faculty of Law graduate from the University of Cairo and former Cairo Prosecutor who received his M.A. and Ph.D. from the

> Université de Montréal. It was his detailed proposal for a Department of Criminology, written while he was an Associate Professor at the Université de Montréal—and his subsequent persistence and not taking "no" for an answer—that enticed the university's Senate to approve the new program in the spring of 1975. His detailed and complete curriculum—completed and adopted by Senate before a single faculty member was hired—operationalized that vision" (p. 17)....
>
> Fattah's original curriculum included 44 different courses.... The intent was to give students a broad overview of justice issues and then allow them to choose one or more specializations—a curriculum model that still exists today. Another element that Fattah included in the original proposal that remains to this day was the imposition of breadth requirements to encourage students to broaden their horizons with courses in political science, philosophy, communications, sociology/anthropology, and so on (pp. 21–22).
>
> The first course, Criminology 101—Introduction to Criminology, was taught in September, 1975, by the founding Director. Professor Fattah recalls it was enormously popular, with registration capped at 475—the capacity of the largest lecture hall available at SFU at that time (Fattah, 15 July 2014). Fattah was adamant that the university show its support by allowing him to hire a core cohort of faculty very quickly—and at one point offered his resignation if he was not allowed eight faculty positions immediately (p. 25).

In a 2014 email, Palys, one of the authors of the above-cited article, wrote to Fattah, saying: "One thing you should be heartened by is how long that original vision of yours has continued providing the basic structure of our department; not many people could come up with a curriculum that would still be relevant 40 years later!"

The Future of Criminology

The Belgian Professor **Tony Peters** (1941–2012) was elected president of the International Society of Criminology in 2006 and remained in that position until his untimely death in March 2012. He and Fattah became the closest of colleagues and the best of friends. With Fattah's book *Criminology: Past, Present and Future* (Reference 14) in mind, Peters asked Ezzat to deliver the closing address at Society's 2008 conference, offering his reflections on the future of criminology. Ezzat warned Peters that his current views were rather unconventional and controversial, as may be seen from the very title of the address: "The Future of Criminology as a Social Science and Academic Discipline: Reflections on Criminology's Unholy Alliance with Criminal Policy and on Current Misguided Attempts to Divorce Victimology from Criminology" (references 120, 121). The address marked a significant metamorphosis in Ezzat's thinking, brought about, no doubt, by the negative changes that followed 9/11, particularly the extreme obsession with security at the expense of human rights and freedoms. The paper's conclusion reflects not only his exasperation with the stagnation of criminology and its failure to radically humanize the criminal justice system, but also his frustration with the exploitation of criminology by politicians and research-funding agencies to turn it into a sub-discipline of security studies and a vehicle to introduce oppressive and undemocratic laws and practices. If criminology is to have a future, Fattah believed, it needs to confine itself to teaching and to scientific research and divorce itself from criminal policy. To stress the difference between criminology and criminal policy he proposed a new definition of each (reference 120):

> Criminology is the search for, and the application of, scientific concepts, methods and theories to the study of the phenomenon of crime, its perpetrators and its victims. This definition affirms criminology's scientific character and its status as an empirical, non-normative, non-speculative social/behavioral science. It is meant, above all, to differentiate the science of criminology from the discipline of criminal policy.... [which] is the application of criminological and other types of knowledge, in practice, to achieve desirable goals in the areas of crime control and prevention, for managing offenders and helping victims.
>
> As this definition makes it clear, criminal policy is an applied discipline with a much broader scope and much wider field of application than criminology. Those include the processes of making, unmaking and reforming the laws related to crime, as well as the processes of enforcing and applying those laws, assessing social reaction to crime, and deciding on the ways and means of controlling and preventing crime, and of helping offenders and victims.

Ezzat went on to deplore the current state of criminology:

> Criminology's stagnation, lack of innovation and its slow adaptation to the realities of the twenty-first century is threatening its very existence as it risks becoming irrelevant to the threats facing post-9/11 society, namely the flagrant abuses of power and the serious violations of human rights and civil liberties.
>
> The politics of expansion have not been beneficial to criminology. Retrenchment is the order of the day. Rather than holding firm to fields and areas that do not belong to or are only at the distant periphery of the discipline, criminology should take a bold step and make several territorial concessions that would ensure its safe return to its natural and logical subject-matter. If criminology is to gain in stature and prestige it has to shed its undeserved European reputa-

> tion as an auxiliary branch of the criminal law and its American reputation as a sub-field of sociology or as a peripheral discipline at the bottom heap of the social sciences. It has to affirm its scientific nature, its own identity, its originality, and its autonomy. It has to affirm its specificity, its objectivity and its neutrality. It has to dissociate itself from the criminal law and to divorce itself from criminal policy. And finally, the time seems to have come to separate the teaching of criminology from the teaching of other professional fields such as law, law enforcement, criminal justice, etc. in the same way that medicine is taught separately from nursing and the science of economics is taught separately from the professional discipline of accounting.

Recognition

Recognition for Fattah's pioneering work came in various ways. Notable among international awards is an honorary doctorate from the University of Liège, Belgium (1995); the Hermann Mannheim Award from the International Society of Criminology (2007); and the Hans von Hentig Award from the International Society of Victimology (2009). Fattah is one of a handful of criminologists elected fellows of the Royal Society of Canada (1990). In 1999 he received the Nora and Ted Sterling Prize for Controversy in recognition of his daring to express unconventional views on a variety of topics related to criminology, victimology and criminal justice. As a young scholar in Montreal, he was awarded the Beccaria Prize by the Quebec Society of Criminology and the Alex Edmison award by the Canadian Association of Professional Criminologists. He also received a Presidential Citation for Outstanding Contributions to the Quality of Criminal Justice in Canada from the American Society of Criminology. In 1992 he was awarded the Commemorative Medal of the 125 Anniversary of the Confederation of Canada. He was repeatedly elected to the board of directors of the International Society of Criminology and served as one of the vice-presidents of the society for over a decade. His work has been published in a dozen languages and he has served a visiting professor at numerous universities and other institutions.

A First-Person Epilogue

Nothing is more normal for an academic in the eighth decade of his life than to think of the intellectual and professional legacy they will leave behind. In addition to published books and papers, some write wills and testaments, others are anxious to put into words what they have achieved and what they want to be remembered for. I thought of this some years ago when lecturing to university students in Leuven, Belgium. I cannot think of a better way to conclude my life story than to say again what I told the audience at the end of that lecture:

I have often been accused of being controversial, even too controversial, as if being unconventional is a sin or a crime. If it is, I plead guilty. I never understood what is wrong with being controversial and I would like to ask you to give me one good reason why an intelligent audience like you should be forced to listen, meeting after meeting, to conventional academics repeating conventional ideas. What is wrong with having different opinions expressed that would stimulate debate and force a rethinking of many of the important issues facing our societies in this era of globalization? ...

[I]f there is to be any hope for a better future, then ... it is up to you, the young generation of criminologists, to ensure that my life and that of other human rights activists have not been in vain....

It is up to you to ensure that the neo-McCarthyism that started after 9/11 is defeated and that the ideals of equality, freedom, liberty and justice remain the ideals of every society on the planet in the twenty-first century. When I specified in my latest will that I want my body cremated, I decided to write my own epitaph and I cannot think of a better time or a better forum than the present to make it known. So here it is:

"He was a sensitive, caring and proud individual who devoted his adult life to the pursuit of a just society. A strong advocate of a mild and humane system of justice, he struggled relentlessly against the barbaric practice of the death penalty. Against all odds, he fought for the abolition of the cruel and unusual punishment of imprisonment. He denounced the primitive notions of revenge and retaliation, pleading for a constructive system of restorative justice anchored in restitution not retribution, in reconciliation not retaliation, in forgiveness not vindictiveness. And having escaped the throes of a dictatorial, repressive regime in his country of birth (Egypt), he struggled incessantly in his adoptive country (Canada) for human rights and civil liberties, for a justice system that respects the dignity of human beings, treats them as equals and is free of prejudice and discrimination. He was a dreamer! He dreamt of a better world, a free and just world. He dreamt of a world without poverty, without hunger, without conflict and without violence. He dreamt of a peaceful and just society. Being an idealist, he believed that human beings were reasonable enough to live side-by-side in harmony and to help rather than fight one another. Alas, it took only the events of a single day, 9/11, to shatter his dreams and to prove that the entire struggle has been in vain."

To those lines I would like to have added the perceptive advice of Benjamin Franklin who is reported to have said: "Those who would give up essential liberty to purchase a little temporary safety deserve neither liberty nor safety."

So, what advice can a veteran criminologist and aging academic offer to the young generation of aspiring criminologists?... Let me start with a warning.

Innocent, idealistic students should to be aware that criminology, more than most other social sciences, is prone to ideological manipulation and is highly susceptible to political exploitation. They have to remain on guard and resist every attempt to use the discipline as an instrument or as a vehicle to achieve ideological or political ends or to obtain financial gain. One of the most shocking and sobering articles that ever came to my attention in my long career as a criminologist is an article by Adam Gopnik (January, 2012), "The Caging of America: Why Do We Lock Up So Many People?" Commenting on the astounding record number of inmates in American prisons and jails, Gopnik finds no more chilling document in recent American life than the 2005 annual report of the biggest of private prisons firm, the Corrections Corporation of America. In its report, the company (which spends millions lobbying legislators) cautions its investors about the risk that somehow, somewhere, someone might turn off the spigot of convicted men. It states: "Our growth is generally dependent upon our ability to obtain new contracts to develop and manage new correctional and detention facilities.... The demand for our facilities and services could be adversely affected by the relaxation of enforcement efforts, leniency in conviction and sentencing practices or through the decriminalization of certain activities that are currently proscribed by our criminal laws. For instance, any changes with respect to drugs and controlled substances or illegal immigration could affect the number of persons arrested, convicted, and sentenced, thereby potentially reducing demand for correctional facilities to house them."

Is it any wonder that the number of Americans in prison continues to rise and has reached a record high?

I still remember vividly how criminologists were manipulated during the conservative era of Ronald Reagan and Margaret Thatcher in the 1980s. In order to sell to the public their harsh and costly crime policies of retribution and incapacitation they decided to use criminologists to show an unsuspecting populace that fear of crime has reached alarming levels. Funds for research on fear of crime became abundant and readily available. And despite serious methodological shortcomings (Fattah 1993) dozens of studies were carried out and hundreds of papers containing questionable results were published. Alarm bells started ringing and fear was used as a pretext to introduce stiffer penalties and harsher sanctions.

In a similar vein great publicity was given to Martinson's (1974) infamous conclusion that "Nothing Works" in an attempt to discredit treatment and rehabilitation programs and to maintain that the only effective way of dealing with offenders was more and longer incarceration! Ridiculous laws such as "three strikes and you are out" gained popularity and were passed in several American states. More recently, in the post-9/11 era, we are witnessing serious and persistent attempts to convert the social science of criminology into a security studies discipline subservient to the whims of those in power. This is happening despite the fact that nothing can be further from criminology's subject-matter than "national security" and "public safety"!

In my closing address to the Barcelona Congress in 2008 (references 120 and 121) I drew attention to criminology's stagnation, lack of innovation and its slow adaptation to the realities of the twenty-first century. I talked at length about its manifest lack of impact on criminal law reform, penal policy, and social justice. I warned that this is threatening its very existence as it risks becoming irrelevant to the threats facing post-9/11 society, namely the flagrant abuses of power and the serious violations of human rights and civil liberties. I argued that criminology should take a bold step and make a number of territorial concessions that would ensure its safe return to its natural, logical and scholarly subject matter. I called upon criminology to fight in order to correct the misperception that it is a peripheral discipline at the bottom heap of the social sciences. I explained how criminology is in urgent need to affirm its scientific nature, defend its own identity, and expose its originality and its autonomy. In response to its detractors, criminology needs to affirm its specificity, its objectivity and its neutrality. And it has to dissociate itself from dogmatic criminal law and divorce itself from criminal policy which for all practical purposes is a purely political exercise and enterprise.

Three years later, on the occasion of the sixteenth World Congress of Criminology held in Kobe, Japan in August, 2011 (reference 130) I offered some personal reflections and impressions on the current state of our discipline. I argued that the time has come for criminology to shift its emphasis from minor offences committed by the poor and the have-nots, the powerless, the helpless, the defenceless, the dispossessed; in other words from offences by society's underdogs, and from drug offences perpetrated by those who are seeking an artificial paradise (or simply an escape from their daily boring, monotonous existence) to the serious and far more damaging crimes committed by the elite, by the rich and powerful, quite often with total impunity. I said it is time for criminology to shift its focus from the petty violations of the criminal code to the horrendous acts of corruption, bribery and other acts of abuse of power committed by elected and unelected politicians, by officials in positions of authority and by corporate executives. It is time for criminology to move from petty thievery to the theft of billions, like those committed by seemingly immune banks, and by dishonest corporations such as Enron or the Madoff empire that faltered like a house of cards.

Criminologists cannot and should not remain silent or idle while basic freedoms are trashed in the name of security. Instead of remaining apathetic and indifferent, criminologists need to affirm in the loudest possible voice that security cannot be purchased at the expense of liberty. Criminologists need to take a strong stand insisting that fundamental human rights cannot be trampled upon for the sake of preventing a vague, undefined and unpredictable threat. Criminologists who decry fear of crime as a nefarious condition reducing the quality of life of the citizenry have to vehemently reject the unscrupulous political exploitation of the threat of terrorism (whether red, yellow, or green) and the continuing use of scare tactics to sell to an unsuspecting public drastic security measures that end up abrogating or curbing the same rights and freedoms that they are supposedly meant to protect. Through the mass media, the social media, through meetings and public forums criminologists need to educate those members of the public who are naïve enough to believe the paradoxical argument according to which restrictions on freedoms are imposed as a means of protecting those freedoms! Criminologists need to ask themselves why it is that while reaction against incumbent/state terrorism is mute, the response to insurgent terrorism and the billions or trillions of dollars being spent on fighting it are totally out of proportion (references 120, 123, 124 and 130).

Criminology's fate would be sealed were criminologists to maintain their present silence, were they to become the tools of oppressive regimes and governments. The demise of criminology will be inevitable if criminologists, out of fear to have their research funds cut, refrain from criticizing those in power and denouncing their abuses and their excesses. The future of criminology would be bleak were criminologists to abstain from expressing critical, unconventional, controversial views, or were they to lack the courage to loudly and publicly defend their views and their convictions.

Final Note

Since moving to British Columbia in 1974 Ezzat Fattah and his wife Jenny have lived in Coquitlam. They have two children. Their daughter Sonia, a family physician, her husband and two children live in Cape Town, South Africa. Their son Eric, a diving computers inventor and founder of Liquivision, lives in Burnaby, B.C.

References

Books by Ezzat Fattah

(1) 1969. *Sondage d'Opinion Publique sur la Justice Criminelle au Québec*. Editeur Officiel du Québec. Co-authored with André Normandeau. 256 pages.

(2) 1969. *Le Rôle de l'Enseignement et de la Recherche Criminologique dans l'Administration de la Justice*. Editeur Officiel du Québec. 115 pages.

(3) 1972. *A Study of the Deterrent Effect of Capital Punishment with Special Reference to the Canadian Situation*. Ottawa: Information Canada. 212 pages.

(4) 1972. *Etude de l'Effet Intimidant de la Peine de Mort à Partir de la Situation Canadienne*. (French translation of the above). Information Canada. 222 pages.

(5) 1975. *The Canadian Public and the Death Penalty: A Study of a Social Attitude.* Monograph prepared under contract with the Research and Systems Development Division of the Ministry of the Solicitor General. Ottawa. 152 pages.

(6) 1975. *Les Canadiens et la Peine de Mort: Etude D'une Attitude Sociale.* (French translation of the above). Ottawa. 178 pages.

(7) 1976. *Deterrence: A Review of the Literature.* Published by the Law Reform Commission of Canada under the title: Fear of Punishment. 119 pages.

(8) 1976. *La Crainte du Chatiment.* French translation of the above. Ottawa. 127 pages.

(9) 1986. *From Crime Policy to Victim Policy.* London: Macmillan.

(10) 1989. *The Plight of Crime Victims in Modern Society.* London: Macmillan.

(11) 1989. *Crime and Victimization of the Elderly* (with V.F. Sacco). New York: Springer Verlag. (Also translated into Chinese and published in the People's Republic of China.)

(12) 1991. *Understanding Criminal Victimization*. Scarborough, Ontario: Prentice Hall Canada

(13) 1992. *Towards a Critical Victimology*. London: Macmillan.

(14) 1997. *Criminology: Past, Present and Future: A Critical Overview.* London: Macmillan.

(15) 1998. *Support for Crime Victims in a Comparative Perspective: A Collection of Essays Dedicated to the Memory of Prof. Frederic McClintock* (edited with Tony Peters). Leuven, Belgium: Leuven University Press.

(16) 2001. *Victim Policies and Criminal Justice on the Road to Restorative Justice: Essays in Honour of Tony Peters* (edited with S. Parmentier). Leuven: University of Leuven Press.

Articles and Papers by Ezzat Fattah

(17) 1966. Quelques Problèmes Posés à la Justice Pénale par la Victimologie. *Annales Internationales de Criminologie* 5:2, pp. 335–61.

(18) 1967. Vers une Typologie Criminologique des Victimes. *Revue Internationle de Police Criminelle* 22:209, pp.162–69.

(19) 1967. Towards a Criminological Classification of the Victims. *International Review of Criminal Police* 22:209, pp.162–69. (English translation of the above.)

(20) 1967. Possibilidades de Una Typologia Criminologica de las Victimas. *Revista Internacional de Policia Criminal* 22:209, pp.162–69. (Spanish translation of the above.)

(21) 1967. La Victimologie: Qu'est-elle et Quel est son Avenir? (premiere partie). *Re-*

vue Internationale de Criminologie et de Police Technique. Génève 21:2, pp.113–124.

(22) 1967. La Victimologie: Qu'est-elle et Quel est son Avenir? (suite et fin). *Revue Internationale de Criminologie et de Police Technique* 21:3, pp.192–202.

(23) 1969. La Politique Législative à l'Égard des Toxicomanies Entre la Punition et la Prévention. Actes du Colloque International sur la Sujetion aux Drogues. (OPTAT-Québec), pp.1–16.

(24) 1969. Towards a New Legislative Policy Regarding Drugs and Drug Addiction. *Proceedings of the International Conference of Drug Dependence*, pp. 1–16 (English version of the above).

(25) 1969. *Pour des Nouvelles Mesures Legislatives sur les Drogues et les Toxicomanies. Toxicomanies* (Québec), 2:1, pp.85–108.

(26) 1969. El Rol de la Victima en la Determinacion Delictiva. *Archivos de Criminologia, Neuro-Psiquiatria y Disciplinas Conexas* (Quito), 17:3, pp. 54–93.

(27) 1970. Le Rôle de la Victime dans la Détermination du Délit. *Canadian Journal of Criminology and Corrections* 12:2, pp. 97–116.

(28) 1971. Le Rapport entre le Cannabis et le Crime: Revue Critique de la Littérature Criminologique sur le Cannabis. *Toxicomanies* (Québec) 4:1, pp. 51–79.

(29) 1971. La Peine est-elle la Solution? *Tocicomanies* 4:2, pp. 147–64.

(30) 1972. The Deterrent Effect of Capital Punishment: The Canadian Experience. In E. Sagarin and D.E.J. MacNamara (eds.), *Corrections: Problems of Punishment and Rehabilitation*. New York: Praeger Publishers, pp. 106–114.

(31) 1973. Le Rôle de la Victime dans le Passage à l'Acte. *Revue Internationale de Criminologie et de Police Technique* (Génève) 26:2, pp. 173–88.

(32) 1973. La Victime est-elle Parfois le vrai Coupable? *Psychologie* (Paris), no.46, pp. 29–35.

(33) 1974. The Canadian Experiment with Abolition of the Death Penalty. In William J. Bowers, *Executions in America*. Lexington, Mass.: Lexington Books, pp. 121–35.

(34) 1975. Why Canada Should "Kill" Capital Punishment. *S.F.U. Week*, 2:13.

(35) 1976. The Use of the Victim as an Agent of Self-legitimization: Towards a Dynamic Explanation of Criminal Behaviour. In E.C. Viano (ed.), *Victims and Society*. Washington, D.C.: Visage Press, pp. 105–129.

(36) 1976. The Use of the Victim as an Agent of Self-Legitimization Towards a Dynamic Explanation of Criminal Behavior. *Victimology: An International Journal* 1:1, pp. 29–53.

(37) 1976. Twenty-Five Years in Here? *S.F.U. Week*, 4:10, March 11.

(38) 1977. Deterrence: A Review of the Literature. *Canadian Journal of Criminology and Correcetions* 19:2 (119 pages).

(39) 1977. L'Effet Dissuasif de la Peine: Une Revue de la Littérature. *Revue Canadienne de Criminologie* 19:2 (120 pages).

(40) 1978. Moving to the Right: a Return to Punishment? *Crime and Justice* 6:2, pp. 79–92.

(41) 1979. Die Opferwerdung-Risiko, Erfahrung und Nachwirkungen. In *Das Verbrechens Opfer*. G.F. Kirchhoff and K. Sessar (eds.). Bochum: Studienverlag Dr. Norbert Brockmeyer (in German), pp.179–97.

(42) 1980. The Limits of Deterrence: A Commentary. In *An Anatomy of Criminal Justice*. C.H. Foust and D.R. Webster (eds.). Lexington: Heath and Co., pp. 78–90.

(43) 1980. Sentencing to Death: The Inherent Problems. In *New Directions in Sentencing*. Brian Grosman (ed.). Toronto: Butterworths, pp. 157–93.

(44). 1980. La Justification de la Peine. In Y. Dandurand and F. Ribordy (eds.), *Crime et Société*. Ottawa: Editions de l'Université d'Ottawa, pp. 41–43.

(45) 1980. La Severité de la Peine et la Certitude d'être Puni Sont-elles Conciliables. In Y. Dandurand and F. Ribordy (eds.), *Crime et Société*. Ottawa: Editions de l'Université d'Ottawa, pp. 48–53.

(46) 1980. Some Reflections on the Victimology of Terrorism. *Terrorism: An International Journal* 3:2, pp. 81–108. (Published also in *Perspectives on Terrorism*. S. Bassiouni (ed.) International Institute of Higher Studies in Criminal Sciences, Siracusa, Italy (pp. 66–115).

(47) 1980. Some Recent Theoretical developments in Victimology. *Victimology: An International Journal*: 4:2, pp.198–213.

(48) 1980. Towards a Better Penal System. *The Howard Journal* 19: pp. 27–41.

(49) 1980. Victimologie: Tendances Recentes. *Criminologie* (formerly *Acta Criminologica*) 13:1, pp. 6–36.

(50) 1980. Crime and the Abuse of Power: Offences and Offenders Beyond the Reach of the Law. Final General Report. Published in English and French by the International Society of Criminology, International Association of Penal Law, International Society for Social Defense, and the International Penal and Penitentiary Foundation. Milan, Italy, pp. 70–92.

(51) 1980. The Child as Victim: Victimological Aspects of Child Abuse. *International Review of Penal Law* 50:3–4, pp. 597–623.

(52) 1981. Terrorist Activities and Terrorist Targets: A Tentative Typology. In Yonah Alexander and John Gleason (eds.), *Behavioral and Quantitative Perspectives on Terrorism*. Pergamon Press, pp. 11–32.

(53) 1981 Becoming a Victim: The Victimization Experience and its Aftermath. *Victimology: An International Journal* 6:1–4, pp. 29–47.

(54) 1981. La Victimologie Entre les Attaques Idéologiques et les Critiques Épistemologiques. Déviance et Société 5:1, pp.71–92.

(55) 1981. Is Capital Punishment a Unique Deterrent? A Dispassionate Review of Old and New Evidence. *Canadian Journal of Criminology* 23:3, pp. 291–311. Reprinted in Wesley Cragg (ed.), *Contemporary Moral Issues*. Toronto: McGraw-Hill, 1983.

(56) 1981. Prisons: Who Should be In Them and What are the Alternatives? *Perception* (Ottawa). Spring-Summer, pp. 19–22.

(57) 1982. Making the Punishment fit the Crime: The Case of Imprisonment. Problems Inherent in the use of Imprisonment as a Retributive Sanction. *Canadian Journal of Criminology*, 24:1, pp. 1–12.

(58) 1982. Public Opposition to Prison Alternatives and Community Corrections: A Strategy for Action. *Canadian Journal of Criminology* 24:4, pp. 371–85.

(59) 1983. Canada's Successful Experience with the Abolition of the Death Penalty. *Canadian Journal of Criminology* 25:4, pp. 421–31.

(60) 1983. Il Dibattito in Corso Sulla Pena di Morte Come Deterrente. In Pier Cesare Bori (ed.), *La Pena di Morte nel Mondo*. Casale Monferrato: Case Editrice Marietti, pp. 195–218.

(61) 1984. Victims' Response to Confrontational Victimization: A Neglected Aspect

of Victim Research. *Crime and Delinquency* 30:1, pp. 75–89.

(62) 1985. The Preventive Mechanism of the Death Penalty: A Discussion. *Crimecare Journal* 1:2, pp. 109–37.

(63) 1987. The Use of the Death Penalty for Drug Offenses and for Economic Crime: A Discussion and a Critique. *Revue Internationale de Droit Pénal*. 58:3–4, pp. 723–35.

(64). 1987. To Abolish or Not to Abolish the Death Penalty: A Report on a Painful Question and a Never-Ending Debate. *Revue Internationale de Droit Pénal* 58:3–4.

(65) 1987. On Some Visible and Hidden Dangers of Victim Movements. In E.A. Fattah (ed.), *From Crime Policy to Victim Policy*. London: Macmillan, pp. 1–14.

(66) 1989. Victims and Victimology: The Facts and the Rhetoric. *International Review of Victimology* 1:1, pp. 1–21.

(67) 1989. The Child as Victim: Victimological Aspects of Child Abuse. In Ezzat Fattah (ed.), *The Plight of Crime Victims in Modern Society*. London: Macmillan, pp. 175–209.

(68) 1989. Victims of Abuse of Power: The David/Goliath Syndrome. In Ezzat A. Fattah (ed.), *The Plight of Crime Victims in Modern Society*. London: Macmillan, pp. 25–69.

(69) 1991. From Crime Policy to Victim Policy: The Need for a Fundamental Change. *International Annals of Criminology* 29:1–2.

(70) 1992. The Need for a Critical Victimology. In E.A. Fattah (ed.), *Towards a Critical Victimology*. London: Macmillan, pp. 3–26.

(71) 1992. Victims and Victimology: The Facts and the Rhetoric. In E.A. Fattah (ed.), *Towards a Critical Victimology*. London: Macmillan, pp. 29–56.

(72) 1992. The UN Declaration of Basic Principles of Justice for Victims of Crime and Abuse of Power: A Constructive Critique. In E.A. Fattah (ed.), *Towards a Critical Victimology*. London: Macmillan, pp.401–24.

(73) 1992. Beyond Metaphysics: The Need for a New Paradigm: On Actual and Potential Contributions of Criminology and the Social Sciences to the Reform of the Criminal Law. In R. Lahti and K. Nuotio (eds.), *Criminal Law Theory in Transition*. Helsinki: Finnish Lawyers Publishing Company.

(74) 1993. La Relativité Culturelle de la Victimisation. *Criminologie*, 26:2, pp. 121–36.

(75) 1993. Doing Unto Others: The Revolving Roles of Victim and Victimizer. *Simon Fraser University Alumni Journal* (Spring),11:1, pp. 12–15

(76) 1993. From a Guilt Orientation to a Consequence Orientation. In F. Denker et al. (eds.), *Beiträge zur Rechtswissenschaft*. Heidelberg: C.F. Muller.

(77) 1993. Internationaler Forschungsstand zum Problem "Gewalt gegen Alte Menschen" und Folgen von Opfererfahrung. Hannover: KFN Forscungsberichte, Nr. 10.

(78) 1993. The Rational Choice/Opportunity Perspective as a Vehicle for Integrating Criminological and Victimological Theories. In R.V. Clarke and M. Felson (eds.), *Routine Activity and Rational Choice*. (Vol. 5 in *Advances in Criminological Theory*), pp. 225–258. Piscataway, N.J.: Transaction Publishers.

(79) 1994. Victimology: Some Problematic Concepts, Unjustified Criticism and Popular Misconceptions. In G.F. Kirchhoff, E. Kosovski and H.J. Schneider (eds.), *International Debates of Victimology*. Mönchengladbach: WSP, pp. 82–103.

(80) 1994. Some Recent Theoretical Developments in Victimology. In Paul Rock (ed.), *Victimology*. Dartmouth: Aldershot, pp. 285–300.

(81) 1994. From Victimization by the State to Victimization by Crime: A Side Effect

of Transition to Democracy. In Uwe Ewald (ed.), *New Definitions of Crime in Societies in Transition to Democracy*. Bonn: Forum Verlag.

(82) 1994. La Victimologie au Carrefour: Entre la Science et L-Idéologie. *Présentations à la Société Royale du Canada*. Vol. 47, pp. 159–72.

(83) 1994. The Interchangeable Roles of Victim and Victimizer (Second Inkeri Anttila Lecture). Published by HEUNI, Helsinki, Finland. 26 pages.

(84) 1994. The Criminalization of Social Problems: Child Abuse as a Case Study. In S. N. Verdun-Jones and M. Layton (eds.), *Mental Health Law and Practice Through the Life Cycle*. Burnaby: Simon Fraser University, pp.7–15.

(85) 1995. La Victimologie au Carrefour: Entre la Science et L'Idéologie. *Revue Internationale de Criminologie et de Police Technique* no. 2, pp. 131–39.

(86) 1995. Restorative and Retributive Justice Models: A Comparison. In H.-H. Kühne (ed.), *Festschrift für Koichi Miyazawa*. Baden-Baden: Nomos Verlagsgesellschaft, pp. 305–15.

(87) 1996. Violence against the Elderly: Types, Patterns and Explanations. *International Annals of Criminology* (1994) 32:1–2, pp.113–34. Translated into Greek and published in a victimology text released in 1996.

(88) 1997. From Crime Policy to Victim Policy: The Need for a Fundamental Policy Change. In M. McShane and F. Williams III (eds.), *Victims of Crime and the Victimization Process*. New York: Garland Publishing, pp. 75–92.

(89) 1997. Toward a Victim Policy Aimed at Healing not Suffering. In R.C. Davis, A.J. Lurigio and W.G. Skogan (eds.), *Victims of Crime* (second edition). Thousand Oaks, CA: Sage Publications, pp. 257–72.

(90) 1997. Los Roles Intercambiables de Victima y Victimario. *Cuadernos de Criminologia* (Santiago, Chile), no. 7, pp. 23–54.

(91) 1997. Victimas y Victimologia : los Hechos y la Retorica. *Victimologia* (Cordoba, Argentina), no. 14, pp. 13–44.

(92) 1998. Restorative and Retributive Justice Models: A Comparison. In Fattah, E.A. & Peters, T. (eds.), *Support for Crime Victims in a Comparative Perspective*. Leuven: Leuven University Press, pp. 99–110.

(93) 1998. From a Handful of Dollars to Tea and Sympathy: The Sad History of Victim Assistance. (In Chinese.) *Journal of Police Science*, 29:1, pp. 151–68.

(94) 1998. Some Reflections on the Paradigm of Restorative Justice and Its Viability for Juvenile Justice. In Lode Walgrave (ed.), *Restorative Justice for Juveniles: Potentialities, Risks and Problems*. Leuven: Leuven University Press, pp. 389–401.

(95) 1999. Prologue: On Some Visible and Hidden Dangers of Victim Movements. In Peggy M. Tobolowsky (ed.), *Understanding Victimology: Selected Readings*. Cincinnati, OH: Anderson Publishing Co.

(96) 1999. Victim Redress and Victim-Offender Reconciliation in Theory and Practice: Some Personal Reflections. *The Hokkaigakuen Law Journal* 35:1, pp. 155–82.

(97) 1999. From a Handful of Dollars to Tea and Sympathy: The Sad History of Victim Assistance. In J.J.M. Van Dijk, Ron G.H. Van Kaam and Joanne Wemmers (eds.), *Caring for Crime Victims: Selected Proceedings of the 9th International Symposium on Victimology*. Monsey, N.Y.: Criminal Justice Press, pp. 187–206.

(98) 1999. Victims' Rights: Past, Present and Future—A Global View. *Proceedings of the National Conference on Victims' Rights*. Sydney, Australia: Sydney City Mission.

(99) 1999. Mediation in Penal Matters. Report for Correctional Services Canada. Ottawa. 44 pages.

(100) 2000. Victimology: Past, Present and Future. *Criminologie* 33:1, pp. 17–46.

(101) 2000. Victim Assistance in Canada. Resource Material Series no. 56. Fuchu/Tokyo: UNAFEI (Asia and Far East Institute for the Prevention of Crime and the Treatment of Offenders), pp. 48–59.

(102) 2000. Victimology Today: Recent Theoretical and Applied Developments. Resource Material Series no. 56. Fuchu/Tokyo: UNAFEI (Asia and Far East Institute for the Prevention of Crime and the Treatment of Offenders), pp. 60–70.

(103) 2000. The Vital Role of Victimology in the Rehabilitation of Offenders and their Reintegration into Society. Resource Material Series no. 56. Fuchu/Tokyo: UNAFEI (Asia and Far East Institute for the Prevention of Crime and the Treatment of Offenders), pp. 71–86.

(104) 2000. Victim Redress and Victim-Offender Reconciliation in Theory and Practice- Some Personal Reflections. Resource Material Series no. 56. Fuchu/Tokyo: UNAFEI (Asia and Far East Institute for the Prevention of Crime and the Treatment of Offenders), pp. 87–101.

(105) 2000. How Valid Are the Arguments Frequently Made Against Mediation and Restorative Justice? In Hedda Giertsen (ed.)., *Albanian and Norwegian Experiences with Mediation in Conflict*. Oslo: Dept. of Criminology, University of Oslo, pp. 25–36.

(106) 2001. Preventing Repeat Victimization as the Ultimate Goal of Victim Services. *International Annals of Criminology* 38, pp. 113–133

(107) 2001. Does Victimology Need Deontology? Ethical Conundrums in a Young Discipline. Proceedings of the Xth International Symposium on Victimology. In A. Gaudreault and I. Waller, *Beyond Boundaries: Research and Action for the Third Millennium*. Montreal: Association Québécoise Plaidoyer-Victimes, pp. 129–54.

(108) 2001. Es Necesaria Una Deontologia Victimológica? Complejidades Éticas En Una Joven Disciplina. In Cuadernos de Criminología, no. 11, Instituto de Criminologia Policia de Investigaciones de Chile, pp. 53–76.

(109) 2001. Victimizing the Helpless: Assaulting Children as a Corrective Measure. In E.A. Fattah and S. Parmentier (eds.), *Victim Policies and Criminal Justice: On the Road to Restorative Justice. Essays in Honour of Tony Peters*. Leuven: University of Leuven Press, pp. 15–34.

(110) 2001. Victims' Rights: Past, Present and Future. A Global View. In Robert Cario and Denis Salas (eds.), *Oeuvre de Justice et des Victimes*. Vol. 1. L'Harmattan, pp. 81–108.

(111) 2002. From Philosophical Abstraction to Restorative Action—From Senseless Retribution to Meaningful Restitution. Just Desert and Restorative Justice Revisited. In H.J. Kerner and E. Weitekanp (eds.), *Restorative Justice, Theoretical Foundations*. Devon, UK: Willan Publishing, pp. 308–21.

(112) 2002. Gewalt gegen 'gesellschaftlich Überflüssige'. In Wilhelm Heitmeyer and John Hagan (eds.), *Internationales Handbuch der Gewaltforschung*. Westdeutscher Verlag, Germany, pp. 958–80.

(113) 2002. Selectivity, Inequality and Discrimination in the Treatment of Victims of Crime. In Gudrun Nordborg & Anna Sigfridsson (ed.), *Våldets Offer—Vårt Ansvar. Nordic Criminology* 38:1–2, pp. 113–33. Conference. Brottsoffermyndigheten. Stockholm, Sweden, pp. 16–36.

(114) 2003. Violence against the Socially Expendable. In Wilhelm Heitmeyer and John Hagan (eds.), *International Handbook on Violence Research*. London: Kluwer Academic Publishers.

(115) 2003. Victims Rights: Past, Present and Future. A Global View. In A. Manganas (ed.), *Essays in Honour of Alice Yotopoulos-Marangopoulos*, Vol. B. Athens: Nomiki Bibliothiki Group Publishing.

(116) 2004. Gearing Justice Action to Victim Satisfaction. Contrasting Two Justice Philosophies: Retribution and Redress. In Hendrik Kaptein & Marijke Malsch (eds.), *Crime, Victims and Justice: Essays on Principles and Practice*. Burlington,VT: Ashgate Publishing Company.

(117) 2004. Positions Savantes et Idéologiques sur le Rôle de la Victime et sa Contribution á la Genése du Crime. In Robert Cario and Paul Mbanzoulou (eds.), "La Victime est-elle Coupable?" Autour de l'æuvre d'Ezzat Abdel Fattah. Collection "Sciences Criminelles". (Les Controverses). *L'Harmattan*, Paris, pp. 23-41.

(118) 2006. Le Sentiment d'insécurité et la Victimisation Criminelle dans une Perspective de Victimologie Comparée. In Michel Born, Fabienne Kéfer and André Lemaître (eds.), *Une Criminologie de la Tradition à L'Innovation. En Hommage à Georges Kellens*. Bruxelles : De Boeck & Larcier, pp. 89–106.

(119) 2007. Is punishment the appropriate response to gross human rights violations? Is a non-punitive justice system feasible? In *Restorative Justice: Politics, Policies and Prospects*, E. van der Spuy, S. Parmentier, A. Dissel (eds.). Published under the auspices of the Faculty of Law, University of Cape Town (JUTA and Co). Reprinted in *ACTA JURIDICA* (Capetown) (2007), pp. 209–227.

(120) 2008. The Future of Criminology as a Social Science and Academic Discipline: Reflections on Criminology's Unholy Alliance with Criminal Policy and on Current Misguided Attempts to Divorce Victimology from Criminology. *International Annals of Criminology* 46:1–2, pp. 137–170.

(121) 2009. Reprint of the above in *Acta Criminologiae et Medicinae Legalis Japonica* 75:4, pp. 89–107.

(122) 2009. Pregiudizi, stereotipi, e biases morali e ideologiche: loro impatto sulle politiche, le strategie e le pratiche di intervento. In Anna Maria Giannini & Barbara Nardi (eds.), *Le Vittime del crimini: Nuovo prospettive di ricerca e di intervento*. Torino: Centro Scientifico Editore. (In Italian.)

(123) 2009. Criminology and Human Rights Challenges in the Post 9/11 Era. *Judicatus* (Mexico) 1:2, Junio, pp. 255–285. (In English.)

(124) 2009. Criminologia Y Derechos Humanos Retos En La Era Posterior Al 9/11. *Judicatus* (Mexico) 1:2, Junio, pp. 220–254. (In Spanish.)

(125) 2010. The Evolution of a Young, Promising Discipline: Sixty Years of Victimology, A Retrospective and Prospective Look. In Paul Knepper, Shlomo Shoham and Martin Kett (eds.), *International Handbook of Victimology*. Taylor and Francis, pp. 43–94.

(126) 2010. Da investigação ao activismo, da academia ao partidarismo e o resultante empobrecimento da Vitimologia (in Portugese) [From research to activism, from scholarship to partisanship and the resulting impoverishment of victimology]. In Sofia Neves and Marisalva Favero (eds.), *Victimologia: Ciencia e Activismo*. Portugal: Almedina.

(127) 2010. Quand Recherche et Savoir Scientifique Cedent le Pas a l'Activisme et au

Parti Pris. *Criminologie* 43:2, pp. 49–88.

(128) 2011. Protecting Children and Preventing their Victimization: From Policy to Action, from Drafting Legislation to Practical Implementation. *Acta Criminologiae et Medicinae Legalis Japonica* 77:2, pp. 28–55.

(129) 2011. Is Restorative Justice a Viable Option in Crimes of Violence? *Keio University Faculty of Law Journal of Law, Politics and Sociology (HOGAKU KENKYU)*, pp. 713–730.

(130) 2012. Reflections and Impressions of a Veteran Criminologist on the Current State of the Discipline on the Occasion of the 16th World Congress in Kobe, Japan, 5–9 August 2011. *International Annals of Criminology* 49:1–2, pp. 21–40.

(131) 2012. The Dawning of a New Era in Social Reaction to Crime: Promise, Potential and Limitations of Restorative Justice. *Archiwum Kryminologii* (Warszawa 2013), pp. 7–42.

(132) 2015. On Some Important Yet Neglected Issues in Victim Research: A Modest Attempt to Revive Interest in Theoretical Victimology. In Tod Tollefson (ed.), *Victimological Advances in Theory, Policy and Services. A Festschrift in Honor of John Peter Joseph Dussich.* Dumont Printing, pp.67-77.

(133) 2016. Under-Researched Theoretical Concepts in Victimology: Proneness and Vulnerability Revisited. Contribution to the Festschrift Honoring Prof. Gerd Kirchhoff (in press).

(134) 1970. L'Alcool en Tant que Facteur Victimogène. *Toxicomanies* 3: 2, pp. 143–73. With A. Raic.

(135) 1971. *La Victime Est-Elle Coupable?* Montreal: Presses de l'Université de Montréal. 256 pages.

(136) 1975. Victims of Violence. In R. Ericson (ed.), *Violence in Canadian Society*. Toronto: Centre of Criminology, University of Toronto, pp. 47–72.

Additional References

(137) 2004. Cario, Robert and Mbanzoulou (eds.), "La Victime Est-Elle Coupable?" Autour de l'oeuvre d'Ezzat Abdel Fattah. Paris: L'Harmattan. (123 pages).

(138) 1977. Christi, N. Conflicts as Property. *British Journal of Criminology* 17:1, pp. 1-19.

(139) 1993. Clark, Ron V. and Felson, Marcus (eds.) *Routine Activity and Rational Choice. Advances in Criminological Theory*, Vol. 5. Transaction Publishers.

(140) 2014. Griffiths, C. and Palys, T. Of Big Tents and Handmaidens: The Origins and Evolution of Criminology at Simon Fraser University. *Annual Review of Interdisciplinary Justice Research* 4.

(141) 1969. Hoefnagels, Peter G. *The Other Side of Criminology*. Kluwer-Deventer, Holland

Additional Unnumbered References

Fattah, Ezzat A. (1993). Research on Fear of Crime: Some Common Conceptual and Measurement Problems. In W. Bilsky et al. (eds.), *Fear of Crime and Criminal Victimization*, pp. 45–70. Stuttgart: Ferdinand Enke Verlag.

Fattah, Ezzat A. (1998). The Elderly's High Fear/Low Victimization Paradox: An Unconventional View. In H.D. Schwind et al. (eds.), *Festschrift für Hans Joachim Schnei-*

der. Berlin: Walter de Gruyter, pp. 415–30.

Gopnik, Adam (2012). The Caging of America: Why Do We Lock Up So Many People? *The New Yorker*, January 30, 2012.

Martinson, R. (1974). What Works? Questions and Answers about Prison Reform. *The Public Interest* 35, pp. 22–54.

FOUR
Jean-Paul Brodeur: A Cosmopolitan Thinker

Benoît Dupont and John Winterdyk

Jean-Paul Brodeur (1944–2010), the son of a police officer, was born in 1944 and by all accounts led a rich and somewhat eclectic life.

In 1975, he completed his Ph.D. in philosophy at the University of Paris-Nanterre. His senior supervisor was the esteemed French phenomenologist **Paul Ricoeur.** Brodeur's dissertation involved a critical analysis of Spinoza's ethics. In his dissertation he was primarily concerned with the idea that good and evil can be understood through a higher form of knowledge that transcends empiricism and theory—not an undemanding subject!

Upon his return to Montreal he accepted a position in the philosophy department at the University of Quebec in Montreal (UQAM). However, in the fall of 1977, while on leave in the small African nation of Benin where his wife was running a cooperative project, he came to the conclusion that philosophy was incapable of offering a compelling explanation of, let alone a remedy for, violence and evil. Much to the dismay of his former colleagues, Brodeur left philosophy to join the then-fledgling field of criminology, a decision that he never looked back on nor regretted. As Dupont (2011) points out, Brodeur was also intrigued by the fact that during the late 1970s a number of activist academics (e.g., the French philosopher and social theorist Michel Foucault [1926–1984], perhaps best recognized for his 1975 book *Discipline and Punish*, and the Dutch scholar Louk Hulsman [1923–2009], primary author of the Council of Europe's influential report on decriminalization [Council of the European Union, Report on Decriminalization, Strasbourg 1980], among other documents) were very critical of the penal system and called for its abolition. Similarly, Georges Leroux (2011) observed that Brodeur left philosophy behind because he felt that postmodern philosophy was too self-absorbed and undermined by "the sterility of its apprehension."

Throughout his academic career, Brodeur was, as Stenning and Roberts (2011) note, a tireless worker and prolific writer. Yet, while he is best remembered for his work in the area of policing, he followed a somewhat unconventional path in criminology, just as he had in his earlier academic work. As a criminologist, he published some 26 academic books and several special journal issues dealing with policing. In addition, Brodeur also served as the associate editor of the *Canadian Journal of Criminology* and was a member of the journal's editorial committee until his passing. He also served as the director of the International Centre for Comparative Criminology (see Box 4.1 above) from 1988 to 1996 and then again from 2004 to 2010, during which time the Centre's budgetary situation was particularly tight. By capitalizing on his effective negotiating and administrative skills, he helped to ensure that the Centre weathered the storm and in fact continued to thrive.

Box 4.1. International Centre for Comparative Criminology

The International Centre for Comparative Criminology was founded in 1969 by Denis Szabo. Today, it serves the largest group of researchers working on criminal phenomena, control and security in the francophone world. Internationally, it is among the leading centres in its field, bringing together more than 40 regular researchers from six Quebec universities, as well as other researchers from public and para-public organizations. At any given time, the Centre supports some 80 collaborators from Quebec, Canada and internationally.

The Centre's website further notes that it serves as an intermediary between U.S. and European research. For example, the CICC has collaboration agreements with academic centres of criminological research (or related fields) from a dozen countries, such as Australia, Belgium, France, Germany, Italy, the Netherlands, South Africa, South Korea, Spain, Switzerland, the United Kingdom, and the U.S. In addition, the Centre regularly organizes and hosts conferences and major international seminars.

Many of the faculty members in the School of Criminology at the University of Montreal are also members of the CICC. This relationship is a strong asset as it provides a venue to support faculty, promote collaborative work, and enable qualified students to work as research assistants in the Centre. In addition, the Centre also offers a number of scholarships to support various research initiatives.

According to Dupont (2011), Brodeur's greatest satisfaction came in completing what he considered with considerable fondness his magnum opus, which represented the sum of his work on policing. This book, *The Policing Web*, was published posthumously in 2010 by Oxford University Press. Sieh (2012) describes the book as richly descriptive in offering Brodeur's theory of policing. Brodeur covered a wide of police-related topics in the book, ranging from the use-of-force paradigm, investigations, and clearance rates to policing issues in relation to people of color, the poor and the disenfranchised.

After the events of 9/11, Brodeur, along with his CICC colleague **Stéphane Leman-Langlois**, published extensively on the topic of terrorism. Together, they contributed to an increased level of theoretical and empirical understanding of the issue. In so doing, they helped to dispel doomsday prophecies often put forth by what Leman-Langlois (2011) described as "self-proclaimed experts."

What justifies including Brodeur as one of the Canadian pioneers in criminology is the fact that his final work represents a modern treatise on policing, one which makes his intellectual heritage accessible to all who contemplate the functions of police activity by furnishing a rich theoretical and empirical framework. It is perhaps somewhat ironic that, as a French Canadian, Brodeur is best known for his pioneering work on policing, as policing as we know it today was created in France in 1667. His first major published work in this field—a study of the history of commissions of inquiry into police in Canada, from 1895 to 1970—remains a major resource on the politics of policing in Canada. In a 1983 article, he pointed out that although most of Canada can trace its policing model back to England, Quebec, because of its historical linkages with France, adopted a model of policing that can trace its roots to seventeenth-century France. The traditional French model was seen as an instrument to advance state interests, rather than being community-oriented.

Another unique aspect of Brodeur's work that is illustrative of his passion and commitment to the discipline was the fact that, instead of restricting himself to the comfortable position of a passive outside observer (i.e., nonparticipant observer), he chose to embrace the opportunity to serve in various advisory capacities (along with **Anthony Doob**) to both law enforcement agencies and, in the late 1980s, to the Canadian Sentencing Commission. In other words, in recognizing his unique professional position, Brodeur embraced the opportunity to offer government and/or criminal justice agencies and organizations advice on policy reforms. He was the quintessential applied social scientist, something of a rarity at the time.

His willingness to bridge academic knowledge and policy reform resulted in the construction of clear principles designed to assist in the creation of a fairer penal policy. His interest in policing was not limited to mainstream policing. In fact, along with **Carol LaPrairie** (1937–2010), he played an instrumental role in the development of policing policy among First Nations communities. Stenning and Roberts (2011) also point out that, along with **Roger McDonnell**, Brodeur conducted critical research into the policing of remote Cree communities in Quebec's James Bay region in the early 1990s that had a lasting impact on these and other First Nation communities.

As Dupont (2011) noted, Brodeur's work with the Cree communities

Box 4.2. Brodeur's High Policing-Low Policing Model

Brodeur argued that the political component is the core ingredient of what he termed "high policing" (from the French term *haute police*). Rather than being a deviant aberration that numerous inquiries, courts and other disciplinary mechanisms tended to focus on and respond to in a punitive manner, "High policing is actually the paradigm for political policing: it reaches out for potential threats in a systematic attempt to preserver the distribution of power in a given society" (cited in McCormick & Visano 1992: 285). Brodeur felt that policing in North America operates largely in accordance with the "high policing" paradigm. The paradigm has four key characteristics: (1) "Control" is accomplished in part by collecting and storing intelligence that might further state policies; (2) Powers extend beyond those as decreed by bifurcated systems that separate the powers associated with legislation from enforcement and the sanctioning of offenders; (3) Protection of the community may be secondary to the use of enforcement to generate more information and hence intelligence; and (4) Extensive use is made of undercover and paid informers and there is a willingness to advertise such a strategy, with part of the motivation in doing so being the amplification of fear among the populace (cited in McCormick & Visano 1992: 286).

"Low policing," in Brodeur's terms, is characteristic of the traditional English model of policing, which focuses more on the protection of the public. In contrast to high policing it focuses on more fundamental aspects of law and order, by addressing such conventional criminal activities as those involving public safety and security as well as street crime.

As René Lévy (2011) noted in his tribute, Brodeur's unique perspective "allowed him to overcome a major 'epistemological obstacle' by reintroducing the notion of political policing in Anglo-American criminology, freeing it from the monopoly exercised upon it by the Neo-Marxist approach."

required considerable patience and a willingness to accommodate opposing points of views. Despite such challenges, Brodeur's pragmatic disposition allowed him to seek out compromises that would often result in a "win-win" outcome. Yet friend and colleague Anthony Doob (2011), in his tribute to Brodeur, points out that their efforts (along with those of other Canadian scholars who dared to venture into the legal and political quagmire) were considerably blunted by a significant shift in criminal justice policies toward the more punitive principles promoted by politicians willing to exploit fear of crime to implement harsher (and less scientific) measures.

Unusually among academics, Brodeur did not shy away from offering comments to the media, especially in relation to matters involving police work and terrorism. He believed the public had the right to be properly informed, thus allowing it the opportunity to more objectively evaluate the facts and discern media sensationalism. For example, he regularly highlighted in the press how the use of police informers, despite obvious benefits, could also have a corrosive effect on the criminal justice system (institutionalizing perjury, discrediting the courts, making the police lazy, helping innocents get convicted), and should therefore be used sparingly. Between 1999 and 2001, Brodeur wrote a bimonthly feature on crime and justice for a Radio-Canada morning program. In addition, between 2001 and 2003, he wrote a bimonthly column for *Le Devoir*. His professional integrity was widely respected and often acknowledged by his media peers. For example, Michel Lacombe of Radio-Canada devoted a long segment of his program to discussing how Brodeur made an effort to bridge the gap between intellectual discourse and the lay public.

Perhaps one of the most poignant expressions of the respect Brodeur had garnered from his media colleagues occurred when Michel Desautels interrupted his radio talk show to announce Brodeur's passing, declaring that Brodeur "allowed [journalists] to appear more intelligent and listeners to be better informed." Brodeur was undeniably a prominent public voice in Quebec whose influence extended well beyond the borders of that province.

Unwilling to shy away from controversy, in 1978 Brodeur became involved in what became known as the Keable Inquiry into the 1970 October Crisis. Together with the controversial yet revealing McDonald Commission, the Keable Inquiry revealed that for several years after the October Crisis, the RCMP in Quebec had committed arson, carried out bomb attacks, dynamite theft, and kidnappings, and even issued fake FLQ communiqués in order to artificially maintain an atmosphere of fear and insecurity harmful to the Quebec independence movement. These events were on par with the Watergate scandal which occurred in the U.S. at the same time, and proved to be a major turning point for the RCMP as well as for Brodeur's academic career. His participation in the Keable Inquiry applied his passion and intellectual prowess from his training as a philosopher to the study of policing, and marked his emergence as a major researcher and thinker on law enforcement.

Even though he was a well-respected and influential figure in Quebec, Brodeur's influence extended to the international stage. He regularly attended the American Society of Criminology's annual conferences, and was a guest professor at many English-speaking institutions within Canada and internationally in addition to authoring entries on police and police technologies in the Encyclopedia Britannica. In 2009, he worked alongside two French scholars on policing, Dominique Monjardet and Frédéric Ocqueteau, to develop international and comparative events for the Paris-based Institut des hautes études de la sécurité intérieure (IHESI—the National Institute of Advanced Studies in Security and Justice). Brodeur also played an important role in the development of police research in Belgium. In 1990 he was named a member of the Royal Society of Canada, and in 2002 was awarded a Killam Scholarship, one of Canada's most prestigious endowments for scholarly activities.

Whether working with decision-makers responsible for reforming the criminal justice system, the heads of public commissions mandated to inquire into the activities of police, military and intelligence institutions, or with a myriad of other discipline-specific institutions, Brodeur's focus was always on trying to improve the quality of public services. Some might have thought that such collaboration would blunt a scholar's critical sense, but, as evidenced by Brodeur's legacy, these interactions instead nourished his thoughts.

As noted in the introduction to this book, it is not necessarily easy to identify the pioneers of Canadian criminology and criminal justice, but Brodeur's work has left its mark and blazed the trail for numerous scholars in his wake.

References

Articles commemorating the work of Jean-Paul Brodeur. (2011). *Canadian Journal of Criminology and Criminal Justice* 53(3).

McCormick, K., and L. Visano (eds.) 1992. *Understanding Policing.* Toronto: Canadian Scholars Press.

Sieh, E. (2012). Jean-Paul Brodeur: The Policing Web. Book Review. *Critical Criminology* 20(3):341–344.

Shearing, C. (2011). Re-considering the field of policing: A review of *The Policing Web. Canadian Journal of Criminology and Criminal Justice* 53(3): 325–341.

Stenning, P.C., and Roberts, J.V. (2011). The scholarship of Jean-Paul Brodeur. *Canadian Journal of Criminology and Criminal Justice* 53(3): 267–272.

Selected Works by Jean-Paul Brodeur

Brodeur J.-P. (1983). High Policing and Low Policing: Remarks about the Policing of Political Activities, *Social Problems* 30(5): 507–520.

Brodeur J.-P. (1991). Justice for the Cree: Policing and alternative dispute resolution. James Bay, Que.: Grand Council of the Crees.

Brodeur J.-P. (2007). De grandes espérances. *Criminologie*, 40(2): 161–166. A stern indictment of the naïveté and inadequacies of French criminology.

Brodeur J.-P. (2010). *The Policing Web*. Oxford: Oxford University Press.

Canadian Sentencing Commission (1987). *Sentencing Reform: A Canadian Approach*. Ottawa: Government of Canada.

Fournier M. (1976). Les conflits de discipline: philosophie et sciences sociales au Québec, 1920–1960. In Panaccio, C. (dir.), *Philosopher au Québec*. Montréal: Les Éditions Bellarmin, pp. 207–236.

Leman-Langlois, S., and Brodeur, J.-P. (eds.). (2009). *Terrorisme et antiterrorisme au Canada*. Montréal: Les Presses de l'Université de Montréal.

Brodeur J.-P. (ed.). (2005). La police en pièces detaches. Special issue of the journal *Criminologie*, 38(2).

Brodeur, J.-P., and Jobard, F. (eds.). (2005). *Citoyens et délateurs: la délation peut-elle être civique?* Paris: Autrement.

Brodeur, J.-P., and Rigakos, G. (eds.). (2005). Security, policing, and governance in Canada. Special issue of *The Canadian Journal of Criminology*, 47(1).

Brodeur, J.-P., Gill, P., and Töllborg, D. (eds.). (2003). *Democracy, Law and Security; Internal Security Services in Contemporary Europe.* Aldershot, UK: Ashgate Publishing Company.

Brodeur, J.-P. (1999). *Comparisons in Policing: An International Perspective*. Brookfield: Avebury.

Brodeur, J.-P. (ed.) 1998. *How to Recognize Good Policing.* Thousand Oaks, CA: Sage Publications.

Brodeur, J.-P. (1997). *Violence and Racial Prejudice in the Context of Peacekeeping, Commission of Inquiry into the Deployment of Canadian Forces to Somalia*. Ottawa: Government of Canada.

Brodeur, J.-P. (ed.) (1984). La police après 1984. Special issue of the journal *Criminologie,* 17 (1).

FIVE

Marc Le Blanc: Career within a New Criminology

Marc Le Blanc

Introduction

In 1960, **Denis Szabo** created the Department of Criminology at the l'Université de Montréal and with it promoted a new definition of that discipline. He taught us that the mission of criminology should be to develop as "an amalgam of a multidisciplinary fundamental science and applied discipline." With this statement in mind, I invite you to join me on my most extraordinary journey, my criminological career.

First, we will travel through the country of apprenticeship—from high school to my doctorate. Second, we will follow an itinerary of choices, opportunities, and accomplishments in the context of the evolution of criminology in Quebec, across North America and in Europe. The theme of the trip is "from juvenile delinquency toward developmental criminology and from program evaluation to program development." It represents the evolution of my research activities and practices over the past 50 years (see Box 5.1).

Apprenticeship: From High School to Doctorate

In 1943, a few hours after giving birth to me, my mother died. My father was away in the army during the Second World War and in his absence, I lived successively with relatives, two couples without children, and my great grandparents. Two-and-a-half years later, I was moved to a distant city to live with my father and his new wife. Adapting to the move was extremely difficult for me. As I reflect on those formative years, I am certain that, as we learn in developmental criminology, such an experience had a significant impact on my personality and career.

The first stop on our journey is apprenticeship. Virtually all French-speaking academics born before the post-war baby boom were trained in a religious institution called the *collège classique* before entering university. I was not admitted to such an institution. I went to a public high school for five years. My parents and teachers thought that I would eventually study engineering

Box 5.1. It All Started When ...

My research activities could not have been undertaken without the open minds and patience of more than 10,000 adolescent girls and boys and more than 1,000 delinquent girls and boys and welfare cases. About 1,700 of them were interviewed many times from their early adolescence until many of them were well into their 50s.

The gathering of data could not have been accomplished without the dedication and the courage of many tens of interviewers, undergraduate and graduate students in criminology, psychology, and psychoeducation. Let's not forget the rigorous and zealous professionals who supervised interviewers and conducted the data organization and statistical analysis of our enormous files. Many colleagues in Montreal were both supportive and also helped to advance my thinking. I acknowledge, among others, Denis Gagné, Maurice Cusson, Marcel Fréchette, Jean Proulx, Michel Janosz, Jacques Dionne, Jacques Grégoire, Gilles Gendreau, Claude Bilodeau, Nadine Lanctôt, Julien Morizot, and Pierrette Trudeau Le Blanc. Colleagues abroad were also very helpful: Michel Born, David Farrington, Anne-Marie Favard, Rolf Loeber, Ray Corrado, Vincent Peyre, and Per-Olof Wikström. I am grateful to all of them; in French we say, *"Mille mercis."*

I also want to express my appreciation to organizations that regularly supported my research activities during the last 40 years: the Social Science and Humanities Research Council of Canada, various federal and provincial ministries, the Killam Fellowship, les Fonds pour la formation des chercheurs et l'aide à la recherche du Québec, le Conseil québécois pour la recherche sociale, the Canadian Institutes of Health Research, private foundations, and, most importantly, l'Université de Montréal.

because my marks in mathematical subjects were always near 100%. Instead, I choose the social sciences! It was probably the career path taken by one of my uncles that impressed me. After serving in the Navy, he studied at the London School of Economics and became a diplomat in the 1950s. He was the only member of my extended family who went beyond high school as we were all part of the working class.

I was admitted into a two-year social sciences program in 1961. The program took the form of an introduction to all the social sciences. The first day, I heard the new word "criminology" and discovered that it was a social science discipline. Denis Szabo grabbed my attention with his enthusiastic presentation of that new science and profession, by his unconventional dress—he was not dressed in a conservative dark suit like other directors—and by his behaviour: he read his mail and a book while the dean and his colleagues introduced the various social sciences.

Two years later, I chose the road to criminology by choosing to study sociology. Szabo taught me a course on deviance that confirmed my interest in criminology. I also took a course on Durkheim's theoretical contributions to sociology that focused on his books *Le suicide* and *L'éducation morale*; they became the foundation of my theoretical work.

In 1964, I obtained my first summer research job at the Ministry of Education in Quebec. My assigned task involved counting (by computer) the pupils in each class and school and reporting for the first time these data in tables. In addition, that year I got married.

In 1965, I entered the master's program in criminology where Denis Szabo recruited me as an interviewer for a study on the use of alcohol in the adult population of Montreal. A year later, I became the father of a beautiful girl who is herself now a university professor in sociology. In the mid-to-late 1960s, Szabo transferred me to the field of juvenile delinquency, which formed the primary interest of most of my academic career. In 1967, I entered the doctoral program and a year later I became the father of a boy who went on to become the engineer that everybody had thought I would be during my formative academic years.

In the master's program, Denis Szabo held a seminar in which one of the main questions was the definition of criminology. He, in effect, "brainwashed" many cohorts of his students in the 1960s with his own definition of criminology! Szabo argued that criminology should be a solidly grounded science, like the natural sciences, and a rigorous profession, like medicine. He advocated that the knowledge of theoretical and applied criminology should be combined. Its subjects have to be the act of crime, the criminal activities of individuals, and criminality in a community. In addition, he felt that both research and applied criminologists should take a multidisciplinary approach, integrating knowledge from three domains: 1) law and justice, 2) the life sciences (i.e., biology, psychology, and psychiatry), and 3) the social sciences, particularly sociology. Szabo felt that criminology should locate itself in the center of this knowledge triangle.

After I had begun work as a member of Szabo's research program in 1966, I became a self-taught methodologist, statistician, and computer programmer. I then started to teach courses on methodology and statistics. I suspect this was a result of my enduring interest and ability in mathematics, first discovered during high school. This evolution is interesting, since during my undergraduate studies I learned only about descriptive statistics, correlations, and chi-squares, as well as how to produce a table with a sorter machine. In fact, even throughout my graduate studies, no class was available on advanced statistics. Being a self-taught methodologist, statistician, and programmer was very exciting and stimulating; I had the sense of creating a new way to "do" science.

In 1969, with the defence of my doctoral thesis, my studies were completed, and I was recruited as an assistant professor at the department. This was not a common practice back then.

The Background of my Apprenticeship: Existing Criminological Research

In the background of this first landscape to be seen along our journey was a chain of mountains—Quebec pioneers in criminology. At the beginning of the twentieth century, **Wilfrid Derome** (1877–1931) created the first forensic laboratory in North America.[18] During his short life, Derome conducted research on toxicology, ballistic, graphology, and judiciary photography, and offered expertise to police departments and courts.

Despite advances in forensic criminology, the formal study of juvenile delinquency did not begin or coincide with the creation of the Department of Criminology in 1960. Research on delinquency was primarily the domain of scholars in the departments of social work and psychology at the l'Université de Montréal, Laval University, and McGill University. Even then, the perspective used to study the characteristics of delinquents and adult criminals was that known as the *ecology of crime*, whose roots are evident in the Chicago school of criminology.

In 1949, **Julien Beausoleil** (of the Department of Psychology) published the first modern empirical study of juvenile delinquents. There were two active centres of criminological research in Montréal starting in the 1950s. The first centre, at McGill University, was composed of a team directed by **Bruno Cormier** (1919–1991), a psychiatrist and true pioneer of forensic psychiatry and clinical criminology. He became the first Canadian fellow of the American Society of Criminology. His team offered psychiatric clinical evaluation in penitentiaries, developed a model prison that was implemented in New York State, and published many empirical works on latecomer and persistent criminals that are now studied by developmental criminologists. Many of their publications appear in the *Canadian Journal of Criminology.*

The second center was the Department of Psychology at the Université de Montréal. **Noël Mailloux** (1907–1997) was the main figure, and he directed many master's and doctoral theses on juvenile and adult delinquents. As a clinician, he was renowned in criminological circles in Europe. In addition, he

[18] In 1929, J. Edgar Hoover from the FBI visited Derome's lab, laying the foundations for the creation of the FBI forensic laboratory.

was associated with Boscoville, which was developing an innovative institution for delinquents. It was a psychoeducational treatment based on the work of Piaget, theoreticians of the self, particularly Rapaport and Erikson, Aichorn's experiment, and the new educational participative philosophy.

A summary of the contributions of these pioneers can be found in the four historical books cited in Box 5.2. In the 1960s, the Department of Criminology (renamed the School of Criminology in early 1970) recruited academics from these centres and professionals in police services, courts and juvenile and adult correctional services, as part-time or full time professors. Furthermore, with

Box 5.2. Empirical Criminology at the University of Montreal

Le Blanc, M., and Cusson, M. (2010). *Traité de criminologie empirique*. 4ième édition. Montréal, Presses de l'Université de Montréal.

Le Blanc, M., Ouimet, M., and Szabo, D. (2003). *Traité de criminologie empirique*. 3ième édition. Montréal, Presses de l'Université de Montréal.

Szabo, D., and Le Blanc, M. (1994). *Traité de criminologie empirique*. 2ième édition. Montréal, Presses de l'Université de Montréal.

Szabo, D. & Le Blanc, M. (1985). *La criminologie empirique au Québec: phénomènes criminels et justice pénale*. Montréal, Presses de l'Université de Montréal.

All the books are comprised of three main sections. The first section focuses on (1) the criminal phenomenon, that is, the changes in the quantity and nature of delinquency and criminality over time, (2) studies of new forms of criminality and deviance that were of interest in the Montréal criminological community, and (3) papers on such topics as adolescent delinquency, female delinquency and crime, etc.

The second section presents a synthesis in the domain of penal justice, that is: (1) the evolution of laws, (2) surveys of the attitudes of the population and agents of the justice system toward law and justice, (3) the state of research on policing and private security, and (4) the functioning of juvenile and adult courts.

The third section covers penal measures, that is: (1) prevention, (2) juvenile and adult alternative measures (community work, victim compensation, etc.), (3) restorative justice, (4) treatment and correctional measures for adults and juveniles, and (5) the management of mental health criminals.

In 2010, for the fiftieth anniversary of the School of Criminology, the series was capped by a list of the most significant publications of the last 50 years in criminology in Québec.

the impulse provided by the new generation of Ph.D.'s, the department gradually invested and concentrated in all the main research fields in criminology with graduate, contracted, and subsidized research activities. The history of this work, up to 2010, appears in four books on the state of empirical criminology with the umbrella title *Treatise of Empirical Criminology*.

I will now focus on the development of research on juvenile delinquency after the creation of the Department of Criminology. In 1964, Szabo launched the research program known as Social Structure and Adolescent Morality. The initiative was innovative for six reasons. First, the team was multidisciplinary; researchers and students came from sociology, psychology, and criminology. Second, it was based on a theory of social change that stated that the advent of mass societies explains the loosening and diversification of morality and changes in the quantity and nature of adolescent deviance. Third, the design was multi-level, because the data collection included both communities and individuals, with a comparison of a French-speaking working class with an upper-class area in Montreal. Fourth, the concepts and metrics came from psychology and sociology. Fifth, deviance was assessed by self-reports (in 1967, to our knowledge, this was the first such survey in Canada) and official statistics. Sixth, sophisticated statistical techniques were used at a time when they were not yet available by using SPSS. In 1968, an article was published on Denis Szabo's theory using some of the empirical findings (Szabo, Le Blanc, Deslauriers, and Gagné 1968). As we will see, during my career I took into account and perfected the characteristics of this program of criminological studies.

In 1968, I was assigned to the measurement and analysis of the distribution of adolescent deviance in Montreal and a comparison of the working and upper-class communities studied. One year later, I delivered two research reports, followed by my Ph.D. thesis. These reports presented the first Canadian data on self-reported delinquency across social classes, compared to official delinquency statistics (Le Blanc 1968, 1969a). In addition, a psychological measure of socialization was used (Gough SO scale) as one might expect, given Szabo's multidisciplinary definition of criminology. The conclusions were surprising. The level of self-reported delinquency and socialization was similar in the lower and upper classes, while it doubled in the lower-class community when official delinquency figures were used. The level of socialization was similarly much lower for the institutionalized delinquents of the two communities.

In my Ph.D. thesis, I added two chapters: an ecological analysis of official delinquency and a study of police criteria to refer a juvenile delinquent to court (Le Blanc 1969b). The Montreal ecological results were unlike those for cities in the United States, where the delinquency rate dropped off as one moved outward through a series of concentric circles surrounding the centre of the city. In Montreal, the distribution followed the topography of the island. It was a reverse "T" whose branches, we found, increased in length and widened over the next several decades. The characteristics of the area with high rates of delinquency were similar to those in other North American cities: physical deterioration, poverty, high rates of immigration, and so on. The last chapter was an incursion in applied criminology, with a focus on decisions by the police, again as we would expect from Szabo's approach to criminology.

At that time, we observed that the criteria for a referral to juvenile court by police were the seriousness of the offense, recidivism, increasing age, and a negative attitude. The conclusions were not much different from those of a recent study by Carrington and Schulenberg (2013).

After my Ph.D., I stood at a turning point in my career. The difficult question for a new academic is always "What should be my next research activity?" I decided to begin new research on the measurement of self-reported delinquency and the exploration of multidisciplinary explanatory factors. As a result, my career unfolded in two parallel trajectories. The first was a focus on fundamental science, from juvenile delinquency toward developmental criminology. The second was work in applied science, from treatment program evaluation toward design and implementation of new program content. In covering these trajectories, I organize my account by decade, from the 1970s to the 2000s. My role in the field of juvenile delinquency was to assume the leadership of two parallel research teams made up of different academics, research professionals, and students. The ensuing body of work formed the foundation of many dissertations and publications in Quebec between 1970s to the 2000s.

My Lifespan Landscape: Fundamental and Applied Science Trajectories

The 1970s: Time to Gather Data

When I look back at that period, I am astonished by the fact that there was no return, or so little, to the academy, funding agencies, and society. There were some reports and publications of minor value. In retrospect, the data sets gathered look like seeds being planted with no certainty whether they would grow. Nevertheless, the work was not in vain.

From Juvenile Delinquency toward Developmental Criminology: This trajectory was launched by reading the most important book in theoretical and empirical criminology of the twentieth century, Travis Hirschi's (1969) *Causes of Delinquency*. Based on his treatise, I choose to test his control theory and replicate his empirical results in a new cultural context, the French-speaking population of Quebec. This replication was done with a random sample of the population of girls and boys 12 to 18 years of age. Hirschi's theoretical and empirical statements were confirmed (Caplan and Le Blanc 1985). We expanded the Nye and Short (1957) self-reported delinquency questionnaire; we added Hirschi's type measures of the bonds to society (attachment, involvement, commitment, and belief) and other important notions in the domain of sociological criminology, such as discipline (rules, supervision, etc.) and informal and formal sanctions by society. To break new ground, I planned a two-wave panel study to observe changes in delinquency in correlation with changes in social controls.

My colleague **Marcel Fréchette**, my office neighbour, was also designing a two-wave panel study of the psychological development of delinquents during adolescence. He gathered data with ten psychological tests and he constructed an interview with numerous questions on family, peers, school and work experiences, friends, sexuality, etc. In addition, he conceived questions on offending that included descriptive indicators, such as participation, frequency, variety, and seriousness, and boundary indicators, such as onset, offset, and duration. These parameters became the foundations of the measurement of criminal activity for the study of the criminal career, or what we later called developmental criminology (Le Blanc and Fréchette 1989). His interview had a section exploring how the delinquent committed his crimes, organized by types of crimes. These data on criminals' modus operandi are described in our books (1987, 1989) and their development along the life course is demonstrated (Kazemian and Le Blanc 2004).

Because of new funding opportunities at the SSHRCC, we decided to merge the above two panel studies when gathering data for the second wave. This meant including common measures of self-reported delinquency, the addition of psychological measures for the representative sample, and new questions for the adjudicated males. Some years later, after writing a book on the comparison of these two sample sets and conducting a developmental analysis of criminal activity, we decided to add additional waves of data. The results will be reported in Le Blanc, Lanctôt, and Morizot (in preparation).

We should remember that these two-wave panel studies were not initially conceived and planned as a long-term longitudinal research program. They became such after a visit by David Farrington at my research center in early 1980s. This research program, now called the Montreal Two Sample Three Generations Longitudinal Studies (MTSTGLS), has led to follow-up of the representative and adjudicated samples until age 50. Along the way, we added several longitudinal samples during the last 30 years in an effort to replicate the results.

From Program Evaluation toward Program Content: Following the chapter on police decision-making in my Ph.D. thesis, I was asked to study the criteria of decision-making by probation officers when they recommend a placement to a training school. The content of the file of a typical case in a training school was set out on index cards, with specific items of information on the individual's crimes, family situation, schooling, gang experience, etc. During the process, probation officers looked at an average of 55 pieces of information. Their strategy changed with the type of training that they had received; criminologists would start with the information on crime, social workers with information on the family. However, after evaluating on average only five pieces of information, their minds were set on whether to recommend a placement or not (Le Blanc and Brousseau 1974).

The government of Quebec created, in 1972, the Batshaw Committee to review all institutions for children and propose adequate policies. My task was to collect data on the characteristics of that population in orphanages, reform schools for delinquents, and child welfare training schools. My conclusion was that half of all these children did not present sufficient need, in terms of dysfunctional family characteristics, difficult school experience, seriousness of their delinquency, etc., to justify placement in such institutions. The committee recommended deinstitutionalization; it took ten years to attain a significant result. Once again, these applied research activities were not career-oriented but were in response to societal demands.

During the same period, a Quebec parliamentary committee was reviewing health and welfare laws. Boscoville, an institution for juvenile delinquents that was associated with the Department of Psychology of the Université de Montréal, presented its psychoeducational treatment as innovative and efficient, based on a recidivism study (Landreville 1966). The president of the committee recommended an independent evaluation to document the changes in treated delinquents. Boscoville asked a group of academics from the School of Criminology to undertake that evaluation. I started in this project as a consultant on methodology and statistics and ended up as the director of the project. I was interested in this project probably because, during the first semester of the master's program in criminology, we visited a new secure institution for adolescents, Cité des Prairies. I have always remembered the image of a boy, 11 or 12 years old, who was holding the bars of his cell door, his head touching them; he looked distraught.

In the early 1970s, criminology offered one experimental treatment program based on a socio-criminological theory; its implementation was evaluated and the recidivism rate was analyzed in depth (Empey and Lubeck 1971a). The authors concluded that the effect of that intervention in an open institution, as a reducer of recidivism and a help to delinquents, was questionable. At the end of the program, there were no significant differences between the experimental and the controls. However, the number of delinquent acts was reduced by 85% for the experimental group and by 63% for the in-program failures.

It should be noted that the design of Boscoville evaluation contrasted with the one by Empey and Lubeck because it was longitudinal, multidisciplinary, multi-level, and with multiple control groups. We evaluated the youths first at arrival, one year later, at departure, one and then three years after leaving the centre, and in adulthood. Second, we gathered self-reported and official delinquency statistics, psychological tests, social control variables, measures of the boys' experience with the justice system, and data on their institutional placements. It is interesting to note that the first three domains of data were like the MTSTGLS samples. Third, we studied individuals, youths and educators—

their milieu (for example, the social climate of the pavilions among other variables) and their behaviours. Fourth, the evaluation design of that psychoeducational treatment involved the test of the psychoeducational four-stages theory of progression during treatment. It was partially confirmed since not every adolescent started at the first treatment stage and all gained at least one stage during the treatment period; however, very few travelled through the four stages. Fifth, the gathering of the same data as in the MTSTGLS meant that it was possible to compare the maturation of Boscoville youths with adolescents in the MTSTGLS samples and with boys in a training school and a youth prison (Le Blanc 1985).

At the same time, authorities recommended that I evaluate the impact of Boys' Farm, an open institution that aided English-speaking delinquents. This program was grounded in the theory of interpersonal maturity and the educators there implemented its classification, philosophy, and differential programming based on the content of the Community Treatment Project (Palmer 1974).

The 1980s: Data Analysis and Conceptual Accomplishments

With all these fields of data in hand, it was clearly time to harvest, as they looked very interesting both from a fundamental and an applied perspective. Remember that we are at the end of the 1970s. Criminology was very theoretically oriented and empirically descriptive and correlational. In criminology, the prevalent models of data analysis in the domain of juvenile delinquency were Nye's on family (1958) and Hirschi on bonding (1969). In these studies, self-reported delinquency was explained within the Durkheimian theoretical tradition that I had studied with Szabo. There was also at that time an animated controversy in the criminological community about the usefulness of the self-reported measure of delinquency. In sociology, the technique for the analysis of longitudinal data was at the level of the cross-tabulation of two waves of data. In psychology, the statistical techniques were the multivariate analysis of variance and covariance. I did not feel that these descriptive and correlational strategies were appropriate for multi-wave data and believed it was time to conceptualize the developmental perspective before starting to analyze longitudinal data.

From Juvenile Delinquency toward Developmental Criminology: From 1975 to 1985, Marcel Fréchette and I independently produced numerous research reports for funding agencies and some articles that described the data from our samples. Since we were trained in the European tradition, our career goal was to publish books rather than articles. To fulfill that goal, during the first half of the 1980s, we decided to write a book synthetizing all the data. The words in the title of our 1987 book *Delinquencies and Delinquents* were pluralized, because we took the position that there were many types of delinquencies and delinquents; we were thinking in terms of typology and trajectory. The book was a departure from most books on juvenile delinquency, which were mostly literature reviews. Apart from some articles on the personality of delinquents, the vast majority of the theoretical and empirical publications were from the sociological-criminological perspective. In contrast, our book had several new features.

First, to my knowledge, the word "development" was used for the first time in criminology for the analysis of the criminal activity. Second, we stated that the most important investment in etiological research should be to produce knowledge on the changes in the nature of offending along the life course and its diverse causes along the life span. We are now arguing for the same goals in understanding all forms of antisocial behaviour (Le Blanc 2015).

Third, in parallel to the statement of the criminal career paradigm (Blumstein, Cohen, Roth, and Visher 1986), we analyzed the development of delinquency through what are now called descriptive (participation, frequency, variety, and seriousness) and boundary (onset, offset, duration) parameters. In addition, we started to look at what would later be called changes in the crime mix and the developmental mechanisms of activation and gradation of the criminal activity. Marcel Fréchette had the brilliant idea of drawing a figure showing the two waves of self-reported delinquency interviews; these descriptors showed clearly the gradation of the criminal activities.

Fourth, we compared the representative and the adjudicated adolescents on structural, social bonds, and internal and external constraints explanatory factors, and we tested family, school, peers, and constraints explanatory models using these concepts. Fifth, we compared personality (now it is more fashionable in criminology to use self-control) and we modeled the impact of a structure of personality traits because of our acceptance of the definition of criminology as multidisciplinary.

Sixth, even if at that time there existed some theoretical and empirical typologies of juvenile delinquents, they did not start with developmental trajectories of self-reported delinquent behaviour. We created one with a panel of judges, using descriptive and boundary parameters from early adolescence until young adulthood.

Overall, we showed empirically that the structural, social bonds, social constraints, and self-control characteristics distinguished these meta-trajectories and sub-trajectories using discriminant function analysis (see Box 5.3).

We then started to move further with our analysis of the development of criminal activity beyond adolescence, up to age 30. It was our 1989 book that advanced our conceptualization of the course of criminal activity along the life span. It was multi-level because we analyzed the evolution of the perpetration of offenses from adolescence through youth; we observed that the modus operandi became more and more organized along the life span (Kazemian and

Le Blanc 2004). It was a developmental perspective because our conceptualization went beyond the presentation of data on the descriptive and boundary parameters of official and self-reported offending. We proposed that the course of offending is constructed through the dynamic interaction between three mechanisms, and this was confirmed with our longitudinal data: (1) Activation is generated through acceleration, diversification, and stabilization (in order, increased frequency, variety, and duration with earlier onset); (2) Aggravation or escalation on a developmental sequence is based on the seriousness and the crime mix; and (3) Desistance manifests itself, before offset, by deceleration, de-escalation on the developmental sequence, reaching a ceiling of seriousness, and specialization (reducing the number of types of crimes).

As this work was progressing, in 1985, at the conference held to mark the 25th anniversary of the School of Criminology, I was fortunate to meet **Rolf Loeber**, who was conceptualizing and analyzing the development of problem behaviour. From 1985 to 1990, I was fortunate to discuss with him the need for an overview of developmental criminology. We thought that the concepts we had put forward so far in our publications were not well-organized in an integrated manner. I have great memories of working with Loeber, and our discussions helped to shape the rest of my endeavours in theoretical and empirical developmental criminology.

Box 5.3. Pivotal Works of the 1980s

Fréchette, M., and Le Blanc, M. (1987, reprinted 1990, 1993, 1996, 2003). *Délinquances et délinquants.* Montreal: Gaétan Morin.

Le Blanc, M., and Fréchette, M. (1989). *Male Criminal Activity, from Childhood through Youth: Multilevel and Developmental Perspectives.* New York: Springer-Verlag.

Loeber, R., and Le Blanc, M. (1990). Toward a Developmental Criminology. *Crime and Justice: An Annual Review,* 12: 373–473.

Le Blanc, M., and Loeber, R. (1998). Developmental Criminology Upgraded. *Crime and Justice Handbook,* 23: 115–198.

In sum, the 1980s was a period of intensive conceptual work on the development of offending, accompanied by an in-depth exploration of the validity of that conceptualization in the existing scientific literature and in our longitudinal data sets.

From Program Evaluation toward Program Content: My applied criminology trajectory in the 1980s was characterized by three main activities: (1) dissemination of the results of our evaluation of the impact of two treatments for delinquents; (2) participation in a collaborative study on the functioning of juvenile justice in Canada; and (3) numerous consultations with social welfare and justice agencies of the governments of Quebec, Canada, and other countries.

From 1973 to early 1980, we conceptualized and implemented the design for the evaluation of the Boscoville and Boys' Farm treatments. Since the space is limited here, I will only outline some results of our program evaluation that are still relevant today for juvenile corrections. Our results for the evaluation of Boscoville are reported in length in Le Blanc (1983a: French and English versions), while the comparison of the homogeneous model of Boscoville and the heterogeneous model of Boys' Farm can be found in Le Blanc (1983b).

At the time of the program evaluation, the duration of the youngsters' stays was long, very often two years or more. Our analyses concluded that the optimum duration was around one year. If the stay was longer, there were no significant additional gains in terms of behavioural, psychological, and social developments. If the stay was less than eight months, there was not enough time to obtain significant changes. Currently, the average stay in the institutional system in Quebec is rarely more than six months, which I believe to be too short (Le Blanc 2011). In sum, treatment for juvenile delinquents needs around a year to be significantly efficient and effective.

In criminology, the standard indicator of success is official recidivism. The rate of self-reported delinquency was lower in the first few years after treatment compared to the ears before arrival at Boscoville. Covering the period between 18 and 30 years of age and taking official criminality into account, 67% of the subjects treated during at least one year at Boscoville recidivated, while 83% of the subjects who stayed less than a year did (respectively 28% and 45% for violent crimes). Not only was recidivism less prevalent for the participants treated, it was also less serious. The boys treated in Boscoville clearly displayed less subsequent delinquency. The boys treated at Boys' Farm had a recidivism rate of 79%, a rate 12% higher than the treated boys of Boscoville.

In summary, I concluded that the psychoeducational treatment of Boscoville was not particularly successful. From all the behavioural, social integration, and psychological results, it was evident that the homogeneous model obtains better results than the heterogeneous model. In addition, no meta-analysis of treatment effects was available to compare the results of Boscoville and Boys' Farm to others programs. However, we know, according to Lipsey landmark data set (1989, 1995), that Boscoville recidivism rates would be among the lowest and its psychological impacts among the highest. When these results were presented to the psychoeducator community and to those involved in juvenile correction in Quebec, they were stunned and devastated. They then asked: What type of program should we propose for the delinquent on whom we have made no significant impact? This question of program content will be addressed in the next section.

My second involvement, in parallel, was to participate in the National Study of the Functioning of the Juvenile Court in Canada (NSFJCC). This study was under the leadership of the Canadian Ministry of Justice and directed by Aaron Caplan, my former Ph.D. student at the School of Criminology. I was invited to join a research project that would examine how juvenile courts operated in six urban areas across Canada (Vancouver, Edmonton, Winnipeg, Toronto, Montreal, and Halifax), several non-metropolitan sites, and selected rural areas. Through direct observations in courts, from court files, and through interviews with justice personnel, baseline data were obtained that would permit a future comparison with juvenile courts operations under the then-proposed Young Offender Act. As often happens with governmental research, the later, post-implementation data were never collected because it was not politically useful and there was not much analysis of the existing data set. There was a follow-up book (Corrado, Bala, Linden, and Le Blanc 1992) and some researchers, including myself, published several articles using the data (see Box 5.4).

In addition, I was involved in intensive consulting activities with juvenile social welfare and correctional agencies. It was a period when the Ministry of Justice was conceptualizing a revolutionary law, the Young Offenders Act of 1982. In Quebec, at the same time, work on a modernized Youth Protection Act (1979, 1984) was underway and I was the head of research for a parliamentary group carrying out this work. In the child welfare and juvenile correction agencies, the ideologies of diversion and deinstitutionalization were most fashionable. I had the opportunity to use the data from MTSTGLS, on self-reported delinquency and its etiology, to justify police and justice diversion and justice and welfare deinstitutionalization. With my data, I defended these policies and argued for the reduction of the lengths of placements in juvenile correction.

Box 5.4. Key Works on Boscoville

Le Blanc, M. (1983a). *Boscoville: la rééducation évaluée.* Montréal: H.M.H.

Le Blanc, M. (1983b). *L'efficacité de l'internat pour la rééducation des jeunes délinquants, modèle homogène, Boscoville, modèle hétérogène, Boys' Farm.* Ottawa, Solliciteur Général du Canada.

Le Blanc, M. (1983c). A retrospective view at a decade of evaluation: Boscoville. In R. Corrado, M. Le Blanc, and J. Trépanier (Ed.), *Current Issues in Juvenile Justice.* Toronto: Butterworths.

The True Effect of Treatment in Residence. In H.J. Kerner (Ed.), *Dangerous or Endangered? Questions of Sanctioning, Treatment and Secure Residential Placement of Serious and/or Repeating Juvenile Delinquents.* Heidelberg: Ruprecht-Karls-Universitat Heidelberg.

In sum, the 1980s were intense periods for data analysis and publication. That period was important in the conceptual formalization of developmental criminology. There were many consultations with decision-makers and practitioners in the legal, welfare, and correctional fields. A lesson learned from that period is that we always have too much data for what we can do with it. As a consequence, society pays for a lot of wasted effort. As a result, I believe secondary data analysis should be a high priority in criminology. For me, that period was also marked by a move for professional reasons, in 1987, from the School of Criminology to the School of Psychoeducation.

The 1990s and the 2000s: Replication, Theory, and Differential Treatment

Our journey is entering its final scenes. The houses are constructed and the environmental planning is complete. It is time to take advantage of all the knowledge that has been produced.

As mentioned earlier, after reading Hirschi's *Causes of Delinquency,* I chose to test his control theory by a replication of his empirical results in a new cultural context. However, around the same time, I was also impressed by two publications on the formalization of discursive theories: Sutherland differential association theory was translated into mathematical set language (De Fleur and Quinney 1966) and Empey and Lubeck's lower-class theory of delinquency was stated with axiomatic rules (1971b). Again, I think my past level of comfort with mathematics enhanced the appeal of these works. I undertook the project of the formalization of Hirschi's theory and the construction of a multilayered and developmental theory of antisocial behaviour. In addition, in the 1990s and beyond, I explored the methodological question of replication. I launched a replication of the 1970s data-set on adjudicated males to test the impact on social change and I added adjudicated females.

In my applied criminology trajectory, I started to respond to the question that stimulated the interest of the psycho-educators after the evaluation of Boscoville treatment. Remember that there was a low-maturity group that improved during its stay but that lost most of its gains after leaving the centre, and there was a non-normative group that improved during treatment and continued to mature after leaving Boscoville. The conclusion of the psycho-educators was that they had a good treatment for delinquents with anxious and neurotic traits, but that it was not that efficient with delinquents with psychopathic traits. My response was to assemble a team of specialists on the treatment of each of these types of delinquents. Then we launched a research and development feasibility pre-test of the implementation of a differential treatment program. That project was completed in 2012, even though I retired in 2004.

From Juvenile Delinquency toward Developmental Criminology: Our exact replication of Hirschi's empirical analysis confirmed his findings on commitment, belief, and involvement, but there were some differences concerning attachment. There seemed to be a cultural difference in the importance of the attachment to school; these measures were associated to a lesser degree with self-reported delinquency in our French-speaking sample

(Caplan and Le Blanc 1985). In the following years, I expanded upon Hirschi's theory with more comprehensive measures of delinquency, some additional measures of bonding, some structural measures, constraint concepts of informal and formal social control, and other ideas drawn from sociological criminology. This process was sustained by the formalization of Hirschi's theory.

That enterprise begun with Caplan's doctoral thesis in 1975 (1978) and it was progressively refined through to its ensuing publication (Le Blanc and Caplan 1993). Analyzing the methods of theoretical formalization available during the early 1970s, we choose Gibbs' (1972) method because it was more elaborated and more complex, and his rules were clear.

During the process of formalization, we identified definitional problems and incomplete specification of relationships between concepts and constructs. The end-product of this dissection was the discursive and formal restatement of the theory with an additional eight axioms, 12 postulates, 13 propositions, nine transformational statements, and 17 theorems. I still think, like Gibbs (1985), that any formal mode is superior to the discursive mode. I hope that somebody will undertake the task of formalizing my multi-layered control theory of the criminal phenomenon (Le Blanc 1997) and my social controls theory of the development of antisocial behaviour (Le Blanc 2016).

Replication took the form of gathering a new sample and analyzing data sets from similar available representative samples gathered by other researchers in Montreal. In addition, I collected a new sample of adjudicated males and gathered data with the same measures as were used in the 1970s. However, we observed some differences between the samples from the 1970s and the 1990s. The homogeneity of the first sample had disappeared because of the increased proportion of immigrants with heterogeneous racial and ethnic characteristics. We are now analyzing if this significant structural change has had any impact on the individual development of antisocial behaviour. It is not easy to disentangle all the factors involved in social change! Replication by reproducing results obtained with our representative sample of the 1970s and a comparable sample in the 1980s did produce comparable results (Le Blanc, Ouimet, and Tremblay 1988). We confirmed a similar longitudinal and multidisciplinary model of explanation of self-reported delinquency that accounted for 55% of the variance cross-sectionally and 62% longitudinally. As a result, we concluded that the delinquent conduct was caused by tenuous social ties (little attachment to persons and commitment to social institutions) and delayed psychological development (low self-control), which makes it difficult to accept social constraints. This main dynamic of control has two effects: delinquent conduct on the one hand, and, on the other, marginality in relation to the social role of the conventional adolescent (marginality in terms of seeking delinquent friends and malfunctioning at school), which, in turn, serves as a powerful support for delinquent conduct.

These steps of formalization, replication, and extension of Hirschi's bonding theory opened the road to the formulation of my own theory. My initial statement of the theory was concerned with the total criminal phenomenon composed of three embedded phenomena, as set out in Szabo's first definition of the subject matter of criminology: the act of crime, the person of the criminal, and the state of criminality (Le Blanc 1997a). The interactional content of my theory was the specification of the links between homologous notions from each layer of the criminal phenomenon and a statement of the principles of development over time, whatever the layer. The formulation of this theory

Box 5.5. Developmental Criminology: Key Works

Lanctôt, N., and Le and Le Blanc, M. (2002). Explaining adolescent females' involvement in general deviance: Towards an integration of theoretical perspectives. *Crime and Justice* 26:113–202.

Le Blanc, M., Ouimet, M., and Tremblay, R.E. (1988). An integrative control theory of delinquent behavior: A validation 1976–1985. *Psychiatry* 51: 164–176.

Le Blanc, M., and Caplan, M. (1993). Theoretical formalization, a necessity: The example of Hirschi's social control theory. *Advances in Criminological Theory* 4: 329–431.

Le Blanc, M. (1997a). A Generic Control Theory of the Criminal Phenomenon, the Structural and the Dynamical Statements of an Integrative Multilayered Control Theory. *Advances in Theoretical Criminology* 7: 215–286.

Le Blanc, M. (1997b). Socialization or Propensity: A Test of an Integrative Control Theory with Adjudicated Boys. *Studies in Crime and Crime Prevention* 6: 200–224.

Le Blanc, M. (2006). Self-control and Social Control of Deviant Behavior in Context: Development and Interactions Along the Life Course. In Wikström, P.-O. & Sampson, R. *The Social Contexts of Pathways in Crime: Development, Context, and Mechanisms.* Cambridge: Cambridge University Press.

Le Blanc, M. (2015). Developmental Criminology: Thoughts on the Past and Insights for the Future. In Morizot, J, & Kazemian, L. *The Development of Criminal and Antisocial Behavior, Theory, Research, and Practice.* New York: Springer.

Le Blanc, M. (2016). An Update of a Theory of the Interconnected Development of Personal Controls and Antisocial Behavior. In Farrington, D.P., Kazemian, L., & Piquero, A.R. *The Oxford Handbook on Developmental Criminology.* Oxford: Oxford University Press.

Le Blanc, M., Lanctôt, N., and Morizot, J. (forthcoming). *Explaining the Growth and Decline of Antisocial Behaviour. The Interactional Development of Self and Social Controls and Antisocial Behaviour. Data from the Montreal Two Samples Three Generations Longitudinal Studies.*

was based on a review of the theoretical and empirical criminological literature and chaos theory.

My second theory was limited to the layer of the criminal (2006, 2016). The reader will note that there is also a move from explaining the criminal phenomenon to a more inclusive dependent variable, individual deviant or antisocial behaviour. In addition, for the first time in criminology, I reviewed the literature on the developmental course of self-controls and social controls along the life span. What is most innovative about the papers was the use of the tools of the "chaos perspective" to model the developmental interactions among self-controls, social controls, and antisocial behaviour in the environmental context of a community. There were tests of this theory in our 1988 and 1997b papers with MTSTGLS samples. We are now testing this model with more than two waves of data.

In Box 5.5 above, I have listed some of the key works related to this recent research and analysis.

FROM PROGRAM EVALUATION TOWARD PROGRAM CONTENT: If the 1990s were marked by energetic theoretical activity, it was also the period of an increased commitment toward program content and, from 2000 on, of involvement in research and development (R&D) on the treatment of antisocial adolescents. In addition, I constructed and validated clinical measures. The 1990s were a preparatory period in terms of program content, the time for a feasibility study and to conceptualize a differential program of treatment. The 2000s were the years of program implementation and evaluation.

If academics and psychoeducators were very active in R&D and evaluative research in the 1960s and the 1970s, these activities progressively collapsed during the 1980s and 1990s. Boscoville was closed in 1996. The application of existing treatment programs in the *centres jeunesse* was declared inadequate by an expert committee (Gendreau, Tardif, Baillargeon, and Bilodeau 1999).

In the early 1990s, I put together a team for a feasibility study for the implementation of differential treatment programming. The team was composed of a psychologist for cognitive behavioural intervention (Jean Proulx), a psychologist and psycho-educator for cognitive developmental intervention (Jacques Dionne), a psycho-educator for general institution programming (Jacques Grégoire), and a criminologist for implementation (Pierrette Trudeau Le Blanc). We had access to half-a-dozen units in three centres with various security levels. The programs were implemented over two years. The result of the feasibility study was the 1998 book. The content of the new program proposed in this book had two layers of content, the milieu and group programming. The first layer involved the general conditions of life in a residential institution that are necessary to support changes in behaviour and psychological and social maturations. The practices recommended were an update of the classic psychoeducational program described above. The second layer was the content of specific cognitive-behavioural activities.

In 2000, the government of Quebec created and provided an annual subsidy for a non-governmental R&D centre with the mission to develop and test new prevention and treatment programs and then train professionals to apply them in various governmental and non-governmental services. This centre was located on the Boscoville campus, which was no longer in use, and was called Boscoville 2000. An interesting feature of this project was the fact that there were no adolescents living on the Boscoville campus itself; they were residing in various youth centres in other cities. However, we added sufficient personnel in the field to train the educators and supervise the implementation of the programs. Research assistants were used to gather data. Some of the positive results were an optimization of the content of the treatment activities with the help of the educators that delivered them, a recognition, by all parties, of an increase in professional self-esteem among personnel, and a high involvement rate by the adolescents. In addition, the level and quality of implementation was very high (Le Blanc 2011). On the negative side of the ledger, the youth centres were not able to offer the conditions for differential treatment—that is, selecting the appropriate adolescents for each program and assigning to each program the educators with the best aptitude for that particular program. The ten years of implementation are reported in two books published in 2014 (see Box 5.6).

Box 5.6. Some Key Works, Post-2000

Le Blanc, M., Dionne, J., Proulx, J., Grégoire, J., and Trudeau-Le Blanc, P. (1998). *Intervenir autrement: le modèle différentiel et les adolescents en difficulté*. Montréal: Presses de l'Université de Montréal.

Le Blanc, M., and Trudeau Le Blanc (2014a). *La réadaptation de l'adolescent antisocial, un programme cognitivo-émotivo-comportemental.* Montréal: Presses de l'Université de Montréal.

Le Blanc, M., and Trudeau Le Blanc (2014b). *Documents d'accompagnement pour l'application du programme cognitivo-émotivo-comportemental.* Montréal: Presses de l'Université de Montréal.

Le Blanc, M. (2015). *MASPAQ: Mesures de l'adaptation sociale et psychologique pour les adolescents québécois. Manuel et guide d'utilisation*. Montréal: École de psychoéducation, Université de Montréal.

Le Blanc, M., and Morizot, J. (2008). IHSAQ: *Inventaire des habiletés sociales pour les adolescents québécois*. Montréal: École de psychoéducation, Université de Montréal.

Le Blanc, M., Trudeau-Le Blanc, P., Lanctôt, N. (1999). *MÉQIGAQ Manuel pour évaluer la qualité et d'adolescents québécois.* Montréal: École de psychoéducation, Université de Montréal.

What I consider a major accomplishment in my applied criminology trajectory was the development of three clinical evaluations for adolescents: MASPAQ, IHSAQ, and MÉGIGAQ. The MASPAQ (Measures of Antisocial Behaviour and Social and Psychological Adaptation for Adolescents) is a clinical instrument composed of an interview protocol, software, a set of scales, and a list of results. It was constructed using my 1980s and 1990s samples with current psychometric methods. The software calculates behavioural, social control, and self-control scales that are normed by gender, and age. There are now six versions of the MASPAQ: French (Quebec, France, Belgium), English, Arab, Spanish, Portuguese (Brazil), and Senegalese. The IHSAQ (Inventory of Social Skills for Adolescents) measures 34 different social skills related to communication, anger control and stress management, and problem-solving, all of which are part of our cognitive behavioural treatment program. The MÉGIGAQ (Manual of Measures to Assess the Quality of Intervention in a Group of Adolescents) was devised to measure the quality of social life in residential units from the points of view of both adolescents and educators (see Box 5.6).

Box 5.7. Awards and Recognition

2015: Festschrift: Morizot, J., & Kazemian, L. *The Development of Criminal and Antisocial Behavior, Therory, Research, and Practice*. New York: Springer, 2014.

2014: Léon Gérin Prize of the Government of Quebec for an Exceptional Contribution to Social Sciences.

2014: Lifetime Achievement Award in Developmental and Life-course Criminology from the American Society of Criminology.

2012: Sellin-Glueck Award for international contribution to criminology, American Society of Criminology.

2008: Doctorate Honorius Causa in Criminology and Psychology from the Univerité de Liège, Belgium.

2000: Beaumont-de Tocqueville Prize from the International Association of French-Speaking Criminologists.

1995: Marcel Vincent prize of l'Association canadienne-française pour l'avancement des sciences for Outstanding Contribution to the Social and Behavioral Sciences.

1993: Elected member, Royal Society of Canada, Academy of Arts and Sciences.

1993: Killam Fellowship, Conseil des arts du Canada.

1971: Beccaria prize of the Société de criminologie du Québec (for young researchers).

Conclusion

Looking back at the road we have travelled together, I find it is filled with many pleasant memories but also sprinkled with numerous surprises. At the beginning of my career, I did not anticipate (nor, probably, did my mentor and my colleagues) the quantity, variety, and continuity of the research activities in fundamental and applied criminology that I would produce throughout my 40 years. Was I a hyperactive criminologist?

I am particularly proud of three aspects of these activities. First, as Professor Szabo urged us to do, I managed to uncover fundamental knowledge on the epidemiology and development of individual criminal activity and apply it to state and institutional policies and the treatment of delinquents. Second, I am pleased with the self-taught methodology that characterizes my studies, which involves a mix of longitudinal, multidisciplinary, and multi-level designs and analysis, the use of replications, and the improvement of self-reported methods. Third, I am also pleased with the fact that I produced empirical studies, theoretical statements, and a paradigmatic formalization in the domain of developmental criminology, and that I conceived, carried out, and evaluated the implementation of a complex milieu and cognitive-behavioural treatment program for antisocial adolescents.

Analyzing my research activity in terms of two parallel trajectories, I realize that there was little planning involved. It developed out of affinities with various people and opportunities in my criminological environment. There were a few initial choices that I made and a desire to bring my already existing work to a higher level. In addition, I should note that criminology was still in an early stage of development when I started my academic career. I was lucky that there were many opportunities and considerable room for creativity. I always had the desire to make things clearer, more complex, and more precise. In a period when criminology was discovering an extremely large amount of new information, my natural attitude of curiosity proved fruitful. It was reinforced by the fact that most of my intellectual tools were self-taught.

In sum, I responded to the excitement of new results and new ideas, a passion for the subject of juvenile delinquency, and the novelty of the developmental criminology perspective. I had enormous fun during my career and still do. I wish the same to future generations of criminologists.

All my empirically based publications conclude with comments on the limits of the research I undertook. If I were an independent biographer, I would discuss the relationships between aspects of my personal life and the activities that characterized my career as well as what occurred in criminology as a worldwide discipline during the same five decades. It seems fitting, however, to leave these analyses to posterity and to simply reflect on the wonderful journey I have had following my passion in criminology.

References

Blumstein, A., Cohen, J., Roth, J.A., and Visher, C.A. (1986). *Criminal Career and "Career Criminals"* (volumes 1 and 2). Washington, D.C.: National Academy Press.

Carrington, P., and Schulenberg, J.L. (2013). *Police Discretion with Young Offenders.* Ottawa: Department of Justice of Canada.

Cavan, R. (1969). *Juvenile Delinquency: Development, Treatment, Control.* Philadelphia: Lippincott.

Corrado, R.R., Bala, N., Linden, R., and Le Blanc, M. (1992). *Juvenile Justice in Canada: A Theoretical and Analytical Assessment.* Toronto: Butterworths.

Corrado, R.R. (1992). Introduction. In R.R. Corrado, N. Bala, N., R. Linden, & M. Le Blanc (1992), *Juvenile Justice in Canada: A Theoretical and Analytical Assessment.* Toronto, Butterworths.

De Fleur, M.L., and Quinney, R. (1966). A Reformulation of Sutherland's Differential Association Theory and a Strategy for Empirical Verification. *The Journal of Research in Crime and Delinquency* 3: 1–21.

Empey, L.T. (1978). *American Delinquency.* Homewood, Ill.: The Dorsey Press.

Empey, L.T., and Lubeck, S.G. (1971a). *The Silverlake Experiment: Resting Delinquency Theory and Community Intervention.* Chicago: Aldine Publishing.

Empey, L.T. and Lubeck, S.G. (1971b). *Explaining Delinquency: Construction, Test, and Reformulation of a Sociological Theory.* Toronto: D.C. Heath.

Hirschi, T. (1969). *Causes of Delinquency.* Los Angeles: University of California Press.

Gendreau, G., Tardif, R., Baillargeon, L., and Bilodeau, C. (1999). *L'intervention en internat: une intervention qui doit retrouver son sens, sa place et ses moyens. Rapport du comité sur la réadaptation en internat des jeunes de 12 à 18 ans.* Montréal: Association des centres jeunesse du Québec.

Gibbs, J. (1972). *Sociological Theory Construction.* Hinsdale, Ill.: Dryden Press.

Gibbs, J. (1985). The Methodology of Theory Construction in Criminology. In R.F. Meyer. *Theoretical Methods in Criminology.* Beverly Hills, Calif.: Sage Publications.

Jensen, G.J., and Rojek, D.G. (1980). *Delinquency: A Sociological View.* Toronto: D.C. Heath.

Landreville, P. (1966). Étude follow-up d'un échantillon de garçons confiés à une centre de rééducation de la région de Montréal. Thèse de maitrise inédite. Département de criminologie, Université de Montréal.

Kazemian, L., and Le Blanc, M. (2004). Exploring Patterns of Perpetration of Crime across the Life Course: Offense and Offender-Based Viewpoints. *Journal of Contemporary Criminal Justice*, 20 (4), 393–415.

Le Blanc, M. (1968). Délinquance juvénile à Montréal: 1960–66. Montréal: Département de criminologie, Université de Montréal.

Le Blanc, M. (1969a). Inadaptation et classes sociales à Montréal. Montréal: Département de criminologie, Université de Montréal.

Le Blanc, M. (1969b). Délinquance juvénile: une perspective épidémiologique et stigmatique. Thèse de doctorat inédite, Département de Criminologie, Université de Montréal.

Le Blanc, M. (1985). De l'efficacité d'internats québécois. *Revue Canadienne de Psycho-éducation* 14: 113–120.

Le Blanc, M. (2011). Vers un modèle renouvelé pour la réadaptation en internat des adolescents avec des difficultés graves d'adaptation. Bilan quinquenal 2005-2011. Montréal: Boscoville2000.

Le Blanc, M., and Brousseau, G. (1974). La prise de décision des agents de probation pour mineurs. Revue Canadienne de Criminologie 16: 373–392.

Lipsey, M.W. (1989). *Juvenile Delinquency Treatment: A Meta-analysis Inquiry into the Variability Effects*. New York: Russell Sage Foundation.

Lipsey, M.W. (1995). What Do We Learn from 400 Research Studies on the Effectiveness of Treatment with Juvenile Delinquents? In J. McGuire (Ed.), *What Works: Reducing Reoffending*. New York: Wiley.

Nye, F.I. (1958). *Family Relationships and Delinquent Behavior.* Westport, Conn.: Greenwood Press.

Nye, F.I., and Short, J.F. (1957). Scaling Delinquent Behavior. *American Sociological Review* 22: 326–331.

Palmer, T. (1974). *The Community Treatment Project: A Review of Accumulated Research in the California Youth Authority.* Sacramento, Calif.: California Youth Authority.

Piquero, A.R., Reingle Gonsalez, J.M., and Jennings, W.G. (2014). Developmental Trajectories and Antisocial Behavior Over the Life-course. In J. Morizot & L. Kazemian, *The Development of Criminal and Antisocial Behavior.* New York: Springer.

Szabo, D., Le Blanc, M., Deslauriers, L., and Gagné, D. (1968). Interprétations psycho-culturelles de l'inadaptation juvénile dans la société de masse contemporaine. *Acta Criminologica* 1: 9–135.

SIX

Tadeusz Grygier: Social Protection Code

John Winterdyk

Tadeusz Grygier (1915–2010) was born on February 10, 1915 in Warsaw, which was then part of the Russian Empire though it was occupied later that year by Germany and remained in German hands until the end of World War I. Throughout his rich and varied life he was a psychologist, criminologist, and avid yachtsman (twice nominated to compete in Olympic sailing competitions), as well as the founder of the Department of Criminology at the University of Ottawa in 1967. Along the way, Grygier held visiting positions at Cambridge, the University of Toronto, the University of Montreal, and several universities in China.

His attraction to criminology evolved from a series of events in his life. At the age of 20, he obtained the equivalent of a B.Sc. (Honours) in political science and economics at Jaqiellonian University in Cracow. The following year he completed and received his Master's of Law (canonical and civil) from the University of Warsaw, was admitted to the bar and became the youngest law graduate and *avocet stagiare* in Poland. Shortly thereafter, he enrolled in a doctoral program to study criminology and psychology under the tutelage of Prof. Stanislaw Batwia and Dr. St. Baley at the University of Warsaw. However, his studies were interrupted by the outbreak of World War II.

In 1939, Adolf Hitler began his campaign of terror across Europe and after establishing his pact with Stalin, Poland was divided between Germany and the Soviet Union. Grygier became a Soviet prisoner and was sent to a labour camp in the Komi Republic where hundreds of thousands were sent to during the period to perform forced labour. It is a harsh and desolate area in northeastern Russia. The natural hardships of life in the camp aside, his life was threatened at least twice but he used his superior intellect and psychological insight to save himself from being executed. His skills did not go unnoticed as the camp allowed him certain freedoms, among them the opportunity to work as a psychiatrist at the local hospital. During this period he proposed a plan to reorganize mental health services in the Komi Republic. However, before the idea was able to come to fruition, the Germans attacked Russia and resources and attention were diverted away from the initiative. Upon his early release on parole, Grygier was kidnapped by the Russian secret police and subjected to

Box 6.1. The Social Protection Code

It is clear from those who knew him and through his writing that Grygier's passion for fair and flexible justice was heavily influenced by his personal life experiences; indeed, how could it not be! He regularly spoke and wrote about the need to replace retributive justice with the concept of protection of society. In 1977 he formalized these ideas in what he referred to as the Social Protection Code (SPC). He was invited to present his ideas to a committee of the House of Commons; although his ideas were well received, no legislative action was taken to implement them.

The Social Protection Code can trace its roots to the works of such great philosophers and thinkers as David Hume, Jeremy Bentham, John Stuart Mill, and other proponents of an ethical theory that is called utilitarianism. The views of the ancient Greek philosopher Epicurus, who viewed the attainment of happiness and a tranquil life as being our most important drive and need, were also influential. Grygier later modified the SPC into what he called the Code of Humanist Justice, which is detailed in his 2008 book *Fairness and Justice: The Essence of Morality, Law and Health*. The Code calls for greater cooperation and trust among the major elements of the criminal justice system, among victims and within society as a whole. Grygier (like many others) argued that laws and legislation seldom lead to greater happiness. One of his former colleagues at the University of Ottawa, Dr. Maria Los, points out that Grygier was arguably among the first to introduce the concept of restorative justice in Canada, as early as 1962.

Underlying Grygier's new Code was the idea that the penal code should replace its retributive elements with constructive rewards that could and would promote the offender's social compliance and legitimate self-definition. Here the reader may see parallels with Harold Pepinsky and Richard Qunney's (1991) book on peacemaking criminology, which advocates a move away from conventional criminal justice to restorative justice. Such ideas when first introduced were slow to gain acceptance but today have garnered considerable support.

Pavlovian-style conditioning. Again, Grygier used his psychological knowledge to foil the interrogators. He survived by defining himself not as a victim but as "lucky" scientist who could observe and analyze the effects of brutal oppression (see Box 6.1, above).

Soon after his release in 1943, he was accused by the Soviets of spying for the Germans. Realizing the risk of what would likely happen to him, he fled first to Kuybyshev, then to Iran. While in Iran, he spent a couple of years working for Polish, British, and American intelligence. After the war, he moved to England, where he decided to continue his Ph.D. studies at London School of Economics (LSE). Among his more prominent mentors were **Herman Mannheim** (law and criminology), **Sir Frederic Bartlett** (experimental psychology),

Sir Karl Popper (philosophy and science), **Sir Claus Moser** (his statistical advisor), **Sir Raymond Firth** (anthropology), and **Edward Shils,** a visiting professor of sociology from Chicago. Grygier's Ph.D. thesis was published as *Oppression: A Study of Social and Criminal Psychology* in 1954 and later reprinted in 1973, 1998, 2001, and 2003 (see Box 6.2). The book, which drew on his experiences in the Soviet camps, is still considered relevant today. In 1960, shortly after completing his Ph.D. in 1960, Grygier was recommended by Mannheim for a position at the University of Toronto. There Grygier taught and conducted research in criminology, psychology, and social work, as well as working part-time as director of research and policy advisor for the government of Ontario. In 1965 he represented Canada at United Nations meetings in Stockholm, and then went on to become a consultant on social defence for the United Nations offices in New York and Vienna.

In 1967, Grygier moved to the University of Ottawa where he was invited to set up a research centre in criminology. Two years later he established two interdisciplinary, bilingual programs, one leading to a Master of Arts (M.A.) in criminological research and the other to the professional degree of Master of Correctional Administration (M.C.A.). At the time, Grygier viewed these programs as the world's first department of applied criminology. The programs reflected Grygier's passion for research and emphasis on the importance of the proper application of criminological knowledge. Later, in 1980, the university established an undergraduate program in criminology, which today is one of the leading such programs in the country.

Box 6.2. *Oppression*

In his 1955 review of *Oppression: A Study of Social and Criminal Psychology,* Elio Monachesi of the University of Minnesota notes that "the research design in its original form is highly ingenious and imaginative" (p. 255) and concluded that the monograph "represents a serious and highly important attempt to study systematically what happens to mankind under the brutalizing conditions of warfare.... it deserves serious study" (p. 256). In an era when terrorism and civil wars seem never-ending, no doubt the book still offers some important insights into the field of forensic psychology.

Grygier's research spanned a wide range of topics, including the use of mathematical models for understanding the impact of various social problems. Many of his earlier publications (1945–1983) were in the fields of psychology and personality assessment. In fact, in 1962, he developed his own personality test, the Dynamic Personality Inventory, which was based mainly on the Freudian model. The Inventory is based on 33 scales which are constructed from factor analysis and the scales measured concepts as tendencies, sublimations, reaction-formations, and defence mechanisms that were believed to be associated with the various patterns of psychosexual development.

In addition to his passion for research, Grygier enjoyed supervising graduate students. Notable students included **Maurice Cusson** (University of Montreal), **Robert R. Ross** (University of Ottawa), **Bill Outerbridge** (chairman of the National Parole Board, 1974–1986), and **Ezzat Fattah**, whose career was covered earlier in this book. Grygier once described his orientation as empirical and eclectic, and, like several other Canadian pioneers, he was motivated more by a desire to seek practical solutions rather than to test theories. In fact, one common theme of his work was his interest in rehabilitation and using a humanitarian approach to achieving justice. He once posed the question (in McGrath 1965:40): "Could we be safer if we were less ruthless?" Throughout his career, he continued to argue that Canada's retributive philosophy be replaced by the concept of the "protection of society"—a concept that was eventually adopted by the Canadian Committee on Corrections in 1969. His scholarly influence reached beyond Canada as well; he was a founding member of the Polish Section of the International Society of Criminology and of the British Sociological Association, and also played an instrumental role, along with G.O.W. Mueller, then working at the United Nations in Vienna, in drafting the Convention of International Crimes and the Statute for an International Criminal Court.

After retiring in 1980, Grygier became an advisor on correctional policy and planning for the government of Canada and served as a guest lecturer at several major universities in China after having been selected by the Ontario-Jiangsu exchange program.

After his passing in 2010, the Department of Criminology at the University of Ottawa established the Tadeusz Grygier Founder's Prize. The description of the prize acknowledges him as "one of the pioneers in criminology in Canada, with innovative contributions to psychology and criminological research, and [a person who was] instrumental in introducing the concept of restorative justice in Canada." The award includes two prizes to outstanding undergraduate and graduate students in the department. The prize "recognizes excellence and [provides] encouragement for future innovative research and policy formation in criminology"—true to the spirit of Grygier's lifelong work in the field.

When, around 2002, I invited Grygier to comment on the state of criminology in Canada, he expressed his disappointment with the general lack of influence that criminological studies have had on legislation. He referred to this shortcoming as "tunnel vision." Grygier believed that the state of the law had changed all too little since the sixteenth century, and that "a criminal law oriented in the past" cannot help to build "a just, peaceful, and safe society."

References

Grygier, T. (1977). *Social Protection Code: A New Model of Criminal Justice.* New York: Fred B. Rothman and Co.

Monachesi, E.D. (1955). *Oppression: A Study in Social and Criminal Psychology* [book review]. *American Sociological Review,* 20(2): 255–256.

Pepinsky, Harold and Richard Quinney (eds.). (1991). *Criminology as Peacemaking.* Bloomington, IN: Indiana University Press.

University of Ottawa. Tribute to Tadeusz Grypier. Retrieved from http://socialsciences.uottawa.ca/crm/tribute-tadeusz-grygier.

University of Ottawa. Biography: Tadeusz Grygier. (2010). Retrieved from http://socialsciences.uottawa.ca/sites/default/files/public/crm/eng/documents/OU_Biography_English_Dec14.pdf.

Selected Publications by Grygier: Books

Oppression: A Study in Social and Criminal Psychology. London: Routledge and Kegan Paul, 1954.

The Likes and Interests Test. London: National Foundation for Educational Research, 1960.

Criminology in Transition (with H. Jones and J. Spencer). London: Tavistock Publications, 1965.

Social Protection Code: A New Model of Criminal Justice. South Hackensack, NJ: Fred B. Rothman, 1977.

Exile: The Road to Knowledge—Fragments of an Intellectual Autobiography. Toronto: Polish Research Institute, 2002.

Selected Publications by Grygier: Articles

Psychiatric observations in the Arctic. *British Journal of Psychology* (1948), 39:84–96.

Psychological problems of Soviet Russia. *British Journal of Psychology* (1951), 42:180–184.

Projected researches on the alleged preventive effect of capital punishment and on methods of prevention of crimes of violence" (with Edward Glover). *British Journal of Delinquency* (1951), 2: 144–149.

Leisure pursuits of juvenile delinquents: A study in methodology. *British Journal of Delinquency* (1955), 5:210–228.

A factorial study of insularity. *Psychological Reports* (1957), 3:613–614.

Homosexuality, neurosis and "normality": A pilot study in psychological measurement." *British Journal of Delinquency* (1958), 9:59–61.

A research scheme into personality interaction in probation. *Canadian Journal of Corrections* (1961), 3:140–152.

Current correctional and criminological research in Canada: Present framework, trends and prospects. *Canadian Journal of Corrections* (1961), 3:423–444.

The teaching of criminology as part of the curriculum of a department of psychology. *Canadian Psychologist* (1964), 5a:35–40.

The concept of "the state of delinquency": An obituary. *Journal of Legal Education* (1966), 18: 131–141.

Juvenile delinquents or child offenders: Some comments on the First Discussion

Draft of an Act Respecting Children and Young Persons. *Canadian Journal of Corrections* (1968), 10:458–469.

A computer-made device for sentencing decisions: Is further counting and thinking really necessary? *Journal of Research in Crime and Delinquency* (1969), 7:199–209.

Sentencing: What for? Reflections on the principles of sentencing and disposition. *Ottawa Law Review* (1975), 7: 267–270.

A Canadian approach or an American band-wagon? *Canadian Journal of Criminology* (1988), 30: 165–172.

Penal reform in Canada. *Euro Criminology* (1996), 10: 57–76.

Terrorists, psychopaths, oppressors, and victims. *Euro Criminology* (1999), 13:45–62.

A realistic approach to drugs. *Euro Criminology* (2000), 14:99–102.

Our Supreme Court. *Justice Report* (2001), 16(2):5–6.

SEVEN
André Normandeau: A Passion for the Study of Crime

John Winterdyk

Professor André Normandeau[19] is a bilingual French Canadian who was born (May 4, 1942) and raised in Montreal.

His childhood was by his own account "normal." Normandeau's father was a banker and his mother was a "traditional" stay at home mother who, Normandeau notes, took very good care of his brother and himself. Although his parents were very supportive of his academic pursuits, Normandeau points out that perhaps the seeds for his passion for the study of crime were inherited: his paternal grandfather was a successful criminal lawyer and, at one point, served as the president of the Montreal bar, and his paternal great-grandfather was a police chief in a Montreal suburb.

After graduating from high school, Normandeau went on to complete a bachelor's degree in sociology at the University of Montreal in 1964. He chose sociology because, at the time, he thought he could "help people," especially young delinquents. While studying at Montreal, he was an active member of the journal *Cité Libre*, which was directed by none other than the father of current Prime Minister Justin Trudeau, Pierre Elliot Trudeau, who went on to become the federal minister of justice and eventually Canada's fifteenth Prime Minister (1968–1979; 1980–84).

After finishing his bachelor's degree, Normandeau moved south to the University of Pennsylvania to pursue his master's degree in criminology. At the time, Pennsylvania was something of a criminological hotbed with such notables as the Swedish American sociologist **Thorsten Sellin** (1896–1994), **Marvin Wolfgang** (1924–1998), and **Freda Adler** (1934–), all American criminology pioneers in their own right. Normandeau also acknowledges the influence of

[19] This chapter was prepared with input from André Normandeau.

Professor **Philip Reiff** (1922–2006), a social theorist and cultural critic whose ideas generally paralleled those of Talcott Parsons (e.g., his classic 1935 book *Toward a General Theory of Action*) and Robert Merton (one of the founding fathers of modern sociology and the strain theory). Reiff is also known for the number of books he wrote on Sigmund Freud and his profound legacy. Normandeau's years at the University of Pennsylvania were marked by a close intellectual relationship between the graduate students and their mentors.

With an almost insatiable thirst to further his knowledge, Normandeau then entered the doctoral program in sociology at the University of Pennsylvania. His dissertation, *Patterns and Trends in Robbery*, was written in the tradition of Wolfgang's work on homicide (see Box 7.1). After completing his Ph.D. in 1968, Normandeau went on to carry out post-doctoral work in criminology at the University of California at Berkeley. There his studied under the esteemed sociologist **Jerome Skolnick** (1931–) who introduced him to police research and the controversial meaning of crime clearance rates.

Box 7.1. Some Commissions on which André Normandeau Served

- Commission Prévost sur la justice pénale au Québec, 1970–72
- Commission Ouimet sur la justice pénale au Canada, 1970–72
- Commission Thiffault sur les prisons au Québec, 1976–1977
- Commission Laplante sur le vol à main armée au Québec, 1980
- Commission Bellemare sur la police et les minorités ethniques au Québec, 1987–1988
- Commission Normandeau sur la police au Canada, 1989–1990
- Commission Ryan sur la prévention de la délinquance au Québec, 1992–1993

While at Pennsylvania, Normandeau especially enjoyed working with Sellin, a criminologist, historian, and penologist whose work and ideas have impacted numerous criminologists over the years. Sellin was fluent in eight languages. From Sellin, Normandeau developed a strong interest in historical knowledge as well as the value of being multilingual and multicultural.

In addition to Sellin, Normandeau credits Marvin Wolfgang as having significantly influenced his academic career. Wolfgang's interest in violence prompted Normandeau to eventually engage in considerable research in such areas as violence (sub-cultural), robbery, the death penalty, evaluation of police and correctional services, and crime statistics (see Box 7.1). In 1970 Normandeau replicated Sellin and Wolfgang's famous index of crime study in Canada. He found that Canadians' perceptions of the seriousness of different crimes and appropriate criminal sanctions were remarkably different from their American counterparts. Most notably, Canadians were far less punitive in their attitudes about what an appropriate sanction should be for a particular crime. Several decades later, in 2006, **Anthony Doob** and Cheryl Webster pointed out that Canada's imprisonment rate has stayed relatively unchanged since 1960, something which they attribute, among other factors, to Canadians' ability to shield themselves from the pressure to act in a more punitive fashion toward offenders.

Normandeau strongly believes in the value of engaging in empirical criminology. Facts and statistics are the backbone of knowledge and key to understanding criminological events and issues, essential to ensuring criminology is a full-fledged social science. The legacy of his orientation towards the study of crime is evident in the School of Criminology at the University of Montreal. He has supervised some 35 master's theses and approximately 15 Ph.D. dissertations, not only in Montreal but also in France and Belgium. Among those former students who have gone on to establish distinguished academic careers in their own right are **Maurice Cusson**, now teaching at Montreal, who has published some 20 books on crime and justice, most in French and who Normandeau describes as a "unique and original thinker," and **Marc Le Blanc,** professor emeritus at University of Montreal, author of numerous books on juvenile delinquency, in French as well as in English, and someone recognized in North America and Europe as a

Box 7.2. Meetings with Jacques Mesrine

Among the many anecdotes of Mr. Normandeau's career are accounts of his meetings with French gangster Jacques Mesrine (1936–1979) in the prison of Saint-Vincent-de-Paul in Laval in 1972. Mesrine "seduced everyone, as much by his words as by his presence," recalls Normandeau, who related how at one point during his incarceration Mesrine managed to convince the prison guards to take action against their employers.

As head of a team of academics for the Prevost Commission, Normandeau had convinced federal management of the prison to put into place a rehabilitation model for the handling of inmates, as opposed to relying on the use of a repressive regime.

But when Mesrine and his accomplice, the Montreal murderer Jean-Paul Mercier, managed to escape from the prison, the federal management officials lost their trust in the efforts of Normandeau and his colleagues and promptly suspended any further implementation of Normadeau's recommendation for eight months while the prison completed an internal inquiry about prison security. And as Normandeau himself acknowledged, public opinion had been right to trust the federal minister, Jean-Pierre Goyer.

(The preceding passage was Google-translated, with some editing for grammar, from a posting on April 10, 2011 on the University of Montreal website commemorating the fiftieth anniversary of the School of Criminology.)

"creative scholar and researcher" as well as an important methodological innovator. Another notable former student that Normandeau acknowledges is **Pierre Landreville**, also now professor emeritus at University of Montreal. He has published five noteworthy books on Canadian corrections. As Normandeau points out, Landreville was a "ferocious critic" of imprisonment and a leader of what was commonly known as the "New Criminology" in the 1970s, '80s and '90s. Landerville also worked for some time in Ottawa for the Law Reform Commission of Canada and is the author of the commission's official report on prison and punishment. Similarly, there was **Guy Lemire**, professor emeritus at University of Montreal. Lemire had served as the director ("warden") of a federal penitentiary in Quebec and as Normandeau acknowledges, Lemire wrote a seminal book on prison, one of the "best works" on the subject in the French-speaking world: *Anatomie de la prison* (1990 and 2010). Beyond the University of Montreal, Normandeau supervised **Yacouba Ballo**, from the Ivory Coast, who undertook his Ph.D. at the University of Toulouse (France) between 2000 and 2005. Ballo has since become professor of criminology at the University of Kinshasa in the Ivory Coast and is one of the most respected scholars in French-speaking Africa. Finally, there is **Guy Tardif**, an ex-RCMP officer who became chief of staff to the director of the Montreal police service. After teaching for a time at the University of Montreal, he served as Quebec minister of municipal affairs under Premier René Lévesque from 1976 to 1985.

During his career, Normandeau has published over 500 articles in some 20 countries and authored or co-authored 15 academic books and official reports. His primary areas of interest include the sociology of policing, community policing, the sociology of prison and prison alternatives, and justice policies. His theoretical orientation could be described as a classical or structural functionalist in a Mertonian style, subscribing to the assertion that crime can be partly controlled by an efficient criminal justice system. Under this functionalist view, society is a complex system whose parts work together to promote solidarity and stability, which are founded on the social elements of customs, institutions, norms, and traditions.

Normandeau has held teaching and/or visiting positions at a host of universities including the University of Paris, the University of Toulouse and Université d'Aix-Marseille. He also serves as a part-time advisor to the Montreal police and has been involved in a number of major policy initiatives aimed at improving policing within the city, including programs targeting shoplifting, breaking-and-entering, and efforts to implement community policing.

During his tenure at Montreal, he served first as director of the School of Criminology from 1970 to 1980 and then as director of the International Centre for Comparative Criminology from 1980 to 1988. While serving as the head of the School of Criminology, he was also director of the review *Criminologie* (a

French-language criminology journal) from 1980 to 1988. Since 1990 and to this day, he has served as the director of the Research Group on Policing in the School of Criminology. He also has served as vice-president of the International Society of Criminology and of the American Society of Criminology, and as president of the Canadian Criminal Justice Association and the Québec Society of Criminology.

In addition to his academic career, Normandeau stood as a Parti Quebecois candidate in six elections (1973, 1976, 1981, 1985, 1998, and 2012). This was not unusual behavior; a number of Quebec criminologists (e.g., Denis Szabo, Jean-Paul Brodeur, Marc Le Blanc, Maurice Cusson, and Pierre Landreville, among others) over the years have become heavily involved in community activities and governmental initiatives—more so than is the case with any other criminology centre in Canada, according to Hackler (1994).

Box 7.3. Snapshot of Major Works

- *Deviance and Crime* (with Denis Szabo), Paris, 1970. In French.
- *Justice and Public Opinion,* with Ezzat Fattah, Quebec City, 1970. In French.
- *Armed Robbery: Cops, Robbers and Victims* (with Thomas Gabor and others), Chicago, 1987.
- *Robbers and Victims Speak their Minds.* Montreal, 1986. In French.
- *Preventing Breaking and Entering* (with Marcel Kabundi), Montreal, 1985. In French.
- *A Vision of the Future of Policing in Canada* (with Barry Leighton), Ottawa, 1990.
- *Justice and Minorities* (with Emerson Douyon), Montreal, 1995. In French.
- *Community Policing, Montreal,* 1998, 2005, and 2010. In French.

Even though some of his former students are now retired, Normandeau continues to pursue his passion for the discipline. In 2016, he was nearing completion of his latest book, *Criminology in French European and African Countries,* which examines the historical development of criminology as an intellectual discipline as well as an applied science in France, Belgium, Switzerland, Congo-Kinshasa, Congo-Brazzaville, and the Ivory Coast. He also continues to be a regular contributor to the Canadian Criminal Justice Association publication the *Justice Report*, ensuring that the voice of Quebec criminologists is heard and shared across the country.

Asked to provide his impressions of the current state of Canadian criminology, Normandeau is somewhat more complimentary than some of the other Canadian pioneers included in this book. He notes, for example, that Canadian criminology is now on par with American criminology. More specifically he feels that English Canadian criminology is more theoretical while Quebec criminology tends to be more applied in its orientation. Normadeau believes that major criminological teaching and research centres in Canada are doing a "great job"—a better job than many of their American counterparts, in fact, because unlike U.S. scholars, who tend to be rather provincial in their research (although admittedly that is changing), Canadian criminologists often integrate knowledge from the United States, Europe, and other parts of the world, as well as Canada.

At the time this chapter was written, Normandeau showed no signs of slowing down, attributing his passion and drive to being a "permanent optimist" by nature. He thinks the future of criminology in Quebec, as well as in Canada, as a whole, is "bright." Criminology is now widely recognized as a respected academic discipline in its own right, no longer the junior cousin to sociology, or any other social science. He notes how journalists regularly turn to criminologists for insight and expertise about a wide range of criminological and criminal justice issues. Normandeau himself continues to provide regular commentary to the media when called upon. He also points out that politicians (not just in Canada but internationally) are increasingly soliciting the views of Canadian criminologists in relation to hate crime, terrorism, human trafficking, organized crime, and other topics. And while politicians may not always agree with what criminologists have to say, their research and opinion is valued—"most of the time," Normadeau quipped.

Selected Publications

Normandeau, A. (1970). *La justice criminelle: Les Québécois s'interrogent sur la criminalité et les mesures correctionnelles.* Québec: Éditeur officiel du Québec.

Fattah, E., and Normandeau, A. (1970). *La justice criminelle: Sondage d'opinion publique sur la justice criminelle au Québec.* Québec: Éditeur officiel du Québec.

Szabo, D., and Normandeau, A. (1970). *Déviance et criminalité.* Paris: Colin.

Thiffault, A., and Normandeau, A. (1978). *L'état des prisons au Québec. Québec: Éditeur officiel du Québec.*

Laplante, L., and Normandeau, A. (1980). *Le vol à main armée au Québec.* Québec: Éditeur officiel du Québec.

Kabundi, M., and Normandeau, A. (1985). *Se protéger contre le vol.* Montréal: Les Éditions de l'Homme.

Normandeau, A. (1986). *Le vol à main armée: Les voleurs parlent, les victimes se prononcent.* Montréal: Les Éditions du Méridien.

Gabor, T., Normandeau, A., Baril, M, Cusson, M., Élie, D. and Leblanc, M. (1987). *Armed Robbery: Cops, Robbers and Victims.* Chicago: Charles C. Thomas.

Bellemare, J., and Normandeau, A. (1988). *Les relations entre les corps policiers et les minorités ethniques. Québec: Éditeur officiel du Québec.* En français et en anglais. In English: Police and Minorities.

Normandeau, A., and Leighton, B. (1990). *Une vision de l'avenir de la police au Canada.* Ottawa: Éditeur officiel du Canada. En deux volumes. En français et en anglais. In English: *A Vision of the Future of Policing in Canada.*

Ryan, C., and Normandeau, A. (1993). *Pour un Québec plus sécuritaire: Partenaires en prévention.* Québec: Éditeur officiel du Québec. En français et en anglais. In English: Partners in Crime Prevention.

Normandeau, A., and Douyon, E. (1995). *Justice et communautés culturelles.* Montréal: Les Éditions du Méridien.

Normandeau, A. (1998). *Une police professionnelle de type communautaire. Montréal: Les Éditions du Méridien.* Réédition en 2005 et en 2010. En deux volumes.

Normandeau, A. (2016–17, in preparation). *Criminology in French European and African Countries.*

EIGHT
Jo-Anne Wemmers: Justice for Victims

Jo-Anne Wemmers

Introduction

It is often said that crime is as old as humankind. But, if crime is an age-old phenomenon, it is only recently that researchers have turned their attention to victims of crime, and victimology is an even newer concept. For years, victims were considered the forgotten party in the criminal justice process. While much progress has been made in recent years, the role of victims in the Canadian criminal justice system still remains that of a witness to a crime against the state. This chapter is in recognition of the pioneers in Canadian victimology. I am both honoured and privileged to have known and worked with many of them. The aim of this chapter is to inform and perhaps even inspire students to work in the field of victimology and help to make the recognition of victims' rights as fundamental human rights a reality.

Evolution of a New Science

The word *victimology* first appeared in a publication in 1948, when the American psychiatrist **Frank Wertham** stressed the need for "a science of victimology" (p. 259) in his book, *The Show of Violence*. Several years later, in 1956, **Benjamin Mendelsohn** (1900–1998) published an article in which he outlined the basis of this new science. The objective of victimology, according to Mendelsohn, was the prevention of victimization as well as therapeutic intervention with victims in order to prevent re-victimization (Mendelsohn 1956, p. 97).

Mendelsohn predicted that as the science of victimology matured, it would need its own institutions and academic journals. Two years after the publication of Mendelsohn's seminal work, Professor **Paul Cornil** (1903–1985) of Brussels organized a first conference on victimology for the Dutch-Flemish Society of Criminology that included participants such as Professor **Willem Nagel** (Leiden, The Netherlands). One year later, the *Revue de droit penal et de* *criminologie* published a special issue on victimology in which several papers from this conference were published (Cornil 1959).

It would take another 15 years before the first international symposium on victimology was held. It took place in Israel in 1973 and was organized by Israel Drapkin. Three years later, in 1976, a second international symposium was organized by Stephan Schafer in Boston. In 1979, the third international symposium on victimology took place in Münster, Germany under the leadership of **Hans Joachim Schneider** (1928–2015) and it was at this symposium that the World Society of Victimology (WSV) was created. Since then, the WSV has organized international symposia on victimology every three years (Wemmers 2009a), most recently in Perth, Australia in 2015. The fifteenth such symposium is to be held in 2018 in China.

World Society of Victimology

Throughout the evolution of victimology, the World Society of Victimology (WSV) has played a key role. Founded in 1979, the Society is a not-for-profit, non-governmental organization with consultative status with the United Nations Economic and Social Council and the Council of Europe.

The WSV sponsors seminars and workshops on victimology in many different countries, the oldest and perhaps best-known of which is the post-graduate course held in Dubrovnik, Croatia. First held in 1976, this two-week course is offered annually in the month of May. During the war in the former Yugoslavia, the course was temporarily (1994–1997) moved to Amsterdam (Kirchhoff 1997). Such seminars and workshops provide a key opportunity for the training of new victimologists. Particularly in the society's early years of the society, when university courses on victimology were rare, the Dubrovnik course offered a unique opportunity to train students from around the world in victimology. The course coincided with the annual meetings of the WSV Executive Committee and members of the committee were expected to lecture at the course. As a result, students were taught by top victimologists from around the world. At the same time, these annual meetings provided a rich forum for academics and practitioners to meet and exchange information. Similar courses were later introduced in Japan (since 1998), Latin America (since 2001) and South Africa (since 2003).

In promoting victims' interests, the Society has been the driving force behind international victim policy. A key achievement of the WSV is the UN *Declaration of Basic Principles of Justice for Victims of Crime and Abuse of Power*. Professor **Irvin Waller** (University of Ottawa) together with other members of the WSV played a key role in the drafting of the UN Declaration. A final draft of the Declaration was presented at the Seventh UN Congress on the Prevention of Crime and the Treatment of Offenders, held in Milan, Italy in 1985 (Fattah 1992). The UN General Assembly adopted the Declaration (resolution 40/34) on November 29, 1985 (see the appendix to this chapter). Originally intended as standards and norms for national governments, the UN Declaration later provided the basis for victims' rights in the International Criminal Court, which opened its doors in The Hague, The Netherlands on July 1, 2002.

In 1987, I had the privilege of attending the WSV post-graduate course on victimology, victim assistance and criminal justice as a student. I had done some contract work translating texts from Dutch into English for Professor Albert Hauber, who taught criminology at Leiden University. He told me about the WSV course and suggested that I attend. I followed his advice and it was a wise decision. Besides enjoying two weeks in the beautiful coastal city of Dubrovnik, I was exposed to the many of the greats in the field including Irvin Waller, Jan van Dijk, Mike McGuire, Leroy Lamborn, Helen Reeves, Bob Figlio and Edna Erez. At the time, the UN Declaration had only recently been adopted and member states, like Canada, worked hard to bring their criminal justice systems in line with these newly established UN standards and develop victim-friendly policies. This was the height of the victims' movement.

Box 8.1. World Society of Victimology Post-Graduate Course

Each year, the WSV in collaboration with Inter-University Centre of Dubrovnik organizes a two-week course on Victimology, Victim Assistance, and Criminal Justice. The course takes place in the month of May and brings together students and experts in victimology from around the world. Dubrovnik is a beautiful old city on the Adriatic Sea and a UNESCO heritage site. Besides the academic program, several excursions to local sites are also planned. Students often fall in love with the city, a popular tourist attraction, and its unique ambiance. Anyone interested in participating in the course can contact one of the course directors: Gerd Kirchhoff; Paul Separovic; Elmar Weitekmap; Marianna Hilf; Dick Andzenge; and Chadley James.

Thanks in part to the efforts of the WSV, interest in victimology and victimological research continues to grow and this has led to the creation of national and regional victimology associations. For example, the European Society of Criminology recently established a Working Group on Victimology and the American Society of Criminology now has a division of victimology. These academic societies offer a place for researchers to meet and share their findings and, hence, promote the advancement of victimology as a science.

Global Citizenship

When I attended the WSV post-graduate course, I was a master's student in social and organizational psychology at the University of Leiden in the Netherlands. However, I was also Canadian. Born and raised in Southern

Ontario in 1964, I had moved to the Netherlands in 1985 after finishing an Honours B.A. in psychology at McGill University. My family is Dutch and, thanks to Canada's favourable attitudes towards multiculturalism, I was able to obtain a Dutch passport and live and study in the Netherlands.

The victims' movement was in full swing and the 1980s was a time of consolidating and institutionalizing victims' services (Van Dijk 1997). In an effort to improve the plight of crime victims, the Dutch government introduced victim-friendly policies throughout the criminal justice system. After completing the WSV post-graduate course, my training in victimology was immediately put to use and I began to conduct victimological research. As part of my master's training, I worked as a research assistant on the evaluation of a pilot program, which integrated victim support services into police stations in The Hague (Hauber and Wemmers 1987). Later, because of my experience in victimology, I was hired as a research assistant at the Dutch Ministry of Justice's Research and Documentation Centre (WODC). There I worked on a series of victimological studies, first as a research assistant and later as a researcher. These studies aimed at meeting the needs of victims and reducing secondary victimization, a theme which continues to dominate my work today.

While I was working as a researcher at the Ministry of Justice, I decided to pursue a Ph.D. I completed my doctorate in criminology under the direction of an expert in victimology, Professor **Jan van Dijk** (1947–) at Leiden University. Van Dijk had been director of the Research and Documentation Centre at the Ministry of Justice and left when he became director of the newly established directorate on crime prevention. He played a key role in the development of victim policy in the Netherlands and internationally, working closely with other key figures in the victims' movement such as Irvin Waller[20] in order to establish international standards for crime victims. Founder of the International Crime Victimization Survey, van Dijk has earned several awards, including the Stockholm Prize in Criminology in 2012. He was an inspirational thesis director. Currently, he is with the School of Law at the University of Tilburg, The Netherlands and is a member of the Group of Experts on Action against Human Trafficking of the Council of Europe.

My thesis combined my prior studies in social psychology with my interest in victimology. I invited Herman Steensma, a professor in social psychology at

[20] Elsewhere in this volume, there is an entire chapter dedicated to Irvin Waller and therefore there is no need to go into much detail on his important career here. However, it is impossible to discuss victimology without mentioning Waller's name. Rock (1986) describes Waller as a "moral entrepreneur" (p. 104) and, as director general of research at the Solicitor General of Canada, Waller was in a key position to raise awareness and sensitize government officials to victims' issues.

the University of Leiden, to be my co-director. Herman had worked extensively on justice research, and it was he who introduced me to procedural justice as a framework for understanding victims' experiences in the criminal justice system. Up until that point, research on procedural justice had focused on citizens' justice judgements (Thibaut and Walker 1975; Tyler 1990) or offenders' experiences (Tyler 1984; Haller and Machura 1995) but not on victims of crime. Examining victims' justice judgements proved to be very important in order to better understand their attitudes and behaviour toward criminal justice authorities (Wemmers 1996). Since then, many other researchers have used procedural justice theory in order to understand victims' reactions in a variety of criminal justice contexts (e.g., Orth 2002; Strang 2002; McGonigle-Leyh 2011; Moffett 2014).

Université de Montréal

In Canada, the School of Criminology at the Université de Montréal played an important role in the diffusion of this new science of victimology (Wemmers 2011a). In 1960, **Henri Ellenberger** (1905–1993), was hired by **Denis Szabo** as a professor at his newly founded School of Criminology at the Université de Montréal. Before coming to Montreal, Ellenberger published an article on the psychological relationship between victims and offenders. In it, he argued that studying this relationship would allow us to explain and, therefore, prevent victimization.

Ellenberger would go on to have an important influence on the development of victimology at the School, where he directed students such as **Ezzat Fattah**, who became a prominent author in victimology. In 1966, Fattah published an article entitled (in English translation) "Some Problems that Victimology Poses for Criminal Justice." Like Ellenberger, Fattah's early work focused on the victim-offender relationship. In 1971, Fattah's doctoral thesis was published under the title (again in English translation) *Is the Victim Guilty?* In it, he examines the role of the victim in cases of armed robbery involving homicide. Fattah went on to publish several books in victimology including *Understanding Criminal Victimization: An Introduction to Theoretical Victimology* (1991).

In the 1970s, Fattah left Montreal in order to found the School of Criminology at Simon Fraser University in British Columbia and Ellenberger, his mentor, retired. But Montreal remained in the forefront of victimology research with the work of a young criminologist, **Micheline Baril**, who was a researcher at the Université de Montréal's International Centre for Comparative Criminology and a professor at the School of Criminology. A talented researcher, her first publication on victims was a study on the effects of robbery on small business owners, which she published in 1977. In 1984, she published a pioneering study entitled (translated from the French) "'But we, the witnesses...'" in which she examined the experiences of victims in the criminal justice system (Baril et al. 1984).

In addition to being a scholar, Baril was something of an activist. In the early 1980s she created the first victim support service in Montreal and in 1984 founded the advocacy group, Association québecoise plaidoyer-victimes (Wemmers 2003). Together with her newly formed association, Baril was instrumental in the creation of a provincial victims' bill of rights in 1988, which institutionalized victim support centres throughout the province. Baril's involvement in the victims' movement is representative of its early days in Canada when it was very much dominated by academics and civil servants (Rock 1986; Roach 1999). Unfortunately, however, Micheline Baril died at an early age in 1993.

Following her death, there was a brief hiatus at the School. While victimology continued to be taught by sessional lecturers, the absence of a professor of victimology at the School led to concerns that its rich tradition of research in victimology would be lost. Hence, in 2000, the School posted a position for a professor specializing in victimology and I joined the faculty.

The Université de Montréal is a French-speaking university and I had never worked in French before. Having grown up in Canada, I knew some French but I was far from bilingual. While the idea of lecturing in French was daunting at first, I had worked in a second language before when I lived in the Netherlands. I could learn French. My first year teaching in French was a challenge. In advance of each class I would write out my lecture notes. Although I hate it when a lecturer reads from their notes, this is exactly what I had to do in the beginning. Within 30 minutes of starting my very first lecture in French, there was a line-up of students complaining to the School's director. But I persisted and by the next year, when I gave the same class, I no longer needed my notes. That is when I contacted the University's publishing company, Les Presses de l'Université de Montréal (PUM), and reached an agreement with them to publish my notes as a book. In 2003, my book, *Introduction à la victimologie*, was published. It has since become a best-seller for the PUM, selling over 8,000 copies worldwide.

Today, victimology is stronger than ever at the Université de Montréal. Victimology is an obligatory course for undergraduate students in criminology. Courses on victimological theories and intervention with victims exist at the graduate level. Since 2011, the University's Faculty of Continuing Education has offered a 30-credit certificate in victimology for students who wish to specialize in the field.

Justice for Victims

Justice is a key concept for victims. As they enter the criminal justice system, victims will often claim to seek justice and demand that "justice be done." But what is justice? And more to the point, what do victims consider to be just and fair? The victims' movement drew attention to the marginalization of victims in the criminal justice system. Victims were the forgotten party. They were effectively witnesses to a crime against the state. Not surprisingly, studies found that victims were often dissatisfied with criminal justice authorities and that even people who had been stopped by police (i.e., offenders) evaluated their experiences with criminal justice authorities more favourably than victims did (Junger-Tas and Zeefkens 1978; Tufts 2000).

Secondary victimization is an important notion in victimology. It refers to insensitive reactions to victims by others, in particular criminal justice authorities, and how such reactions can worsen the victim's suffering (Symonds 1980; Wemmers 2003). As a result of their exclusion, victims are often profoundly disappointed with the criminal justice system, which fails to provide them with a sense of justice (Shapland, Wilmore, and Duff 1985; Wemmers 1996; Herman, 2003; Parsons and Bergin 2010). A central theme in my research is to better understand victims' experiences in the criminal justice system in order to identify their needs and reduce the risk of secondary victimization.

While victimologists focussed on secondary victimization, elsewhere, legal scholars developed the concept of *therapeutic jurisprudence* (TJ). TJ draws our attention to the emotional and psychological side of law and the legal process as it envisions law as an instrument of healing and rehabilitation. TJ is an interdisciplinary approach that views legal rules, legal procedures and the roles of legal actors as social forces that produce behaviours and consequences, which are either positive (therapeutic) or negative (anti-therapeutic) (Wexler and Winick 1996; Winick 2000; Erez, Kilchling, and Wemmers 2011). Hence, TJ views secondary victimization as an anti-therapeutic effect of the plight of victims in criminal justice.

How legal actors and procedures affect victims is addressed by *procedural justice theory*, which plays an important role in understanding what is therapeutic and anti-therapeutic for victims in the criminal justice system (Wemmers 1996; Waldman 1998; Wemmers 2009b, 2010a; Laxminarayan 2012). Procedural justice theory shows how one might improve the role of victims in the criminal justice system so that it becomes more therapeutic and less anti-therapeutic, hence reducing the risk of secondary victimization.

Justice judgements are based on several factors. In particular, both procedures and outcomes are important (Van den Bos and Lind 2002; Van den Bos, Lind, and Wilke 2001; Wemmers 2010). Thus, while outcomes, or the ability of law enforcement to catch and convict offenders, are important, they represent only one factor. The police are unable to solve all cases and even if a suspect is apprehended, there is no guarantee that this will lead to a conviction. Although victims cannot be guaranteed favourable outcomes, they can be assured that criminal justice procedures will be fair. Research on fair procedures and outcomes reveals that what comes first matters (Van den Bos and Lind 2002). Typically, people receive procedural information before they know the outcome, and when procedural information precedes outcome information, it has a stronger impact on the individual's overall judgement of fairness. Hence, procedural justice is very important in order to restore victims' sense of justice.

In addition, procedural fairness can contribute to restoring victims' confidence in the criminal justice system and authorities (Tyler 1990; Wemmers 1996; Bradford 2011). Victims look to fairness information in order determine whether or not they can trust authorities (Tyler and Lind 1992). This is particularly important following abuses of power by corrupt governments, which weaken confidence in authorities (Wemmers and Manirabona 2014). Besides individual justice judgements, justice is important at the level of the social group. Gross violations of human rights often target the members of a particular social group, such as ethnic or religious minorities. Justice is a key indicator for members of the victimized community as it sends a message about the authority's integrity and reflects the extent to which a new government has embodied change (Wemmers 2011b)

Box 8.2. Editing Scholarly Journals

Over the years I have and continue to be involved in several different journals in the area of criminology and, in particular, victimology. As a Ph.D. student, I became involved in the editing of the WSV newsletter, *The Victimologist*. Since 2004, I have been an editor for the *International Review of Victimology*. I am currently on the Editorial Advisory Board of the *Canadian Journal of Criminology and Criminal Justice*, the *International Journal of Comparative and Applied Criminal Justice*, as well as the *Journal of Criminological Research, Policy and Practice*. In addition to these English publications, I am and have been involved in several non-English journals, including *Journal international de victimologie* and *Temida*, which is published by the Victimology Society of Serbia. I was the first anglophone to be appointed director of the French journal, *Criminologie*. Publishing is a rapidly changing field due to major advancements in technology and the emergence of open-access journals. I strongly encourage students to take any opportunity to participate in the publication of academic journals. It is a wonderful way to learn about the profession, develop an international network and to stay up-to-date on the newest research in the field.

My research interests focus on victims in the criminal justice system in the broadest possible sense. While a large part of my work focuses on victims in domestic criminal law, in recent years international criminal law has gained tremendous importance. Tragic events in the 1990s such as the war in the former Yugoslavia and the Rwandan genocide put a spotlight on heinous crimes such as genocide, war crimes and crimes against humanity. Following the creation of several ad hoc tribunals for war crimes and crimes against humanity, in 1998 the international community adopted the Rome Statute, which established a permanent International Criminal Court (ICC). A unique feature of the ICC is its recognition of victims' right to participation, reparation and legal representation. However, the integration of victims has proven to be perhaps one of the biggest challenges for the new court (Wemmers 2009b; Hébert-Dolbec 2014; Moffett 2014). While the ICC recognizes victims' legal rights and allows them to seek legal representation in order to enjoy their procedural rights of participation and reparation, the many decisions and appeals regarding victim participation and reparation are a reflection of the strong resistance within the Court towards a substantive role for victims (Wemmers 2010b). Victims' rights are repeatedly blocked by concerns about the distribution of power and possibility of infringing upon the rights of the accused (Wemmers 2009c). By studying victims' experiences in the criminal justice system, we will better understand their needs and develop ways to improve their role in the criminal justice system and reduce the risk of secondary victimization while respecting justice values such as equality and the rights of the accused. In 2015, I was awarded a *Certificate of Appreciation* by the WSV for my contribution to victimology and to the Society (see Box 8.2).

Future

In recent years, both domestic and international criminal law have begun to explore ways in which victims might possibly be given a greater role in the criminal justice system. In Canada, the recent adoption of Bill C-32 and the Canadian Victims Bill of Rights, which introduced victims' rights into the country's Criminal Code, is an example of this trend. However, as the experience of the ICC illustrates, the integration of victims' procedural rights in criminal law is not an easy task. Canada's Victims Bill of Rights stops short of providing enforceable rights for victims of crime. Without enforceable rights, nothing changes. Having worked in the area of victimology both nationally and international for almost 30 years, I feel more has to be done for victims. The status quo is unacceptable.

While victims' rights might be a relatively new concept in criminal law, they are nonetheless human rights (Wemmers 2012). The United Nations' Universal Declaration of Human Rights, which was adopted in 1948, specifies that everyone has the right to recognition everywhere as a person before the law (Article 6). This gives rise to the notion of victim participation and procedural rights for victims. It suggests that victims must not be treated as mere evidence, but must be regarded as subjects with personal, individual and independent standing at the criminal trial (Walther 2011).

Education is vital for the advancement of any science, including victimology. Today, several colleges and universities across Canada not only offer undergraduate and graduate courses in victimology but also certificates in victimology (e.g., Algonquin College and Université de Montréal). These developments hold promise for the future, as growing numbers of young people will be educated in victimology. Tomorrow's professionals will be sensitive to victims' issues and understand the importance of victims' rights. It is only a matter of time before a greater recognition of victims' rights will be achieved. It is my hope and aspiration that one day, victims will finally be recognized as humans with rights before the court. Until that time, victimologists will continue to study victims and victimizations, and, through their research, contribute to the prevention of further suffering.

Appendix: United Nations Declaration of Basic Principles of Justice for Victims of Crime and Abuse of Power

A/RES/40/34
29 November 1985
96th plenary meeting

A. Victims of Crime

1. "Victims" means persons who, individually or collectively, have suffered harm, including physical or mental injury, emotional suffering, economic loss or substantial impairment of their fundamental rights, through acts or omissions that are in violation of criminal laws operative within Member States, including those laws proscribing criminal abuse of power.

2. A person may be considered a victim, under this Declaration, regardless of whether the perpetrator is identified, apprehended, prosecuted or convicted and regardless of the familial relationship between the perpetrator and the victim. The term "victim" also includes, where appropriate, the immediate family or dependants of the direct victim and persons who have suffered harm in intervening to assist victims in distress or to prevent victimization.

3. The provisions contained herein shall be applicable to all, without distinction of any kind, such as race, colour, sex, age, language, religion, nationality, political or other opinion, cultural beliefs or practices, property, birth or family status, ethnic or social origin, and disability.

Access to justice and fair treatment

4. Victims should be treated with compassion and respect for their dignity. They are entitled to access to the mechanisms of justice and to prompt redress, as provided for by national legislation, for the harm that they have suffered.

5. Judicial and administrative mechanisms should be established and strengthened where necessary to enable victims to obtain redress through formal or informal procedures that are expeditious, fair, inexpensive and accessible. Victims should be informed of their rights in seeking redress through such mechanisms.

6. The responsiveness of judicial and administrative processes to the needs of victims should be facilitated by:

(a) Informing victims of their role and the scope, timing and progress of the proceedings and of the disposition of their cases, especially where serious crimes are

involved and where they have requested such information;
(b) Allowing the views and concerns of victims to be presented and considered at appropriate stages of the proceedings where their personal interests are affected, without prejudice to the accused and consistent with the relevant national criminal justice system;
(c) Providing proper assistance to victims throughout the legal process;
(d) Taking measures to minimize inconvenience to victims, protect their privacy, when necessary, and ensure their safety, as well as that of their families and witnesses on their behalf, from intimidation and retaliation; (e) Avoiding unnecessary delay in the disposition of cases and the execution of orders or decrees granting awards to victims.
7. Informal mechanisms for the resolution of disputes, including mediation, arbitration and customary justice or indigenous practices, should be utilized where appropriate to facilitate conciliation and redress for victims.
Restitution
8. Offenders or third parties responsible for their behaviour should, where appropriate, make fair restitution to victims, their families or dependants. Such restitution should include the return of property or payment for the harm or loss suffered, reimbursement of expenses incurred as a result of the victimization, the provision of services and the restoration of rights.
9. Governments should review their practices, regulations and laws to consider restitution as an available sentencing option in criminal cases, in addition to other criminal sanctions.
10. In cases of substantial harm to the environment, restitution, if ordered, should include, as far as possible, restoration of the environment, reconstruction of the infrastructure, replacement of community facilities and reimbursement of the expenses of relocation, whenever such harm results in the dislocation of a community.
11. Where public officials or other agents acting in an official or quasi-official capacity have violated national criminal laws, the victims should receive restitution from the State whose officials or agents were responsible for the harm inflicted. In cases where the Government under whose authority the victimizing act or omission occurred is no longer in existence, the State or Government successor in title should provide restitution to the victims.
Compensation
12. When compensation is not fully available from the offender or other sources, States should endeavour to provide financial compensation to: (a) Victims who have sustained significant bodily injury or impairment of physical or mental health as a result of serious crimes; (b) The family, in particular dependants of persons who have died or become physically or mentally incapacitated as a result of such victimization.
13. The establishment, strengthening and expansion of national funds for compensation to victims should be encouraged. Where appropriate, other funds may also be established for this purpose, including those cases where the State of which the victim is a national is not in a position to compensate the victim for the harm.
Assistance
14. Victims should receive the necessary material, medical, psychological and social assistance through governmental, voluntary, community-based and indigenous means.
15. Victims should be informed of the availability of health and social services and other

relevant assistance and be readily afforded access to them.
16. Police, justice, health, social service and other personnel concerned should receive training to sensitize them to the needs of victims, and guidelines to ensure proper and prompt aid.
17. In providing services and assistance to victims, attention should be given to those who have special needs because of the nature of the harm inflicted or because of factors such as those mentioned in paragraph 3 above.

B. Victims of Abuse of Power

18. "Victims" means persons who, individually or collectively, have suffered harm, including physical or mental injury, emotional suffering, economic loss or substantial impairment of their fundamental rights, through acts or omissions that do not yet constitute violations of national criminal laws but of internationally recognized norms relating to human rights.
19. States should consider incorporating into the national law norms proscribing abuses of power and providing remedies to victims of such abuses. In particular, such remedies should include restitution and/or compensation, and necessary material, medical, psychological and social assistance and support.
20. States should consider negotiating multilateral international treaties relating to victims, as defined in paragraph 18.
21. States should periodically review existing legislation and practices to ensure their responsiveness to changing circumstances, should enact and enforce, if necessary, legislation proscribing acts that constitute serious abuses of political or economic power, as well as promoting policies and mechanisms for the prevention of such acts, and should develop and make readily available appropriate rights and remedies for victims of such acts.

References

Selected Publications by Jo-Anne Wemmers

Wemmers, J. (1996). *Victims in the Criminal Justice System: A Study into the Treatment of Victims and its Effects on Their Attitudes and Behaviour*. Amsterdam: Kugler Publications.

Wemmers, J. (2003). *Introduction à la victimologie*. Montréal: Les Presses de l'Université de Montréal.

Wemmers, J. (2014). *Reparation for Victims of Crimes Against Humanity: The Healing Role of Reparation*. London: Routledge.

Wemmers, J. (2010). The meaning of fairness for victims. In: P. Knepper & S. Shoham (eds.), *International Handbook of Victimology* (pp. 27–43). Boca Raton, FL: Taylor & Francis Group.

Wemmers, J. (2012) Victims' rights are human rights: The importance of recognizing victims as persons. *Temida* 15(2): 71–84.

Wemmers, J. (2009) Victim reparation and the International Criminal Court. *International Review of Victimology* 16 (2). (Guest editor for special issue)

Other References

Baril, M. (1977). *Le citoyen victime de vol qualifé: Sa place dans le processus judiciaire*. Montréal: Centre international de criminologie comparée.

Baril, M., et al. (1984). *Mais nous les témoins: Une étude exploratoire des besoins des témoins au Palais de justice.* Ottawa: Ministère de la Justice Canada.

Bradford, B. (2011). Voice, neutrality and respect: Use of victim support services, procedural fairness and confidence in the criminal justice system. *Criminology and Criminal Justice* 11(4): 345–366.

Cornil, P. (1959). Contribution de la "victimologie" aux sciences criminologiques. *Revue de droit penal et de criminology* 39(7): 587–601.

Erez, E., Kilchling, M., and Wemmers, J. (2011). *Therapeutic Jurisprudence and Victim Participation in Justice: International Perspectives*. Durham, NC: Carolina Academic Press.

Fattah, E.A. (1966). Quelques problèmes poses à la justice pénale par la victimologie. *Annales internationales de criminologie* 5(2): 335–361.

Fattah, E.A. (1971). *La victime: est-elle coupable?* Montréal: Les Presses de l'Université de Montréal.

Fattah, E.A. (1991). *Understanding Criminal Victimization: An Introduction to Theoretical Victimology*. Scarborough: Prentice-Hall Canada.

Fattah, E.A. (1992). The United Nations Declaration of Basic Principles of Justice for Victims of Crime and Abuse of Power: A constructive critique. In: E.A. Fattah (ed.), *Towards a Critical Victimology* (pp. 410–424). New York: St. Martin's Press.

Hauber, A. R., and Wemmers, J. (1987). An experiment of victim assistance in police stations in the Hague. WSV *Newsletter* 6(2): 68–70.

Hébert-Dolbec, Marie-Laurence. (2014). *De l'émergence d'un espace participatif pour les victimes devant la cour pénale internationale: Quelle émancipation de la victime ?* Faculté de droit, UQAM.

Herman, J.L. (2003). The mental health of crime victims: Impact of legal intervention. *Journal of Traumatic Stress* 16(2): 159–166.

Junger-Tas, J., and Zeefkens, A.A. (1978). *Publiek et politie: Ervaringen, houdingen en wensen. Een onderzoek onder de Nederlandse bevolking*. Den Haag : Ministerie van Justitie, WODC.

Kirchhoff, G.G. (1997). *Worldwide Victimology : The WSV Book, Directory 1997*. Mönchengladbach: WSV Publishing.

Haller, V., and Machura, S. (1995) Procedural and distributive justice as seen by German defendants. *Social Justice Research,* pp. 197–215.

Laxminarayan, M. (2012). *The Heterogeneity of Crime Victims: Variations in Legal Preferences.* Nijmegen, The Netherlands: Wolf Legal Publishers.

McGonigle-Leyh, B. (2011). *Procedural Justice? Victim Participation in International Criminal Proceedings.* Antwerp: Intersentia.

Mendelsohn, B. (1956). Une nouvelle branche de la science biopsycho-social: La vicitmologie. *Revue Internationale de criminologie et de police technique* 10(2): 95–110.

Moffett, L. (2014). *Justice for Victim : Before the International Criminal Court.* Oxon: Routledge.

Orth, U. (2002). Secondary victimization of victims by criminal proceedings. *Social Justice Research* 15(4): 313–26.

Parsons, J., and Bergin, T. (2010). The impact of criminal justice involvement on victims' mental health. *Journal of Traumatic Stress* 23(2): 182–188.

Roach, K. (1999). *Due Process and Victims' Rights: The New Law and Politics of Criminal Justice.* Toronto: University of Toronto Press.

Rock, P. (1986). *A View from the Shadows: The Ministry of the Solicitor General of Canada and the Justice for Victims of Crime Initiative*. Oxford: Oxford University Press.

Shapland, J., Willmore, J., and Duff, P. (1985). *Victims in the Criminal Justice System.* Aldershot: Gower Publishing.

Strang, H. (2002). *Repair or Revenge*. Oxford: Clarendon.

Symonds, M. (1980). The second injury. *Evaluation and Change, Special Issue*, pp. 36–38.

Thibaut, J., and Walker, L. (1975). *Procedural Justice: A Psychological Analysis*. Hillsdale, NJ: Wiley.

Tufts, J. (2000). Public Attitudes toward the criminal justice System. *Juristat* 20(12).

Tyler, T. (1984). The role of perceived injustice in defendant's evaluations of their courtroom experience. *Law and Society Review* 18: 51–74.

Tyler, T. (1990). *Why People Obey the Law*. New Haven: Yale University Press.

Tyler, T., and Lind, E.A. (1992) A relational model of authority in groups. In M.P. Zanna (Ed.), *Advances in Experimental Social Psychology,* Volume 25 (pp. 115-191). San Diego: Academic Press.

Van den Bos, K., and Lind, E.A. (2002). Uncertainty management by means of fairness judgements. *Advances in Experimental Social Psychology* 34: 1–59.

Van den Bos, K., Lind, E.A., and Wilke, H. (2001). The psychology of procedural and distributive justice viewed from the perspective of fairness heuristic theory. In *Justice in the Workplace: From Theory to Practice*, Volume 2, ed. R. Cropanzano (pp. 49–66. Mahwah, NJ: Lawrence Erlbaum Associates

Van Dijk, J.J.M. (1997). Het victimologische perspectif in het verleden, heden en toekmst, *Tijdschrift voor criminologie* 39(4): 292–309.

Waldman, E. A. (1998). The evaluative-facilitative debate in mediation: Applying the lens of therapeutic jurisprudence. *Marquette Law Review* 82: 155–170.

Walther, S. (2011). Victims' rights : Procedural and constitution principles for victim participation in Germany. In E. Erez, M. Kilchling, and J. Wemmers (Eds.), *Therapeutic Jurisprudence and Victim Participation in Justice: International Perspectives* (pp. 97–112). Durham, NC : Carolina Academic Press

Wemmers, J.M. (1996). *Victims in the Criminal Justice System*, Amsterdam: Kugler.

Wemmers, J.M. (2003). *Introduction à la victimologie*. Montréal: Les Presses de l'Université de Montréal.

Wemmers, J. (2009a). A short history of victimology. In O. Hagemaan, P. Schafer & S. Schmidt (Eds.), *Victimology, Victim Assistance and Criminal Justice : Perspectives Shared by International Experts at the Inter-University Centre of Dubrovnik* (pp. 33–42). Mönchengladbach: Hochschule Niederrhein.

Wemmers, J. (2009b). Where do they belong? Giving victims a place in the criminal justice process. *Criminal Law Forum* 20: 395–416.

Wemmers, J. (2009c) Victims and the International Criminal Court: Evaluating the Success of the ICC with Respect to Victims. *International Review of Victimology*, 16(2):211–227.

Wemmers, J. (2010a). The meaning of fairness for victims. In P. Knepper & S. Shoham (Eds.), *International Handbook of Victimology* (pp. 27–43). Boca Raton, FL: Taylor & Francis Group.

Wemmers, J. (2010b). Victims' rights and the International Criminal Court: Perceptions within the Court regarding victims' right to participate. *Leiden Journal of International Law* 23(3): 629–643.

Wemmers, J. (2011a). 50 years of victimology in Quebec : Past, present and future developments. *Porte ouverte*, Bulletin de l'Association des services de réhabilitation sociale du Québec, octobre, pp. 40–43.

Wemmers, J. (2011b). Victims' need for justice: Individual versus collective Justice. In R. Letschert, R. Haveman, A.M. de Brouwer and A. Pemberton (Eds.), *Victimological Approaches to International Crimes: Africa.* (pp. 145–152). Antwerp: Intersentia.

Wemmers, J. (2012). Victims' rights are human rights: The importance of recognizing victims as persons. *Temida* 15(2): 71–84.

Wemmers, J. (2014). *Reparation for Victims of Crimes against Humanity: The Healing Role of Reparation*. Oxon: Routledge.

Wemmers, J. and Manirabona, A (2014) Regaining trust: The importance of justice for victims of crimes against humanity. *International Review of Victimology* 20(1):101–09.

Wertham, F. (1948). *The Show of Violence*. New York: Doubleday.

Wexler, D., and Winick, B. (1996). *Law in a Therapeutic Key: Developments in Therapeutic Jurisprudence*. Durham, NC: Carolina Academic Press.

Winick, B. (2000). Redefining the role of the criminal defense lawyer at plea bargaining and sentencing: A therapeutic jurisprudence/preventive law model. In D. Stolle, D. Wexler and B. Winick (eds.), *Practicing Therapeutic Jursiprudence: Law as a Helping Profession* (pp. 245–308). Durham, NC: Carolina Academic Press.

NINE
Gwynne Nettler: "Broad Interests and Serious Beliefs"

John Winterdyk

Gwynne Nettler[21] was born in Manhattan on July 7, 1913, but grew up in Los Angeles, California. He earned a bachelor's degree in history from UCLA in 1934, followed by a master's degree in psychology from Claremont College in 1936. In 1946, at the age of 33, he earned his Ph.D. in psychology and sociology from Stanford University. For his dissertation, entitled *The Relationship between Attitude and Information Concerning the Japanese in America*, Nettler invented the concept of "known-group" validation. This procedure was first reported in the *American Journal of Sociology* in 1946; the entire dissertation has since been reprinted in a series edited by Robert Merton and Harold Zuckerman in 1980.

In his early years in the United States, before settling in Canada, Nettler enjoyed a colorful array of life experiences. He worked in Hollywood as a stuntman in the early Tarzan movies; he performed as a guest stuntman appearance in the 1935 iconic movie *Mutiny on the Bounty*; he also worked as a radio news commentator, a clinical psychologist, and taught at several schools throughout the United States. He even served, for a short time, as a marriage counselor—perhaps somewhat ironic, considering that over the course of his life he himself married and divorced four times. However, his sense of humour was evident when he once remarked that he could teach courses in sociology of the family simply by sharing anecdotes from his married life.

In 1963, seeking a return to teaching, reading and writing, Nettler accepted a joint appointment with the Departments of Psychology and Sociology at the University of Alberta in Edmonton. Shortly after arriving at the university, he moved to Sociology full time, claiming that two "halves" proved to be more

[21] Nettler's first name was usually spelled with an 'e' ("Gwynne"), but on some of his publications, including *Explaining Crime*, the 'e' was dropped ("Gwynn").

than one whole, and also because criminology was then taught largely within the discipline of sociology, and this was of particular interest to him. In 1966 Nettler was promoted to full professor. He remained in the department until 1978, retiring as one of the pre-eminent criminologists in North America.

It was noted in a tribute to Nettler's life and times that during his tenure at the University of Alberta, the department produced more Ph.D.'s in sociology than any other university in Canada. Today, Nettler's academic offspring occupy high government offices, the legal profession, and even a provincial Supreme Court (Madam Justice Carol Ross, Supreme Court of British Columbia). His former students include R. Gillis, B. Silverman, W. Avison, J. Hagan, and T. Hirschi.

Nettler's long and distinguished career was not limited to criminology. His primary area of academic interest and research, in fact, was related to the boundaries of social scientists' competence. That is, what and how can social scientists contribute to the understanding of social issues? Nettler credits the influence of a broad range of scholars, including astronomer A. Leonard, sociologist W.F. Ogburn, psychologist S.I. Franz, as well as several philosophers, including A.J. Ayer, John Mackie, and George Santayana.

In 1975 Craig Boydell reviewed *Explaining Crime*, concluding by stating that the book "is well geared for undergraduate audiences in such courses as social problems, deviance and criminology" (p. 232). Boydell also notes that the book was well received by his students.

Nettler began publishing in the 1940s. Although many of his works bridge the literature of psychology and sociology, his books on crime have been repeatedly cited and referenced by criminology scholars as well as by criminologists and students across Canada and the United States, particularly during the 1970s and 1980s. His book *Explaining Crime* (McGraw-Hill), first published in 1974, is perhaps his most notable work of criminology. However, it was a 1961 article, "Good Men, Bad Men, and the Perception of Reality," that drew international attention, and laid the foundation for *Explaining Crime* and subsequent work. Nettler famously concluded in his article that, "It appears that good people see the world at least as inaccurately—to put it mildly—as bad ones"; for this reason, he argues that the "the conception of evil action is questionable" (pp. 289, 291).

Explaining Crime went through three editions and Nettler wrote nearly a dozen other major scholarly books throughout his academic career. *Explaining Crime* became a standard textbook in most criminology and deviance courses across the country. His final book, *Boundaries of Competence: How Social Sciences Make*

Feeble Science was published when he was 90. Roberts (1990) describes Nettler's work as "an intellectual challenge," recommending that "any intelligent person interested in criminological topics can profit from exposure to the issues presented in this book ... the volume is both instructive and a delight to read ... (and) deserves our serious attention" (p. 357). (It was Roberts who described Nettler as "a scholar with broad interests and serious beliefs," from which description we have taken the phrase used in the chapter title.)

In 1982 Nettler was the recipient of the prestigious E.H. Sutherland Award from the American Society of Criminology. The same year he also became a Fellow of the Royal Society of Canada.

Nettler returned to San Diego, California in retirement. He continued to give occasional lectures and to produce works of scholarship until his passing on October 5, 2007. Fittingly, his final book reiterated his concerns about the scientific limits of social "science." In attribute to Nettler, his former student, Ron Gillis, and former University of Alberta colleague, Bob Silverman, noted that the instructions he left for his body were "easy to predict: He donated his organs to others. He went the way he lived—with class." And to this point, William Avison (2007), a former M.A. and Ph.D. student under Nettler, noted that Nettler had even written his own obituary, in which he described the donation as "an exercise in continuity."

Among his more notable graduate students, Nettler cited **John Hagan** (formerly at the University of Toronto and now at Northwestern University in Chicago) and University of Toronto Professor Emeritus **Ron Gillis**. Other former students include University of Western Ontario scholar **William Avison** and University of Calgary Professor Emerita **Marlene MacKie**. **John Evan** became the director of research in the Department of Justice; formerly he had been president of Management and Policy International, Inc. **Carol Ross** went on to become a prominent attorney and judge in Vancouver. In 2007, Avison wrote that Nettler "was a great teacher. He taught us about sociology and criminology, but more importantly, he taught us about life. He introduced some of us to jazz. He introduced others to the pleasures of a fine cigar and a glass of scotch. He introduced still others to high performance gliding, to the glorious sights of the Monterey Peninsula, and to opera. His stories expanded our horizons and stretched our minds ... (and) to this day, alumni from the University of Alberta still recall Nettler's courses." In 1986, former University of Alberta colleagues Timothy Hartnagel and Robert Silverman compiled a special collection entitled *Critique and Explanation: Essays in Honor of Gwynne Nettler*. The book includes nine chapters, many by former colleagues and/or students of Nettler. The overarching theme focuses on the need for criminological inquiry to rely on careful observation and measurement, and to avoid abstract speculation(s) of criminality.

Many of Nettler's awards and honours were bestowed following his retirement in 1978. In 1982 he received the E.H. Sutherland Award from the American Society of Criminology and in the same year he also became a Fellow of the Royal Society of Canada. But long before being recognized by his peers, Nettler engaged in another practice that reflects his unique personality. As Averson noted in his tribute to Nettler: "Gwynne Nettler lived life on his terms. Every 15 or 20 years, Gwynne would sell or give away much of his library and *objets d'art* so that he could start again. He found it 'reinvigorating.' His prodigious intellect, his keen appreciation of humor, and his unsentimental view of the world allowed him to savour life for over 90 years."

In 2002, I asked Nettler to comment on the state of Canadian criminology. He noted that, as a discipline, it was weak. He argued that criminology and sociology were heavily ideological. That is, these two disciplines confused political preferences with science. He argued that political commitment is hostile to truth-seeking and truth-telling. While criminology presented itself as a policy science, its impact on criminal activity and governmental response to crime was minimal. Criminologists' most useful talent, he claimed, lay in assessing the results of programs that others develop (for example, evaluating the efficacy of offender-rehabilitation and the utility of the death penalty).

References

Avison, W.R. (2007). Gwynne Nettler (1913–2007). *Canadian Journal of Sociology Online*, November-December 2007. http://www.cjsonline.ca/soceye/nettler.html.

Boydell, C. (1975). Gwynn Nettler. *Explaining Crime.* [book review]. *Canadian Review of Sociology and Anthropology* 12(2):231–232.

Gillis, A.R. and Silverman, B. (2007, Oct. 31). Gwynne Nettler. *Globe and Mail.* http://www.theglobeandmail.com/life/gwynne-nettler/article697009/.

Roberts, L. (1990). Nettler: Criminology lessons. *Canadian Journal of Criminology* 32(2):353–357.

Selected Publications by Gwynne Nettler

Netter, G. (1961). Good men, bad men, and the perception of reality. *Sociometry* 24(3):279–294.

Nettler, G. (1989). *Criminology Lessons: Arguments about Crime, Punishment, and the Interpretation of Conduct.* Cincinnati: Anderson Pub. Co.

Nettler, G. (1976). *Social Concerns.* New York: McGraw-Hill.

Nettler, G. (1974; 1978; 1984). *Explaining Crime.* Toronto: McGraw-Hill Ryerson.

Nettler, G. (1972). Knowing and doing. *American Behavioral Scientist* 17:5–25.

Nettler, G. 1959. Antisocial sentiments and criminality. *American Sociological Review* 24:202–218.

Avison. W.R., and Nettler, G. (1976). World views and crystal balls. *Futures* 8: 11–21.

TEN
Jim Hackler: "A Lucky Life in Canadian Criminology"

Jim Hackler

Few students of Canadian criminology may be interested in a detailed description of the lives of those of us involved in this discipline in the twentieth century. However, some of the ideas that evolved during this period, and the way governments and societies responded to those ideas, may provide insights. I will be very brief with my personal history.

Growing Up in a Favorable Environment

I was born in Stockton, California on 15 June 1930 to Helen Ashton and James Fred Hackler. My father drove construction equipment, but when a tractor ran over his foot in 1931 that ended such work. He ended up selling used cars and slowly gained economic security. We later moved to San Francisco and then to San Bruno on the San Francisco Peninsula.

For me, life was fortunate. Growing up, I was taught to be careful with money, but I never felt anxiety. I worked at a variety of jobs, and enjoyed a wide range of experiences; this provided a comfortable childhood and adolescence. I was too young for World War II, but found many job opportunities. When I graduated with a degree in business from the University of California in 1952, I began my military service, which was required of young men during the Korean conflict.

I saw a recruiting poster for the U.S. Army. Men with a master's degree in business and three years of experience were invited to apply for commissions as officers in the Medical Service Corps. I had a business degree and no experience; so I applied. One of the questions I was asked by the board of Army officers interviewing me was as follows: "You have walked into a bar. A woman at the other end of the bar smiles and says, 'What are you doing, big boy?' What do you do?" I don't recall my answer, but I became an Assistant Battalion Surgeon in the U.S. Army.

Life as a Soldier

A medical platoon has about 35 men who support a medical doctor and provide initial emergency medical care for a battalion of 1,000 soldiers. In reality, one rarely sees a doctor during training. An Assistant Battalion Surgeon, usually a "wet behind the ears second lieutenant," organizes ambulances, trucks, mess halls, housing, a small hospital tent, and a large generator.

Hackler, an avid cyclist, often brought his bicycle to conferences (cartoon supplied by the author).

In one exercise, our battalion was to hike 100 miles from Colorado Springs to Camp Hale in the Rocky Mountains, where we learned how to remove injured men in stretchers from cliffs. On the hike we had been assigned a doctor—a young lung surgeon, who was pleasant and content with his assignment. During our first sick call, the doctor came over to me and asked, "Jim, how do you treat blisters?" Few were in need of lung surgery.

One day the battalion was camped around a mountain lake. I told my men that I would be taking my fishing rod. Many of my men realized that, with nine ambulances and several trucks, there would be room for fishing rods.

How did the officers and men from the battalion respond to medics who thought of bringing fishing rods? With envy and amusement. Of course, we used our generator to provide lighting for the headquarter tents of the commanding officer and all of the company commanders. We were also generous with a commodity that sergeants appreciated—adhesive tape. Our strategy was this: wear your helmet liner with a red cross, do your job well, and ask for help from the highest officer around. Basically, those wearing red crosses who were working hard at their job did not get hassled.

In the winter, our platoon returned to Camp Hale and established a 15-bed hospital in tents in the snow. The battalion learned to ski and performed winter maneuvers. Six doctors and one dentist were assigned to the hospital. They all outranked me, but I was the one who was in charge of the hospital, the mess hall, etc. We had lots of equipment, manuals of instruction, but no enlisted men with experience using the equipment. The doctors helped as best they could, but between treating broken legs and sprains, they got in a lot of skiing.

Learning to use all this equipment was a challenge. We relied a lot on manuals. I was able to check my blood to see if I had adjusted to the altitude; a man with a dislocated shoulder had it snapped back in place by a doctor when we experimented with an over-the-nose device to relax his muscles, and so on. We learned many things, but we would have required much training from skilled instructors before we could realistically be seen as being able to provide satisfactory emergency care.

Running a small mess hall was an asset. We were classified as "hazardous duty" and thus I could order or purchase extra items for the mess hall. By having the best mess hall on base, we attracted officers and other helpful people, such as the military police. If one of my men got in trouble in the nearby town of Leadville, it was useful if the military police called me first. We avoided some difficult situations.

Back at our main base at Fort Carson, medical service officers performed other duties. I became part of the military justice system. The Army had Summary, Special, and General Court Martials. A General Court Martial could give the death penalty. An investigation was required before proceeding to a General Court Martial to determine if the highest military court were appropriate.

One case I dealt with involved a soldier from a native Indian band who went AWOL to cut wood for the winter for his grandmother. After cutting enough fuel so she would not freeze, he turned himself in to the police. The first time he did this his company commander asked for a Special Court Martial. The next year he again went AWOL to cut wood for his grandmother. This time his company commander asked for a General Court Martial. When I interviewed the soldier, I asked him if he had spoken to a chaplain, or someone in authority; he responded that he got no support. He admitted that he was shy, and that he did not understand the white man's world, or the military. I recommended against the General Court Martial and he went before a Special Court Martial a second time.

According to U.S. Military Criminal Law it is illegal for someone to interfere with or intimidate an officer doing a General Court Martial investigation. This soldier's commanding officer raged at me and tried to intimidate me, deliberately and knowingly violating the law.

Every investigation I performed seemed to me to be a case of overkill. I recommended that each case be handled by the lower court. No other commanding officer had behaved in an illegal manner.

I also sat on the court of Special Court Martials. At the end of a trial, each member votes secretly, writing his decision on a piece of paper. No one is allowed to influence another member of the court. However, the chair of the court (in my case a full Colonel) would always comment with something like, "This bastard is guilty as hell and deserves the maximum of six months."

When he opened the pieces of paper from the junior officers he might comment, "Who is this pansy who is only recommending three months?" Intimidation was the norm. Although I was involved in less than 30 trials, I never saw a vigorous defense or any defendant found "not guilty."

When carrying out a defense, the relevant officer could remove one member of the court without cause. Other members could be removed for cause. I felt that it would be advantageous to remove this one particular full colonel who had no respect for the law. He was outraged that this young lieutenant would kick him off the court, and resisted. The first time it was difficult to get him to leave. The second and third time he was also clearly displeased. Did I have an obligation to report this blatantly illegal behaviour? I wimped out and did not "rock the boat." Later, when studying corporate crime, I was able to sympathize with whistle blowers.

Fortunately, I was not sent to Korea to rescue patients from mountain cliffs. My military experience was a reasonable two years and the GI Bill paid for my graduate work at the University of Washington.

Changing the World Wasn't So Easy

While working on my Ph.D. at the University of Washington, Leroy Gould and I felt certain that we were pretty smart. Surely, we could apply our new knowledge and cure delinquency. In the 1960s, we put together a funding request for the Opportunities for Youth Project, received money from the Ford Foundation, the Seattle Housing Authority, and the Boeing Corporation. Leroy decided it would be wiser for him to finish his Ph.D. dissertation and take a job offer at Yale. The funding came through and I became the research director of the Opportunities for Youth Project in Seattle.

Herb Costner was my thesis supervisor and provided statistical and other expertise; **Clarence Schrag**, who had been the Director of Corrections for the State of Washington, was optimistic about applying science and knowledge in an effort to actually reduce crime and delinquency.

Opportunities for Youth was very sophisticated but overly complex. We had eight experimental groups, eight control groups, and 49 measures of success. Would this elaborate and sophisticated research design, incorporating ideas from Cloward and Ohlin and other recent research, result in a reduction of delinquency? Of the 49 measures of success, 24 were positive, 25 were negative: clear evidence that we had NO IMPACT.

The local citizenry, who had assumed that there would be success, were not happy. However, the Ford Foundation was not surprised. The most sophisticated of their projects were showing little success. The poorly evaluated ones *claimed* success, but a meta-evaluation of 100 delinquency prevention programs indicated that only two met the qualifications for adequate evaluation. Opportunities for Youth was one of those two. So in 1965 I fled to Canada and the University of Alberta as a new assistant professor of sociology.

It is important to note that more skilled scholars gradually were able to tease out factors that could make a difference, but in the 1960s prevention programs did not look promising.

Modest Skills Are Rewarded If One Arrives at the Right Time

It was a good time to enter academia. And the University of Alberta was a good place to be. Did I make a splash in criminology? When I presented my "causal model of delinquency" at a meeting it was misspelled, listed as a "casual" model rather than "causal." I was the only person to notice the mistake in spelling. The resulting article has been cited about one time ("Testing a Causal Model of Delinquency," *Sociological Quarterly* 11 (Fall 1970): 511–522.)

Crime statistics have long been difficult to interpret. They don't mean the same thing in different places. I believed that I had worked out a strategy for improving such comparisons. My article "Analyzing Juvenile Justice Statistics in Metropolitan Areas," with Wasanti Paranjape, was published in the *Canadian Journal of Criminology*, 25 (October 1983):447–462. I made an attempt to apply this strategy to Australian statistics. ("Improving Crime Statistics by 'Correcting' them for System Characteristics," with Dianne Dagger was published in *Australian and New Zealand Journal of Criminology* (26[1993]:116–126). I even tried to sell this strategy in my criminology textbook, but was told by reviewers that students found it dull. I was advised to drop it. I don't believe any of these ideas have been cited by another criminologist.

My other hopes for scholarly fame were also overlooked, but the University of Alberta was good to those who kept trying. And we were blessed with some outstanding graduate students. I managed to hang on to the coat-tails of people like John Hagan and Rick Linden.

If one is reasonably reliable, modest success is sometimes possible in organizations. I was the executive secretary of the American Society of Criminology, a great-sounding title. In fact, most of the important tasks, such as treasurer and program chair, had long ago been given separate roles. My job was to help the newly elected president remember things. When one is looking for dozens of people to serve on committees and chair various tasks, it is useful to know who ran for office, including those who lost. Admittedly, most of the presidents I served with—along with myself—could barely remember who had won the elections, let alone who had lost. Essentially, I was an assistant to Sarah Hall, the much-loved office manager of the American Society of Criminology, and Chris Eskridge, who did everything. It was a very enjoyable role.

Another grand-sounding title was president of the Sociology of Deviance (Research Committee) of the International Sociological Association. This actually required work, but it provided many interesting contacts.

Let me now turn to some of the events that took place in criminology after the 1960s.

Has Criminology Helped?

Have criminologists helped us understand crime? Have our contributions led to changes that benefit society? There are at least two questions here. First, have we learned very much? And, second, have policy makers used this knowledge, or have those of us in the field had any significant impact on policy makers? Others have addressed these questions more thoroughly, but I'd like to comment on a few personal experiences.

Locking People Up

For about 50 years the U.S. locked up more people each year. About halfway through this process, criminologists had pretty much demonstrated that this was a poor strategy. Other countries paid attention to the research and resisted such extensive incarceration. As California spent increasing amounts on prisons (and increasingly less on education), both society and budgets suffered. North America learns slowly.

Much of my research has focused on juvenile justice systems. Earlier in my career I served on committees when Alberta was considering juvenile prisons (using other names in place of "prison"—e.g., "Young Offender Centre"). They decided to build one in Edmonton and one in Calgary. I was the only one who argued against them. I believed that far less space should be allocated to locking up juveniles. I pointed out that Toulouse, France, with a population of 1,100,000, had three boys in prison. I was a minority of one on the Alberta committees. Twenty years later, it was clear that there was overcapacity.

When I retired to Victoria in 1996, I served on the Family Court Committee. The city was considering a new juvenile lock-up. I was the only one who voted against it. It was expensive, built with high levels of security. After almost 20 years, given its underuse, it was closed. Many citizens objected, but the government was acknowledging the findings from the rest of the world. Put simply, juvenile prisons yield a poor return.

Admittedly, it is very difficult for government to resist the reaction of citizens to serious crime. Newspaper coverage rarely generates sympathy, or insights, for the average reader. Alternatives to long prison terms involve risk and careful planning. Even a progressively minded government will have trouble putting such programs in place. But Canada tends to follow the U.S., and this is an area where public policy is slow to build on knowledge.

Can a researcher in criminology make an impact on a citizen's committee after he retires? Despite the claim that research knowledge is useful, citizen's committees are very often guided by what is popular. Fifty years of research has demonstrated that a juvenile program does not work, yet our committee in Victoria has consistently supported it. It prevents neither juvenile crime, nor drug use, nor a variety of other juvenile problems. Citizen's committees happily buy into the claims of those involved in these programs, people who claim that they were "saved." Enthusiastic practitioners look for people to be "saved" and claim success. Such claims lead policy-makers astray. Carefully controlled research, with control groups, finds that those who are left alone do just as well as those who are treated.

Being a researcher on citizen's committees is probably a waste of time. It is interesting that when I was paid to speak to an audience (sometimes to knowledgeable people, such as juvenile court judges), people paid attention. When an expert provides the same information free to local groups, he or she is usually ignored. My conclusion is that being an "expert" on a citizens' committee may well be a waste of time.

There are, however, a number of programs that do show promise. I will mention them later. But in general, the public gets on a bandwagon of popular activities. Popularity and so-called "common sense" outweigh serious research.

Universities can in fact contribute to the problem. In the social sciences, the research for most theses is carried out with small budgets; the limited budget can rarely support the costs and the time required for rigorous evaluations. The hard sciences are better able to group thesis work, compartmentalize elements of a study, and resist some of the weaknesses that plague other university departments. While much social science research can add knowledge, some can generate misleading information. Restorative justice illustrates some of these problems.

Juvenile Justice Systems: A Significant Contribution?

Studying juvenile justice systems in different parts of the world has been an interesting specialty for me. It is worth noting that the ideas developed from this research have had little impact on Canadian systems; in that sense, they have not been particularly significant. Instead of finding some overarching principles, I found considerable diversity; often times the factors at work were far from visible. Perhaps I have offered a cafeteria of ideas that could help us look at our own juvenile justice systems more critically.

For example, in Vienna, I noticed that when Mrs. Pavlik, a senior "youth officer," appeared in court, the defendant always received probation. Since the parole office was six kilometres from court, parole officers only occasionally came to court. But whenever they did appear, the juvenile always received probation. Although I was assured by the judges that they made their decisions independently, it seemed that the decision had been made in advance.

When the judges were unsure about a case, they would usually talk with Mrs. Pavlik, who knew all of the other youth officers in Vienna. Did she recommend a solution? Mrs. Pavlik was not even on any organizational chart.

However, I felt this "liaison" role was the most important and most crucial to the key decisions made in the Vienna Juvenile Court. (See "Informelle Kommunikationsstrukturen im Strafverfahren," *Kriminologisches Journals* 4 (1974): 307-312.)

In other words, many informal and poorly understood features of a juvenile court system (or for that matter, many of the systems and bureaucracies we study) are major factors in influencing outcomes.

In Edmonton an experienced parole officer was located at the juvenile court. Frequently, parole officers (and police officers) would spend many hours waiting at the court when in fact they needed to spend only a few minutes at the court proceedings. This liaison parole officer at court was often able to handle these matters as well as advise on many cases so that regular parole officers did not have to waste time in court and would only appear when they were really needed.

Often, liaison roles are not understood by those who are reorganizing courts. Since the Edmonton position was not clearly defined, it was eliminated to save money. Actually, it cost the province a great deal more since they had to use more staff in a less efficient manner.

In Paris each of the judges is assisted by an *educateur* (correctional social worker). One judge had an educateur who spoke Arabic and enjoyed good relations with a unit from the police that focused on Arab-speaking juveniles. This link made a major difference in the way this judge served her particular geographical area. Thus, even though the law may be the same, different areas, different bureaucratic situations, and different individual characteristics can have a tremendous impact on outcomes. For more information, see "Locking Up Juveniles in Canada: Some Comparisons with France," with Antoine Garapon, Chuck Frigon, and Ken Knight, *Canadian Public Policy* 13 (1987):477–489, and "Practicing in France What Americans Have Preached: The Response of French Judges to Juveniles," *Crime and Delinquency* 34 (1988):467–485.

Promising Ideas

Restorative Justice: Are We Using It Effectively? When I first arrived in Edmonton in 1965, I taught an evening class on criminology alongside my daytime classes. The students were mainly people working in the justice and correctional systems. The criminology classes I taught in the 1960s usually included lectures on what would be referred to as "restorative justice." That term was not used in 1965, but the principles have been known for several hundred years. I used the experiences of the Plains Indians to illustrate my lectures. These lectures were well received, but could not be sold to government in the 1960s.

The core idea behind what was later called restorative justice (RJ) is to bring someone whose behaviour has been unacceptable, and who has been rejected by society, back into normal society. What I found particularly promising about these ideas was that they applied to crimes which cause us considerable concern, such as violence in the family. Unfortunately, those in RJ programs prefer to focus on teen-age shoplifters.

Research carried out in the U.S., England, and Australia, using control groups and careful analysis, showed promise. Today, such programs are popular in Canada and elsewhere. Unfortunately, the type of research which focuses on WHY any changes take place with young offenders who participate in any of the programs is not being carried out in Canada, nor is it happening in the majority of RJ programs. The assumption is simply made that RJ must be good. The WHY remains a sort of "black box" phenomenon.

The problem is that many RJ programs focus heavily on teenage shoplifters. However, most teenage thieves are not "outside" the society. Most of them are not alienated from the society. Are teenage outpourings of guilt about shoplifting at Walmart really sincere? Or is such crime part of growing up? Learning to "con" adults is a useful skill.

In addition, we have new and troubling knowledge that those who are more talented are also more likely to cheat on income tax, drive through pedestrian-protected zones, etc. It is disturbing that those who are most likely to get into law and medicine and other high-status professions are also those who are most likely to "cut corners" in order to get ahead in society.

Admittedly, RJ does work on teenage shoplifters. But is it because these young people learn that their futures will be endangered by continuing such practices? Is this restorative justice, or simply that most teenagers become aware of the risks?

The old-fashioned warning from a police officer may serve the same purpose, but asking forgiveness of a circle of sympathetic adults is good practice for deceiving other adults in the future. It also gives these adults a sense of success. Are we rewarding those young people who are gaining skill at conning adults? We simply don't know. In Canada we are patting ourselves on the back. But we are not doing research on "why" things are happening. Volunteers in RJ report that the process is less rewarding and more difficult to use when working with violent offenders; this is where society should be concerned. Volunteers prefer to work with young people, preferably attractive ones. It makes us feel better.

None of the restorative justice programs in Canada have built-in sophisticated research components that help us understand the difficult and important questions regarding how the programs might in fact help the offender and victim. While some RJ practitioners do assess whether the procedures were competed, for the most part Canadian RJ conferences are almost always self-congratulatory. RJ has great promise for those violent crimes which should most concern society. But we may be using it on those where it is least needed and deceiving ourselves that compliance is true success.

Next, I would like to focus on a truly promising crime prevention idea that developed by David Olds who works at the University of Colorado Health Sciences Center, where he directs the Prevention Research Center for Family and Child Health. His research and ideas reflect what I feel holds considerable promise as it is based on sound research and scientific evidence. To date, the evidence shows that over the 30-odd years the program has been operating, along with the three longitudinal studies (see below) that have been undertaken, that it has been assessed as one of the best evidence based prevention programs for not only the prevention of child maltreatment but in providing a child with a greater likelihood of success later in life.

Creating Better Mothers: A Truly Promising Approach: For many decades we have been accumulating considerable evidence that providing a better quality of life for children reduces a variety of social ills, including criminal behaviour. Medical and social science research focusing on child development makes it clear that providing effective support to vulnerable first-time mothers helps children become less troubled and less troublesome young adults.

Having the basic knowledge of what we should be doing is not the same as actually designing an action program that can be put in place in different communities, carried out with different ethnic groups, and then evaluated in a systematic and scientific way. David Olds and his colleagues have done just that. Working with pregnant mothers who had few resources and were at risk, these programs utilized public health nurses (i.e., the Nurse-Family Partnership program (NFP) to deliver the sort of information and support that could potentially be made available in most communities.

The NFP differs from many mental-health, substance-abuse, and crime-prevention interventions in that it focuses on improving prenatal health, reducing child abuse and neglect, and enhancing family functioning in the first two years of the child's life. Other programs have concentrated on school-aged children in the pre-adolescent or adolescent age range, but these seem to be less effective than programs designed to reduce socio-emotional risks for children at a very early age. The details and strategy used in these programs are summarized elsewhere (see D.L. Olds (2007), "Preventing Crime with Prenatal and Infancy Support of Parents: The Nurse-Family Partnership," *Victims and Offenders* 2:205–225). I simply wish to note some of those results and suggest that these findings provide clear guidelines for social policies—policies that would reduce crime and other undesirable social behaviour, enrich the lives of many people, and save the taxpayers a great deal of money.

The strategy of these programs has a basic theme—to support first-time mothers to become effective parents. The public health nurses helped women to identify health issues, achieve a healthy diet, stop smoking, etc. After delivery, the nurses helped mothers and other caregivers improve the physical and emotional care of their children.

The Elmira, Memphis, and Denver studies: The 400 young mothers in the Elmira, New York sample were primarily white single mothers. Compared to their control group, the nurse-visited women improved their diets, smoked 25% fewer cigarettes during pregnancy, suffered from fewer kidney infections, and produced heavier babies. During the first two years of the child's life, nurse-visited children born to low-income, unmarried teens had 80% fewer cases of child abuse and neglect than did their counterparts in the control group.

Clearly, these young mothers were performing better, but did this translate into less crime for their children when they became adolescents? By the time these children were 15 years of age, they were performing better than the comparison group. Those visited by nurses had 69% fewer convictions, 58% fewer sexual partners, smoked 28% fewer cigarettes, and consumed alcohol on 51% fewer days. Not only were there fewer arrests, there were fewer adjudications as Persons in Need of Supervision (PINS) and fewer violations of probation. These effects were greater for children born to mothers who were poor and unmarried at registration. Clearly, better parenting did lead to better social performance in the children (Olds et al. 1997).

Did being a better mother help the mother to become a better citizen? At the 15-year follow-up, poor unmarried women continued to show a number of enduring benefits. In contrast to their counterparts in the comparison condition, those visited by nurses both during pregnancy and during the infancy of the child averaged fewer subsequent pregnancies, fewer subsequent births, longer intervals between the birth of their first and second children, fewer months on welfare, and fewer months receiving food stamps. There was a 79% reduction in child abuse and neglect, a 44% reduction in maternal misbehaviour due to alcohol and drug use, and 69% fewer arrests. Obviously, becoming a better mother has a major payoff for the mother as well as for the child, not to mention for society.

The Elmira study focused on young unmarried white women living in a semi-rural area. Would the same strategy work for young disadvantaged black women in an urban setting? The Memphis sample focused on such a population.

During the first two years after birth there was an 80% reduction in the number of days in hospital for injuries and ingesting something dangerous compared to the control group. By age six there were fewer behavioural and mental health problems. Grades were better in grades one to three in the nurse-supported sample.

At age 12, about 5% of the comparison group children had used tobacco, alcohol, or marijuana in the past 30 days. For the nurse supported group, it was roughly 1.7%. The numbers for depression followed a similar pattern.

So the public health nurse advocacy strategy had a major impact on young white and black families. Would it also work for Hispanic families?

The Denver sample involved primarily Hispanic families. Again, those who were visited by public health nurses did better than the comparison groups. Instead of providing more statistics, let me note a different feature of the Denver study. Paraprofessionals, instead of trained nurses, were also used to deliver services similar to those provided by the public health nurses. The results were not as good as they were when the nurses did the visitations. For policy-makers, this may become an issue. David Olds and his colleagues are very cautious about using strategies that do not meet the standards achieved by well-trained public health nurses.

Policy Implications for Canada

The policy implications of these carefully evaluated scientific studies should be obvious. If public health nurses can dramatically change the lives of white, black, and Hispanic families, might they have the same impact on Aboriginal families in Canada? Or immigrant families struggling in large cities? Each study showed that the most significant improvements were seen in high-risk, low-resource families. These are the very families that many people claim are hopeless, beyond help. And yet psychologists have shown that when people recognize that there is hope, they can and do change. These nurse visitation programs offer such hope.

Fortunately, the potential for public health nurse visitation programs in Canada is rather good—assuming the appropriate political leaders will act on the evidence that is available to them.

Leaving at a Good Time

I have been blessed with good timing. Having fortunate experiences while young, moving to Canada when there was a demand for sociologists, having excellent graduate students, and experiencing a rewarding professional life has certainly made me one of the lucky ones.

Publications by Jim Hackler

(with brilliant insights largely overlooked by other scholars)

Hackler, J. (1966). Boys, blisters, and behavior: The impact of a work program in an urban central area. *Journal of Research in Crime and Delinquency* 3:155–164.

Hackler, J. (1971). A developmental theory of delinquency. *Canadian Review of Sociology and Anthropology* 8:61–75.

Hackler, J., and Bourgette. P. (1973). Dollars, dissonance, and survey returns. *Public Opinion Quarterly* 37:276–281.

Hackler, J., and Hagan, J. (1975). Work and teaching machines as delinquency prevention tools: A four year follow-up. *Social Service Review* 49:92–106.

Hackler, J. (1979). "The dangers of political naivete and excessive complexity in evaluating delinquency prevention programs. *Evaluation and Program Planning* 1:273–283.

Hackler, J., and Hansen, C. (1985). Police killings. *Canadian Journal of Criminology* 27:227–232.

Hackler, J. (1987). Stealing conflicts in juvenile justice: Contrasting France and Canada. *Canadian Journal of Law and Society* 2:141–151.

Hackler, J. (1988). Practicing in France what Americans have preached: The response of French judges to juveniles. *Crime and Delinquency* 34:467–485.

Hackler, J., and Don, K. (1989). Screening juveniles and the central city phenomenon: Understanding the dynamics of police systems. *Canadian Police College Journal* 13:1–17

Hackler, J., and Dagger, D. (1993). Improving crime statistics by 'correcting' them for system characteristics. *Australian and New Zealand Journal of Criminology* 26:116–126

Hackler, J. (1984). Implications of variability in juvenile justice," pp. 213–233 in Klein, M. (ed.), *Western Systems of Juvenile Justice*. Beverly Hills: Sage.

Hackler, J. (1996). Anglophone juvenile justice: Why Canada, England, the USA, and Australia are behind other developed countries." In Winterdyk, J. (ed.), *Issues and Perspectives on Young Offenders in Canada.* Toronto: HBJ-Holt Canada.

ELEVEN

Anthony N. Doob: Champion and Pioneer of Evidence-Based Policy Research

John Winterdyk

In 2013, the *Canadian Journal of Criminology and Criminal Justice* published a rare Festschrift in honour of Professor Emeritus Anthony (Tony) Doob. This special issue consists of a collection of articles written by former students as well as several national and international scholars. The introduction to this collection observes that Anthony Doob is "one of the most prolific criminologists in Canada. One cannot read about criminological issues within Canada without discovering some of his scholarship" (p. 458). He has not only produced scholarly work on a wide range of issues and topics, but he has also arguably contributed to the evolution of Canadian criminology and criminal justice.

Much of this summary is drawn from the 2013 Festshrift (with page numbers in parentheses).

The Early Years

Anthony Doob was born in Washington, D.C., in 1943. A social psychologist by training, he obtained his undergraduate degree from Harvard University in 1964, followed by a Ph.D. in psychology at Stanford University in California in 1967. In 1968 he joined the department of psychology at the University of Toronto; in the early 1970s Doob was invited to offer a course in the university's newly established master's program in criminology. Over the next decade, he gradually drifted into criminology on a full-time basis. After a sabbatical year in Cambridge, England, in 1978–79, Doob returned to Toronto to become the new director of the Centre of Criminology.

Blazing a Trail

Like many pioneers whose work is described in this book, Doob followed an eclectic path until finally joining the University of Toronto in 1968. At the invitation of Martin Friedland (then a commissioner on the Law Reform Commission of Canada, now professor emeritus of law at Toronto), Doob worked for the now-defunct Law Reform Commission of Canada. The commission comprehensively and systematically reviewed different aspects of Canadian law. Topics included such subjects as evidence, mental disorders in the criminal process, sexual offences, criteria for the determination of death, euthanasia (including aiding suicide and cessation of treatment), and arrest. Doob's work at the law commission involved conducting "social science research to inform the validity of the then-current approaches and to provide an evidentiary basis for formulating proposals to reform the existing law" (Sprott and Roberts in Festschrift, p. 458).

Box 11.1. *Youth Crime*

Published in 2004, *Responding to Youth Crime in Canada* was one of the first books to consider the country's response to *Youth Criminal Justice Act*, which took effect April 1, 2003.The authors suggest the youth justice system has had a comparatively modest impact on youth crime because of the complex nature of such crime, and call for a shift away from believing that the youth justice system can "solve" youth crime toward an examination of how the system can better respond to it. **Jim Hackler**'s review of the book noted that it would "help any professional taking on responsibilities which require an awareness of key issues in the youth justice system."

The move to evidence-informed legal policy research was not only innovative, but a pioneering contribution to establishing new legal policy in Canada. Doob's work, carried out with Julian Roberts, on public views of sentencing led to his appointment to the Canadian Sentencing Commission in 1984. In 1987, Doob and others published a major report of over 630 pages. Saskatchewan Judge **Omer Archambault** served as the chairman; **Jean-Paul Brodeur** and Julian Roberts were part of the expert research staff. The commission's report resulted in an extensive list of recommendations that covered the entire spectrum of sentencing practices in Canada. For example, the report notes out that the problems of sentencing practices in Canada had less to do with the people who were making decisions than with the overall structure in which sentencing decisions were being made. The commission's report was a watershed event that helped to bring about major reforms in how Canada examined, amended, or revised sentencing policies. Doob's work positioned him to become one of the first Canadian sociology-criminology scholars to help serve as a bridge between the commission and the academic research community. Doob's firm belief in the important of research evidence to inform sentencing policies continues to influence Canadians today.

Sentencing and Sentencing Policy

Doob's greatest contribution to Canadian criminology and criminal justice may well be his pioneering work around sentencing and sentencing policy, work that dates back to the early 1970s (see Box 11.1). As Michael Tonry notes, while the United States has undergone numerous sentencing reforms, Canada has undergone far fewer such reforms. American sentencing reforms tend to be largely punitive, and time has shown many of them to be counter-productive. One of the great insights in the 1987 report was that "solutions being proposed in other jurisdictions, though perhaps useful to examine, cannot be imported unchanged in Canada" (p. xxv).

Tonry observes in a comparison of Canadian and American legal reforms that Doob's research on sentencing influenced Canadian sentencing reforms to be undertaken as "humanely and effectively as they can" (p. 474). It is perhaps an interesting irony that in spite of the sheer volume of work produced by American criminologists and legal scholars, the state of the criminal justice system can still be characterized as being "unhealthy" and slow to reform. While we have historically looked to our neighbours to the south for guidance regarding the administration of criminal justice, they could learn something from their neighbours to the north, too. The insightful work of Doob and colleagues (such as **Cheryl Webster, Jane Sprott**, and **Julian Roberts**) would be a good starting point (see Box 11.2).

Other scholars have observed that Doob and his colleague Jean-Paul Brodeur played a key role in ensuring that the Commission "recognized the need to enhance sentencing policy and practice by developing more accurate statistical information and fostering an active program of empirical research" (p. 496). Moreover, Doob continued to champion, and at times spearhead, "the need to achieve a greater degree of uniformity in sentencing decisions across Canada" (ibid.). For example, much of Doob's research emphasized the need to adhere to the principle that sentencing should be proportionate to the relative gravity of the offence: "Let the punishment fit the crime." Scholars have also noted how Doob's work has influenced such diverse areas as the sentencing of individuals with neurocognitive impairment (e.g., FASD, ADHD, PTSD, etc.), the preliminary inquiry process, and how public attitudes should inform criminal justice policy. His research influenced the evolution of preliminary inquiries, ensuring that they be used in a constructive manner, not only in order to determine that there is sufficient evidence to bring a case to trial, but also to "reduce the use of expensive court resources" (p. 526).

The Festschrift entry by Doob's former student, **Valerie Hans**, considers his jury-related research. Hans highlights Doob's instrumental and novel work on the role of Canadian jury decision-making. Doob was among the first to conduct research "on questions of relevance to the Canadian jury" (p. 533). She notes that his work—particularly the research taken while working for the Commission—helped to lay the foundation for subsequent jury research in Canada. Hans also recalls a case in the early 1970s, when Doob worked in the psychology department at U of T. He received an urgent call from a defence lawyer seeking assistance for his client. The lawyer genuinely believed that his client was innocent, but felt that the witness who had identified his client in a line-up must somehow have been biased (see Box 11.3). The lawyer involved was R. Roy McMurtry, who later became the Attorney General of Ontario and the Chief Justice of Ontario. Along with one of his undergraduate students, Hershi Kirshenbaum, Doob "devised an innovative way to test the fairness of line-ups" that was instrumental in demonstrating that the line-up had likely been biased. This study sparked a renewed interest on the part of psychologists in the problem, well identified within the law, of wrongful convictions resulting from (honest) errors in suspect identification.

Box 11.2.
Justice for Girls

In response to apparent concern about female delinquency and criminality, *Justice for Girls* (Chicago: University of Chicago Press, 2009) offers a unique comparative insight into how the U.S. and Canada have responded to female and in particular adolescent female crime. The authors also examine how the alleged apprehension about the (as they argue) exaggerated extent and nature of "girl crime" in both countries has affected the treatment of both girls and boys.

Doob was one of those rare academics who were able to integrate his sociological work into the legal arena. He was one of the first Canadian academic pioneers to engage in what can be called applied criminal justice research. His research continues to influence many contemporary researchers.

Other scholars observe that Doob's research on public perception in Canada "has fundamentally shifted academic and policy approaches to understanding public views of crime and punishment" (p. 549). Doob's notable contribution includes important work on methodology, work that has "influenced a burgeoning literature internationally, most notably in the United Kingdom, United States, Europe, Australian and New Zealand"

(p. 550). It is worth noting that during the years Stephen Harper was prime minister, many of Doob's ideas and policy influences were "dismantled," replaced instead by more "punitive criminal justice policies" (p. 550).

The Lord Chief Justice of England, Gordon Hewart, is credited with the now famous 1922 aphorism: "Not only must Justice be done; it must also be seen to be done." Doob and his colleagues have helped not only to examine public perception of crime and punishment, but to also demonstrate that when the public is provided with correct and consistent information about how to respond "to questions about crime and justice matters," they will favour "approaches that are meaningful and those which use justice resources sensibly" (Varma and Marios 2013:558).

Youth Justice and Evaluation Research

Another area of influence is youth justice. Doob's interest dates back to the mid-1970s when the Centre of Criminology was asked to perform a review of what was known about the diversion of youth from the youth justice system.

Box 11.3. University of Toronto Centre for Criminology

In 1984 along with the esteemed Canadian criminal lawyer **Edward Greenspan**, Doob assembled a collection of articles on the influence of **John Edwards**, founder of the University of Toronto Centre of Criminology. In honour of Edwards' role in the creation of the criminology program and eventually the Centre for Criminology, the University has since 1995 hosted the annual John Edwards Memorial Lecture. At the inaugural lecture the presenter was Professor Andrew Ashworth, King's College, University of London, whose lecture was entitled "Mens Rea and Statutory Offences." Also see A.N. Doob and E.L. Greenspan (eds.), *Perspectives in Criminal Law: Essays in honour of John Ll. J. Edwards* (Toronto: Canada Law Book, 1985).

From 1997 Doob also founded and edited the journal *Criminological Highlights* (*CH*). Published six times per year, each issue includes eight one-page summaries of high-quality articles from a wide range of sources, primarily research that is relevant to policy-makers and practitioners. *CH* is available free by subscription, and is read in more than 45 countries.

In 1999, Doob served as an expert witness for the Canadian Foundation for Children, Youth and the Law; his testimony was "critical in highlighting the conditions of confinement for adolescent males in secure facilities throughout the province [Ontario] and essential to the 119 recommendations that arose from the inquiry" (p. 564). Doob's 1999 report, "The Experiences of Phase II Male Young Offenders in Secure Facilities in the Province of Ontario," was instrumental in changing how institutionalized young offenders were treated. Doob and his colleagues explored how the overuse of custody for minor and non-violent young offenders under the Young Offenders Act desperately required reform.

Doob and Tonry also edited a collection on youth justice as part of the *Crime and Justice* series (#31). The book includes 11 perspectives from international scholars on their national youth justice systems, including Canada, Denmark, Germany, Great Britain, the Netherlands, New Zealand, Sweden, as well as other western countries. This collection compares and contrasts current youth justice laws.

Scot Wortley and Rosemary Gartner also describe Doob's significant contributions to the "underdeveloped state of evaluation research on crime prevention and policy in Canada" (p. 577). He has been a relentless champion of interventions in the criminal justice system that are informed "by sound empirical evidence as their effectiveness" (p. 578). Wortley and Gartner observe that Canadian evaluation research "is not that impressive" (p. 580), for a variety of reasons, including ideological differences between community perceptions and academics, a lack of resources, resistance from funders, and the challenge for academics of communicating their research to the community. Furthermore, Doob has observed that in the United States many crime prevention or intervention programs have received funding without proper evaluation and they have later been proven ineffective. Doob has led the way in Canada in the effort to ensure that money is wisely spent and that programs are careful evaluated. Nevertheless, Doob continues to blaze a trail, and his contributions to crime and Canadian criminal justice policies have been profound. A 2007 study by Ellen Cohn and David Farrington found that Doob was "the most widely cited criminologist in Canada" (p. 588).

In 2011 Doob received the University of Toronto's Carolyn Tuohy Impact on Public Policy award, and in 2014 he became one of the few Canadian criminologists to receive the Order of Canada.

Rosemary Gartner summed up Doob's impact in her introductory remarks to his 2014 John Edwards Lecture, describing him as "an irritating gadfly to those in power who favour rhetoric and political expediency over evidence-based, coherent criminal justice policies."

References

A Festschrift in Honour of Anthony N. Doob. (2013). *Canadian Journal of Criminology and Criminal Justice*, 55(4).

Cohn, E., and Farrington, D. (2007). Changes in scholarly influence in major international criminology journals. *Australian and New Zealand Journal of Criminology* 40(3):335–359.

Doob, A.N., and Greenspan, E.L. (eds.) *Perspectives in criminal law: Essays in honour of John Ll. J. Edwards*. Toronto: Canada Law Book, 1985.

Hackler, J. (2005). How should we respond to youth crime? (book review). *Canadian Journal of Law and Society* 20(1):193–208.

Sentencing Reform: A Canadian approach. (1987). Ottawa: Ministry of Supply and Services Canada.

Selected Publications: Anthony Doob

Webster, C.M., and A.N. Doob (in press). American punitiveness "Canadian style"? Cultural values and Canadian punishment policy. *Punishment & Society*.

Doob, A.N., and C.M. Webster (in press). A criminal justice agenda for Canada. *Policy Options* 36(3).

Murphy, Y., J.B. Sprott, and A.N. Doob (2015). Pardoning people who once offended. *Criminal Law Quarterly* 62: 209–225.

Doob, A.N., and C.M. Webster (2014). Creating the will to change: The challenges of decarceration in the United States. *Criminology & Public Policy* 13(4): 547–559.

Doob, A.N., C.M. Webster, and A. Manson. (2014) Zombie parole: The withering of conditional release in Canada. *Criminal Law Quarterly* 61(3): 301–328.

Sprott, J.B., and A.N. Doob. (2014). Confidence in the police: Variation across groups classified as visible minorities. *Canadian Journal of Criminology and Criminal Justice* 56(3): 367–379.

Webster, C.M., and A.N. Doob (2014). Penal reform "Canadian style": Fiscal responsibility and decarceration in Alberta, Canada. *Punishment & Society* 16(1): 3–31.

Sprott, J.B., C.M. Webster, and A.N. Doob. (2013). Punishment severity and confidence in the criminal justice system. *Canadian Journal of Criminology and Criminal Justice* 55(2): 278–292.

Doob, A.N. (2012) Principled sentencing, politics, and restraint in the use of imprisonment: Canada's break with its history. *Champ Penal/Penal Field*, IX. http://champpenal.revues.org/8335.

Webster, C.M., and A.N. Doob. (2012). Maintaining our balance: Trends in imprisonment policies in Canada. In Ismaili, Karim, Jane Sprott and Kimberly Varma (eds.). *Canadian Criminal Justice Policy*. Toronto: Oxford University Press, pp. 79–109.

Doob, A.N., and C.M. Webster. (2012) Back to the future? Policy development in pre-trial detention in Canada. In Ismaili et al. (eds.), *Canadian Criminal Justice Policy*, pp. 30–57.

Doob, A.N., and A.E. Gross (1968). Status of frustrator as an inhibitor of horn-honking responses. *Journal of Social Psychology* 76: 213–218.

Doob, A.N., and D.T. Regan (eds.). (1971). *Readings in Experimental Social Psychology*. New York: Appleton-Century-Crofts.

Doob, A.N., and H.M. Kirshenbaum. (1972). Some empirical evidence on the effect of S. 12 of the Canada Evidence Act upon an accused. *Criminal Law Quarterly* 15(1): 88–96.

Doob, A.N. (1983). The organization of criminological research: Canada. In M. Tonry and N. Morris *Crime and Justice: An Annual Review of Research.* Volume 5. Chicago: University of Chicago Press.

Doob, A.N., and J-P. Brodeur. (1995). Achieving accountability in sentencing. In Philip Stenning (ed.), *Accountability for Criminal Justice: Selected Essays.* Toronto: University of Toronto Press, pp. 376–396.

Hans, V.P., and Doob, A.N. (1976). S.12 of the Canada Evidence Act and the deliberation of simulated juries. *Criminal Law Quarterly 18*(2): 235-253.

Sprott, J.B., J.M. Jenkins, and A.N. Doob. (2005). The importance of school: Protecting at-risk youth from early offending. *Youth Violence and Juvenile Justice* 3(1): 59–77.

TWELVE

Richard V. Ericson: Institutions, Crime and Deviance

Kevin D. Haggerty, Aaron Doyle and Janet Chan

Introduction

This brief introduction to the scholarship of Richard V. Ericson (1948–2007) highlights the continuing value of his research as well as his remarkable abilities as an interdisciplinary scholar.[22]

Richard earned a bachelor's degree in the social sciences at the University of Guelph, followed by a master's degree in sociology at the University of Toronto. From there he went to Cambridge University in the UK where he completed his Ph.D. at the Institute of Criminology under the supervision of Derick McClintock.

Over the course of his career Ericson served as a professor of criminology and sociology, of sociology and law, and of criminology and law. His first academic position was at the University of Alberta, where he helped found the *Canadian Journal of Sociology.* He then accepted a position at the Centre of Criminology at the University of Toronto, where he eventually served multiple terms as director. For more than 20 years Ericson fostered the Centre's interdisciplinary vision of criminology. Later, he became the founding principal of Green College, an interdisciplinary graduate residential college at the University of British Columbia. He held this post for its first 10 years (1993–2003). Under Ericson's leadership, Green College evolved as a rich intellectual environment, an achievement that he felt was perhaps his most meaningful and important (see Box 12.1). David Garland (2007) called Green College Richard's "individual masterpiece."

Ericson's theoretical orientation falls broadly under the catch-all category of social constructionism. This encompasses an intellectual trajectory that

[22] This chapter draws from a larger overview of Richard's work (see Haggerty, Doyle, and Chan 2011).

commenced with labeling theory, pioneered in the late to mid-1960s by the likes of the American sociologists Edwin Lemert and Howard Becker, combined with symbolic interactionism that originates in the works of sociologist Max Weber (1864–1920) and philosopher George Herbert Mead (1863–1931). Over the years, Ericson's interests broadened to include a diverse array of influences drawn from media/cultural studies, risk theory, and post-Foucauldian analysis of governmentality. He undertook many large empirical projects that were deeply informed by theory.

Ericson's work was also important in a variety of disciplines: each of his books has been reviewed in more than a dozen journals by scholars from criminology, sociology, political science, law, and (for the media books)

Box 12.1. An Institutional Approach to Crime

Perhaps surprisingly for a criminologist, Richard studiously avoided etiological questions about why people might or might not commit crime. He always believed that crime is not a naturally given phenomenon, but that certain acts *become* crimes through highly variable institutional practices of categorization, monitoring, and processing. To understand crime, we must therefore understand the institutions that define it. Richard consequently practiced what is known as an "institutional approach" to criminology (Ericson and Shearing 1991). This involved a strong commitment to interdisciplinary research that focused on criminal justice institutions. Such institutions include the police, courts, and corrections, but also encompass a diverse array of other institutions that shape crime control, including law reform bodies, economic institutions, the news media, and also the increasing role played by science in governing crime (Ericson and Shearing 1986). These inquiries address a wide range of concerns about how such institutions reproduce the existing social order, advance a distinctive vision of morality, and shape social hierarchies relating to class, race, and gender.

journalism, communications, and cultural studies (see selected references at the end of this entry). Ericson's scholarship brought together criminology and sociology with many other disciplines and subfields such as media studies. His work on insurance played a key role in creating the emerging interdisciplinary field of insurance studies, while his theoretical work on surveillance (Haggerty and Ericson 2001) was also seminal in the emerging discipline of surveillance studies (Wood 2002).

Across all of his scholarship Ericson continually returns to questions about the power and paradoxes of official knowledge. This includes his analyses of the production of official accounts, the structures for communicating knowledge, shifts in the how institutions use knowledge to govern populations, and how institutions operate in contexts of uncertainty.

Another aspect of Richard Ericson's scholarship is his commitment to empirical research. While many academics avoid the rigors of undertaking empirical research, particularly later in their careers, Ericson continued to undertake field research throughout his working life. His methodological orientation was largely qualitative, and typically involved face-to-face interviews with those who placed different roles within the institutions he was studying. Ericson's major projects also often featured direct ethnographic observation.

His politics were broadly progressive, and he was unafraid to take a strong normative position. For example, he challenged police repression of protest at the APEC international summit at the University of British Columbia in 1997 (Ericson and Doyle 1999). Although Ericson's research was not a vehicle for advocacy, he did, nonetheless, believe that sound empirical scholarship could serve as a critical political force. It is worth nothing, however, that he saw the impact of academic knowledge on policy as being by and large more oblique and unpredictable than academic activists might wish (Ericson 2006:366).

Ericson's Major Works

From 1972 to 2007 Richard Ericson published 12 book-length research studies, plus five shorter research monographs, eight edited volumes, and over 100 journal articles and book chapters. This scholarship covered a range of topics from more conventional criminology such as law, justice, policing, and crime control to broader social, cultural, and economic issues such as the news media, risk, security, or insurance. These works were highly cited as influential across diverse fields. Cohn and Farrington (2007) observe that along with other notable scholars such as John Braithwaite (i.e., restorative justice), David Garland (i.e., studies of penal institutions and governability), and Ken Pease (i.e., his work on crime prevention), Ericson was among the top 50 scholars cited in three of the four journals surveyed.

The diversity of Ericson's subject matter was a consequence of both his personal curiosity and his explicit desire to avoid intellectual stagnation, something he did by re-inventing himself academically approximately every decade.

The Courts

As a junior faculty member at the University of Toronto, Richard oversaw a team of researchers examining the operation of Canada's criminal justice system. One book that emerged from this research was *The Ordering of Justice* (Ericson and Baranek 1982), a significant study of the day-to-day operations of criminal courts. Based on what Katherine Van Wormer characterizes as "painstakingly extensive research" (1982:1825), the book examines how the accused person moves through the criminal justice process. In conjunction with Ericson's policing books, *The Ordering of Justice* corrects the claim that the criminal justice system is skewed in advantage of defendants. The book provides a disturbing image in which "once the mold is set by law enforcement agents there are few resources available to the accused to shape his destiny within the criminal process" (Ericson and Baranek 1982:28). Defendants are actually "dependents," disadvantaged as "one shot" players who lack the all-important relationships and experience or "recipe knowledge" available to repeat players such as police, lawyers, and judges. Consequently, the role of the defendant is institutionally and interactionally structured towards passivity and cooperation. The defendant is subject to rules and processes designed to enable law enforcement personnel to control him or her; the large picture that emerges has Kafkaesque overtones of disempowered defendants moving through an alien and alienating process. In his review of the book Thornton (1983) described the approach as "unique," observing that while there have been numerous similar accounts of the criminal process from the lens of the various agents (police, lawyers, correctional officers, etc.), the defendant is the only one who "remains with a case from beginning to end" (p. 1269). Van Wormer concluded that the book sharply refutes the official image of the adversarial system, in the process revealing that the "emperor has no clothes" (1982:1827).

Policing

Ericson's early research at the University of Toronto also produced two books on the police. Here, individual associations of police officers are seen as a subset of policing more generally, understood as governmental efforts to control, develop, shape, and refine the population. *Reproducing Order* (1982) focuses on police patrol work, while *Making Crime* (1981) is a study of detectives. These works established Ericson as the "pre-eminent Canadian scholar" undertaking research on the police (Chappell 1984:219). And while these books detail differences between several forms of police work, the image that emerges from both studies is of policing as involving little of what might be called "crime work." Instead, police are called upon to deal with many different forms of disorder. They use rules—often creatively—to exert control over the production of knowledge; this becomes a process of transforming human complexity into a simple authoritative account on which other players in the criminal justice system ultimately depend. By using vague laws and their own low occupational visibility as enabling resources, officers transform troublesome situations into a normal and efficient state, in the process reproducing the existing social order.

A famous incident in the annals of policing research involves Ericson's own research. The Board of Commissioners of Police objected to how it was portrayed in *Making Crime*, particularly in areas of police discretion, "rule breaking," and other forms of deviance. The Board tried to halt the book's publication. With the support of the University of Toronto, and following extensive negotiations, the monograph was published accompanied by a fascinating—if at times confusing—12-page response by the Board of Commissioners of Police, as well as a reply by Ericson himself. In addition to this unusual exchange, *Making Crime* also included an extended section on the realities of police research; Ericson attributed the difficulties of conducting research to the fact that the presence of researchers threatened the police's control over producing authoritative accounts. The book remains not just a fascinating resource, but also a cautionary account for researchers studying any institution.

Ericson took an almost 20-year hiatus from police research, returning to it with *Policing the Risk Society*, with Kevin Haggerty (1997). This book employed a substantially different orientation than in his earlier volumes. *Policing the Risk Society* is one of the most cited monographs on police published in the past twenty-plus years. In a recent review of "classics in police research," Pat O'Malley (2015) characterizes it as a landmark study representing a "watershed" in policing scholarship. The book situates the police in the context of ascendant risk-based forms of governance. Here, the emphasis is on how the police, through their increasingly regimented, formatted, and controlled information work, serve the risk-management needs of a host of institutions external to police organizations. Using a qualitative methodology, Ericson and Haggerty trace the flows of police-generated information through and beyond the walls of the police organization, interviewing many key players throughout. Rather than being primarily agents of state-directed violence, the book demonstrates the remarkable amount of knowledge-work performed by the police: "The police are now deployed in a manner similar to social science researchers. They are equipped with extensive closed-ended systematic observation reports along with coding instructions. These communication formats serve the dual purpose of effecting certainty and closure in police work and providing the requisite knowledge of risk to external institutions" (Ericson and Haggerty 1997:429). The book also draws attention to a population that had typically been ignored in policing scholarship; the large cadre of mid-level police managers, whose role is dominated by structuring, processing, categorizing, and conveying risk-relevant knowledge.

The News Media

Following his initial studies on criminal justice institutions, Ericson produced three volumes on the news media (Ericson, Baranek, and Chan 1987, 1989,

1991), which Peter Manning (1990:785), describes as "exemplars of theoretically sensitive team research." These three volumes are some of the most important and most-cited ethnographies of news production. The three books are set against the larger backdrop of a theory of the knowledge society, wherein power-knowledge represents the key dimension of hierarchy. The three books were based on ethnographies of six major urban print and broadcast news organizations, as well as qualitative and quantitative analysis of their content. The research included extended direct observation of the news-making process. It also involved interviews with news personnel at various organizational levels as well as with 93 key news sources in four institutional arenas: the police, courts, legislature, and private sector. One of the key contributions of these books involved the author's ability to shift the focus from researching media influence on individual audience members to understanding media influence on institutional audiences like the police or government.

The first book in the trilogy, *Visualizing Deviance* (1987), broadened our understanding of crime in the media by arguing that the primary element of news is the social construction of deviance (broadly defined) and control. This is particularly true in respect of deviance from procedural propriety, although it also includes deviance from "common sense." Journalists are vital workers in a knowledge society, helping to transform specialized bureaucratic knowledge into so-called common sense. Yet their legitimacy often depends on that of the powerful "authorized knowers" whom they quote. Journalists "visualize" events for audiences in ways that are inherently political, drawing upon implicit understandings of social order. Journalism offers a closed circle in which reporters often draw on other outlets for information, but they do not overtly criticize or question the claims made by other news organizations. However, while other accounts portray the media as monolithic, in fact conflict within news organizations over what stories to cover (and how to cover them) is also rife. This conflict involves not only with interpersonal biases and sharing of resources, but also disagreements grounded in ideological differences.

Their second media book, *Negotiating Control* (1989), explores the role of official news sources in journalism, in particular how the media's complex interconnections with other institutions involve an ongoing dialectical struggle of power and knowledge. Peter Manning's (1990:786) review of the book characterizes it as "a model of ethnographic work carefully located in relevant social structures and a major contribution to the literature of deviance and control and media studies." The book explores the politics of this knowledge through an analysis of both enclosure and disclosure in front and back-regions of these institutions. The detailed ethnographies allow a much more nuanced account of the relationship between source and journalists. The relationship defined in *Negotiating Control* was so detailed that it replaced the previous model of "primary definers" described in Hall et al. (1978). For example, "inner circle" police reporters tend to be close to police sources and reflect police ideology to a large extent as being self-censoring in order to maintain close ties with police sources. In the outer circle, there is a much less cozy relationship with the police, and much more emphasis on police and organizational deviance.

The final book in the media trilogy, *Representing Order* (1991), contains rich data on how news of crime, law, and justice varies by media and market, focusing on the quantitative and qualitative study of media content, both longitudinally and cross-sectionally. This varies considerably, for example, in choice of topics or type and number of sources used, and in degree of personalization, by market (quality, popular) and by medium (i.e., television, newspapers, radio). Yet, as the authors demonstrate, accounts of crime and deviance dominate all news media with items about crime, law, and justice making up roughly one half of all the news. Considering the question of "balance," all outlets tend to provide only one side in the majority of stories. "Journalists and their sources are too concerned about making moral judgments, and effecting social control on the basis of those judgments, to avoid taking sides" (Ericson et al. 1991:179). Another important common facet across all media outlets is that deviance is almost always individualized and personalized, with structural causal explanations of deviance given almost no play.

Insurance

Following *Policing the Risk Society*, Ericson's focus turned to insurance, an institution of comparable scope and importance to the criminal justice system and the news media, but one much less in the public and academic spotlights. It is a topic that is much less "sexy" in academic terms; it had never been the subject of such a research project. Ericson's two books, *Insurance as Governance* (Ericson, Doyle, and Barry 2003) and *Uncertain Business* (Ericson and Doyle 2004), provide a painstakingly detailed analysis of insurance as a vital institution of modern governance. Ericson and his collaborators demonstrate that insurance has long been overlooked as a key institution of governance, and that private insurance becomes particularly prominent as the state progressively withdraws from direct service provision. Again, these developments are set in the context of a "risk society," composed of intersecting institutions that organize in relation to the production and distribution of knowledge of risk. Given the hidden importance of insurance, there has in fact long been a "risk society"; today the influence of insurance organizations is particularly profound and multifaceted. Insurers involve themselves in governance through producing knowledge about risks and making such risks calculable, using actuarialism to create risk pools, binding populations together legally, protecting against loss of capital, managing risks through surveillance, and serving as a social technology of justice. Jonathan Simon concluded that *Insurance as Governance* "is one of the most original and far-reaching works of sociological research that I have ever read. Ericson, Doyle, and Barry present enough new findings to fill a small subfield, and produce our most compelling analysis to date of how the tactics and strategies of insurers help govern our risk society."

While the façade of actuarial science provides insurance with a scientific public face, the second major insurance study, *Uncertain Business*, reveals the limits of such knowledge, even in a context that is ostensibly all about rational calculation. While much previous scholarship on risk emphasized the modern capacity to assess and calculate risk, this study by contrast revealed how elusive and illusory it is. Companies insure many things for which they do not have good knowledge of risk, as *Uncertain Business* demonstrates with studies of life, disability, earthquakes, and terrorism insurance. In the absence of such knowledge, insurers move away from governance through risk and towards governance in conditions of uncertainty. While this presents difficulties for insurers, it also provides a context for ingenious solutions about how to proceed in a context of imperfect knowledge. The book demonstrates this by showing how each kind of risk entailed its own logic of governance. These books helped to bring the study of insurance to a wider sociological audience. Scholar Tom Baker wrote: "No serious scholar writing empirically about insurance or government beyond the state will be able to ignore this book.... Indeed, it is the most important recent book in the field."

A Final Word

One of Ericson's final books, *Crime in an Insecure World* (2007), provides an excellent entry into his larger oeuvre. This book is a departure from his usual approach; it is not based on new empirical research, but rather features a more overt sense of moral urgency and a deliberate attempt to reach out to a broader audience. *Crime in an Insecure World* offers an extensive narrative crosscutting institutions and nation states (especially the UK, the U.S., and Canada), tracing the history of liberalism and of risk and uncertainty. Here, Ericson argues that the problem of uncertainty has now replaced the problem of order and is central to neo-liberal governance. Criminalization has become the leading response to such uncertainty, something that becomes mobilized through what Richard calls "counter-law" (see Box 12.2). He examines this process across the realms of national, social, corporate, and domestic security. This short book is a kind of short capstone statement that draws upon a lifetime of research and thinking.

Richard as Colleague and Mentor

Ericson was known among friends as a person of great human compassion, as

Box 12.2. Counter Law

As a society, we are increasingly uncertain of our ability to produce accurate, actionable knowledge about the many interpersonal, social, and environmental risks that we face. At the same time, we are also losing faith in our ability to effectively govern such risks. In such a situation, a form of precautionary thinking has emerged, characterized by two types of counter-law. These counter-laws aim to introduce greater certainty in the process of governing by eroding or bypassing longstanding legal practices and protections:

1. *Law against laws* refers to a proliferating number of rules that elide or reduce due process and criminal law provision, themselves seen as too cumbersome or producing unpredictable outcomes. For this reason, they may "get in the way" of pre-empting imagined sources of harm. Law against laws eases due process protections and facilitates easier processing of risks, often through streamlined process of arrest and conviction. The result is a constant "state of exception," as rules are developed to avoid or provide exceptions to existing rules. Examples include using local bylaws to manage homeless or transient populations, using the lower legal thresholds characteristic of immigration laws to target criminals, mandatory sentencing provisions (here we recall the "three strikes" laws), and the development of strict liability laws that eliminate the need to prove criminal intent.

2. *Surveillant assemblages* refers to the escalation in monitoring of individuals and organizations; such monitoring becomes a de facto alternative form of regulation and punishment. This includes the focused surveillance of particular individuals (through such things as surveillance cameras), but also increasingly involves monitoring large population groups through aggregate statistical measure (now often referred to as "big data" or "dataveillance"). All such monitoring allows for the prospect of repressive forms of social control, but also aims to enhance the security and prosperity of certain populations. For example, organizations use surveillance in the first instance to distinguish what individuals belong (as employees, customers, clients, etc.) from those who will be excluded. Those individuals who are included within the organization's remit undergo an ongoing second order of surveillance designed to ensure that they can maintain their membership, and to determine the level of services they are to receive. In the name of "accountability," however, these organizations are themselves increasingly subject to surveillance through audits, inspections, accountability provision, and the unrelenting proliferation of assorted metrics.

well a possessor of a sharp sense of humor. David Garland observed that "For someone who was so accomplished and successful, he was surprisingly modest and self-deprecating. He told stories against himself. He refrained from name-dropping. He made no effort to impress. He seemed very secure and never the least bit pompous or self-important" (2007:xi).

Ericson's sense of irony often focused on paradoxes in official knowledge and behaviour, and on the hypocrisy of official accounts. He searched for moments of irony as sociologically revealing. He also loved language, and used word play to illustrate such ironies: for example, "accountability" became instead "account ability" (Ericson 1995), meaning the ability of institutions, when called to account, to produce self-serving official narratives and to have them accepted by others as legitimate. Publishers and others on occasion saw "account ability" as a typo rather than a sly shift and insisted on reconnecting the two words.

Ericson was also an excellent mentor to generations of graduate students, incorporating them into a litany of large empirical research projects. He excelled at using the first-hand involvement of his doctoral students in his empirical research as a teaching opportunity while simultaneously serving as a model of scholarly integrity. Richard Sparks' memories of Ericson include many instances of thinking "so that's how it should be done" and "that's what supervision is ..." (in Garland 2007:xiii). Those of us who were Ericson's students all benefitted enormously from his formal mentoring, and undoubtedly even more from the myriad impromptu lessons that he offered. The book *57 Ways to Screw Up in Grad School* (Haggerty and Doyle 2015) is dedicated to Ericson as it was he who originally showed us the nuances of how to navigate our way through graduate school. It was only after his death, however, that we learned about the full extent of his generosity towards his students, which included a series of "above and beyond" initiatives, such as putting up a student in a hotel after he found himself temporarily homeless, and paying for meals to be delivered three times a day to a student who was recovering from cancer treatments.

On occasion Ericson joked while patting one of his voluminous books, in reference to what he called the "weight of the evidence." Students were constantly impressed by Richard's encyclopedic knowledge of criminological and social theoretical literatures as well as a vast range of other works. We were also amazed by the meticulous way he kept notes of his readings and his analysis of qualitative data. He had a set of filing cabinets filled with transcripts, institutional documents and photocopied academic articles, along with his large library. All of this was organized on thousands of index cards that dated back at least to the early 1970s. Without the benefit of search engines, Richard would retrieve every quote or note he had ever recorded from his readings. He often lent us his books; on every page was an underlined phrase, as well as notes, observations, and responses. So the "weight of the evidence" was not just in the printed pages, but in Ericson's overall approach to scholarship.

We recall the meticulous attention and sharp ethnographic eye Richard brought to the quotidian, to what others might find mundane and not worthy of remark: interviewing a police bureaucrat about changes in official forms, or observing how an insurance adjuster examined a damaged car and then negotiated the claim. When he was unable to accompany students on interviews or field research due to his numerous other academic and administrative responsibilities, he was nonetheless eager for an account immediately following our fieldwork experiences, asking if there were "any nuggets" or "any gems."

Other important works of scholarship not mentioned here include Ericson's observations on the disciplines of criminology and sociology (see Ericson and Carriere 1994, Ericson 2003, 2006) and his influential theoretical work on surveillance (Haggerty and Ericson 2000; 2006). Ericson's authored or co-authored books alone total more than 3,500 published pages, an astounding quantity of scholarship that remains relevant to this day.

References

Not Attributed to Ericson

Challell, D. (1984) "Review of *Reproducing Order: A Study of Police Patrol Work.*" *Canadian Journal of Sociology* 9(2): 219–222

Cohn, E. G., and D.P. Farrington (2007). "Changes in Scholarly Influence in Major International Criminology Journals." *The Australian and New Zealand Journal of Criminology* 40(3): 335–359.

Garland, D. (2007). "Richard Ericson: An Appreciation." *Canadian Journal of Sociology* 32(4): xi–xviii.

Haggerty, K. D., and A. Doyle. (2015). *57 Ways to Screw Up in Grad School: Perverse Professional Lessons for Graduate Students.* Chicago: University of Chicago Press.

Haggerty, K.D., A. Doyle, and J. Chan (eds.) (2011). *Crime, Institutional Knowledge and Power: The Rich Criminological Legacy of Richard Ericson.* Surrey: Ashgate.

Hall, S., C. Critcher, T. Jefferson, J. Clarke, and B. Roberts. (1978). *Policing the Crisis.* London: Macmillan.

Manning, P. (1990). "Review of *Negotiating Control: A Study of News Sources.*" *American Journal of Sociology* 96(3): 784–786

O'Malley, P. (2015). "Revisiting the Classics: 'Policing the Risk Society' in the Twenty-First Century." *Policing and Society* 25(4): 426–431.

Thornton, W.E. (1983). "Review of *The Ordering of Justice.*" *Social Forces* 61(4): 1269–1271.

Van Wormer, K. (1982). "Review of *The Ordering of Justice.*" *Journal of Criminal Law and Criminology* 73(4): 1825–1827.

Wood, D. (2002). "Foucault and Panopticism Revisited." *Surveillance and Society* 1(3): 234–239.

Selection of Richard V. Ericson's Scholarly Works

Ericson, Richard V. (1981). *Making Crime: A Study of Detective Work.* Toronto: Butterworths.

Ericson, Richard V. (1982). *Reproducing Order: A Study of Police Patrol Work.* Toronto: University of Toronto Press.

Ericson, Richard V. (2003). "The Culture and Power of Criminological Research." In *The Criminological Foundations of Penal Policy: Essays in Honour of Roger Hood*, edited by Lucia Zedner and Andrew Ashworth, 31–78. London: Oxford University Press.

Ericson, Richard V. (1995). "The News Media and Account Ability in Criminal Justice." *Accountability for Criminal Justice: Selected Essays* edited by Philip C. Stenning, 135–161. Toronto: University of Toronto Press.

Ericson, Richard V. (2006). "Publicizing Sociology." *British Journal of Sociology* 56(3): 365–372.

Ericson, Richard V. (2007). *Crime in an Insecure World.* Cambridge: Polity.

Ericson, Richard V., and Patricia Baranek. (1982). *The Ordering of Justice: A Study of Accused Persons as Dependents in the Criminal Process.* Toronto: University of Toronto Press.

Ericson, Richard V., Patricia Baranek, and Janet Chan. (1987). *Visualizing Deviance: A Study of News Organization.* Milton Keynes: Open University Press.

Ericson, Richard V., Patricia Baranek, and Janet Chan. (1989). *Negotiating Control: A*

Study of News Sources. Milton Keynes: Open University Press.

Ericson, Richard V., Patricia Baranek, and Janet Chan. (1991). *Representing Order: Crime, Law, and Justice in the News Media*. Toronto: University of Toronto Press.

Ericson, Richard V., and Kevin Carriere. (1994). "The Fragmentation of Criminology." *The Futures of Criminology*, edited by David Nelken, 89–110. London: Sage.

Ericson, Richard V., and Aaron Doyle. (1999). "Globalization and the Policing of Protest: The Case of APEC 1997." *The British Journal of Sociology* 50(4):589–608.

Ericson, Richard V., and Aaron Doyle. (2004). *Uncertain Business: Risk, Insurance, and the Limits of Knowledge*. Toronto: University of Toronto Press.

Ericson, Richard V., Aaron Doyle, and Dean Barry. (2002). *Insurance as Governance*. Toronto: University of Toronto Press.

Ericson, Richard V., and Kevin D. Haggerty. (1997). *Policing the Risk Society*. Toronto: University of Toronto Press, and Oxford: Oxford University Press.

Haggerty, Kevin D., and Richard V. Ericson. (2000). "The Surveillant Assemblage." *British Journal of Sociology* 51(4): 605–622.

Ericson, Richard V., and Clifford Shearing. (1986). "The Scientification of Police Work." *The Knowledge Society*, edited by G. Böhme and Nico Stehr, 129–159. Dordrecht and Boston: Reidel.

Ericson, Richard V., and Clifford D. Shearing. (1991). "Introduction: An Institutional Approach to Criminology." *Criminology: A Reader's Guide*, edited by Jane Gladstone, Richard Ericson and Clifford Shearing, pp. 3–19. Toronto: Centre of Criminology.

Haggerty, Kevin D., and Richard V. Ericson (eds.) (2006). *The New Politics of Surveillance and Visibility* Toronto: University of Toronto Press.

THIRTEEN

Irvin Waller: Harnessing Criminological Data to Stop Violent Crime, Implement Victim Rights and Reduce Incarceration across the World

Irvin Waller

This is your world. Shape it or someone else will.

My Introduction to Criminology as a Solution to Problems

It was my father's passion for justice that started me towards criminology as a solution to injustice. I was born in 1944—just prior to the end of World War II—while my father was still finishing tours of duty as a pilot. I was brought up in Newcastle upon Tyne, on the north-east coast of England. My father was a barrister and later a judge, who believed deeply in justice and, in particular, the fairness of the British system of criminal justice.

At the age of 17, I left my protected family and school environment to spend six months on a British freighter in the Pacific Ocean in order to see the world. It was during this period that my life was transformed by a brutal attack on me. I was attacked by an apprentice/trainee on the ship; this person's attack, I realized later, had all the characteristics of someone disposed to violence. He had experienced much violence as a child and used violence as the way to get what he wanted with women, other sailors and unfortunate cats who got on board the freighter. He was a callous bully and his jealousy of my privileged background got the better of him. I was saved by other apprentices but not before I had endured a near-death experience. Tragically, a few weeks later another of my fellow apprentices was murdered by this apprentice, who sat opposite us at meals.

Little did I realize at the time that these experiences would play a role in the career path I have followed. I would realize only decades later that I knew what it was like to be a victim of extreme violence. Intellectually I wanted to understand these events. I wanted to find solutions. I did not want punishment for the perpetrators.

I entered Cambridge University as a student and a chance meeting there introduced me to a group of fellow undergraduates who were prison visitors. I joined them on their visits and began by visiting a uniquely British prison, Hollesley Bay. The prison was established to rehabilitate young men from British slums through mentoring and fresh air on farms. It was an opportunity to get to know some of their life experiences and to understand something about what it meant to be sentenced to this three-year indeterminate sentence, served in the country side. I learned later on that it was the largest prison farm in the British prison system. It was also made famous by the autobiographical book *Borstal Boy* by Brendan Behan (1971).

I completed my first degree, a bachelor's in mathematics and economics, in 1965.

I spent the summer of 1965 as a marshal to a high court judge, an experience that introduced me to real cases of horrible crimes, and the realities of the sentencing process as an arbitrary and ineffective reaction to violence.

Getting Educated to Use Empirical Data to Influence Policy

The Cambridge diploma in criminology and the Institute of Criminology were the invention of **Sir Leon Radzinowicz** (1906–1999), a Polish immigrant to England who had degrees from universities across Europe. While at the Institute of Criminology in Rome, he studied under the esteemed Italian criminologist Enrico Ferri, who had been a student of Cesare Lombroso. Radzinowicz was the quintessential internationalist and believer in evidence, both strong influences on my life. He happened to be in England when Hitler invaded Poland in 1939 and so stayed. He spent time after the war looking at criminology across Europe before founding the now world-famous Institute of Criminology from where many renowned criminologists have influenced criminology internationally. Radzinowicz became a very successful even if unlikely member of the British elite. By 1959 he was a professor in the Law Faculty at Cambridge, and in 1970 he was knighted by Queen Elizabeth II.

For Radzinowicz, criminology was about influencing public policy by being pragmatic and carrying out empirical research to collect criminological data. His personal role was more about using criminological data to influence policy than producing the data, but he brought together a dream team of criminological empirical researchers who produced an impressive library of monographs. These included the likes of Roger Hood, Derek McClintock, and Donald West. Each would publish multiple monographs on path-setting criminological studies.

Professor Radzinowicz wanted to educate and train criminologists who would become researchers and practitioners in order to care better for offenders and transform policy to be more humanitarian, logical, and effective.

The Radzinowicz diploma was tailor-made so that if he thought you needed three lectures on how to interview female prisoners, then you got the best person in the world to deliver those three lectures. If you needed 12 lectures on criminological data on juvenile delinquency, then you got 12 lectures from the best person in the world on that. You could not call yourself a Radzinowicz criminologist without actually tasting the real world. The students had various types of one-week placements with the police, in prisons and so on. The courses we took combined with these practical experiences should be compulsory for anyone teaching or practicing criminology.

I firmly believe that if only criminology were taught in a similar manner today, criminologists would be more motivated to change the world and less inclined to pursue careers without measurable impact on the real world of harm to victims, policing that too often accepts over-expenditure and violations of rights, and incarceration conditions that have shown little improvement for prisoners and even less for rehabilitation.

The teachers included the Institute staff, but Radzinowicz was able to attract the best from across Britain and the world to teach their favorite subject in the way that was needed. He attracted top criminologists from the United States who were looking for a location for a sabbatical. For example, Marvin Wolfgang was just one of those prominent American criminologists who spent time teaching at Cambridge during the era of Radzinowicz. But many of the lecturers were persons working in the system, such as police officers, judges and prison administrators. My father taught the sentencing course for a time, while also being on advisory groups for the reform of criminal justice.

I received the diploma in criminology from the Law School, University of Cambridge, in 1966.

Empirical Research to Provide Evidence for Policy Reform, 1966-1974

I was recruited from Cambridge in 1966 to join **John Edwards**[23] at the new Centre of Criminology at the University of Toronto.

I became the principal investigator on the component that followed the data on, and experiences of, 423 men incarcerated in federal prisons in Ontario during the final weeks of their incarceration and the first three years following their release. This became my Ph.D. thesis and the second book in English on criminology in Canada, *Men Released from Prison*. In 1973, I was awarded my

[23] For an overview on the history of the Centre for Criminology and Sociological Studies at the University of Toronto and the influence of John Edwards see http://criminology.utoronto.ca/about-us-2/history/.

Ph.D., Criminology (Law), University of Cambridge, Cambridge.

The book was about outcomes in terms of reduction of recidivism. It

Box 13.1. Commissions and Task Forces on which Waller Served

Hugessen Task Force on Release of Inmates, 1972 (member). One of four members of the task force that reviewed, for the Solicitor-General of Canada, the status of sentencing, parole decision-making, and parole effectiveness. It recommended specifics for better data to guide, evaluate, and justify parole, some of which are still waiting for action. It used evidence and human rights principles to make several significant recommendations, which have sustained parole until today. They were implemented in the 1970s to protect rights of parole applicants and include members of the parole board from a broad set of experiences to encourage greater support and greater coordination with courts.

Quebec Task Force on Crime Prevention, 1994 (member of executive committee). The task force brought together a broad spectrum of leaders in policing, judiciary, corrections, municipalities, and the nongovernmental sector across the province of Quebec. It reached a consensus that Quebec should have a national crime prevention council and centre and invest in effective prevention strategies, particularly at the municipal level. Some of this has materialized at the municipal government level in Montreal and Quebec City.

National Criminal Justice Commission, U.S., 1994 (member and one of three non-US citizens). The commission was established in 1994 by the National Center on Institutions and Alternatives to examine criminal justice policy in the United States and recommend ways in which that policy can make the country safer. Commission members included leading citizens, criminal justice specialists, community leaders, national and international scholars, professors, and authors. The project provided a "comprehensive assessment of crime policy in America and offered solutions to violence prevention, victim care and mass incarceration." Its collective report was *The Real War on Crime*.

White Paper Task Force on Community Safety, South Africa, 1996 (member). I was recruited by the South African Minister of Safety and Security to join a task force of leading South Africans to propose evidence-based ways to reduce the high rates of violence faced by the Mandela government. The recommendations included establishing a crime prevention board and investing at the local/community level in crime prevention initiatives. As of 2016, South Africa was still implementing some of these recommendations but the transition remains slow and so violence remains an endemic problem.

Policy Paper for UK Government on Less Crime, Less Costs, 2009 (co-author). This paper proposes evidence-based ways for the UK to reduce crime while reducing costs. "Policy Exchange" is a think tank that prepared a vision for the Conservative Party in opposition. It was written in collaboration with Max Chambers and Ben Ullmann under the leadership of Gavin Lockhart. The report was discussed with a number of key politicians who would later become cabinet members.

Opportunities for Open Society Institute to Promote Violence Prevention and Reparative Justice, 2008 (principal author). The Open Society Institute asked for reasoned proposals as to how they could use foundation money and skills to promote violence prevention in the United States, Latin America, and elsewhere. The report was prepared collaboratively with OSI, discussed for a full day with the Deputy Head of the OSI and led to some funding going into violence prevention and homicide reduction in Latin America.

Policing Canada in the 21st Century: New Policing for New Challenges, 2014 (member). The Council of Canadian Academies brought together leading academics from Canada and abroad to review the evidence on policing and its future. The report provided a new vision for policing, including that police are just one player in a multi-sectoral strategy to reduce crime and that there was little evidence that increased expenditures on policing were a significant contributor to reductions in crime.

Expert Advisory Groups, 2013– (member). Some progressive initiatives have established expert advisory groups. In Saskatchewan, Deputy Minister McFee established an expert advisory group the provincial program to Build Partnerships to Reduce Crime (see http://saskbprc.com/), which seeks advice on its innovative best practices and evidence. In addition, the RCMP has a Federal Witness Protection Program that seeks advice through an Advisory Committee appointed by the Commissioner of the RCMP.

showed that the prison system not only failed to achieve these outcomes, but it was too late to make any major differences given that these men arrived at the prison gates with so many negative life experiences that it would have taken a miracle to change their life course significantly. The study led to multiple journal articles and chapters and even headlines in the major national newspapers. It did not, however, lead to the policy reform for which I had hoped in carrying out the study.

The study also introduced me to some of the most dedicated reformers of my time, not just in Canada but in the world. These include **Frank Miller** (1927–2000), the father of parole in Canada; **John Braithwaite**, the deputy head of the Corrections Service of Canada and the head of the U.S. Correctional Association; and **Bill Outerbridge** (1926–2012), who pioneered the international prisoner exchanges and was chair of the Parole Board. These were quintessential Canadians committed to real outcomes for real people because they cared about those people, but somehow frustrated by politicians and public servants committed too much to the survival of organizations and not enough to people or outcomes.

My involvement in the study also started me on one of many governmental commissions that allowed me to influence public policy using criminological data (see Box 13.1). I was appointed to the Hugessen Committee in 1973, designed to reorganize parole in Canada. This led to my appointment as the first Director General of Research and Statistics for what is now Public Safety Canada (see Box 13.2). Justice Hugessen was a remarkable individual who also had those quintessential Canadian qualities of caring and wanting to make Canada the best in the world. The Hugessen Committee transformed parole in Canada from its original roots in the Parole Act of 1959 into a system that provided some human rights protections for the applicant and some broader involvement of different perspectives, such as victims on the board itself to provide greater public support.

In early 1970, John Hogarth—whom I admired—received national publicity for comparing the rate at which inmates were *admitted* to prisons in Canada with the rate for the number of persons incarcerated on an *average day* in other countries. There are many more admissions than persons incarcerated on an average day. This made Canada look wrongly much more punitive than these other countries. I was astonished at both the lack of quantitative research skills of John Hogarth and the incompetence and gullibility of the journalists who were so quick to believe that Canada was more punitive than the United States—only a cursory glance would have shown this not to be true. It was also astonishing to see the impact of these miscalculated statistics on political debate at the time, fortunately discouraging U.S. punitiveness to come to Canada.

I undertook a careful study to show how to compare rates of incarceration between different countries. Academically, this became a bestseller; it was adopted as the leading textbook in the United States and the new Ministry of

> **Box 13.2. Organizations to Influence Policy Spearheaded by Waller**
>
> **First Director General, Research Division of Solicitor-General of Canada (now Public Safety).** As Director General, I was responsible for the establishment of the research division as well as the files for the abolition of the death penalty, the gun safety program, dangerous offender legislation, and research-based policy for the Solicitor-General of Canada. The Solicitor-General was the federal ministry responsible for reform of Canadian criminal justice policy as well as the RCMP, Corrections Service of Canada and the National Parole Board. I pioneered funding for policy relevant criminological research, including at the Universities of Montreal, Simon Fraser and Toronto. These actions shifted Canada to a more evidence based and compassionate policy on crime as well as investing in research that would be used to educate Canadians about crime and punishment.
>
> **First Director General, International Centre for the Prevention of Crime Canada, 1974.** As Director General, I was responsible for establishing the ICPC, convincing leading national crime prevention organizations to join its board and expand the funding for its activities. The ICPC was a clearing house for evidence and best practices in the prevention of crime across the world. It was also a hub for the development of national and local policies between governments and leading nongovernmental organizations from every continent. By 2000, it had recurring financial and substantive support from Belgium, Canada, France, the Netherlands, Quebec, South Africa, United Kingdom, and the United States. It worked in English, French and Spanish. It has influenced North American, European, Latin American and other countries efforts to prevent crime, particularly through urban policies. It influenced the resolutions on crime prevention from the 1995 and 2000 UN Congresses on Crime Prevention and Criminal Justice as well as the development of the Safer Cities Program for UN-Habitat.
>
> **Joint Author of Safer Cities Program of UN-Habitat, 1996.** The Safer Cities program is a UN Habitat program to reduce violence in cities across the world. It was based on the principles, such as those in the UN ECOSOC Guidelines for Urban Safety as well as the multi-sectoral approach at the municipal level that tackled problems of youth violence and violence against women. I wrote most of the substantive parts of the proposal and collaborated with the successful efforts to get initial funding from the Dutch Foreign Ministry. The first programs were launched in Johannesburg and in Dar-es-Salaam where it quickly spread across Tanzania. The program has spread throughout Africa and is being considered on other continents.
>
> **Founding Director, Institute for the Prevention of Crime, University of Ottawa, 2006.** The Institute was set up to harness effective preventive strategies in Canada. With significant initial funding, my colleague Ross Hastings and I developed a journal on crime prevention, proposals for a Canadian national strategy, and the national municipal network for crime prevention. We advised and prepared reports for several provinces on effective crime prevention strategies, of which the most exciting was the Alberta strategy that coordinated the spending of $1 billion over six years on both enforcement and prevention. The Canadian Municipal Network for Crime Prevention (renamed from the National Municipal Network) has recently received three year funding to foster greater capacity for Canadian municipalities to harness evidence based crime prevention among the 15 cities who are current members and 15 new cities planned to join.

the Solicitor-General translated it into French. No surprise, however, that the media were not interested in the real numbers—just the mistaken calculation that created the myth that Canada was more punitive than the United States. Canada has a penchant for accepting gross distortions that show itself in a bad light.

However, it is my way of measuring incarceration rates that has become the international standard used by the International Centre for Prison Studies.

This measure is regularly quoted to show the U.S. with incarceration rates that grew from double ours at 200 per 100,000 to 700 per 100,000. During this time, ours has hardly changed.

John Edwards also hosted leading personalities from criminology research institutes in North America, where I met **Denis Szabo**. I had three things in common with him: I spoke some French when he was still having difficulty with his English; I came from England but had spent time in Belgium and France and so was an internationalist; and his Ph.D. Supervisor was the father of my first wife. As a result, I would get regular invitations to Montreal and was inspired by Denis Szabo's world vision. In 1971, I spent three months in the Ivory Coast as one of Szabo's criminological emissaries. This opened my eyes to West Africa and the world as well as the potential for criminology to make a real-world difference.

In 1972, I was required to apply for new research funds to pay for my salary. *Men Released from Prison* showed the limits of corrections. So I shifted my research program to focus on why men are put in prison and whether there were more effective ways of meeting those needs. I received a significant grant (about $1.3 million over 2 years in 2016 dollars) from the Canada Council (now SSHRC) to develop a questionnaire and do a survey of the public (including victims) focused on residential burglary as well as examining the geographic distribution and census data correlates of 5000 police recorded burglaries in Toronto. My next book was *Burglary, the Victim and the Public* (1978), the third book in English on criminology in Canada.

This pioneering research on the needs of crime victims and their protection confirmed that burglary was largely preventable. The research also showed that victims had needs, most of which were not for punishment of offenders. It led to a model way to undertake victimization surveys and methods for assessing gaps in services for victims and prevent victimization. Most of the methodology was later adopted by the British Home Office for their Crime Survey. Not so in Canada.

During my time, we started a graduate course in criminology that brought together experts from different departments at the university—a modest version of the Cambridge Diploma in Criminology. We wanted our graduates to experience the system as well. I was its graduate secretary and we achieved some of the flavor of Cambridge.

Before I left the University of Toronto, I attained a tenure track position as an associate professor in the Law School in 1973. My role was to introduce law students to the realities of the human processes of crime, policing and corrections. I had already taught a joint course with one of Canada's foremost criminal law professors, Alan Mewett, but I would move onto Ottawa before I taught classes on my own.

Working in Government to Harness Evidence for Policy Reform, 1974-1980

I was the founding Director General of the Research Division (later the Research and Statistics Division) of what is now Public Safety Canada during the Pierre Elliot Trudeau years (1969–1979; 1980–1984). We began to use criminological data to support the political efforts to abolish the death penalty, control firearms, and stop femicides. We obtained significant funds for the ministry to provide better evidence to guide policy. However, given political priorities, only some of the funds were used to invest in evidence-based policies to reduce crime and violence in Canada.

We also innovated a publication called *Selected Trends* on crime and justice, designed for politicians to access data on crime and criminal justice for Canada as well as conclusions from criminological research data from Canada and elsewhere. We prepared video versions to present the data. These initiatives

Box 13.3. UN GA and ECOSOC Resolutions and Actions to Change World Crime Prevention and Criminal Justice Policy Influenced by Waller

Much of this advocacy was undertaken through my leading role in the World Society of Victimology and the International Organization for Victim Assistance, both of which organizations held special consultative status with the UN. I continue to be involved in advisory and collaborative work with the World Health Organization's Violence Prevention Alliance and the Safer Cites Program of UN-Habitat.

1985: UNGA resolution to adopt the Declaration on Basic Principles of Justice for Victims of Crime and Abuse of Power (pioneered);
1996: ECOSOC acceptance of Urban Crime Prevention Guidelines (fostered);
2002: ECOSOC acceptance of Crime Prevention Guidelines (fostered);
2005: ECOSOC acceptance of the Guidelines on Justice in Matters involving Child Victims and Witnesses of Crime (mentored);
1985: UNODC Planned governmental workshops and lobbied UN Congresses on Crime Prevention and Criminal Justice) in Milan (1985), Havana (1990), Cairo (1995), Vienna (2000), Bangkok (2005), San Salvador (2010), Doha (2015).

later inspired other documents such as the *British Home Office Digest* and the *ICPC Digest* that in turn influenced policy across the Western world.

These initiatives set Canada on a paradigm shift to positive results (less violence), consistent with humane values (no death penalty, less incarceration), and so less waste of lives and taxes—all influenced by criminological evidence. These illustrate not only that criminology can contribute to a better world, but also the importance of empirical criminological data to that influence and the vital role that criminologists must play.

All our work for the Trudeau government was about evidence and results, helping Canada to become a model for other Western nations. The British government came to look at our system of using criminological data generated to foster innovations in preventive policing, diversion, and prevention generated by a companion branch with funds for innovation. The Dutch government set up an exchange with us so that they could learn and use our vision of research and innovation.

During my time with the Solicitor-General, I was the lead for Canada in negotiating our position as an observer with the Council of Europe's Group on Crime Problems. I regularly travelled to Strasbourg and was impressed by the thinking of some key bureaucrats from European countries such as **Louk Hulsman** (1923–2009), a Dutch legal scientist and criminologist, who became a hero for young Canadian theorists on prison abolitionism, and **Ole Ingstrup** who twice (1988–92; 1996–2000) became head of the Correctional Service of Canada. It was the broad range of contacts from across Europe that would turn out to help me in my international career, particularly influencing change through intergovernmental organizations such as the United Nations (see Box 13.3).

At the third International Symposium for Victimology in Munster, Germany in 1979, I was elected to the founding executive of the World Society of Victimology, and subsequently served for five consecutive six-year terms. I served as president, three times as secretary general, and co-organized with **Arlène Gaudreault** (see Chapter 15) of Plaidoyer-Victimes the Montreal Symposium in 2000, which was attended by over one thousand delegates from more than 60 countries.

In 1979, I was invited to be the visiting professor in the Department of Criminal Justice at the State University of New York (SUNY) in Albany, where I met many fine scholars including Leslie Wilkins, Michael J. Hindelang, Rita Warren, and Lawrence Sherman. SUNY had an impressive compulsory graduate course on planned change. This course focused on how you can influence policy and programs. It stressed the importance of the appointments made by politicians to be the heads of agencies, legislation and funding, data and evidence, and emotional influences such as movies or the news. Auditing the course taught me why monographs, however intelligent, do not change the world on their own. I realized that my role in Public Safety Canada had been influential because I had access to those political decision-makers. It also gave me the logic to see what I had to do next as I left government. Every criminology student should take a compulsory course like this to shape the world.

Working in Canada Internationally for Policy Reform, 1980 to 1992

In 1980 I moved to the University of Ottawa because I wanted to stay near my children from my first marriage, which was breaking up. I became an associate professor and in 1982 I was promoted to full professor. The quick promotion was based on the fact that I already had brought in significant research funds, published two seminal monograph books, had been a senior bureaucrat using evidence to influence a major paradigm shift, and could teach graduate classes in both English and French.

I was also lucky enough to meet my new life partner, Susan Tanner, who is a strong and very successful advocate for women and the environment, trained in both law and planned change. She has encouraged my commitment to working with the decision-makers who create change and not assuming that rational arguments on their own change anything.

As I look back, it was a positive time to move as the department at the University of Ottawa was committed to producing graduate students who cared about people, could help offenders and victims, and were committed to policy reform and acting on it. It was also an environment where the rector wanted to make a difference. So, the tone of the university was very much to support my national and international ambitions to make a difference.

From 1980 to 1985, I was involved in pioneering and advocating for the victim Magna Carta adopted in 1985 by the UN General Assembly. This was a venture that started small but caught fire rapidly and was the first and most important of my actions to influence crime policy across the world (see Box 13.4). I was inspired in a major way by Marlene Young, executive director of the U.S. National Organization for Victim Assistance (NOVA). I was elected to the board of NOVA from 1980 to 1986. It was here that I met Leroy Lamborn, a U.S. professor of law, with whom I enjoyed working closely over several years. His special skill was finding the wording of the UN General Assembly resolution on victims.

Box 13.4. Keynote Speeches and Government Consultations by Waller

Africa (7): Egypt, Ivory Coast, Kenya, Morocco, South Africa, Tunisia, Zaire.

Middle East, Asia and Australasia (14): Australia, China, India, Israel, Japan, Mongolia, New Zealand, Palestine, Qatar, Saudi Arabia, Sharjah, Singapore, Thailand, Turkey.

Europe (18): Austria, Belgium, Croatia, Denmark, England, Finland, France, Germany, Hungary, Ireland, Italy, Malta, Norway, the Netherlands, Portugal, Russia, Scotland, Spain, Sweden.

Latin America (10): Argentina, Brazil, Colombia, Costa Rica, Cuba, Ecuador, El Salvador, Guatemala, Mexico, Venezuela.

North America (2): Canada, United States.

Denis Szabo had always wanted a Canadian to play a greater role internationally and he introduced me to **Irene Melup**,[24] who at the time served as the UN public servant committed to rights for victims of abuse of power. As a result, I partnered with her and was coached on how to work with the UN system. We were the quarterbacks for a network that successfully pioneered the movement to get the UN General Assembly to adopt the resolution calling for effective prevention and the implementation of the Basic Principles of

[24] See Vetere, E. & David, P.R. (eds.) (2005), *Victims of Crime and Abuse of Power (Bangkok, 18–25 April 2005): Festschrift in Honor of Irene Melup.* New York: United Nations.

Justice for Victims of Crime and Abuse of Power. There were many partners but one of the most important was a magistrate from France called Marie-Pierre de Liege who had come out of the magistrate's union from 1968 to be an influential and energetic French official able to stir France to take a leadership internationally on both victims and prevention.

To my surprise, I received awards from the World Federation for Mental Health and the U.S. National Organization for Victim Assistance for my work leading to the UN General Assembly resolution. This has influenced services

Box 13.5. Recognition for Role in Influencing Policy

- Paul Rock, *A View from the Shadows: The Ministry of the Solicitor-General of Canada and the Making of the Justice for Victims of Crime Initiative* (Oxford: Clarendon, 1986). Book identified Irvin Waller as a moral entrepreneur in Canadian victim movement.
- Donald Santarelli Award, National Organization for Victim Assistance (U.S.), 1987. For contributions to victim policy in the world in recognition of contributions to the UN General Assembly Resolution GA/34 on Crime Prevention and Victim Rights.
- Marlene Young Award, World Federation for Mental Health, 1987, for contributions to victim mental health concerns internationally.
- Captain of Crime Prevention Award, Ministry of the Interior, Belgium, 1996.
- Recognition by Belgium, Canada, France, the Netherlands, and the province of Quebec with letter of appreciation from Bureau of Justice Assistance, U.S. Department of Justice, 2001, for contributions as founding Director General of the International Centre for prevention of crime affiliated with UN.
- Friend of Chair, United Nations Intergovernmental Meeting, 2002, Expert Group to Propose Guidelines on Crime Prevention; later adopted by ECOSOC.
- Pioneer of Victim Movement in the U.S., 2003, (only non-U.S. citizen and one of few academics), included in Oral History for U.S. Department of Justice, Office for Victims of Crime.
- Distinguished International Criminologist, 2004; one of seven (and only Canadian) included in *Lessons from International/Comparative Criminology/Criminal Justice,* edited by J. Winterdyk and L. Cao, chapter on "Harnessing Criminology and Victimology Internationally."
- Stephen Schafer Award, National Organization for Victim Assistance (U.S.), 2004, for outstanding contributions to the victims' movement in the field of research.
- Premio Internacional de Victimología y Defensa de las Víctimas, 2005, annual prize awarded by the Crime Victim Foundation of Spain.
- Tribute to Irvin Waller for His Contributions to Violence Prevention and Crime Victim Rights in Mexico and Latin America, 2016, two-day event organized by the Instituto Nacional de Ciencias Penales, Attorney General of Mexico.

and rights for victims across the world, including the International Criminal Court and numerous pieces of national legislation and the European Union Directive on Victim Rights (see Box 13.5).

Starting around 1986, I became more focused on crime prevention through social development. I was invited to speak on crime prevention through social development at a Council of Europe meeting on the role of local government in crime prevention in Strasbourg, where I met **Gilbert Bonnemaison,** who was the treasurer of the French Socialist party and then Speaker (Questeur) of the French National Assembly. He was a humanist who cared about the social conditions that led to crime, the locking-up of so many young men and the reality that the crime bureaucracies were not meeting the needs of people on the streets of France. I will never forget him getting up from an expensive dinner that he was hosting for dignitaries from Europe and the U.S. to go to the riots occurring near the French National Assembly to plead with the young men to stop burning cars. He later became the first president of the International Centre for the Prevention of Crime. But first, I became his link to the non-French speaking world and helped develop the major meeting of mayors and local government in Barcelona, where Gilbert founded the European Forum for Urban Safety with me as his scientific adviser. He asked me to explore ways to hold a meeting in North America.

In time, I worked in many initiatives internationally. With time and effort, support grew for the creation of an international centre for the prevention of crime affiliated with the United Nations. The mayor of Montreal in 1989 had asked us to develop a proposal for its creation. Today the International Centre for Prevention of Crime (ICPC) is the only global non-governmental organization in the program network of the UN Office on Drugs and Crime focused exclusively on crime prevention and community safety. It is committed to using evidence and good practice to shape the world.

Working from Canada for Policy Reform, 1993-2000

Between 1993 and 2000, I was founding executive director of the ICPC. Its creation was a specific recommendation of the Horner Committee in Canada and those major conferences that had been held just a few years earlier.

The ICPC was to be a clearing house to promote crime prevention across the world. We brought together the criminological research in an annotated bibliography used by the U.S. National Commission on Crime and Justice. We edited a digest, as well as examples of best practices, to engage governments and cities in shifting towards effective and cost effective ways of reducing and dealing with crime. The key to our funding was our vision but also our collaboration with governments interested in evidence-based policy and reform. The ICPC was not only a clearing house for evidence on best practices but also a hub for governments to learn from each other and develop UN guidelines (see Box 13.3, above). The quinquennial Congress on Crime Prevention and Criminal Justice in 1995 started government workshops that fostered exchanges between governments, experts and practitioners. These were organized by governments and the ICPC. The meetings involved the sharing of research results, best practice and ways to implement crime prevention. The success of these workshops led to similar workshops being organized by other members of the UNODC program network, such as HEUNI in Europe and UNAFEI in Asia.

The ICPC was also a hub for leaders in the non-governmental world. For example, **Nigel Whiskin** had engineered the remarkably successful Crime Concern in the United Kingdom as a vehicle to promote effective crime prevention and **Jack Calhoun** had been the chief executive of the U.S. National Crime Prevention Council who added youth crime prevention and even some urban strategies to the famous "Take a Bite Out of Crime" situational prevention. Together and independently they became important champions for the ICPC with government and long-term friends and inspiration for me. Michel Marcus, the head of the European Forum for Urban Safety and a pioneer of the unique multi-sectoral crime prevention policies of France, was an important architect of our work and success.

During my stint at the ICPC, I also developed the Safer Cities program with UN Habitat that has multiplied successful crime reduction strategies across Africa. During this time I worked on national commissions on criminal justice in South Africa and the United States (see Box 13.1). To work for the Mandela government was an inspiring experience which has led to some long-term changes but not before momentum was lost as the police bureaucracy took advantage of publicity for crime prevention, instead of the investment going to the agencies that could effectively tackle the problems.

Writing for Policy Reform, 2000-2014

In 2000, my youngest son was nearly killed in a traffic crash. This brought me back once again to the importance of my children and the need to balance the excitement of influencing world changes with family. So I left ICPC and was awarded a transitional contract from the new National Crime Prevention Centre to bring together a list of national and international crime prevention contacts for them and gather information for what later became the basis for my book *Less Law, More Order.* This book was my first attempt to write a book in a language that was accessible to ordinary citizens and politicians. It became an important calling card for invitations as an author to contribute to shaping policy reforms across the world (see Box 13.6).

I developed a proposal to the National Crime Prevention Centre (NCPC) to harness evidence-based crime prevention in Canada at the University of Ottawa. This was approved in 2006 as part of a shift to more evidence-based crime prevention by the Canadian NCPC.

Our proposal and contract included: (1) The development of the first three issues of a journal on the best Canadian and international evidence and research related to preventing crime and violence. This was successfully developed by Ross Hastings and an exceptional Ph.D. student, Mélanie Bania; (2) Bringing together a group of leaders from government, municipalities, academe and the NGO sector to propose a national strategy for Canada; and (3) Creating a network of representatives from 14 municipalities from coast to coast to develop comprehensive crime prevention strategies tackling the problems and risk factors that lead to crime at the local level.

From about 2007 forward, we worked with various provinces to promote evidence-based crime prevention strategies. The most successful province was Alberta. They invested about $1 billion over seven years in the implementation of the strategy. The Alberta initiative inspired new comprehensive community

Box 13.6. Media, Social Media, and Books Debating Violence Prevention and Victims' Rights

I have written three major books specifically to reach politicians and the public as well as participating in a task force on the future of policing. These books are the basis of my active work in media and with the Canadian Municipal Network for Prevention of Crime.

Council of Canadian Academies (2014). *Policing Canada in the 21st Century: New Policing for New Challenges*. Ottawa: Council of Canadian Academies. (One of 12 academic members.)

Waller, Irvin (2013). *Smarter Crime Control. A Guide to a Safer Future for Citizens, Communities and Politicians*. New York: Rowman and Littlefield.

Waller, Irvin (2010). *Rights for Victims of Crime: Rebalancing Justice*. New York: Rowman and Littlefield.

Waller, Irvin (2006). *Less Law, More Order: The Truth about Reducing Crime*. Westport, CN: Praeger.

Action Briefs for the Canadian Municipal Network for the Prevention of Crime that share knowledge with stakeholders who can decide investments in prevention. safercities.ca.

Op-eds. With Michael Kempa. *Toronto Star*, beginning in 2015.

TEDx: Smarter Crime Control, Less Law, More Order (2013). http://www.youtube.com/watch?v=FgVorJJa2cM.

Website, blogs and social media. http://www.irvinwaller.org.

Canadian listserv. Scientific and best-practice developments are distributed about once a month to interested persons, including Canadian public servants and some media.

Radio, newspaper and television (beginning in 1980). Interviews on average every couple of weeks including ones with the Canadian Press, *Globe and Mail*, *Ottawa Citizen*, CBC, Radio-Canada and other French-language outlets, with occasional interviews in Spanish, particularly in Latin America.

safety strategies in cities such as Edmonton (i.e., REACH).

It was at this Institute that I rediscovered **Rick Linden,** one of Canada's most successful writers of criminology textbooks and a criminologist who had taught police chiefs, designed guides to prevention and been the catalyst to successfully reduce auto theft in Winnipeg by 85%. His calm focus on outcomes and working with the establishment has inspired me in different ways. I am proud to be a contributor on victim rights to his textbook.

Less Law, More Order did indeed lead to multiple invitations across the world (see Box 13.5). The Spanish version of *Less Law, More Order* influenced the pioneering national crime prevention legislation of Mexico as well as generating media headlines in Argentina, Colombia, Ecuador, Mexico, and Venezuela. These involved many presentations and advice to governments across Latin America, including to the Senate Committees in Colombia and Mexico. It also led to presentations and advice across Europe and further afield, including to the European Union and to the crime prevention conference in Germany with some 3,000 participants.

In 2009, the World Society of Victimology and the International Victimology Institute in the Netherlands got together to develop a draft convention to encourage the UN to implement services and rights for victims. Building on this, I developed and wrote *Rights for Victims of Crime: Rebalancing Justice* (2011) (in 2 languages), which included specific recommendations for actions that governments could take and a model law.

I was also fortunate enough to have **Veronica Martinez Solares** join me as a visiting research fellow for a year in Ottawa in 2006. She was to serve as an advisor to key players in the Mexican Parliament and the Office of the Mexican President. This brilliant young woman had left law because she cared about victims and wanted to make a difference for victims and for violence prevention. She had done a master's degree in victimology at INACIPE where she got a grade of 100% in a course guided by the internationally renowned Dr. Maria de la Luz Lima Malvido. She was influenced, as I am, by Dr. Lima and her husband Luis Manzanera, both criminologists dedicated to working in government at senior levels and in academe in efforts to change policy. The mission of Dr. Martinez was to stop violence, help victims and eliminate femicide. While visiting at the Institute, I persuaded her to spend some time in England before returning to Mexico. Upon returning to Mexico, she has worked as a catalyst for some of the most important innovations in Latin America in relation to violence prevention and victim rights (see Box 13.5).

In 2014, I wrote my third book for legislators as well as for informed members of the public and potential victims: *Smarter Crime Control: Less Law, More Order* is now available in six languages, and *Rights for Victims of Crime* and *Smarter Crime Control: A Guide to Safer Futures for Citizens, Communities and Politicians* are available in English and Spanish and in translation to Chinese.

I am now president of the new and still small International Organization for Victim Assistance in consultative status with the UN. I am also working increasingly on panels and advisory committees. In Canada, these included the Council of Canadian Academies Panel on the Future of Policing (2014), the Advisory Group to the Deputy Minister of Police and Prisons of Saskatchewan, and the Advisory Group to the RCMP on the Federal Witness Protection Program. I also continue to make regular appearances in front of House of Commons and Senate Committees for the Parliament of Canada.

While most people in their seventh decade might like to take life a bit easier, I want to consolidate and sustain my work to share the latest developments in crime prevention and victim assistance in Canada through a list-serv and do the same internationally on Twitter with a dream of influencing the broken criminal justice and crime prevention policies of the United States.

In Sum

My father's profession, my traumatic experience of violence on a freighter, and my skills with data reinforced chance decisions to engage in criminology at Cambridge, studies that were empirical and focused on policy reform. This led to my recruitment to Canada to work on my major evaluation of prison and parole, which left me with no doubt that prisons were not and could not be the solution to crime. I also became convinced that newspaper headlines about the results of research make policy reform difficult. My major study of victims and prevention left no doubt that focusing on the needs of victims and prevention were the solutions. But the combination of my reflections on the two monographs guided my contributions in government to the most significant reform in Canadian crime policy ever and one clearly reinforced by empirical data and a positive vision about prevention and victim assistance.

The challenge from Denis Szabo to make Canada a centre of UN policy reform, the inspiration of Leslie Wilkins and a course on planned change, and the international contacts developed while in the Canadian government led me to influence an important shift towards prevention and victim rights in Canada, at the UN and so across the world. The collaboration on victims with Irene Melup and Marlene Young and with Gilbert Bonnemaison and Claude Vezina and later Jack Calhoun and Nigel Whiskin on prevention led to many important milestones as has the collaboration with Claudio Stampalija, Luis Manzanera and Maria de la Luz Lima and Veronica Martinez.

In 1966, neither prevention nor victim rights were on any agenda anywhere in the world nor at the heart of modern criminology at Cambridge. Fifty years later, they are very much on the agenda in Canada and across the world. This is particularly evident in Europe, Latin America, and now China. They are the only solution to reduce police repression and over-use of incarceration and particularly the epidemics of violence, such as we see in Latin America, among blacks in the United States, and among Canada's Indigenous peoples. Ironically, it is the United States that has produced such an abundance of criminological data but which is so far behind in its use for prevention or making criminal justice decent. It is increasingly recognized by Obama (2015) as having a racist and broken approach; consider books such as *The New Jim Crow* (Alexander 2012).

Where to Go from Here?

It is sad to see how little has changed in Canada from 1980 to today in dealing with offenders with greater decency, despite all the lamenting by criminologists and the teaching of ephemeral American criminological theory to mass undergraduate classes. Crime rates went up and have come back down; but this fluctuation is not because of criminology. Property crime is apparently only at 1960s levels (this level was unacceptable then and even more unacceptable now given all the advances in our lives) and violence is not even below 1980 levels. This is unimpressive compared to any successful area of public policy. Our prisons are just modern-technology versions of the old. In fact, the overcrowding and numbers of prisoners on pre-trial is far worse than anyone could have imagined 35 years ago. Policing is likely generally better but we do not know for sure. Innovations such as Tasers and body cameras and particularly ubiquitous cell phone cameras must all help to reduce brutality; but the 911 system is not about prevention, just reaction.

But change is happening to prevent crime and so avoid the $50 billion or more of harm to victims in Canada each year. The criminological data accumulated over the last 50 years is now accessible and used to recommend specific actions that policy makers can take (Waller 2014). It is endorsed by UN agencies such as WHO and Habitat and put into guidelines that Canada supports internationally. The UN General Assembly has adopted 17 sustainable development goals to be achieved by 2030, including reducing violence against women, safer cities, and fewer homicides. They also include a goal on implementation that might have been inspired by the SUNY planned change course.

There is much more work to be done by the next generations of criminologists to get governments to invest in initiatives that are cost-effective, decent, and compassionate. They must do more than lamenting our broken criminal justice system and its biases against Indigenous peoples. This can only be done by investing in Canada upstream in the proven strategies that stop violence and provide services and rights that victims of crime need. It is time for Canada and Canadian criminology to focus on harnessing this evidence to stop street violence, shootings, and intimate partner and sexual violence. It is time to put into place targets to reduce incarceration to the levels of countries like Germany and Sweden or better. As an Ontario Minister of Community Safety liked to say in his brief sojourn in that portfolio, you cannot solve twenty-first-century social problems with nineteenth-century reactive policing.

The dream is achievable if enough criminologists care about people and have the energy to fight for reforms by using evidence, modern media, and the skills to effect planned change. They will be helped by visionary local and national politicians who want to deliver real outcomes to benefit the public. For young criminologists and victimologists, there are great opportunities if you choose to lead rather than follow. Ask not what your government can do for you but what you can do for your government. You must engage with government. You must develop your own non-governmental groups. You must get into politics, the media and use your power, of which you may not yet be aware. You must become the pioneers of criminology for the twenty-first century. This is your world. Shape it or someone else will.

References

Major Publications by Irvin Waller

Smarter Crime Control: A Guide to Safer Futures for Citizens, Communities and Politicians, New York: Rowman and Littlefield, 2013 (published in Spanish and translated into Chinese).

Rights for Victims of Crime: Rebalancing Justice. New York: Rowman and Littlefield, 2010 (published in Spanish and translated into Chinese).

Less Law, More Order: The Truth about Reducing Crime. Westfield, CN: Praeger, 2006 (in paperback Manor House, 2008) (published in Bengali, Chinese, French, German, and Spanish).

With B.C. Welsh, and D. Sansfaçon. *Crime Prevention Digest 1997: Successes, Benefits and Directions from Seven Countries.* Montreal: International Centre for Prevention of Crime, 1997 (in French and informally translated into Czech).

With Norm Okihiro. *Burglary, the Victim and the Public.* Toronto: University of Toronto Press, 1978 (Centre of Criminology Series, Volume 3).

Men Released from Prison. Toronto: University of Toronto Press, 1974 (paperback, 1979) (Centre of Criminology Series, Volume 2).

With J. Chan (1974). Prison use: A Canadian and international comparison, *Criminal Law Quarterly,* 17(1):47–71. Reprinted in R. Carter, D. Glaser and L. Wilkins (eds.), *Correctional Institutions,* Second Edition. Philadelphia: Lippincott, 1977 (also published in French).

Other References

Alexander, Michelle (2010). *The New Jim Crow: Mass Incarceration in the Age of Color Blindness.* New York: The New Press.

Behan, Brendan (1958). *Borstal Boy.* New York: Korni (also made into a film of the same title).

Bonnemaison, Gilbert (1983). *Face à la délinquance: prévention, répression, solidarité: rapport au Premier ministre.* Commission des Maires sur la Securite (France), la Documentation française.

Canadian Council on Social Development (1983). *Crime Prevention through Social Development.* Ottawa.

Canadian Council on Social Development (1981). *Rights and Services for Victims of Crime.* Ottawa.

Calhoun, Jack. http://www.harrywalker.com/speaker/John-A-Calhoun.cfm?Spea_ID=778.

Hogarth, John (1970). *Sentencing as a Human Process.* Toronto: University of Toronto Press.

Hood, Roger and Richard Sparks (1970). *Key Issues in Criminology.* New York: McGraw-Hill.

Hood, Roger G. (1974). *Crime, Criminology and Public Policy: Essays in Honour of Sir Leon Radzinowicz.* New York: The Free Press.

Horner, Bob (1993). *Crime Prevention in Canada: Towards a National Strategy: 12th report of the Standing Committee.* Ottawa: House of Commons.

International Centre for Prison Studies. http://www.prisonstudies.org/.

Justice Canada (1982). *Criminal Law in Canadian Society.* Ottawa.

Lima Malvido, Maria de la Luz. http://www.inacipe.gob.mx/ investigacion /investigadores/titulares/maria_de_la_luz_lima_malvido.php.

Loeber, Rolf and David Farrington (2012). *From Juvenile Delinquency to Adult Crime: Criminal Careers, Justice Policy and Prevention.* Oxford: Oxford University Press.

Mannheim, Hermann and Leslie T. Wilkins (1955). *Prediction Methods in Relation to Borstal Training*. London: Home Office

McClintock, Derek (1995). Obituary. *British Journal of Criminology* 35 (1): 134–137.

Melup, Irene, Eduardo Eduardo and David Pedro (2005). Victims of Crime and Abuse of Power: Festschrift in Honour of Irene Melup. New York: United Nations.

Obama, Barack (2015). http://www.nytimes.com/2015/07/15/us/politics/obama-calls -for-effort-to-fix-a-broken-system-of-criminal-justice.html?_r=0.

Radzinowicz, Sir Leon (2000). Obituary. http://www.theguardian.com/news/2000 /jan/01/guardianobituaries.

Rutherford, Andrew (1993). *Criminal Justice and the Pursuit of Decency*. Oxford: Oxford University Press.

Sherman, Lawrence (2016). http://www.crim.cam.ac.uk/people/academic_research/ lawrence_sherman/.

Solicitor-General of Canada. *Selected Trends*. Ottawa.

Szabo, Denis. http://classiques.uqac.ca/contemporains/szabo_denis/szabo_denis_ photo/szabo_denis_photo.html.

UN Habitat. http://unhabitat.org/urban-initiatives/networks/global-network-on-safer-cities/.

U.S. Department of Justice. crimesolutions.gov.

Waller, Irvin (2014). *Smarter Crime Control: A Guide to Safer Futures for Citizens, Communities and Politicians*. New York: Rowman and Littlefield (translated into Spanish and in translation into Chinese).

Waller, Irvin (2014). Implementing evidence-based policy to deal with crime in Canada. In Shaun Young (ed.), *Evidence Based Policy-Making in Canada*. Toronto: Oxford University Press, pp. 118–149.

Waller, Irvin (2012). Victimology, victim services, and victim rights in Canada. In R. Linden (ed.), *Criminology: A Canadian Perspective*, 7th (2012) and 8th editions (2015). Toronto: Nelson.

Waller, Irvin (2012). Convincing governments to invest in prevention: Reducing crime, protecting victim rights. In Marc Coester and Erich Marks (eds.), *International Perspectives of Crime Prevention 4* (pp. 9–16). Monchengladbach, Germany: Forum Verlag Godesberg GmbH.

Waller, Irvin (2010). *Rights for Victims of Crime: Rebalancing Justice*. New York: Rowman and Littlefield (translated into Spanish and in translation into Chinese).

Waller, Irvin (2006). *Less Law, More Order: The Truth about Reducing Crime*. Westfield, CN: Praeger (in paperback Manor House, 2008) (translated into Bengali, Chinese, French, German, and Spanish).

Waller, Irvin (2003). *Crime Victims: Doing Justice to Support and Rights*. Helsinki: European United Nations Institute for Crime Prevention and Criminal Justice (in English and Russian) and in Spanish: *Apoyo gubernamental a las victimas del delito*. Mexico: Instituto Nacional de Sciencias Penales, Attorney General, Mexico, 2004.

Waller, Irvin, B.C. Welsh, and D. Sansfaçon (1997). *Crime Prevention Digest 1997: Successes, Benefits and Directions from Seven Countries*. Montreal: International Centre for Prevention of Crime (in French and translated into Czech).

Waller, Irvin (1991). *Putting Crime Prevention on the Map*. Paris: European Forum for Urban Safety (in English, French, and Spanish), and Moscow: Academy of Ministry of Interior (in Russian); Rat fur Kriminalitatsverhutung in Schleswig-Holstein (in German).

Waller, Irvin and Norm Okihiro (1978). *Burglary, the Victim and the Public*. Toronto: University of Toronto Press.

Waller, Irvin (1974). *Men Released from Prison*. Toronto: University of Toronto Press (paperback, 1979).

Waller, Irvin and Chan, J. (1974). Prison use: A Canadian and international comparison. *Criminal Law Quarterly*, 17(1):47–71. Reprinted in R. Carter, D. Glaser and L. Wilkins (eds.), *Correctional Institutions*, second edition. Philadelphia: Lippincott, 1977 (Also in French).

Waller, Irvin and Veronica Martinez (2016). Smarter crime control: Putting prevention knowledge into practice. In John A. Winterdyk et al. (ed.), *Crime Prevention: International Issues and Perspectives*. Boca Raton, FL: CRC Press.

West, Donald. https://en.wikipedia.org/wiki/Donald_J._West.

Wilkins, Leslie (2000). http://www.theguardian.com/news/2000/jul/03/guardian obituaries.

World Health Organization (2014). *Global Status Report on Violence Prevention*. Geneva.

Young, Marlene. NOVA, http://www.iovahelp.org/About/MarleneAYoung/.

FOURTEEN

Patricia L. Brantingham and Paul J. Brantingham: Environmental Criminologists

Patricia L. Brantingham
and Paul J. Brantingham

Introduction

Patricia (Matthews) Brantingham was born in 1943 in St. Louis, Missouri, the daughter of a corporate executive. She grew up in Massachusetts and New Jersey as her father's career as a physical chemist and senior corporate executive prospered and prompted moves to more demanding jobs in new locations. She did her undergraduate studies at Barnard College, the women's college at Columbia University, where she majored in theoretical mathematics and played on the intercollegiate basketball team.

Paul Brantingham was born one day later than Patricia in 1943 and was raised in Long Beach, California, one of four sons of a podiatrist. He completed his undergraduate work at Columbia College, the men's college at Columbia University, where he majored in Government, played football, threw the hammer on the track team, and won the Eisenhower Watch for maintaining the highest grade point average among varsity athletes.

Columbia University

Pat and Paul met during their first year at university and dated during their undergraduate years with the relationship becoming much more serious as they entered their graduate studies. Patricia took a master's degree in theoretical mathematics at Fordham University while Paul studied law at Columbia University's school of law. They married in 1967. Paul became a member of the California Bar in 1969.

Patricia's degrees in mathematics initially led her into a career in business, working as a systems analyst for several major corporations. As a systems analyst at Johnson and Johnson she designed accounting, shipping and accounts receivable subsystems within an overall management information system. At Technicon Corporation she was a systems analyst on a team that designed a transplantable hospital laboratory information system. This was a modular system that controlled laboratory equipment, scheduled work, handled quality control, and carried out result reporting. At Hunt-Wesson Foods (known for Hunt's tomato paste and as the American franchisee for Canada Dry ginger ale) she headed a team of 24 analysts and programmers and was primary designer on a management information system that handled sales, shipping, inventory, production scheduling, and accounting.

Paul had studied criminal law under Herbert Wechsler, who was a former director of the American Law Institute and is widely recognized for the creation of the Model Penal Code, and criminal procedure under Monrad Paulsen who, among other scholarly attributes, was a champion of importance of university law schools and the function and role they play in bridging legal scholarship with universities and the community at large (see Graetz and Whitebread II 1981). That experience touched off a life-long interest in understanding criminal events. During his third year at Columbia Law School Paul took an elective seminar in criminology led by Sir Leon Radzinowicz (1906–1999), the founding director of the Institute of Criminology at Cambridge University. Paul won a Ford Foundation fellowship for study in the criminology post-graduate diploma course at Cambridge University.

Pat and Paul moved to Cambridge and lived in Clare Hall, a new graduate-students-only college, while he took the post-graduate diploma course. Professor Roger Hood had sponsored them at Clare Hall. Paul's overall course of study was supervised by Prof. Donald West. Paul's principal written paper (similar to a master's thesis) analyzed new trends in British juvenile justice.

Paul studied along with **Richard Ericson** (1948–2007), one of the pre-eminent criminologists of his time, and Keith Couse, who was then Director of John Howard Society of Ontario. Pat, in view of her background in mathematics and computing, was pulled onto several research projects to handle computing and statistical analysis, notably Roger Hood's study of magistrates' sentencing in motoring offences and a study of violent crime in England and Wales conducted by F.H. McClintock and Anthony Bottoms. Pat spent considerable time utilizing the computing facilities at the Institute for Theoretical Astronomy, where the Institute of Criminology had computing privileges. She often crossed paths with **Irvin Waller** who was then completing his doctorate and also using Theoretical Astronomy's computing facilities. (The key-punch machines were in a shed in the middle of a sheep pasture on Theoretical Astronomy's grounds). Along the way their son Jeffrey was born at Mill Road Maternity Hospital and spent some of his first year of life living in Clare Hall.

Florida State University

Following completion of the Cambridge Diploma Course, Paul was hired as an Assistant Professor of Criminology by Florida State University (FSU). His initial teaching assignments included courses in criminal law, criminal procedure, juvenile justice, and international and comparative criminology. He shared an office with Fred Faust (new assistant professors were not given individual offices at FSU in those days) who had completed his Ph.D. in sociology at Ohio State under Walter Reckless. Fred had been director of the Ohio Juvenile Justice system prior to pursuing an academic career. Together they edited a juvenile law casebook (Faust and Brantingham 1974, 1979) that went through two editions. Florida State criminology had many luminaries on faculty at that time including Vern Fox, C. Ray Jeffery, Ron Akers, Harry Allen, and Tom Blomberg. Paul and Fred were in the office next to Ray Jeffery, who coined and formulated the term CPTED (Crime Prevention through Environmental Design). During the preparation and publishing of the first edition *of Crime Prevention through Environmental Design* in 1971, the three of them spent much time discussing ideas about crime reduction. This led to development and publication by Paul and Fred (with key contributions from Patricia) of the conceptual model of crime prevention as occurring at three levels—primary, secondary and tertiary—and setting out the ways that different institutions and segments of society could play roles in all three levels of crime prevention (Brantingham and Faust 1976; see Figure 14.1 below).

Figure 14.1. The Conceptual Model of Crime Prevention
Crime Prevention Roles at the Primary, Secondary and Tertiary Levels

Agency	Primary	Secondary	Tertiary
	PUBLIC SECTOR		
Police	General deterrence through presence and patrol. Community policing. Citizen education programs. Advice on situational prevention strategies.	Crime and intelligence analysis. Emergent hot spot policing. Problem oriented policing programs (POP).	Established hot spot policing. Arrest and charge. Prolific offender management.
Courts	General deterrence through exemplary sentences.	Diversion. Conditional discharges and probation.	Sentences aimed at incapacitation. Prolific offender management.
Corrections	General deterrence through existence.	Probation. Community supervision.	Incapacitation. Prolific offender management.
Schools	School time frame management. School access control. After-school programs such as sports and drama.	Situational prevention programs on school grounds.	Remedial education programs.

Urban Planners	Crime prevention through environmental design. Routine activity management through social, temporal and physical planning.	Hot spot redesign. Traffic flow control.	Institutional design.
Health Agencies	General health programs. Anti-drug education.	High-risk persons identification and intervention.	Drug abuse rehabilitation. Prolific offender management.
Social Agencies	Community development.	Social services for high-risk individuals and groups: social housing, job placement, domestic abuse interventions.	Social interventions in established cases of domestic abuse, prolific offender management.
Agency	**Primary**	**Secondary**	**Tertiary**
	PRIVATE SECTOR		
Businesses	CPTED. Security and loss prevention. General situational prevention.	Employee screening. Security focus on hot spots. Hot spot focus for situational prevention. Participation in POP.	Prosecution of offenders. Hiring and management of ex-offenders. Environmental modifications aimed at situational prevention.
Churches and Religious Organizations	Moral and ethical education.	Programs for the disadvantaged. Crisis intervention. Participation in POP.	Aftercare services.
Other NGOs	Recreation programs. General social work.	Participation in POP.	Aftercare services.
Communities	Neighbourhood Watch and similar programs. Neighbourhood-based sports programs (e.g., Little League, minor hockey).	Neighbourhood clean-up projects designed to "fix broken windows." Participation in POP.	Cocooning and other community-supported repeat victimization interdiction programs.
Families	Good parenting: supervision; temptation reduction. Rule-setting and consistent enforcement.	Closer supervision. Therapy support.	Aftercare support. Therapy support.
Individual Private Citizens	Household and business security precautions. General charity.	Participation in Neighbourhood Watch, POP and similar programs.	Crime site modifications.

Patricia pursued additional graduate work at Florida State, taking both a master's and a Ph.D. in Urban and Regional Planning. Her master's field project helped decide where to place stations on the route of the new Atlanta subway system then being developed. Discussions over lunch with Paul and his colleagues raised Patricia's interest in crime prevention through planning. Her master's research thesis utilized point set topology to build a new mathematical approach to understanding the structure of neighbourhoods and regions. Applied to the distribution of crime in space and time in joint articles with Paul (Brantingham and Brantingham 1975, 1978) this approach established our long-term commitment to the application of mathematics to the understanding of crime and urban form.

During the course of her graduate studies Patricia worked for the Southeast Regional Census Processing Center that was housed at Florida State and carried out the first successful implementation of a new GIS system, GRIds, developed by the U.S. Census Bureau (the GRIds system eventually grew into the TIGER files that have so strongly facilitated the growth of computerized mapping in the U.S.). The implementation of GRIds made it possible to generate a computerized point map of burglary in Tallahassee using data provided by the Tallahassee Police Department. This was one of the first computerized crime maps published in the field of criminology (see Brantingham and Brantingham 1975). That study enabled the use of a new computer mapping system to create statewide crime maps structured into isomorphic areas and analyze patterns at many levels of spatial aggregation (Brantingham, Dyreson, and Brantingham 1976).

Patricia became interested in computer simulation modelling as a way both to understand the operation of complex systems and as a tool for conducting experiments assessing the impact of different planning and policy options on those systems. Using Dynamo IV, she built a dynamic simulation model of the entire Florida criminal justice system which was used by the state Department of Corrections to analyze the resource impact of different policy options at a time when the system was under substantial resource strains. At the time, it was one of the largest dynamic simulation models extant. This set up a long-term interest in using computer simulation and laid the groundwork for developing computational criminology.

Simon Fraser University

In early 1977, we were recruited by **Ezzat Fattah** to join his criminology department at Simon Fraser University (SFU) in Burnaby, British Columbia. The department looked exciting, we had had a long interest in Canada (we had honeymooned at Expo 67) and Vancouver then, as now, was a marvellous city. So, in September of that year we moved to Vancouver and started teaching at SFU. Except for a six-winter sojourn in Ottawa, we have been at Simon Fraser ever since.

The Evolution of Crime Pattern Theory

Upon arriving at SFU we learned that the university's computing resources could not handle large simulation models and had to set that interest aside for the time being. We began a series of theoretical studies on the character of criminal events at a time when most of Canadian (as well as American) criminology was focused on understanding individual criminal motivation. We elaborated the idea that a crime, a criminal event, had at least four elements: an offender, a target (or victim), a location in space-time and a legal prohibition. We thought that study of the location of criminal events in space-time held the most promise both for better understanding crimes and for devising ways to prevent them. It followed, for us, that understanding how the offender went about selecting the time and place at which to take criminal action against a target (or victim) should become a major subject for theoretical development and empirical research. In *A Theoretical Model of Crime Selection* (1978) we developed the concept of a hierarchical target search process grounded in an offender's awareness of space and structured by a satisficing rather an optimizing strategy. We also organized a series of panels addressing crime and space for an international criminological conference held in Stockholm that year under the auspices of the International Division of the American Society of Criminology and the National Council for Crime Prevention Sweden (BRA). Many of the papers from that conference were subsequently included in *Environmental Criminology* (1981). Our own paper, "Notes on the Geometry of Crime," has become one of our more widely cited works and forms the conceptual framework on which crime pattern theory has developed.

"Notes on the Geometry of Crime"

This paper was a formal, mathematically structured development of a theory describing the movement patterns inherent in criminal events. It focused on the offender's journey to crime in a world structured by the physical and social environments and by the distribution of criminal opportunities across those environments. It proceeded to develop propositions in twelve steps, beginning with the simplest possible case—a single offender situated at a single location which was surrounded by uniform distribution of identical criminal opportunities—and progressing at each subsequent step to add one further complicating factor and move closer to the complexities of real behaviour in the real world. We elected to present these formal steps as diagrammatic illustrations rather than as equations. The third proposition, Step 3 in the formal development, produced a diagram which is often cited: it considered the case of an offender who led a more normal life, travelling between home, work, and various recreational and shopping anchor points and indicated the probable crime sites that would be selected by that offender. Crime was posited to occur in greater density around the anchor points and with less density along the pathways between (see Figure 14.2 on the next page; note that lighter colours indicate greater density of crimes).

"Nodes, Paths and Edges"

We expanded on the geometry of crime in "Nodes, Paths and Edges" (1993) by distinguishing between environmental impacts on the psychology, activity patterns and decision patterns of individuals, including criminals, and environmental impacts on aggregate crime patterns. At the individual level, the physical environment and social routines shape the individual's awareness space, pathways through the awareness space affect where criminal opportunities will be sought or perceived, and the individual's personal crime template structures the decision to commit a crime. At the aggregate level, activity nodes such as schools, business districts, shopping centres, entertainment venues, as well as offenders' home neighbourhoods and the pathways between them structure where offenders as a group travel and find targets.

Moreover, crimes concentrate along edges between different kinds of neighbourhoods because many different people use those edges to access many different kinds of land uses and activities. This suggests that neighbourhood insiders are generally responsible for crimes within homogenous neighborhoods, that both neighborhood insiders and outsiders commit crimes on edges of neighbourhoods, but that most outsider crime is committed on or near the edges. Empirical testing in Greater Vancouver has confirmed this concentration of crime on neighbourhood edges (Beavon et al. 1994; Song, Spicer, and Brantingham 2013; Song, Spicer, Brantingham, and Frank 2013).

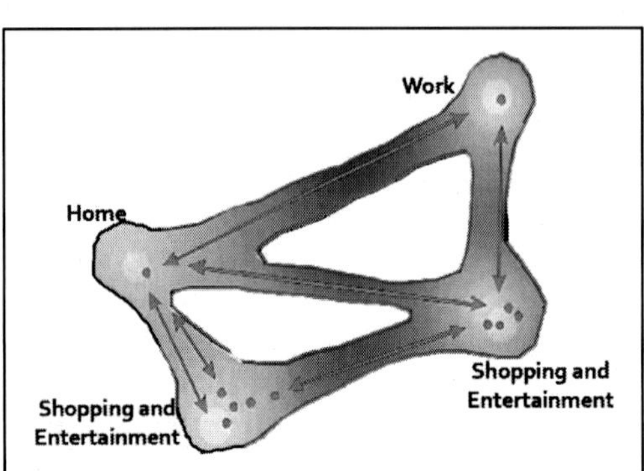

Figure 14.2. Awareness Space/Individual Offender (courtesy the authors).

Toward a Pattern Theory of Crime

We also sought, in 1993, to develop a formal synthesis of the geometry of crime with routine activity theory as fully developed by Marcus Felson and with rational choice theory and the situational crime-prevention model as developed most extensively by Ronald Clarke. Crime Pattern Theory, which results from the synthesis, addresses a wider range of criminological issues than any of the three theories can address on their own. The synthesis emphasized that criminal events need to be understood in terms of offender template and readiness to commit a crime, the structural and activity backcloths of the city, the specific features of crime locations, and the specific triggering events that match some target and situation to the offender's crime template in a way that elicits criminal action at that time and place. We showed how crime pattern theory could be used to analyze crimes as diverse as pilfering of office supplies, household burglary, and serial rape.

Articulation of crime-pattern theory allowed us to propose new analyses of important aspects of crime. We were able to explain how land uses, pathways, and human activity spaces can converge to create persistent crime hot spots in

"Criminality of Place" (1995) and in a more fully developed "Theoretical Model of Crime Hot Spot Generation" (1999). We could use crime-pattern theory to predict spatial and temporal patterns of crime displacement following a hot spot intervention in "Anticipating the Displacement of Crime Using Environmental Criminology" (2003). We could show how controlling crime and controlling fear of crime often require difficult trade-offs in "Planning Crime Reduction Strategies" (1997) and articulate a formal theory of target search (Song, Spicer, and Brantingham 2013).

In 2008, we contributed a chapter to Richard Wortley and Lorraine Mazerolle's book on environmental criminology and crime analysis, in which we summarized the *rules of crime pattern theory* in ten statements (specifically one assumption and nine rules):

Crime and Normal Behavior

The criminal event is comprised of an action by an offender against a target in violation of a criminal law at a site and time in which the situation does not prevent or deter the action.

Because the criminal offender is only one element of the criminal event, it is possible to reduce crime by understanding and changing any of the other elements necessary to the event.

Most crime is a by-product of normal, legal behaviour.

Understanding the patterns in normal behaviour can explain the patterns in most crime.

Rule 1: Crime Decision Templates

As individuals move through a series of activities they make decisions.

When activities are repeated frequently, the decision process becomes regularized.

This regularization creates an abstract guiding template.

For decisions to commit a crime this is called a ***crime template***.

The template specifies suitable targets, sites, situations, and crime techniques.

The crime template structures later crime decisions.

Crime templates evolve over time, but relatively slowly.

Rule 2: Social Networks Matter

Offenders sometimes make crime decisions and undertake criminal actions on their own.

Most people do not function as atomic individuals, but have a network of family, friends, and acquaintances.

These linkages have varying attributes and influence the decisions of others in the network.

These linkages structure who might be involved as offenders in any given criminal event.

These linkages structure decisions about criminal target, site, situation and technique.

Rule 3: Crime Patterns

When individuals are making their decisions independently, individual decision processes and crime templates can be treated in a summative fashion, that is, average or typical patterns can be determined by combining the patterns of individuals.

When individuals are influenced by a social network, the patterns must be understood in terms of the network.

Rule 4: Criminals Learn from Criminal Events

Individuals or networks commit crimes when there is some triggering event and some process by which an individual or network member can locate a target or a victim that fits within a crime template.

Criminal actions change the offender's bank of accumulated experience and alter future actions.

Rule 5: Nodes, Paths, Edges and Routines

People have a range of daily, weekly, monthly, and annual routines that structure their position and movements in space-time.

These routines shape both the directionality of the journey to crime and the temporality of criminal events.

Activity occurs at routine nodes and along the normal pathways between these nodes. Such nodes may include: home and the homes of relatives and friends; work and school sites; shopping and entertainment venues; or transportation junctures.

Activity is constrained by physical and social edges between neighborhoods. Edges can be simple or complex. Crime builds along edges. This tends to create crime ridges running between major crime nodes.

Rule 6: Awareness Spaces and Crime

People develop activity spaces composed of the nodes and paths they routinely utilize.

People develop an awareness space based on their activity spaces.

People who commit crimes have normal spatio-temporal movement patterns like everyone else.

The likely location for a crime is near this normal activity and awareness space.

Awareness spaces evolve over time. This can change the criminal activity spaces of individuals and networks.

Rule 7: Space-Time Intersections

Criminal opportunities present when the space-time locations of potential targets and victims intersect the activity spaces of potential offenders.

The potential targets and victims become actual targets or victims when: the potential offender's willingness to commit a crime has been triggered; and the potential target or victim fits the offender's crime template.

Rule 8: Urban Form as a Constraint

The prior rules operate within the built urban form which structures human movement into nodes and paths.

The built form sorts crime hot spots into: **Crime generators** which are created by high flows of people through and to nodal activity points; **Crime attractors** which are created when suitable targets are known by potential offenders to be concentrated at specific nodes. Potential offenders travel to a crime attractor for the specific purpose of committing a crime there; **Crime neutral areas** which do not see high flows of people and which do not have a public reputation for concentrations of suitable targets.

The built form channels crime nodes and paths.

Rule 9: The Backcloth Matters

Criminal events play out across a backcloth composed of social, economic, political, and physical dimensions.

All the backcloth dimensions affect the location and clustering of crimes.

Analysis of the backcloth is important to understanding and comparing crime patterns across places and times.

Development of crime pattern theory is an ongoing concern. As we learn more about the characteristics of criminal events we continue to improve the theory.

Research on Criminal Justice Policy and Criminal Justice System Operations

Another extended stream of research that has occupied us since coming to Simon Fraser University has been research on the structure, policy, operations, and cost of different components of the Canadian criminal justice system.

Police Studies

Much of our work on police organization and operations has gone forward in government reports. Patricia served as one of the commissioners on British Columbia's Task Force on Public Order (1992) which explored the causes and handling of a number of public order incidents in the province, notably a riot during the Penticton Peach Festival in 1991,[25] and which recommended a series of changes in the way police need to handle large scale disturbances. Paul has worked on a series of major studies tracking how the policing function has increased in complexity and cost over time: these studies have demonstrated that the amount of time needed to properly deal with such diverse matters as burglary and drunk driving has massively increased and that the amount of administrative time required by each constable to properly document each police activity has also increased substantially over the past 30 years. We have

[25] According to Sarah Efron, a journalist for *Vice Magazine*, the riot "apparently broke out after 20 teenaged misfits, hyped up on (MC) Hammer, began chucking rocks at a traffic cop. The tally: over 50 arrests, 60 injuries, and one shamed, pathetic rapper in an oversized, purple jumpsuit." It ranked among the top 10 riots in Canada (see http://www.sarahefron.com/stories/Riot.shtml).

also conducted a series of studies on the rising costs of policing in context: these studies have demonstrated that across Canada in general, and in British Columbia particularly, the rise in police costs have been consistent with the rise in costs for delivery of other public services. Put another way, at the national level, the rise in police costs over the past three decades has been consistent with the rise in costs for health care and education. In British Columbia the share of municipal operating expense devoted to police services has remained relatively stable at around 15% over the past 30 years. These findings have proven very important to the discussion of police funding in the wake of declines in the official crime rate.

Legal Aid Studies

During 1979–1981, Patricia, in conjunction with Peter Burns (then Dean of the Faculty of Law at the University of British Columbia; he later served on the B.C. Law Reform Commission, 1985–92), conducted an in-depth evaluation of an experimental public defender office situated in Burnaby, British Columbia. The experimental office was operated under the auspices of the Legal Aid Society of British Columbia and the federal Department of Justice and compared the cost-effectiveness and cost-efficiency of the staff public defender office against the provision of criminal legal aid through more traditional judicare procedures in which private practitioners were hired on a case by cases basis to represent certain defendants and remunerated according to a fixed tariff.

The public defender research was followed by Patricia and Paul conducting an evaluation of the entire legal aid system in British Columbia for the Department of Justice during 1982–1985. Subsequent studies for the Department of Justice and the Legal Services Society of British Columbia followed through the 1980s and 1990s. Pat and Paul worked with colleague Stephen Easton to develop a series of studies on cost and efficiency in delivery of legal aid services (1994). Paul participated in a major international development project in which Canada, through the United Nations' International Centre for Criminal Law Reform, provided expert technical assistance to the People's Republic of China in creating a criminal legal aid system aimed at improving the standards of justice in China (2002).

Government of Canada Operations

Patricia and Paul spent much of the 1980s on leave from Simon Fraser University, working for the Government of Canada in Ottawa. Initially asked by the Department of Justice to conduct a comprehensive program evaluation of the litigation sector of the Department (1987) they also became involved in a series of additional studies, in particular an evaluation of legal services provided to the other departments of government and an audit of security within the department.

Patricia served as Director of Program Evaluation in the Department of Justice from 1985 through 1989. Paul became Director of Program Evaluation and Special Reviews at the Public Service Commission of Canada from 1985 through 1988. They returned to Simon Fraser University over the course of 1988–1989.

Following their return to Simon Fraser University, they developed a method for profiling the work of Department of Justice lawyers in providing civil legal services to federal government departments through Departmental Legal Services Units (1990) and conducted a series of studies that led to the creation of information systems for tracking and controlling the work of federal Crown Agents in handling both criminal prosecutions and civil advice and litigation work on behalf of the government of Canada (1991).

The Institute for Canadian Urban Research Studies (ICURS)

During 1992, Patricia and Paul founded the Institute for Canadian Urban Research Studies (ICURS) as a multi-disciplinary institute at Simon Fraser University. Members of the institute were drawn from many different departments within the university including Business Administration, Computing Science, Criminology, Economics, Geography, and Mathematics. The focus of the institute has been the interactions between built and natural environments on the one hand and social and behavioural patterns on the other. ICURS has maintained a physical presence in the School of Criminology and much of its work has been in expanding the knowledge base in environmental criminology. Since 2005 ICURS has maintained a secure computing facility that houses extensive secure research data collections in criminology and criminal justice. ICURS now has research agreements in place with university research centers across Canada, in the United Kingdom, in Australia, and the United States. In 2016, ICURS developed a secure High Performance Computing facility with support from Compute Canada and the Canadian Foundation for Innovation.

Evidence-Based Criminology

Over the years, we have been heavily involved in empirical research aimed at establishing evidence-based understandings of different crime types and the structure of crime patterns. These studies have paid attention to breaking and entering (known as burglary in most of the rest of the world) and motor vehicle theft. We have also been very involved in understanding how urban form and the built environment shape crime patterns. In particular, we have demonstrated the empirical reality of neighbourhood edge effects (Song, Spicer, and Brantingham 2013) as predicted by crime pattern theory, have identified a crime concentration pattern quite different from usual hot spot patterns that we call "crime ridges" (Song, Spicer, Brantingham, and Frank

2013; Curman, Andresen, and Brantingham 2015), have examined how street networks and land uses interact to concentrate crime (Brantingham, Brantingham, and Molumby 1977; Beavon, Brantingham, and Brantingham 1994; Kinney et al. 2008); and have established the strong directionality in persistent offenders' journeys to crime (Frank, Andresen, and Brantingham 2012, 2013).

The directionality finding is particularly useful in understanding repeat offending. Analysis of thousands of persistent offender crime trips demonstrated that they almost always head in the same direction when they leave home: a single 30° angle radiating from an offender's home will capture 50% of all the offences they are known to have committed; 90% of their crimes can be captured with a single 110° angle radiating from home.

Computer Simulations in Criminology and Criminal Justice

Over the years we have been very interested in the use of computer simulation as a method of describing the operation of the criminal justice system (see Brantingham, Brantingham, and Dyerson 1976). The transition from the computing environment at Florida State University to the computing environment at Simon Fraser University necessitated our setting simulation modeling aside until technological advances again made use of large-scale computing feasible. We then returned to exploration of the possibilities offered by this approach to research (Brantingham and Brantingham 2004; Brantingham et al. 2008; Alimadad et al. 2008). In addition to modeling the operation of the criminal justice system under many different policy and resource conditions, computer simulations of various kinds can be used to test criminological theory. We have worked with colleagues in the fields of computing science, mathematics, and geography to test several propositions in environmental criminology and crime pattern theory (e.g., Brantingham et al. 2005; Malleson and Brantingham 2009; Brantingham et al. 2011). We have also worked with colleagues from the SFU School of Interactive Arts and Technology to explore the use of computer generated virtual environments to test theory and to explore dimensions of the fear of crime (e.g., Park et al. 2008, 2010, 2012).

In 2005, in recognition of her contribution to creation of the field, Patricia was appointed to the world's first endowed chair in computational criminology and has since served as RCMP University Professor of Computational Criminology at Simon Fraser University. Paul has served as RCMP University Professor of Crime Analysis at the same time.

New Techniques of Measurement and Analysis

Topology: Patricia and Paul have long been committed to finding new techniques for measuring and analyzing crimes and patterns in crime. They have, led by Patricia, been particularly interested in using the branch of mathematics called *topology*—the generalized science of geometry in n-dimensional space—to understand the structure of neighbourhoods and how that structure shapes where crimes concentrate (Brantingham and Brantingham 1975, 1978; 1994; 2015; Brantingham et al. 2009; Frank et al. 2010). This type of analysis has proven particularly useful in understanding crime patterns in Greater Vancouver. In addition, it has begun to prove useful in looking at the structure of organized criminal groups in Canada (see Brantingham et al. 2012; Tayebi et al. 2014).

Location Quotients of Crime (LQC): Another innovation in measurement stems from recognized recognition that the *location quotient*, a standard analytic tool used by geographers and regional planners to measure how the economic activities of different communities within a larger region differ from the average economic activity pattern of the region as a whole, could be used to understand how the crime patterns of a particular community differ from the average crime patterns of that community's province or how a provincial or territorial crime pattern differs from Canada's overall crime pattern, the *location quotient of crime*, or *LQC* (see Brantingham and Brantingham 1995, 1997). Use of the LQC can help explain why crime patterns mapped at different spatial resolutions look so different from one another (Brantingham, Dyreson, and Brantingham 1976). LQC analysis has proven particularly useful in understanding the very different crime patterns that are seen in the large cities of southern Canada and the small cities and rural areas of northern Canada (Carlton, Brantingham, and Brantingham 2014).

Crime Gravity Scores: The Crime Gravity Score (CGS) represents an alternative to the standard crime rate and the crime severity index produced by the Canadian Centre for Justice Statistics at Statistic Canada. The standard crime rate is a measure of the unweighted count of criminal events recorded in the Uniform Crime Reports system per unit volume of population and is useful for making comparisons between communities of different size or for the same community over time. The standard crime rate has some imperfections: murder, motor vehicle theft, and possession of cannabis are treated equally—a crime is a crime is a crime. The Crime Severity Index (CSI), developed by the Canadian Centre for Criminal Justice Statistics, utilizes crime weights derived from the average sentences handed down by the courts to persons convicted of specific types of crime, again per unit volume of population. The CSI improves on the standard crime rate as an aggregate measure by treating different crimes differently: murder carries a weight of 7401.75 per crime, motor vehicle theft carries a weight of 84.44 per crime, while possession of cannabis carries a weight of 6.71 per crime. The index is constructed by multiplying the count of each crime type by its weight, summing the resultant numbers, dividing the summed result by jurisdictional resident population and standardizing by first multiplying to a unit volume of population then indexing the result to the calculated 2005 CSI value for Canada as a whole set to an index value of 100. Obviously one murder has the same impact on the crime severity index score as 83 motor vehicle thefts or more than one thousand cannabis possession crimes. This is an improvement over the standard crime weight but still correlates with the standard crime rate at $r = 0.9$. Paul has developed the CGS which provides an alternative view of the gravity of the group of crimes which must be handled by police. It begins by using crime counts and their severity weights, just as the calculation of the CSI does, but divides by the total number of crimes rather than by population. The CSI measures the severity of the crimes risked by any individual resident of a community; the CGS measures the gravity of the average crime handled by the police. It is a better measure of police criminal workload. Note that the crime gravity score declined much less sharply than the crime rate or the crime severity index scores between 1998 and 2014.

Thoughts on Canadian Criminology

Over the past 40 years or so, Canadian criminology has evolved from a scattering of people with an interest in crime issues spread across schools of law, departments of sociology, social work and psychology, and a few university programs largely devoted to producing personnel for Correctional Services Canada into a well-grounded, evidence-driven discipline committed to scientific analysis of crime and criminals and to use of those analyses to shape both criminal policy and criminal justice system operations. Reflecting this evolution, the premier Canadian scholarly journal in the field has changed its name from its original *Canadian Journal of Corrections* (1958–1969) to *Canadian Journal of Criminology and Corrections* (1970-1977) then to the *Canadian Journal of Criminology* (1978–2002) and is now (since 2003) the *Canadian Journal of Criminology and Criminal Justice.*

The Canadian criminal justice system has evolved from a strictly blue-collar set of occupations to one which increasingly is staffed by university-trained professionals. The expansion of university degree programs across the country—but particularly in Quebec and British Columbia—has, over this time, created a criminal justice system that increasingly works with university researchers in looking for policies and practices, based on better empirical understandings of criminal events and the people involved in them, that will reduce the quantum of crime and improve our ability to deal with the crimes that do occur.

In our view, Canadian criminology and criminal justice now operates in several different but interrelated intellectual areas: crime analysis; crime prevention; equitable and cost-effective justice operations; offender management; and evidence-driven policy formulation.

In the ***crime analysis*** area, researchers—often working in collaboration with criminal justice agencies—are continually developing better empirical understandings of Canadian crime patterns. We now understand that a very large proportion of all crimes are committed by a very small but persistent portion of the total population (see, e.g., Carrington, Matarazzo, and de Souza 2005) and that repeat victimization is also a major element in the overall crime pattern (see, e.g., Frank, Brantingham, and Farrell 2012). Most offenders commit their few crimes at relatively young ages, then desist. Persistent offenders, in contrast, continue to commit crime over very long careers. Most crimes carry relatively light CSI seriousness weights; very serious crimes are rare. In British Columbia in 2014, for instance, the five most frequently reported offences, accounting for 53% of all reported offences, were theft of $5,000 or under from a motor vehicle with seriousness weight of about 37, mischief with a seriousness weight of 30, disturbing the peace with a seriousness weight of 9, other theft of $5,000 or under with a seriousness weight of 37, and breaking and entering with a seriousness weight of about 187. In contrast, murder, the most serious offence with a weight of about 7042, accounted for just two one-hundredths of one percent (0.02%) of reported offences in 2014. Robbery, which has a seriousness weight of 583, accounted just eight tenths of one percent (0.8%) of reported offences.

We also understand that most crimes are committed very close to the offender's anchor points, usually the home anchor point (see, e.g., Andresen, Felson, and Frank 2012) and that most journeys to crime vector are in the same direction (Frank, Andresen, and Brantingham 2012, 2013). This tells us that crime clusters into corridors and ridges rather than into simple "hot spots" (Song et al. 2013; Curman, Andresen, and Brantingham 2015) and is most intense along edges between different types of neighbourhoods (Song, Spicer, and Brantingham 2013).

An important development in recent years has been the migration of crime from the relative visibility of the street to the relative invisibility of the internet. Internet-based theft, extortion, impersonation, bullying, harassment, and emotional assault are growing problems with remarkably low rates of reporting to the police. Criminal conspiracies ranging from international terrorism to child pornography are facilitated by computer communication. Canadian criminologists and Canadian criminal justice personnel need to develop a whole new set of skills grounded in mathematics and computer science in order to research and address this new dimension of crime.

The ability for criminologists to provide detailed empirical analysis of crime has been made possible through the development of computerized databases by Canadian criminal justice agencies and the development of research- and data-sharing partnerships between agencies and universities. The creation of secure high-performance research computing facilities such as the one at the Institute for Canadian Urban Research Studies (ICURS) at Simon Fraser University means that Canadian criminologists will be able, increasingly, to do better and more detailed research using big data.

In the ***crime prevention*** area, Canadian criminologists have been able to develop focused prevention models that operate at the primary, secondary, and tertiary levels of intervention for both the domain of the criminal event and the domain of criminality (Brantingham 2010). Combinations of situational and developmental prevention strategies are likely to substantially reduce the volume of crimes faced by Canadians while deflecting many potential offenders from ever becoming involved in committing a crime (Brantingham and Brantingham 2012). Better prediction methods will allow criminologists and intervention agencies to anticipate the patterns of displacement following a preventive intervention, and put resources in place to prevent that displacement from occurring (Brantingham and Brantingham 2003).

In the area of ***equitable and cost-effective criminal justice operations***, Canadian criminologists are increasingly able to provide evidence on how to make the operation of the criminal justice system both fairer and more effective. It is worth noting that we now know that public expectations of police range far beyond crime fighting—only about 20% to 30% of calls for police service involve a recordable criminal event. Most police activity is centered on protection of public safety and preservation of community tranquility. As crime rates have dropped since the mid-1990s, the amount of time it takes to try any criminal case has expanded such that backlog issues and questions of fairness have become matters of substantive concern. Hence, a major challenge for the next generation of criminologists will be finding ways to help the criminal courts become both better and more efficient fact finders providing speedier and more accurate resolution of criminal cases.

In the area of ***offender management*** we have learned that the majority of offenders can be managed with minimal sanctions and still prevented from committing further offences. Restorative justice initiatives combined with community correctional supervision hold much promise, but require careful evaluation and further research.

We have also learned that there is a small group of persistent and prolific offenders who are responsible for most crimes. Persons with mental health and drug addiction issues comprise one sub-group of persistent offenders. These people require assistance with their multiple problems through multi-agency cooperation between police, courts, health agencies, and social agencies. University-based criminologists can provide a working forum in which these agencies can research joint answers and conduct evaluations of assistance programs. A second group of persistent, prolific offenders cannot be deterred and must be managed, again through multi-agency programs that include incarceration, training, community surveillance, and social assistance. Much research is needed into such programs.

In terms of *evidence-driven policy development,* criminological research into specific crime patterns can have important effects in producing policy that provides for less crime and more community tranquility. We sense that current and future decision makers in all parts of the Canadian criminal justice system are interested in research that can help them do their jobs more effectively.

In sum, we believe that the future for Canadian criminology is one that is both challenging and exciting. There is a real demand for trained criminologists to work at all levels of the criminal justice system as data and policy analysts as well as operational personnel.

References

Selected Publications and Papers

Given that our academic careers span several decades and we have engaged in a wide range of issues, we have grouped publications into several sub-headings.

Crime Pattern Theory

(1978) P.J. Brantingham, and P.L. Brantingham, "A Theoretical Model of Crime Site Selection," pp. 105–118 in M. Krohn and R.L. Akers, *Crime, Law and Sanctions: Theoretical Perspectives*. Beverly Hills, Calif.: Sage Publications

(1981) P.L. Brantingham, and P.J. Brantingham, *Environmental Criminology*. Beverly Hill, Calif.: Sage Publications.

(1981) P.L. Brantingham, and P.J. Brantingham, "Mobility, Notoriety, and Crime: A Study in the Crime Patterns of Urban Nodal Points," *Journal of Environmental Systems* 11:89–99.

(1981) P.L. Brantingham, and P.J. Brantingham, "Notes on the Geometry of Crime," pp. 27–54 in P. Brantingham and P. Brantingham, *Environmental Criminology*. Beverly Hills, Calif.: SAGE.

(1984) P. Brantingham, and P. Brantingham, *Patterns in Crime*. New York: Macmillan.

(1991) P. Brantingham, and P. Brantingham, *Environmental Criminology*. (2d ed.) Prospect Heights, Illinois: Waveland Press.

(1993) P.L. Brantingham, and P.J. Brantingham, "Environment, Routine and Situation: Toward a Pattern Theory of Crime," *Advances in Criminological Theory* 5:259–294.

(1993) P.L. Brantingham, and P.J. Brantingham, "Nodes, Paths and Edges: Considerations on the Complexity of Crime and the Physical Environment," *Journal of Environmental Psychology* 13:3–28.

(1995) P.L. Brantingham, and P. J. Brantingham, "Criminality of place: Crime generators and crime attractors," *European Journal on Criminal Policy and Research* 3: 5–26.

(1997) P.J. Brantingham, and P. L. Brantingham. "Understanding and Controlling Crime and Fear of Crime: Conflicts and Trade-Offs in Crime Prevention Planning," pp.43–60 in S. P. Lab, *Crime Prevention at a Crossroads*. Cincinnati: Anderson Publishing.

(1999) P.L. Brantingham, and P.J. Brantingham, "A Theoretical Model of Crime Hot Spot Generation." *Studies on Crime and Crime Prevention* 8: 7–26.

(2003) P. J. Brantingham, and P.L. Brantingham, "Anticipating the Displacement of Crime Using the Principles of Environmental Criminology," *Crime Prevention Studies* 16: 119–148

(2008) J.B. Kinney, P.L. Brantingham, K. Wuschke, M.G. Kirk, and P.J. Brantingham, "Crime Attractors, Generators and Detractors: Land Use and Urban Crime Opportunities." *Built Environment* 34(1): 62–74.

(2008) P.L. Brantingham, and P.J. Brantingham "Crime Pattern Theory." In Richard Wortley and Lorraine Mazerolle (eds.), *Environmental Criminology and Crime Analysis*, pp. 78–93. Cullompton, U.K.: Willan Publishing.

(2010) P. L. Brantingham, "Crime Pattern Theory." In B. Fisher and S. Lab (eds.),

Encyclopedia of Victimology and Crime Prevention. Beverly Hills: Sage Publishing.

(2013) P.J. Brantingham. and P.L. Brantingham, The Theory of Target Search. In Cullen, F. and Wilcox, P. (eds.), *The Oxford Handbook of Criminological Theory.* New York: Oxford U Press, 2013. Pp. 535–553,

EVIDENCE BASED CRIMINOLOGY

(1975) P.J. Brantingham, and P.L. Brantingham, "The Spatial Patterning of Burglary," *The Howard Journal of Penology and Crime Prevention* 14: 11–24.

(1977) P.J. Brantingham, and P.L. Brantingham, "Housing Patterns and Burglary in a Medium-Sized American City," pp. 63–74 in J. Scott and S. Dinitz, *Criminal Justice Planning.* New York: Praeger.

(1977) P.J. Brantingham, P.L. Brantingham, and T. Molumby, "Perceptions of Crime in a Dreadful Enclosure," *Ohio Journal of Science* 77:256–261.

(1980) P.J. Brantingham, and P.L. Brantingham, "Crime, Occupation, and Economic Specialization: A Consideration of Intermetropolitan Patterns," pp. 93–108 in D.E. Georges-Abeyie and K.D. Harries, *Crime: A Spatial Perspective.* New York: Columbia University Press.

(1994) D.L.K. Beavon, P.L., Brantingham, and P.J. Brantingham, "The Influence of Street Networks on the Patterning of Property Offenses," at pp. 115–148 in Clarke, R. V. (ed.) *Crime Prevention Studies*, vol. 2. Monsey, NY: Criminal Justice Press.

(1994) Z.P.L. Fleming, P.L. Brantingham, and P.J. Brantingham, "Exploring Auto Theft in British Columbia," at pp. 47–91 in Clarke, R. V. (ed.) *Crime Prevention Studies,* vol. 3. Monsey, NY: Criminal Justice Press.

(1994) P.L. Brantingham et P.J. Brantingham, "La Concentration Spatiale Relative de la Criminalité et son Analyse: Vers un Renouvellement de la Criminologie Environmentale," Criminologie 27: 81–97.

(1996) P. Barclay, J. Buckley, P.J. Brantingham, P.L. Brantingham, and T. Whinn-Yates, "Preventing Auto Theft in Suburban Vancouver Commuter Lots: Effects of a Bike Patrol." *Crime Prevention Studies* 6: 133–161.

(2007) M. Andresen, and P.J. Brantingham, *Hot Spots of Crime in Vancouver and Their Relationship with Population Characteristics.* Ottawa: Department of Justice.

(2008) G. Jenion, and P.J. Brantingham, *Project 6116 National Study of Youth Offender Involvement in Auto Theft Final Report: British Columbia 2004–2005.* Windsor: NCE Auto21.

(2010) A.H. Ghaseminejad, and P.J. Brantingham, "An Executive Decision Support System for Longitudinal Statistical Analysis of Crime and Law Enforcement Performance." *Proceedings of IEEE-ISI Vancouver.*

(2012) Frank, R., Andresen, M.A. and Brantingham, P.L. Criminal directionality and the structure of urban form. *Journal of Environmental Psychology* 32(1): 37–42.

(2012) Frank, R., Brantingham, P.L., and Farrell, G. Estimating the True Rate of Repeat Victimization from Police Recorded Crime Data: A Study of Burglary in Metro Vancouver. *Canadian Journal of Criminology and Criminal Justice*, 54: 481–494.

(2012) Patricia L. Brantingham, Paul J. Brantingham, Uwe Glässer and Mohammad A. Tayebi. *An Analysis of RCMP "E" Division Data to Estimate Possible Criminal Organizations: Final Descriptive Report.* Ottawa: Public Safety Canada

(2013) Frank, R., Andresen, M.A. and Brantingham, P.L. Visualizing the directional bias in property crime incidents for five Canadian municipalities. *Canadian Geographer*, 57(1): 31–42.

(2013) Song J, Spicer V., Brantingham P., Frank, R. Crime Ridges: Exploring the Relationship between Crime Attractors and Offender Movement. *2013 European Intelligence and Security Informatics Conference.* IEEE; 2013: 75–82.

(2013) Song, J., Spicer, V., & Brantingham, P.L. The edge effect: Exploring high crime zones near residential neighborhoods. *2013 IEEE Inernational Conference on Intelligence and Security Informatics.* 2013: 245–250.

(2014) Carleton, R., Brantingham, Patricia L., and Brantingham, Paul J. Crime Specialization in Rural British Columbia, Canada. *Canadian Journal of Criminology and Criminal Justice* 56 (5):595–621.

(2015) Curman, Andrea S. N., Andresen, M.A., and Brantingham, Paul J. Crime and Place: A Longitudinal Examination of Street Segment Patterns in Vancouver, BC. *Journal of Quantitative Criminology.* 31:127–147 (published online, May, 2014).

Crime Analysis

Topological Analysis

(1975) P.L. Brantingham, and P.J. Brantingham, "Residential Burglary and Urban Form," *Urban Studies,* 12: 273–284.

(1978) P.L. Brantingham and P.J. Brantingham, "A Topological Technique for Regionalization," *Environment and Behavior,* 10: 335–353.

(1994) P.L. Brantingham et P.J. Brantingham, "La Concentration Spatiale Relative de la Criminalité et son Analyse: Vers un Renouvellement de la Criminologie Environmentale," *Criminologie* ,27: 81–97.

(2009) P.L. Brantingham, P.J. Brantingham, M. Vajihollahi, and K. Wuschke, "A Topological Technique for Crime Analysis at Multiple Scales of Aggregation." In D. Weisburd, W. Bernasco and G. Bruinsma (eds.) *Putting Crime in its Place: Units of Analysis in Spatial Crime Research.* New York: Springer-Verlag.

(2010) R. Frank, A. Park, P.L. Brantingham, J. Clare, K. Wuschke, and M. Vajihollahi, "Identifying High Risk Crime Areas using Topology". *Proceedings of IEEE Intelligence and Security Informatics-Public Safety and Security Conference, Vancouver, May 2010.*

(2015) P.L. Brantingham, and P.J. Brantingham, Understanding Crime with Computational Topology. In Martin A. Andresen and Graham Farrell (eds.) *The Criminal Act: The Role and Influence if Routine Activity Theory.* Pp. 131–145. New York: Palgrave Macmillan.

Location Quotients

(1995) P.L. Brantingham, and P.J. Brantingham, "Location Quotients and Crime Hot Spots in the City," at pp. 129–150 in Carolyn Rebecca Block, Margaret Dabdoub and Suzanne Fregly (eds.), *Crime Analysis Through Computer Mapping.* Washington, D.C.: Police Executive Research Forum.

(1997) P.L. Brantingham, and P.J. Brantingham, "Mapping Crime for Analytic Purposes: Location Quotients, Counts, and Rates," *Crime Prevention Studies,* 8: 259–284.

(2014) R. Carleton, P.L. Brantingham, and P.J. Brantingham, Crime Specialization in Rural British Columbia, Canada. *Canadian Journal of Criminology and Criminal Justice,* 56 (5): 595–621.

Other Techniques

(1976) P.J. Brantingham, D.A. Dyreson, and P.L. Brantingham, Crime Seen Through a Cone of Resolution, *American Behavioral Scientist,* 20: 261–273.

(2008) M.A. Andresen, and P.L. Brantingham, "Visualizing ambient population data within census boundaries: A diasymetric mapping procedure." *Cartographica,* 43(4): 267–275.

(2009) M.A. Andresen, K. Wuschke, J.B. Kinney, P. Brantingham, and P.L. Brantingham. "Cartograms, crime, and location quotients," *Crime Patterns and Analysis,* 2(1): 31–46.

(2013) P.J. Brantingham, Crime Rates, the Crime Severity Index and Crime Gravity Scores. ICURS Technical Note 1.1. Burnaby, B.C.: Institute for Canadian Urban Research Studies.

(2014) A. Reid, R. Frank, N. Iwanski, V. Dabbaghian, and P.L. Brantingham, Uncovering the Spatial Patterning of Crimes: A Criminal Movement Model (CriMM). *Journal of Research in Crime and Delinquency,* 51: 230–255.

(2014) M. Tayebi, M. Ester, U. Glässer, and P.L. Brantingham. Spatially embedded co-offence prediction using supervised learning. *KDD 2014 Proceedings of the 20th ACD SIGKDD International conference on Knowledge and Data Mining,* pp. 1789–1798.

Crime Prevention

(1976) P.J. Brantingham, and F.L. Faust, A Conceptual Model of Crime Prevention, *Crime and Delinquency*, 22: 284–296.

(1980) P.L. Brantingham "Crime Prevention Through Environmental Design: An Overview, *Proceedings of the Seminar on Crime Prevention Through Environmental Design*. Vancouver: Regional Consultation Centre, Ministry of the Solicitor General and British Columbia Association of Chiefs of Police.

(1980) P.L. Brantingham. "Crime Prevention Through Urban Planning, "Proceedings of the Seminar on Crime Prevention Through Environmental Design." Vancouver: Regional Consultation Centre, Ministry of the Solicitor General and British Columbia Association of Chiefs of Police.

(1984) P.L. Brantingham, and P.J. Brantingham, "Burglar Mobility and Crime Prevention Planning," in R.V.G. Clarke and T. Hope, Coping with Burglary: Research Perspectives on Policy. Boston: Kluwer-Nijhoff.

(1986) P.L. Brantingham. "Trends in Canadian Crime Prevention," pp. 103–112 in Kevin Heal and Gloria Laycock (eds.), *Situational Crime Prevention: From Theory to Practice*. London: HMSO.

(1988) P.L. Brantingham, and P.J. Brantingham. Situational Crime Prevention in British Columbia, *Journal of Security Administration.* 11: 17–27.

(1989) P.L. Brantingham. Crime Prevention: The North American Experience, at pp. 331–360 in D. J. Evans and D.T. Herbert (eds.), *The Geography of Crime*. London: Routledge.

(1990) P.L. Brantingham, and P.J. Brantingham, "Situational Crime Prevention in Practice," *Canadian Journal of Criminology,* 32: 17–40.

(1995) P.J. Brantingham, and P.L. Brantingham, "Environmental Criminology and Crime Prevention," at pp. 207–240 in P.-O. H. Wikstrom, R. V. Clarke and J. McCord (eds.), *Integrating Crime Prevention Strategies: Propensity and Opportunity.* Stockholm:

National Council for Crime Prevention Sweden.

(1996) P.L. Brantingham. " Crime Prevention: The Future" at pp. 113–138 in Serge Brochu, *Perspectives actuelles en criminologie.* Montréal: Centre international de criminologie comparée, Université de Montréal.

(1997) P.J. Brantingham and P.L. Brantingham, "Understanding and Controlling Crime and Fear of Crime: Conflicts and Trade-Offs in Crime Prevention Planning," at pp. 43–60 in S. P. Lab (ed.) *Crime Prevention at a Crossroads.* Cincinnati: Anderson Publishing Co.

(1998) P.J. Brantingham, and P.L. Brantingham, "Environmental Criminology: From Theory to Urban Planning Practice." *Studies on Crime and Crime Prevention* 7: 31–60.

(2000) P.L. Brantingham, and P.J. Brantingham, "Police Use of Environmental Criminology in Strategic Crime Prevention." *Police Practice and Research* 1: 211–240.

(2001) P.J. Brantingham, and P.L. Brantingham, "The Implications of the Criminal Event Model for Crime Prevention" in *Advances in Criminological Theory* 9: 277–303 (The Process & Structure of Crime: Criminal Events & Crime Analysis, edited by R.F. Meier, V. Sacco and L.W. Kennedy). New Brunswick, N.J.: Transaction Press

(2005) P.L. Brantingham, P.J. Brantingham, and W. Taylor, "Situational Crime Prevention as a Key Component in Embedded Crime Prevention." *Canadian Journal of Criminology and Criminal Justice*, 47: 271–292.

(2010) Paul J. Brantingham. "Domains of Crime Prevention." In B. Fisher and S. Lab (eds.), *Encyclopedia of Victimology and Crime Prevention.* Beverly Hills: Sage Publishing.

(2012) Paul Brantingham and Patricia Brantingham. Situating Situational Crime Prevention: Anchoring a Politically Palatable Crime Reduction Strategy. In Nick Tilley and Graham Farrell, *The Reasoning Criminologist: Essays in Honour of Ronald V. Clarke.* Cullompton, U.K.: Willan Publishing.

Criminal Justice Operations

Police

(1992) W. Snowdon, P. Brantingham, S. Simpson, and G. Strathdee. *Report of the Task Force on Public Order for the Province of British Columbia.* Victoria: Ministry of the Attorney General.

(2007) Aili E. Malm, Nahanni Pollard, Paul J. Brantingham, Darryl Plecas, Patricia L. Brantingham, and J. Bryan Kinney. Utilizing Activity-Based Timing to Analyze Police Service Delivery. *Law Enforcement Executive Forum,* 7(5): 1–20.

(2010) F. Young, R.C. Bent, J. Clare, R. Frank, P.J. Brantingham, and P.L. Brantingham. *Feasibility Study on the Development of a Policing Complexity Index.* Institute for Canadian Urban Research Studies for British Columbia Ministry of Public Safety and Solicitor General and Statistics Canada.

(2014) ICURS Staff. *Economics of Policing: Complexity and Costs in Canada, 2014.* Burnaby: Institute for Canadian Urban Research Studies, Simon Fraser University.

(2015) P.J. Brantingham. Notes on the economics of policing in context. The Second Summit on the Economics of Policing and Public Safety: Innovation and Partnerships 2015. Ottawa.

COURTS AND THE LEGAL SYSTEM

Law

(1974) F.L. Faust, and P.J. Brantingham. *Juvenile Justice Philosophy.* St. Paul, Minn.: West Publishing Co.

(1979) F.L. Faust, and P.J. Brantingham. *Juvenile Justice Philosophy* (2d ed.). St. Paul, Minn.: West Publishing Co.

(1979) P.J. Brantingham, and J.M. Kress. *Structure, Law, and Power: Essays in the Sociology of Law.* Beverly Hills, Calif.: Sage Publications.

The Courts

(1979) P. Brantingham, and T. Blomberg. *Courts and Diversion: Policy and Operations Studies.* Beverly Hills, Calif.: Sage Publications.

(1985) P.L. Brantingham, "Sentencing Disparity: An Analysis of Judicial Consistency," *Journal of Quantitative Criminology,* 3: 281–305.

(2011) P.J. Brantingham, A.H. Ghaseminejad, and P.L. Brantingham. "The Distribution of Event Complexity in the British Columbia Court System: An Analysis Based on the CourBC Analytical System." *Proc. European Intelligence and Security Informatics Conference (EISIC).* Athens, Greece.

(2014) A. Reid, G. Farrell, S. Mu, W. Richter, A. Ghaseminejad, P.J. Brantingham, and P.L. Brantingham. A Matrix of Measures of Court Caseload. *Canadian Bar Review,* 92: 105–122.

Legal Aid

(1981) N. Maxim, and P.L. Brantingham. *The Burnaby, British Columbia Experimental Public Defender Project. Report 6: Relationship Analysis.* Ottawa: Department of Justice.

(1981) P.L. Brantingham and N. Maxim. *The Burnaby, British Columbia Experimental Public Defender Project. Report 3: Cost Analysis.* Ottawa: Department of Justice.

(1981) P.L. Brantingham, and R. Corrado. *The Burnaby, British Columbia Experimental Public Defender Project. Report 4: Client Satisfaction Analysis.* Ottawa: Department of Justice.

(1981) P.L. Brantingham. *The Burnaby, British Columbia Experimental Public Defender Project. Report 1: Summary. Ottawa*: Department of Justice.

(1981) P.L. Brantingham. *The Burnaby, British Columbia Experimental Public Defender Project. Report 2: Effectiveness Analysis.* Ottawa: Department of Justice.

(1981) P.L. Brantingham. *The Burnaby, British Columbia Experimental Public Defender Project. Report 5: Tariff Analysis.* Ottawa: Department of Justice.

(1981) P.L. Brantingham. *The Burnaby, British Columbia Experimental Public Defender Project. Report 7: Distributional Impact.* Ottawa: Department of Justice.

(1981) P.L. Brantingham. *The Burnaby, British Columbia Experimental Public Defender Project. Report 8: Technical Appendix.* Ottawa: Department of Justice.

(1983) P.L. Brantingham, P.J. Brantingham, and D.J. Beavon. *Sentencing in Two Canadian Courts.* Ottawa: Department of Justice.

(1984) P.L. Brantingham, and P.J. Brantingham. *An Evaluation of Legal Aid in British Columbia.* Ottawa: Department of Justice.

(1985) P.L. Brantingham. Public Defender and Judicare: Case Outcome Differences, *Canadian Journal Criminology, 27*: 67–81

(1989) P.L. Brantingham, and P.J. Brantingham. "L'aide juridique au Canada, en Angleterre et aux Etats Unis: une comparison," *La Revue de Droit Penal et de Criminologie.*

(1990) P.J. Brantingham, and P.L. Brantingham. *Strategic Options in the Evaluation of Legal Aid in Canada*. Ottawa: Department of Justice.

(1992) P.J. Brantingham, P.L. Brantingham, and L. Fraser. *A Technical Planning Tool for the Legal Services Society of British Columbia: A Background Study.* Vancouver: Legal Services Society of British Columbia.

(1992) P.L. Brantingham, P.J. Brantingham, and P. Wong. *Patterns in Legal Aid, Second Edition*. Ottawa: Department of Justice.

(1994) S. Easton, P.J. Brantingham, and P.L. Brantingham. *Cost and Efficiency in Canadian Legal Aid.* Ottawa: Ottawa University: Queen's Economic Projects, Government and Competitiveness Seminar.

(2002) P.J. Brantingham. "Canadian Legal Aid Evaluations: Cost Efficiency and Cost Effectiveness Lessons." Pp. 343–366 in International Centre for Criminal Law Reform and Criminal Justice Policy, *Breaking New Ground: A Collection of Papers in the International Centre's Canada-China Cooperation Programme.* Vancouver: ICCLR. [English version of a 1999 article published in Chinese.]

Department of Justice Canada Operations

(1987) P.L. Brantingham, and P.J. Brantingham. *An Evaluation of Litigation Services in the Department of Justice.* Ottawa: Department of Justice.

(1990) P.L. Brantingham, P.J. Brantingham, L. Fraser, and P. Wong. *An Approach to Work Profiling in the Legal Services Sector of the Department of Justice.* Ottawa: Department of Justice.

(1991) P.L. Brantingham, P.J. Brantingham, J. Brockman, F. Dorsemaine, S. Easton, L. Fraser, and P. Wong. *Crown Agent (Criminal Law) Management: A System Design Study*. Ottawa: Department of Justice.

(1991) P.L. Brantingham, P.J. Brantingham, J. Brockman, F. Dorsemaine, S. Easton, L. Fraser, and P. Wong. *Crown Agent (Civil Law) Management: A System Design Study.* Ottawa: Department of Justice.

Computer Simulation of Criminal Justice Operations

(1976) P.L. Brantingham, P.J. Brantingham, and D.A. Dyreson, "MODPOP: An Approach to Policy Planning in Criminal Justice Through Dynamic Simulation Modeling," pp. 94–109 in V. Fox, *Proceedings, 21st Annual Southern Conference on Corrections.* Tallahassee: Florida State University.

(2004) P.L. Brantingham, and P.J. Brantingham. "Computer Simulation as a Tool for Environmental Criminologists," *Security Journal,* 17(1): 21–30.

(2005) P.L. Brantingham, P.J. Brantingham, and U. Glässer. "Computer Simulation as a Research Tool in Criminology and Criminal Justice." *Criminal Justice Matters,* 58: 19–20.

(2005) P.L. Brantingham, U. Glässer, B. Kinney, K. Singh, and M. Vajihollahi. Modeling Urban Crime Patterns: Viewing Multi-Agent Systems as Abstract State Machines. In D. Beauquier, E. Börger and A. Slissenko (eds.), *Proc. 12th Intl. Workshop on Abstract State Machines*, Paris, Mar. 2005, pp. 101–117.

(2008) A. Alimadad, P.L. Brantingham, P.J. Brantingham, V. Dabbaghian-Abdoly, R. Ferguson, E. Fowler, A.H. Ghaseminejad, C. Giles, J. Li, N. Pollard, A. Rutherford, and

A. van der Waall. "Using Varieties of Simulation Modeling for Criminal Justice System Analysis." In Lin Liu and John Eck (eds.), *Artificial Crime Analysis Systems: Using Computer Simulations and Geographic Information Systems*, pp. 372–412. Hershey, PA: Idea Group Publishing.

(2008) P.L. Brantingham, U. Glasser, P. Jackson, B. Kinney, and M. Vajihollahi. "Mastermind: Computational Modeling and Simulation of Spatiotemporal Aspects of Crime in Urban Environments." In Lin Liu and John Eck (eds.), *Artificial Crime Analysis Systems: Using Computer Simulations and Geographic Information Systems*, pp. 252–280. Hershey, PA: Idea Group Publishing.

(2008) A. Park, T. Calvert, P.L. Brantingham, and P.J. Brantingham. The Use of Virtual and Mixed Reality Environments for Urban Behavioural Studies. *PsychNology* 6(2): 119–130.

(2009) N. Malleson, and P.L. Brantingham. "Prototype burglary simulations for crime reduction and forecasting." *Crime Patterns and Analysis,* 2(1): 47–66

(2010) A. Park, V. Spicer, M. Guterres, P. L. Brantingham, and G. Jenion. Testing Perception of Crime in a Virtual Environment. *Proceedings of IEEE Intelligence and Security* Informatics: Public Safety and Security Conference, Vancouver, May 2010.

(2011) V. Dabbaghian, V. Spicer, S.K, Singh, P. Borwein, and P.L. Brantingham. The Social Impact in a High-Risk Community: a Cellular Automata Model, *J of Computer Science,* 2: 238–246.

(2011) P. L. Brantingham, K. Wuschke, R. Frank, and P.J. Brantingham. "Crime Emergence and Simulation Modeling: Modeling Crime Space." In Jean Marie McGloin, Christopher Sullivan and Leslie Kennedy (eds) *Crime Emergence: Reducing Uncertainty in Theory and Research.* Chapter 11, pp. 198–224. New York and London: Routledge

(2012) A. Park, J. Clare, V. Spicer, P.L. Brantingham, T. Calvert, and G. Jenion. "Examining context-specific perceptions of risk: exploring the utility of "human-in-the-loop" simulation models for criminology." *Journal of Experimental Criminology* 8 (1): 29–47, 2012

THE COST OF CRIME

(1996) P.J. Brantingham and S. Easton. *The Crime Bill: Who Pays and How Much?* Vancouver: Fraser Institute.

(1998) P.J. Brantingham and S. Easton. *The Costs of Crime: How Much and Who Pays?* Vancouver: Fraser Institute.

(2014) S. Easton, H. Furness, and P.J. Brantingham. *The Cost of Crime in Canada: 2014*. Vancouver: Fraser Institute.

References in Addition to the Brantinghams' Selected Bibliography

M. Andresen, M. Felson, and R. Frank. (2012). The Geometry of Offending and Victimization. *Canadian Journal of Criminology and Criminal Justice,* 54: 495–510.

P. Carrington, A. Matarazzo, and P. de Sourza. (2005). *Court Careers of a Canadian Birth Cohort.* Ottawa: Statistics Canada. Catalogue 85-561-MIE 2005006.

M.J. Graetz, and C.H. Whitehead II. (1981). "Monrad Paulsen and the idea of a university law school." Faculty Scholarship Series, Yale University: Yale Law School.

FIFTEEN

From Indifference to Engagement: A Victims' Advocate Reflects on the Evolution of Victims' Rights in Canada

Arlène Gaudreault

The Dawning of Humanitarian Victimology

As I look back on my career, I consider myself fortunate to have been part of the first cohort of criminology students in the early 1970s. I chose this avenue of study because I wanted to help people in trouble. Criminology, then in its infancy, offered a wide array of possibilities for young professionals, the majority of whom were preparing for a career working with offenders. From the outset, I wanted to become involved in areas of intervention requiring innovation, developing new services, and thinking outside the box—at least by the standards of the time. This is what led me at the beginning of my career to work in a range of settings such as a halfway house, a group home for adolescent girls, and a school for children who were experiencing behavioural problems or had been victims of physical or sexual abuse. In 1984, I was hired as program head and field placement coordinator at École de criminologie de l'Université de Montréal. I held that position until 2009. I was also a lecturer on victimology from 1993 to 2010 for students enrolled in the bachelor's program as well as those enrolled in the master's and certificate program in criminology at the university. From 2000 to 2012, I was a visiting professor at Université de Pau in France in their master's program on the rights of victims.

I also served as president of the Association professionnelle des criminologues du Québec for 10 years (1974–1984). This position allowed me to interact with various criminal justice services (e.g., intervention, parole, youth probation centres, and prison settings) and to reflect on the ethical issues of our profession. I was very proud of my profession and I wanted it to be acknowledged and to contribute to the advancement of a more humane justice—a justice more respectful of the rights of offenders and victims.

I have also had the privilege of serving as community board member of the

Commission québécoise des libérations conditionnelles, in addition to serving on numerous work groups and boards of directors. All these experiences contributed to my personal and professional growth. But above all, my involvement in the field of victimology, more particularly with Association québécoise Plaidoyer-Victimes, is what most profoundly influenced my career path and remains the work I am most passionate about.

Initially, my university training had not prepared me to work with victims, as it was focused on helping and controlling both young and adult offenders. Recall that, in the early 1970s, victimology was practically absent from not only the Université de Montréal criminology curriculum, but from any criminology or criminal justice program in Canada. Humanitarian victimology was still in its early stages. As **Ezzat Fattah** (1991) noted, people at that time were more concerned with the victims' role in the offence and their relationship to the offender than with the recognition of their rights and of our responsibilities toward them.

In Canada, the first initiatives in favour of victims and their loved ones did not appear until the 1970s (Gaudreault 1996). Influenced by what was being done in the United States and New Zealand, a few provinces began implementing victim compensation programs with a view to assisting victims of crimes against the person.[26] For example, it was not until 1967 that Saskatchewan established the first victims' compensation program and not until 2014 did Canada enact the Canadian Victim's Bill of Rights.

During the 1970s, Canada along with several other countries witnessed the emergence of the feminist movement. It marked the beginning of a broad mobilization aiming to advance the rights of women: shedding light on violence against women, exposing inequalities and prejudices, demanding social and legislative changes, implementing community-based services, and transforming justice practices.

The physical and sexual abuse of children, long hidden from sight, was at the heart of the work of the Study Committee on Sexual Offences Against Children and Youth, Sexual Offences Against Children (Badgley Report 1984). The committee, which was chaired by Professor Robin Badgley of the University of Toronto, formulated several recommendations aiming to better protect children and youth, and to provide them with assistance services. Around the same time, the Federal-Provincial Working Group on Justice for Victims of Crime (1983) presented a grim portrait of the situation of victims in relation to both the assistance and treatment provided to them within the criminal justice system. There were many shortcomings, and it became clear there was

[26] For a detailed chronological overview of the victim's rights movement in Canada see the appendices to this chapter and also https://crcvc.ca/wp-content/uploads/2011/10/victims-rights_paper_DISCLAIMER_Feb2015.pdf.

much work to be done in the area of child protection.

These early initiatives brought us face to to face with the lack of resources available to victims, the lack of consideration shown to them when they cooperate with the criminal justice system, as well as our indifference toward them. The voices of victims' associations began to emerge, calling for action.

At this milestone in the development of assistance to victims, two criminologists emerged as leaders in Canada: **Micheline Baril**, then a professor at École de criminologie de l'Université de Montréal, and **Irvin Waller** of the University of Ottawa's Department of Criminology. Both were part of the Canadian delegation that participated in the drafting of the United Nations *Declaration of Basic Principles of Justice for Victims of Crime and Abuse of Power* (1985). Both contributed to work around the issue of victims' rights in the international community. They engaged in a veritable crusade to convince governments to implement major reforms in order to ensure that victims, those "orphans of the criminal justice system," were better treated (Waller 1981) and had access to services.

In Quebec, Micheline Baril (1941–1993; photo, below left) had a determining influence on my professional career and remains a major source of inspiration for many workers and researchers. In 1983, she introduced victimology as a field of study and practice at École de criminologie de l'Université de Montréal. At the same time, she initiated research and gave a voice to victims as a means of documenting—not to mention better understanding—their paths within the criminal justice system as they sought assistance (Baril 1983). Baril spoke to different groups, arguing that victims be treated with respect and compassion, regardless of their circumstances. Focusing on action, she was able to secure the funding necessary to establish the first Centre d'aide pour les victimes d'actes criminels in Quebec, an agency for which I was privileged to serve as coordinator (Gaudreault 1996). In 1984, convinced that victims needed a voice, she founded Association québécoise Plaidoyer-Victimes (AQPV), of which I was a member along with a few colleagues.

Baril, an energetic and visionary figure, seized every opportunity to demand services, policies, and legislation that would take into account the needs and concerns of victims and their loved ones. She passed away in the prime of life and, unfortunately, her work remains little known or poorly understood beyond the borders of Quebec and among younger generations of criminologists. Yet she handed down a precious inheritance in victimology and became renowned within the francophone community for her rigorous work and her ability to mobilize numerous workers in her quest of justice for victims (Cario and Gaudreault 2003).

Many people became engaged in the fight for victims' rights. At the time, governments provided virtually no funding for victim assistance. Nor were they sensitive to victims' voices. Unfortunately, many forms of violence were ignored, misunderstood, or trivialized. Victims were the target of prejudices and often perceived as being responsible for their own plight, as accepting of their fate, or as being overwhelmed by sorrow or anger. Changing attitudes toward them was only one of the challenges to be met. From an intervention perspective, we had much to learn to improve the way in which we treated, listened to, and accompanied victims. We also had much to do to ensure that their rights became rooted in our institutional practices and within our criminal justice system. There was no research or practical experience to draw upon at this time.

These obstacles, however, did not dampen our ambitions. On the contrary, this was an exciting time; we continued to operate in a context that provided an opportunity to innovate and contribute to change, to influence decision-makers as well as social and criminal justice policy-makers. It was an opportunity to develop new policies and to invest in new fields of research. We were driven by a profound conviction that members of society, collectively and individually, needed to demonstrate greater accountability toward victims and their loved ones. Those objectives remain central to the mission of Association québécoise Plaidoyer-Victimes (AQPV).

Association québécoise Plaidoyer-Victimes (AQPV): A Leader in Quebec and in Canada

AQPV has been instrumental in bringing the concerns of victims before several parliamentary commissions, committees, and task forces in both Quebec and the rest of Canada as well as in the tabling of legislation and actions plans aiming to improve the situation of victims and to better acknowledge their rights. AQPV's many publications, analyses, and position papers all demonstrate its expertise and its credibility with a range of authorities (www.aqpv.ca). This work also demonstrates that the recognition of victims' rights has taken place step-by-step.

AQPV members have spoken widely to groups and organizations, such as the Conférence des juges du Québec, the Bar of Quebec, the Fédération professionnelle des journalistes du Québec, the National Parole Board (NPB), the Canadian Institute for the Administration of Justice (CIAJ), the Quebec Society of Criminology (QSC) and the Canadian Criminal Justice Association (CCJA). Drawing upon mutual consultation with its membership and contributors, AQPV has also sponsored its own symposiums, workshops, and discussion forums. In the year 2000, under the auspices of the World Society of Victimology, the Association hosted the tenth International Symposium on Victimology in Montreal. The symposium attracted some 1,300 participants from around the world. I had the pleasure of co-chairing this event with Irvin Waller.

AQPV also produced and made available many documents to foster a better understanding of criminal victimization, to support the work and research of professionals in the field, and to improve the training of students interested in victimology or preparing for a career in this field. Since 2012, AQPV has begun to make available a series of manuals designed to provide better tools for victims and their loved ones, as well as recourse within the criminal justice system. AQPV has also provided a number of training activities that have contributed to the transfer and update of knowledge, to the improvement of the skill sets of professionals providing assistance to victims, and to the critical analysis of intervention-related issues. This contribution is significant in view of the many changes that have reconfigured victim assistance. Also, AQPV's training activities help with the specialization and professionalization of services.

It is difficult to do justice to the work of AQPV and to gauge its impact. One thing is certain: its achievements have contributed to promoting the expertise we developed in Quebec and across Canada in the field of victimology. Collectively, the various initiatives reflect AQPV's influence, its leadership, its ability to innovate and to mobilize partners from various sectors. In spite of limited resources, it has successfully built on the work of a competent team of people committed to its mission, and it has inspired and fuelled a vast movement of solidarity toward victims since the early 1980s. AQPV has been unrelenting in advocating for justice that is more respectful and more compassionate toward victims and their loved ones, all the while avoiding a vengeful justice. These values have served to guide its action and commitment and remain at the heart of its mission.

A Collective and Mobilizing Process

Some 30 years later, what progress has been made in the area of victim assistance? And where should we focus our energies in the future?

Let us first recall that, for many years, victim assistance organizations were supported by volunteers and low-paid professionals, most of them women (Gaudreault 2001). In Quebec and elsewhere in Canada, their contribution was invaluable. These pioneers called for stable and recurring funding for quality, accessible services. At the end of the 1980s, amendments were made to the Criminal Code in hopes of making it possible for the courts to impose victim-fine surcharges and for the provinces to establish Victim Assistance Funds. These initiatives were instrumental in breathing new life into existing organizations and in the establishment of new resources. As well, several subsidy programmes were created within various government departments and agencies to support several field projects and programs. These efforts fostered the growth and diversification of services. Victims now have access to a broader range of organizations able to meet their basic needs. They may also turn to professionals who have developed expertise, approaches, and programs for persons or groups with special needs. This is the case, for example, for many organizations working in the field of family and sexual violence with adults, adolescents, and children. Unfortunately, it is difficult to situate the various victim assistance programs, for the data available to us remain incomplete, varying from one province to the next (Dawson 2010).

We have also made major strides around intervention. We now have a better understanding of criminal victimization, its impact on people and on the communities that deal with the fallout; we also better understand victims' needs and the factors contributing to their recovery. Victim services have adapted their practices in order to account for the complexity and diversity of victims' needs. For example, pornography and sexual exploitation on the Internet, cybercrime, violence in the intimate relations of youth, victimization within gangs, harassment in the workplace, and terrorism are some of the realities confronting professionals today. These professionals have developed new knowledge and diversified their approaches in order to address these emerging problems. They have formed alliances with other partners with a view to providing a better continuum of services. Today, hospitals, health centres, and agencies providing psychosocial services to families, youth and immigrants all offer assistance to victims within their respective mandates and have established or improved services to address their needs. Agencies devoted to victim assistance have also developed partnerships with professionals in the fields of research and academia. The sharing of their expertise has enabled the integration of the points of view of the various actors, fostered a collective reflection about the numerous issues related to victim assistance, and led to the carrying out of numerous action-research projects.

The care of victims is now based on a multidisciplinary and professional approach. It has, in fact, been considerably enriched through the dialogue and networking of numerous agencies and people concerned with the cause of victims. Workers within assistance and compensation services, police officers, Crown counsel, professionals in the field of health and social services, analysts, and civil servants from various ministries have pooled ideas, knowledge, and resources. Their efforts have also led to the creation of new services or the improvement of existing ones, to the implementation of co-operation protocols, and to the development of programs that have fostered the transfer of knowledge, the training of workers, public education, and the evolution of our policy and legislation. In Quebec, the work being done in consultation has been one of the dynamic forces underlying the development of assistance to victims.

Victims and the associations representing them have also played an active role in this vast movement. They have spoken at numerous forums on the lack of compassion and understanding they experienced on the part of institutions, of their feeling of being left in the lurch, of the complexity of procedures, and of the imbalance between their rights and those of offenders. Citizens United for Safety and Justice (CUSJ), Victims of Violence, Child Find Canada, Mothers Against Drunk Driving (MADD), Canadians Against Violence Everywhere Advocating Its Termination (CAVEAT), the Canadian Resource Centre for Victims of Crime (CRCV), l'Association des familles de personnes assassinées ou disparues (AFPAD): these organizations have shown the determination to demand the recognition of victims' rights at the social, legislative, and judicial levels.

The Era of Legislative Reforms

Since its inception, the victim's assistance movement has made immense strides with a host of legislative reforms that have helped to promote the rights of victims and bring them up to date. In addition, the Criminal Code of Canada and the Corrections and Conditional Release Act were amended on several occasions to ensure that victims were better protected and to enhance their experiences within the criminal justice system (see Appendix 1 to this chapter). A number of judgments and decisions were handed down by the Supreme Court of Canada and by the lower courts on issues pertaining to the rights and interests of victims. Several provincial laws or decisions handed down by administrative tribunals have contributed to improved access, notably to programs that could assist in recovery, in obtaining redress, and in being compensated.

In April 2015, the federal government broadened the legislative arsenal with the adoption of the Canadian Victims Bill of Rights (CVBR). It should be recalled that, in 1988, Canada had set off on this path with the adoption of the Canadian Statement of Basic Principles of Justice for Victims of Crime, an example that was followed by all provinces and territories. While the CVBR was generally well accepted, certain concerns were raised during the consultation process leading to its enactment. Several groups and experts deplored the fact that the rights outlined in this bill remained largely subject to the discretionary power of the courts and agencies responsible for the administration of justice. Also, the remedies available to victims lacked a clear definition and were difficult to enforce. Such constraints considerably limit the bill's scope and enforceability. Its implementation also raises significant challenges. It requires the allocation of resources and the commitment of governments, particularly those of the provinces and territories, for the administration of justice rests on their shoulders. It assumes that the various actors in the criminal justice system will better fulfill their obligations and will put in place mechanisms and means to make their commitments known, to account for them, and to evaluate them periodically (AQPV 2013). In this respect, the Office of the Federal Ombudsman for Victims of Crime is a key player that assists victims whose rights have been infringed. Although this agency is relatively new, it has already made significant strides in bringing victims' concerns forward to various bodies. Despite its limitations, the CVBR is an important lever contributing to the advancement of victims' rights. To paraphrase Professor Alan Young (2005), the bill is a living tree that can evolve and develop to better reflect reality from a social, historical, and political perspective.

Remaining Focused on Victims' Rights

Today, the issue of victims' rights is now part of the public agenda. Victims are not as marginalized as they had been in the past. Governments and institutions with responsibilities toward them have mobilized. The movement that was launched back in the 1980s is not about to be stifled. It will continue to evolve and move forward. In many respects, the intense activity observed over the past several decades is encouraging, both in terms of the legislative framework as well as from the perspective of the development of services. With the changes and reforms, the criminal justice system is now better able to take into account the diverse needs of victims and their loved ones.

Yet we have not won all our battles: far from it! We should not be blind to the problems victims face when trying to obtain emotional support, advice on how to better protect themselves or on how to obtain compensation. We must continue to improve access to services that make it possible for them to rebuild their lives and to carry on with dignity. In most instances, this process occurs outside the criminal justice system, which does not constitute the only nor the best response to victims' needs (see Appendix 2 in this chapter).

Despite all the advances, the protection of the fundamental rights of victims is not guaranteed. Much remains to be done before victims can know, understand, and exercise their rights. Protecting their interests requires continued analysis of and action on issues from a systemic and long-term perspective. For that to happen, we must have mechanisms to influence the development of laws and policies pertaining to victims and we must be able to ensure the existence of a citizen presence and voice. This means that we must support organizations like Association québécoise Plaidoyer-Victimes that devote considerable energy to achieving such objectives.

Summary

I have had the privilege of being involved in and contributing to this solidarity movement, which has given rise to major social transformations in Canadian society. All those years of teaching, of being in contact with several student cohorts, and of exchanges and joint endeavours with partners from various sectors, more particularly with my colleagues at L'Association québécoise Plaidoyer-Victimes, have provided room to reflect, and have influenced and guided my actions and my engagement. They forced me to challenge myself. Victims, however, have also played a vital role in my evolution. Through their resilience and combativeness, they have inspired me to keep working, as there is still much that can and should be done to support victims of crime not only in Canada but around the world.

Biographical Notes

In addition to the biographic details provided in the main text. Arlene is the recipient of many awards and citations recognizing her contributions to the development of initiatives supporting victims and promoting their rights, including:

- Prix de la justice du Québec, ministère de la Justice du Québec, June 1997;
- Personnalité de la Semaine, *La Presse*, June 1997;
- Personnalité de l'Année in the Humanisme, courage et développement personnel category, Gala de l'excellence de *La Presse*, October 1997;
- Award of Excellence, Canadian Criminal Justice Assocaition, Vancouver, 2003;
- Robert Sauvé Award, Commission des services juridiques, Québec, 2007;
- Tribute Award, Quebec Society of Criminology, 2013;
- Tribute Award, Murdered or Missing Person's Families' Association (MMPFA), 2015.

Appendix 1: Key Dates of Victims' Rights Legislation

1983: Bill C-127, amending the Criminal Code in relation to sexual offences and other offences against the person. The amendments replace the crime of rape with sexual assault offences that focus on the violent nature of the crime rather than its sexual aspect. They amend substantive rules and the rules of evidence applicable to sexual offences. The new legislation also provided that a spouse could be charged with sexual assault.

1983: Bill C-89, amending the Criminal Code with respect to restitution orders, the Victim Impact Statement, and the recovery of stolen goods and their restitution.

1983: Bill C-15, amending the Criminal Code and the Canada Evidence Act to better protect youth from sexual exploitation.

1992: Bill C-49, amending the Criminal Code to define consent in the context of sexual assault cases and establish new rules regarding evidence about a complainant's past sexual conduct.

1992: Bill C-36, concerning the Corrections and Conditional Release Act (CCRA), recognizing the need for victims of crime to have access to information about the offender who harmed them, and to be allowed to provide information to be considered

in decisions regarding offenders' conditional release.
1993: Bill C-126, creating the new offence of criminal harassment.
1995: Bill C-41, amending the Criminal Code to restructure the principles of sentencing and affirm that sentencing serves to provide reparations for harm done to victims or the community.
1997: Bill C-27, amending the Criminal Code (juvenile prostitution, sexual tourism affecting children, criminal harassment, and female genital mutilation) by including provisions to facilitate the testimony of young victims and witnesses and strengthen the stalking provisions.
1997: Bill C-46, amending the Criminal Code to guarantee that only relevant documents from the personal and confidential records of complainants and witnesses will be made available to the accused in prosecutions for sexual offences.
1999: Bill C-79, amending the Criminal Code to facilitate the participation of victims and witnesses in the criminal justice system.
2002: Bill C-15, amending the Criminal Code and other legislation accordingly, by creating new offences and law enforcement measures related to the sexual exploitation of children (particularly in juvenile pornography, Internet luring and sex tourism).
2005: Bill C-2, amending the Criminal Code and the Canada Evidence Act to provide an improved response to family violence. The Act increases the sentences for offences committed against children (abuse, neglect and sexual abuse), and facilitates testimony by victims, more vulnerable witnesses and children through several measures (screen, closed-circuit television, and a trusted adult).
2005: Bill C-46, amending the Corrections and Conditional Release Act, by creating new measures intended for victims. These measures include financial assistance for victims who wish to attend the hearings of the Parole Board of Canada and the creation of a National Office for Victims with an information and support mission.
2005: Bill C-2, amending the Criminal Code, notably by ensuring better protection for youth and increasing the age of consent to sexual activity from 14 to 15 years.
2005: Bill C-27, creating the specific offence of "trafficking in persons" within the Criminal Code of Canada, and broadened its definition to include the movement of persons within Canada.
2010: Bill S-2, amending the Criminal Code to enhance police investigation of crimes of a sexual nature and enable police services to proactively use the national database to prevent crimes of a sexual nature.
2012: Bill C-10, amending the Criminal Code to enshrine victims' right to present a victim impact statement at parole hearings (previously only a policy).
2015: Bill C-32, enacting the Canadian Victims Bill of Rights and proposing changes to the *Criminal Code* and *Corrections and Conditional Release Act* to increase victims' rights to information, protection, participation, and compensation in the criminal justice system.

Reference for Appendix 1: Boudreault, J., Poupart, L., Leroux, K., and Gaudreault, A. (2011). *Introduction to Intervention With Crime Victims*. Montréal: Association québécoise Plaidoyer-Victimes.

Appendix 2: Key Dates of Victims' Rights Initiatives

1981: Creation of the Federal-Provincial Task Force on Justice for Victims of Crime.
1988: Adoption of the Canadian Statement of Basic Principles of Justice for Victims of Crime.
1998: Publication of *Victims' Rights: A Voice, Not a Veto*, the Report of the Standing Committee on Justice and Human Rights, which examined the victim's role in the criminal justice system.
2000: Creation of the Policy Centre for Victim Issues within the Department of Justice Canada, and creation of the Victims Fund.
2003: Adoption of the Canadian Statement of Basic Principles of Justice for Victims of Crime.
2005: Creation of the National Office for Victims.
2007: Creation of the Office of the Federal Ombudsman for Victims of Crime.

References

Association québécoise Plaidoyer-Victimes. (2014). Bill C-32, *An Act to enact the Canadian Victims Bill of Rights and to amend certain Acts,* House of Commons, 2nd session, 41st legislature. Brief presented to the Standing Committee of Justice and Human Rights, October 31, 2014.

Baril, M., Durand, S., and Gravel, S. (1983). Mais nous les témoins... Une étude exploratoire des besoins des témoins au Palais de justice de Montréal. *Collection Victimes d'actes criminels, document de travail n° 10.* Ottawa: Ministry of Justice.

Baril, M., Durand, S., and Gravel, S. (1983). Mais nous les témoins ... Une étude exploratoire des besoins des témoins au Palais de justice de Montréal. *Crime Victims: working paper no. 10.* Ottawa: Ministry of Justice.

Baril, M. (1983). *L'envers du crime.* Montréal: Les Presses de l'Université de Montréal.

Cario, R., Gaudreault, A., and Lopez, G. (2002). *Avant-propos de l'envers du crime.* Paris: L'Harmattan.

Dawson, M. (2010). Documenting the Growth of Resources for Victims/Survivors of Violence. *Victims of Crime Research Digest No. 3.* Ottawa: Department of Justice of Canada.

Fattah, E. (1991). *Understanding Criminal Victimization: An Introduction to Theoretical Victimology.* Scarborough, ON: Prentice-Hall Canada.

Gaudreault A. (1996). "Les premiers centres d'aide aux victimes d'actes criminels : lorsque la mémoire refait surface." Dans Coiteux, J., Campeau, P., Clarkson, M.M., & Cousineau, M.M. (eds.). *Question d'équité: l'aide aux victimes d'actes criminels.* Montréal: Association québécoise Plaidoyer-Victimes, chapitre 7, pp. 181–205.

Gaudreault A. (1996). L'Association québécoise Plaidoyer-Victimes : Regard sur une décennie. Dans Coiteux, J., Campeau, P., Clarkson, M.M., and Cousineau, M.M. (eds.). *Question d'équité: l'aide aux victimes d'actes criminels.* Montréal: Association québécoise Plaidoyer-Victimes, chapitre 2, pp. 33–81.

Gaudreault, A. (2001). "L'aide aux victimes d'actes criminels au Québec et au Canada: esquisse d'un parcours." Dans Cario, R., and Salas, M. (eds.). *Oeuvre de Justice et Victimes, Vol. 1.* École nationale de la magistrature. Paris : l'Harmattan, chapitre 6, pp. 109–122.

Gaudreault, A. (2010). "Les lois et chartes qui enchâssent les droits des victimes d'actes criminels: réflexions autour de l'expérience canadienne," Les Cahiers de PV—Antenne sur la victimologie, no. 6, pp. 2–9.

Gaudreault, A. (2013). *" Des initiatives pour mieux répondre aux besoins des victimes d'actes criminels: l'expérience du Canada," Cahiers de la Sécurité intérieure: Les victimes de la délinquance, Revue trimestrielle,* pp. 135–142.

Gaudreault, A. (2013). *"Renforcer les droits des victimes au Canada: un rêve illusoire,"* Ressourcez-vous, Société de criminologie du Québec, pp. 13–23.

Federal-Provincial Working Group on Justice for Victims of Crime. (1983). Ottawa, Department of Supply and Services.

Study Committee on Sexual Offences against Children and Youth, Sexual Offences Against Children (Badgley Report). (1984). Ottawa: Justice Canada.

Waller, I. (1981). Les victimes d'actes criminels: besoins et services, Canada/États-Unis, *Déviance et Société 3:* 277–282.

Waller, I. (2011). *Rights for Victims of Crime: Rebalancing Justice.* Toronto: Rowman & Littlefield Publishers.

Young, A.N. (2005). Crime Victims and Constitutional Rights, *Criminal Law Quarterly, vol. 49:* 443–450.

SIXTEEN
Pioneers of the Canadian Legal System

Ritesh Dalip Narayan

Introduction

The term "living tree doctrine" refers to the need for interpretations of the Canadian Charter of Rights and Freedom to evolve alongside our changing times (see *Edwards v. Canada [Attorney General]*). This doctrine can be extended to the Canadian legal system if we imagine that the legal system is a kind of living tree, transforming itself as social values, security needs, and demographics change. Caretakers of our living tree have made the Canadian legal system into a model for legal systems around the world (Rule of Law Index 2015).

The Canadian legal system is the umbrella for law and justice in Canada. Law enforcement, corrections, and other facets of legal administration are all dependent on the legal system for the interpretation of laws and prosecution of criminals. The system as we know it today is the product of not one but many groups of individuals that include politicians, judges, lawyers, and academics. This chapter considers some key pioneers of the Canadian legal system.

History of the Canadian Legal System

The Magna Carta of 1215 laid the foundation of democracy in Britain. Other legal pronouncements that affect Canada include the Royal Proclamation of 1763, the British North America Act (BNA Act) of 1867 and the Constitution Act of 1982. The Royal Proclamation set provisions for British laws and courts. The BNA Act was passed to set the legal ground rules for Canada, and to divide up power between the provinces and the federal government (Boyd 2015; see Box 16.1). Section 91 of the BNA Act lists the powers the federal parliament can exercise as well as the powers of the provincial legislatures. Unless the parties agree otherwise, the federal government must not make laws dealing with matters of provincial jurisdiction, and vice versa. If one party does pass a law that intrudes on the jurisdiction of the other, the courts will strike it down. In 1982, under the leadership of Prime Minister Pierre Elliot Trudeau, the power to amend Canada's Constitution was repatriated—that is, "brought home" to

Canada from Britain—and the new Act, called the Constitution Act, 1982, came into existence.

Two years after the enactment of the BNA Act authorized the government in establishing a Court of Appeal for Canada, the government of the day decided that a Supreme Court was "essential to our system of jurisprudence and to the settlement of constitutional questions" (Saywell 2002:2). In spite of skepticism from several provinces and scrutiny from the judicial committee, the Supreme Court of Canada was established.

This brings us to the issue of sources of Canadian criminal law. The main sources of criminal law in Canada are statues and judicial decisions, known as "common law." The enactment of the Canadian Charter of Rights and Freedom as part of the Constitution Act was a significant event, and questioned the notion of "parliamentary supremacy." The Charter gave decisive powers to the judiciary to decide on the validity of a law made by parliament. "Canadian judges have demonstrated their willingness to use this far reaching power where they believe that it is absolutely necessary to do so" (Verdun-Jones 2015:11).

Box 16.1. The Birth of Canada's Criminal Code

After Confederation in 1867, the first prime minister, Sir John A. Macdonald, was adamant that Canada should not long suffer the fragmented existing arrangement, under which each province had its own criminal code. Macdonald believed in the need for a single, uniform regime of criminal law for the entire country. In fact, the Canadian constitution—which he helped write—gave the federal government the explicit authority to codify the criminal law. An initial set of nine statutes was passed by the House of Commons in 1869 to consolidate the laws regarding coinage offences, forgery, offences against the person, larceny, malicious injuries to property, perjury, and procedure. A complete Criminal Code was finally achieved in July 1892, under the leadership of Sir John Sparrow David Thompson (1845–1894), then the Minister of Justice and later Canada's fourth prime minister. This was a major event in Canadian legal history.

Since the enactment of the Charter, the judiciary has been diligently examining cases, not only in the attempt to correctly interpret statues, but also to determine how the Charter must be interpreted and applied in view of our changing social demographics and needs. Landmark cases such as *Carter v. Canada (AG)*, which looked at the right to physician-assisted dying, and cases interpreting the traditional definition of marriage are two examples of such action by Supreme Court of Canada justices. In the next section, we profile judges who have acted as pioneers of change within the Canadian legal system.

Justices as Pioneers of Change

Chief Justice Bora Laskin (1912–1984)

Bora Laskin was born in Fort William (now Thunder Bay), Ontario, on October 5, 1912. After graduating with a B.A. from the University of Toronto in 1933, he enrolled at Osgoode Hall Law School. From 1933 to 1936, he articled and continued to study at the University of Toronto, earning an M.A. in 1935 and an LL.B. in 1936. The following year, he received an LL.M. from the Harvard Law School. Upon his return to Toronto that year, he was called to the bar and began his legal career writing headnotes for *The Canadian Abridgement*. In 1940 he embarked on a teaching career that spanned 25 years, mostly at the University of Toronto except for four years at Osgoode Hall (1945–49). He was the author of many legal texts, including *Canadian Constitutional Law*. He was also associate editor of *Dominion Law Reports* and *Canadian Criminal Cases* for 23 years. Laskin was appointed to the Ontario Court of Appeal in 1965 and to the Supreme Court of Canada on March 19, 1970. On December 27, 1973, he was named Chief Justice of Canada; he served on the Supreme Court for 14 years in total.

Bora Laskin in 1935 (LAC).

More often than not, Laskin found himself on the minority side of decisions. On matters of Canadian federalism under the Constitution Act, 1867, Laskin was seen as the most aggressive supporter of federal power of any justice since Confederation. This made for a stark contrast with fellow justices who were often strong proponents of provincial powers under the Constitution (Saywell 2002).

Laskin often took a position that was later adopted by a majority of the Court. Among his most famous dissents was his opinion in *Murdoch v. Murdoch*[27] where he was the sole judge who would have ruled in favour of a wife's application for an equal division of property acquired during the course of the marriage. The outcome of the case was highly controversial. It triggered reforms to matrimonial laws across the country, leading to the adoption of Laskin's view of property equality between husband and wife.

Chief Justice Brian Dickson (1916–1998)

Robert George Brian Dickson was born in Yorkton, Saskatchewan, on May 25, 1916. After his family moved to Winnipeg, he attended the University of Manitoba and graduated with an LL.B. in 1938. He worked for two years in the investment department of the Great-West Life Assurance Company and then was called to the bar in 1940. Before practicing law, he enlisted in the armed forces during the Second World War and served overseas, where he was severely wounded in 1944. Upon his return to Winnipeg in 1945, he joined the law firm of Aikins, Loftus, MacAulay, Turner, Thompson, and Tritschler. He also lectured at the Faculty of Law at the University of Manitoba for six years, until 1954. In 1963 he was appointed to the Court of Queen's Bench of Manitoba and four years later was elevated to the Manitoba Court of Appeal. He was appointed to the Supreme Court of Canada on March 26, 1973 and became its Chief Justice on April 18, 1984, serving a total of 17 years in all before retiring on June 30, 1990. Chief Justice Dickson died on October 17, 1998, at the age of 82.

Dickson's appointment to the Supreme Court of Canada coincided with the Court's early encounters with the Charter; he quickly became a key voice in the interpretation and application of the Charter. Dickson wrote the decision in *R v. Oakes* framing the Court's interpretive approach to section 1 of the Charter. (Section 1 is the provision declaring that Charter rights are subject to such reasonable limitations as can be demonstrably justified in a free and democratic society.) He wrote one of the opinions in the second *R. v. Morgentaler* abortion rights case that attempted a limited, procedurally oriented invalidation of Canada's abortion law, allowing Parliament room to develop another law more consistent with the priorities of women seeking abortions. In their review of Dickson's private papers, Sharpe and Roach (2003) reveal that Dickson authored the Court's unanimous, unsigned judgment that struck down Quebec's unilingual commercial sign law. But the same decision essentially established as a constitutional principle the fact that Quebec is a distinct society possessing the constitutional room to preserve and promote its particular linguistic character within the Canadian federation.

These were among the most remarkable decisions of the Charter era. Dickson's objective was to seek consensus on the Court and to draft his own opinions in such a way as to attract the agreement of colleagues. Occasionally, his papers reveal, his post-hearing ruminations produced an about-face. At all times, he tried to write clearly so the intelligent layperson, the trial judge, and the juror could all apply constitutional law consistently, and he was consistently praised for his legal writing (Sharpe and Roach 2003). According to Sharpe and Roach, probably the most prominent accomplishment for Dickson was facilitating the Canadian legal system's movement from an older, formalist model in which law was confined to formulaic adjudication of disputes between individuals, to the new era in which law is viewed as a tool for general social reform.

Sharpe and Roach also suggest that Dickson held "progressive views" (p. 77) all his life and needed only the correct legal influences to embody them in his decision-making. Dickson was the product of a practitioner's legal education in Manitoba and spent his earlier career in isolation from the growing academic ferment in legal education (Bateman 2004). However, his service on the bench provided him with a second legal education, this time oriented to the academic study of law, a pedagogy that situates law in social and political context. Adjudication and judicial review necessarily possess a policy-making dimension, according to the new pedagogy, and law students are encouraged to pursue these connections. This new paradigm represents a functional approach.

Dickson's second legal education took place while he was on the bench, through the reading of academic analyses of law in submissions to the court and in his own research. His clerks, all of them recent products of contemporary legal education, were of tremendous assistance in this respect (Saywell 2002). However, Dickson remained the bridge between the two worlds. He combined the contextualism of the new approach to law with reverence for the rule of law—the need for clear, stable rules to guide all and sundry. His military formalism combined with his sensitivity to context in matters ranging from the definition of the "reasonable person" to the reception of new types of evidence in criminal cases to vitiate criminal responsibility. Of the latter, the use of the concept of battered woman's syndrome in *R. v. Lavallee* is among the most instructive (Bateman 2004).

Louise Arbour (1947–)

Louise Arbour was born two years after the end of World War II in Montreal, Quebec, on February 10, 1947. She received a law degree with distinction from the Université de Montréal in 1970. She was promoted quickly, first clerking for Mr. Justice Louis-Philippe Pigeon of the Supreme Court of Canada in 1971; she served as a research officer at the Law Reform Commission of Canada in 1972–73, and was a law professor at Osgoode Hall from 1974 to 1987, serving as associate dean in her final year. As vice-president of the Canadian Civil Liberties Association (1985–1987) she represented the association in cases where she contested the law shielding rape victims from revelations about their sexual history.

Louise Arbour (Global X/flickr)

Arbour was appointed to the Supreme Court of Ontario (High Court of Justice) in 1987 and in 1990 was elevated to the Court of Appeal for Ontario. In 1995–96 she conducted a difficult enquiry into the conditions in the Prison for Women in Kingston, Ontario. That role was followed by three high-profile years as the United Nations' chief prosecutor for the International Criminal Tribunal for the former Yugoslavia and for Rwanda (see Box 16.2).

Prime Minister Jean Chrétien appointed Arbour to the Supreme Court of Canada on June 10, 1999. On June 30, 2004, she retired, and was appointed High Commissioner for Human Rights at the United Nations.

She made many headlines as High Commissioner and it may be that she is best known for her criticisms of the United States. More recently as a lawyer in Montreal she has advocated against Canada's "addiction" to solitary confinement (*Globe and Mail*, December 14, 2014).

In 2015, Arbour made news again, speaking out against government handling of the Syrian refugee crisis and arguing that Canada must take in more Syrians. She had equally strong words for the government's controversial anti-terror legislation, Bill C-51, which became law in June 2015. Arbour expects constitutional challenges to the legislation, and said she found the position of the Liberal Party—which voted for the bill but vowed to repeal or amend parts of it—to be "enormously disappointing" (CBC, September 5, 2015).

Box 16.2. The Hague

In 1996, at Richard Goldstone's recommendation, Louise Arbour was appointed as his replacement as Chief Prosecutor of the International Criminal Tribunal for Rwanda in Arusha, and of the International Criminal Tribunal for the former Yugoslavia (ICTY) in The Hague. She indicted then-Serbian President Slobodan Milošević for war crimes, the first time a serving head of state was called to account before an international court. Others indicted were Milan Milutinović, President of the Republic of Serbia, Nikola Šainović, Deputy Prime Minister of the Federal Republic of Yugoslavia, Dragoljub Ojdanić, Chief of the General Staff of the Armed Forces of the Federal Republic of Yugoslavia, and Vlajko Stojiljković, Minister of Internal Affairs of the Republic of Serbia.

The International Criminal Tribunal for Rwanda (ICTR) was an international court established in November 1994 by the United Nations Security Council. Arbour as the tribunal's chief prosecutor indicted 93 individuals considered responsible for serious violations of international humanitarian law in Rwanda in 1994. Those indicted include high-ranking military and government officials, politicians, businessmen, as well as religious, militia, and media leaders.

With its sister international tribunals and courts, the ICTR has played a pioneering role in the establishment of a credible international criminal justice system, producing a substantial body of jurisprudence on genocide, crimes against humanity, war crimes, as well as forms of individual and superior responsibility. Canada should be proud of Arbour's work on the international stage.

Murray Sinclair (1951–)

Murray Sinclair was born and raised in north Winnipeg. He graduated as valedictorian of his high-school class, as well as athlete of the year in 1968, and participated in air cadets for several years. Murray also served as a special assistant to the Attorney General of Manitoba. He then continued his academic career at the University of Winnipeg, studying sociology and history. Following his bachelor's degree, Murray attended the Faculty of Law at the University of Manitoba, graduating in 1979. He was called to the Manitoba bar in 1980.

By the time that Murray was given a judicial appointment, he was known for his representation of Aboriginal people as well as his knowledge of Aboriginal legal issues. Sinclair was the first Aboriginal judge in the province following his appointment as associate chief justice of the Provincial Court of Manitoba in March 1988. He was also appointed co-commissioner of Manitoba's public inquiry into the administration of justice and Aboriginal people (the Aboriginal Justice Inquiry).

Sinclair also carried out an inquiry into the deaths of 12 children in the pediatric cardiac surgery program of the Winnipeg Health Sciences Centre in 1994. His report, issued in 2000, led to significant changes to pediatric cardiac surgeries in Manitoba, as well as the study of medical error in Canada.

Murray Sinclair served as a legal counsel for the Manitoba Human Rights Commission. He has been an adjunct professor of law and an adjunct professor in the Faculty of Graduate Studies at the University of Manitoba. In January 2001 he was appointed to the Court of Queen's Bench of Manitoba and in June 2009 was also appointed chair of Canada's Indian Residential Schools Truth and Reconciliation Commission (see Box 16.3). Its objective was to document the stories of residential school survi-

Box 16.3. Truth and Reconciliation

The Truth and Reconciliation Commission of Canada was unique. Created by the Indian Residential Schools Settlement Agreement, which settled the class action suits, the Commission spent six years travelling across Canada to hear from Aboriginal people who had been taken from their families as children—on some occasions forcibly—and placed for much of their childhoods in residential schools. The Commission heard from more than 6,000 witnesses, most of whom had survived the experience of living in the schools as students. The stories of that experience are horrifying, particularly in Canada, a country that takes pride in its long-standing democratic processes and generosity. In these residential schools, children were abused, physically and sexually; children died in the schools in numbers that would not have been tolerated in any other school system anywhere else in the country. But the commission's mandate was less about finger-pointing than revealing the truth and laying the foundations for moving forward. "Now that we know about residential schools and their legacy, what do we do about it?" (Honoring the Truth, Reconciling for the Future 2015).

vors as well as those of their families and communities. Murray has received many awards, including the A.J. Christie Prize in Civil Litigation and the National Aboriginal Achievement award.

Chief Justice Beverley McLachlin (1943–)

Serving as not only Canada's first female Chief Justice on the Supreme Court of Canada but also the Chief Justice with the longest tenure, Beverley McLachlin continues to perform an integral role in the evolution of the Canadian legal system. Born in Pincher Creek, Alberta on September 7, 1943, McLachlin's judicial career began with an appointment to Vancouver County Court in 1981. She was soon elevated to the B.C. Supreme Court, the B.C. Court of Appeal and, in 1989, to the Supreme Court of Canada. Not only has Chief Justice McLachlin made distinctive judicial decisions, but she has been instrumental in interpreting laws and rendering decisions on numerous landmark cases.

Landmark Supreme Court Decisions under Chief Justice Beverley McLachlin

Case	Issue
R. v. Darrach [2000] 2 S.C.R. 443, 2000 SCC 46	Rape shield law
R. v. Morrisey [2000] 2 S.C.R. 90, 2000 SCC 39	Cruel and unusual punishment
R. v. Starr [2000] 2 S.C.R. 144, 2000 SCC 40	Hearsay exception
R. v. Latimer [2001] 1 S.C.R. 3, 2001 SCC 1	Assisted suicide
R. v. Sharpe [2001] 1 S.C.R. 45, 2001 SCC 2	Defense of duress
R. v. Nette [2001] 3 S.C.R. 488, 2001 SCC 78	Criminal causation
Sauvé v. Canada (Chief Electoral Officer) [2002] 3 S.C.R. 519, 2002 SCC 68	Right to vote for prisoners
R. v. Buhay [2003] 1 S.C.R. 631, 2003 SCC 30	Exclusion of evidence, search and seizure.
Canadian Foundation for Children, Youth and the Law v. Canada (A.G.) [2004] 1 S.C.R. 76, 2004 SCC 4	Spanking allowed under Charter
R. v. Mann [2004] 3 S.C.R. 59, 2004 SCC 52	Section 8 search and seizure
R. v. Tessling [2004] 3 S.C.R. 432, 2004 SCC 67	Privacy rights, section 8, thermal imaging
R. v. Turcotte [2005] 2 S.C.R. 519, 2005 SCC 50	Right to silence
R. v. Labaye [2005] 3 S.C.R. 728, 2005 SCC 80	Defining "indecent" in Criminal Code
Multani v. Commission scolaire Marguerite - Bourgeoys [2006] 1 S.C.R. 256, 2006 SCC 6	Freedom of religion; banning kirpans in school
R. v. Khelawon [2006] 2 S.C.R. 787, 2006 SCC 57	Hearsay evidence
R v. Nur [2015] S.C.R., 2015 SCC 15	Constitutionality of mandatory minimum sentences for various firearm offences
Carter v. Canada (AG) [2015] S.C.R., 2015 SCC 5	Right to physician assisted dying

Chief Justice McLachlin has established a consensus-building court that often presents unanimous decisions and a unified front. Her belief that the public is entitled to understand the reasons for Supreme Court decisions and procedure is apparent not only in the quality of written decisions but also in her speeches and public interviews (Mackinnon 2014). McLachlin has also offered advice to the Canadian government while subsequently being scrutinized by Parliament. This included giving advice to then Justice Minister Peter Mackay about a potential constitutional issue involving the appointment of a Federal Court judge. McLachlin has been called "more than just a 'sitting judge'" given that she also heads the judicial branch and is a member of the Privy Council (Mackinnon 2014).

Lawyers as Pioneers of Change

Edward L. Greenspan (1944–2014)

Edward L. Greenspan was one of Canada's most famous criminal lawyers. Born on February 28, 1944, in Niagara Falls, Ontario, Greenspan was the son of a scrap metal dealer and a school secretary. He decided early on in life that he wanted to pursue a legal career. He earned his B.A. from the University of

Box 16.4. Edward Greenspan's Academic CV

- 2013: Lecturer, Brock University, fourth-year political science course on politics and the criminal process.
- 1972–1999: Lecturer on criminal procedure, then advanced criminal law at the University of Toronto Law School.
- 1986–1989: Lecturer on advanced evidence in criminal cases at Osgoode Hall Law School, York University.
- 1989: Delivered the Hugh Alan Maclean Lecture at the University of Victoria Faculty of Law.
- 1986: Delivered the Culliton Lecture, University of Saskatchewan Law School.
- 1983: Delivered the Isaac Pitblado Lecture (Manitoba).
- 1983: Practitioner–in–Residence, Faculty of Law, University of Western Ontario.
- 1982: Milvain Chair of Advocacy, University of Calgary Law School.
- 1972–1981: Lecturer on criminal procedure, Osgoode Hall Law School, York University.
- 1971–mid–1980s: Lecturer on criminal law, Bar Admission Course.

Toronto in 1965, his LL.B. from Osgoode Hall Law School in 1968, and was called to the Ontario Bar in 1970. He practiced in Toronto and throughout Canada and was named a Queen's Counsel in 1981. Greenspan had an extensive background in academia as well, teaching in several post-secondary institutions (see Box 16.4).

Greenspan was a member of the Ontario Judicial Council and the Judicial Ethics Advisory Committee. He was vice-president of the Canadian Civil

Liberties Association for an extended period and also served as editor-in-chief of *Canadian Criminal Cases* and of *Martin's Criminal Code*. Greenspan received an honorary LL.D. from the Law Society of Upper Canada, University of Windsor, and Assumption University. He is the recipient of the Advocates' Society Medal for lifetime achievement as an advocate. As well as his high-profile career as a defence lawyer, he was the host and narrator of the award-winning CBC series *Scales of Justice*, which aired on CBC Radio from 1982 to 1990 and on CBC Television from 1990 to 1994. Over the course of his 44-year career, Greenspan represented several high-profile clients. He defended theatre impresario Garth Drabinsky, disgraced media baron Conrad Black, former Nova Scotia premier Gerald Regan and Karlheinz Schreiber, a German financier with dealings in Canada. He also represented Saskatchewan farmer Robert Latimer, convicted of the mercy killing of his daughter, in a case that would spark a national debate on euthanasia.

An aspect of Greenspan's tactical litigation skills and unconventional analysis was evident in the 1981 case of *R. v. Scopelliti* where he successfully defended Antonio Scopelliti on murder charges. The Orillia convenience-store owner shot and killed two 17-year-olds, Michael McRae and David Sutton, who were trying to rob the store. He claimed he acted in self-defence, and Greenspan won the case by characterizing the men as aggressive and raising prior instances of assault in court. Until then, courts did not typically allow such evidence if the defendant had not known about it at the time of the incident; however, in Scopelliti's case, the judge allowed it. Greenspan's client was acquitted by a jury.

Box 16.5. Selected Publications by Edward Greenspan

- Foreword to J. Patrick Boyer, *Raw Life: Cameos of 1894 Justice from a Magistrate's Bench Book* (2012).
- "The Impact of the Warren Court in Canada," chapter in Harry N. Scheiber, ed., *Earl Warren and the Warren Court: The Legacy in American and Foreign Law* (2007).
- "The Law of Evidence: Lowering the Threshold for Admissibility of Defence Evidence in a Criminal Case," Law Society of Upper Canada Special Lectures (2003).
- *The Case for the Defence*. With George Jonas (1987).
- "The Future Role of Defence Counsel," *Saskatchewan Law Review* 51 (1986–1987).
- Introduction to George Jonas, ed., *Scales of Justice* (1983).

Greenspan's contribution to the Canadian legal system has been immense. Not was he been a great litigator, but he was also an important advocate for law and civil rights. He wrote extensively and his writings form an integral part of learning and understanding law in Canada, as Box 16.5 demonstrates.

Hersh E. Wolch, QC (1940–)

Born on April 18, 1940, in Winnipeg, Wolch remains a prominent Canadian lawyer and advocate for the wrongfully convicted. For half a century, he has been a passionate advocate for his clients, as well as for the legal profession itself. Wolch received his Bachelor of Commerce degree from the University of Manitoba in 1962 and his law degree in 1965. He was called to the bar of Manitoba in 1965, Saskatchewan in 1972, and Alberta in 1978.

He was a crown prosecutor for the province of Manitoba from 1965 to 1971 and for the federal Department of Justice from 1971 to 1973. Wolch was director of the Bar Admissions Course for Manitoba as well as director of education for the Law Society of Manitoba. He is a past president of the Manitoba Trial Lawyers' Association as well as a board member of the Canadian Association of Criminal Defence Lawyers. In 1982 he was made a Queen's Counsel, and in 2015 received the Distinguished Service Award from the Law Society of Alberta and the Alberta branch of the Canadian Bar Association.

Wolch's cases "have influenced the development and interpretation of the law. Hersh has been credited as instrumental in advocating for and helping to

Box 16.6. Wolch and the Exonerating the Wrongfully Convicted

David Milgaard was charged with the 1969 murder of Saskatoon nursing aide Gail Miller and in January 1970 was sentenced to life in prison. Appeals to the Saskatchewan Court of Appeal and Supreme Court of Canada in the two years after his conviction were unsuccessful. Milgaard's mother, Joyce, believed from the day he was arrested that her son was innocent. She kept his case alive as Milgaard spent more than two decades in prison. In 1991, Justice Minister Kim Campbell directed the Supreme Court of Canada to review the conviction, which was set it aside in 1992. Five years later Milgaard was cleared through the use of DNA evidence. The Saskatchewan government awarded Milgaard $10 million for his wrongful conviction in 1999, the same year Larry Fisher was found guilty of the rape and stabbing death of Gail Miller.

Steven Truscott was sentenced to be hanged in 1959 at age 14 for a schoolmate's murder, becoming Canada's youngest death-row inmate. After the original conviction, he spent four months in the shadow of the gallows until his death sentence was commuted to life imprisonment. Paroled in 1969, Truscott disappeared into an anonymous existence in a southern Ontario city. On August 28, 2007, 48 years later, the Ontario Court of Appeal unanimously overturned Truscott's conviction and acquitted him, declaring the case "a miscarriage of justice" that "must be quashed." In July 2008, the Ontario government announced it would pay Truscott $6.5 million in compensation for his ordeal.

develop many of the principles that now form part of the Canadian Charter of Rights and Freedoms and our justice system in general" (*Calgary Herald*, February 22, 2015). His most satisfying work may well have been his efforts for the Association in Defence of the Wrongly Convicted (see Box 16.6), working on high-profile cases involving the likes of David Milgard, Steven Truscott, and Donald Marshall.

Wolch has said that when he and his colleagues began working on Milgaard's case, following Milgaard's serving 23 years for crime he did not commit—the brutal rape and murder of a Saskatoon nurse in 1969—very few people would listen. Eventually, thanks to the efforts of the Association in Defence of the Wrongly Convicted, Milgaard was exonerated and the real killer, Larry Fisher, was convicted.

Politicians as Pioneers of Change

Pierre Elliot Trudeau (1919–2000)

The original Canadian constitution was an Act of the British Parliament; this meant that it could only be changed by Britain. For many years, Canada's prime ministers had been looking to "bring the constitution home." When Trudeau's opportunity came to make history by doing so, he would make the task even more challenging by also wanting to include a Charter of Rights in the Constitution.

Born in Montreal on October 18, 1919, Pierre Trudeau served nearly 16 years as the country's fifteenth prime minister. His charismatic personality matched the revolutionary ideas of the 1960s. After graduating from the elite Jesuit preparatory school, Collège Jean-de-Brébeuf, Trudeau went on to receive a law degree from the University of Montreal. Shortly after graduating, he became a desk officer for the Privy Council. From 1951 to 1961, he practiced law, specializing in labour and civil liberty cases.

In 1961, he joined the staff of the University of Montreal as a professor of constitutional law. Four years later, Liberal Party leaders were searching for potential candidates, and Trudeau and two of his colleagues were invited to run. All three men won election that year; Trudeau became minister of justice. Within a year, he had reformed divorce laws and liberalized laws on abortion and homosexuality.

Immediately following his election as prime minister, he began advocating for universal health care. He also worked to reform governmental caucus meetings in order to make them more efficient. The 1970 "October Crisis" tested his stance against terrorists; he invoked the War Measures Act, giving the government overarching power to arrest without trial. On domestic matters, he championed the official implementation of bilingualism. Perhaps the two most significant events that occurred during the Trudeau administration were the first referendum on Quebec independence and the patriation of the

Constitution from Great Britain.

To keep Quebec within Confederation, Trudeau assured the province that its rights would be protected under a new constitutional arrangement. In October 1980, he asked the British government to amend the BNA Act by adding an amending formula and a Canadian Charter of Rights and Freedoms. By November 1981, the prime minister had brought nine provinces—all except Quebec—into his plan to bring home the Constitution, which occurred the following year.

The Canada Act, 1982 has two parts: the Constitution Act, 1982, and the British North America Act, 1867 (later renamed the Constitution Act, 1867). It is the Constitution Act that includes the Canadian Charter of Rights and Freedoms. Because the Charter is part of the constitution, no part of it can

Box 16.7. Other Notable Figures

Kent Roach, professor of law at the University of Toronto, is the author of 12 books and more than 200 articles. His works include *Constitutional Remedies in Canada, Due Process and Victims' Rights, The Supreme Court on Trial* (both shortlisted for the Donner Prize), *Brian Dickson: A Judge's Journey* (winner of the Dafoe Prize; co-authored with Robert J. Sharpe), and *The 9/11 Effect: Comparative Counter-Terrorism* (winner of the David Mundell Medal).

Simon Verdun-Jones, professor of criminology at Simon Fraser University, has written extensively on criminal law, procedure and evidence, criminal law reform and international criminal justice.

Clayton Charles Ruby, lawyer and activist, has devoted his professional career to ensuring that those who are underprivileged and face discrimination are given equal access to the legal system of this country. Many of his cases have been high profile, including representing Donald Marshall Jr., who spent 11 years in jail after being wrongly convicted of murder, at the Royal Commission on the Donald Marshall Jr. Prosecution.

Nathalie Des Rosiers, an academic and politician with expertise in constitutional law, served as general counsel for the Canadian Civil Liberties Association (CCLA), a national organization that acts as a watchdog for the protection of human rights and civil liberties in Canada, from 2009 to 2013.

Barry Stuart, former chief justice of the Territorial Court of Yukon (now retired), a faculty member of numerous Canadian law schools, and an internationally respected leader in multiparty conflict resolution, pioneered the use of peacemaking circles for public processes in North America. In the 1970s, he played an important role in shaping environmental law in Canada.

be changed by a federal or provincial government acting unilaterally. The House of Commons, the Senate, and two-thirds of the provinces representing over 50% of Canadians must approve any changes to the Charter or any other part of the constitution. The enactment of the Charter brought with it a new era of legal interpretation. It also challenged Parliament to be prudent when making laws, as it gave the Supreme Court power to overturn laws that infringed upon the Charter.

Academics as Pioneers of Change

Peter Wardell Hogg (1939–)

Peter Wardell Hogg, CC, QC, FRSC was born on March 12, 1939, in Lower Hutt, New Zealand. Hogg attended Nelson College (Nelson, New Zealand) from 1952 to 1956 and earned his LL.B. from the University of New Zealand in 1962, his LL.M. from Harvard University in 1963, and his Ph.D. from Monash University in Melbourne, Australia in 1970.

In 1970, he was appointed professor of law at Osgoode Hall and in 1998 was appointed dean of the law school. In 2003, he accepted a position as scholar in residence at the law firm of Blake, Cassels & Graydon LLP. He is a co-author of *Liability of the Crown*, 4th ed. (Carswell) and *Principles of Canadian Income Tax Law*, 7th ed. (Carswell), as well as the author of numerous articles and publications, including *Constitutional Law of Canada*, now in its fifth edition (this is the only comprehensive treatise on constitutional law). His writings have been frequently cited by the Supreme Court of Canada. He also appears as counsel in constitutional cases.

In 2004, he was lead counsel for the Canadian government in the same-sex marriage case heard by the Supreme Court. Hogg also advised the committee that studied Marshall Rothstein's nomination to the Supreme Court, arguing that the creation of the committee was important to Canada's legal history, and that it should refrain from posing political questions about abortion and same-sex marriage.

Perhaps Hogg's most influential stance was his position on the notwithstanding clause included in the Charter. This section of the Charter allows Parliament or a legislature to enact legislation that overrides section 2 or sections 7–15 of the Charter for a five-year period. Hogg has questioned "whether it is meaningful to speak about rights when the principal provisions of the Charter can be overcome by the enactment of an ordinary statute containing a notwithstanding declaration" (Hogg 1997, p. 36). The use of the notwithstanding mechanism has less frequent than it might otherwise have been thanks to Hogg's relentless criticism of it.

Dr. Nicholas Bala (1952–)

Born in Montreal, Dr. Bala is a leading authority on bullying and family and children's issues. He holds law degrees from Queen's and Harvard, has been a professor in the Faculty of Law at Queen's University since 1980, where he also served as associate dean for five years, and is presently academic director of the Osgoode Hall Law School's part-time LL.M. in family law. He twice won

Law Student Society teaching awards at Queen's and in 2006 was the winner of the Queen's University prize for excellence in research.

Bala has published extensively in the areas of family and children's law, authoring or co-authoring 13 books and over 125 book chapters and articles in journals of law, psychology, social work, and medicine. His work is regularly cited by the courts. He frequently presents at continuing education programs for lawyers, doctors, police, psychologists, and other professionals, as well as at academic and law reform conferences. Since 1999 he has led an interdisciplinary research team funded by the Social Sciences Research Council of Canada that is studying child witness issues.

His first co-authored book in the youth justice field was *The Young Offenders Act Annotated* (1984). He wrote *Youth Criminal Justice Law* (Irwin Law, 2003) just before the Youth Criminal Justice Act (2002) came into force, and has written a number of articles about the new act since then.

Bala has worked as a consultant on youth justice and other child and family law issues for the federal government as well as for aboriginal groups and the governments of Ontario and the Yukon. He has also appeared as a witness before parliamentary committees dealing with youth justice reform and other issues related to family and children's law. In February 2006 he testified as an expert witness at the Nova Scotia inquiry into the youth justice system (the Nunn Commission).

Conclusion

The Canadian legal system had its origins in British law, but has gradually evolved into its own separate entity with its own identity. Judges are the ultimate interpreters of law; their decisions also reflect security needs, changing demographics and the social mood of Canadians.

Numerous Canadian lawyers have become advocates and key players in the administration of law, contributing greatly to the country's legal system.

Former Prime Minister Pierre Elliot Trudeau was a major force in the evolution of the legal system. Not only did he "bring home" the constitution, but he also successfully incorporated into it the *Canadian Charter of Rights and Freedom*.

Academics contribute to the legal system's evolution through research, publications, teaching and presentations. In doing so, they affect public perceptions of the legal system.

References

Bateman, T.M.J. (2004). Review of *Brian Dickson: A Judge's Journey*, by Robert J. Sharpe and Kent Roach. www.lawcourts.org/LPBR/reviews/Sharpe-Roach204.htm.

Biography of Edward Greenspan. (2014). http://www.greenspanpartners.com/lawyers/edward-l.-greenspan-q.c.html.

Boyd, N. (2015). *Canadian Law: An Introduction*, 6th ed. Toronto: Nelson Education.

Hogg, P.W. (1997). *Constitutional Law of Canada*, 4th ed. Scarborough, ON: Carswell.

Living Justice Press. (2016). Barry Stuart. www.livingjusticepress.org.

Mackinnon, L. (2014, May 6). "Chief Justice Beverley McLachlin more than just a 'sitting judge.'" CBC News: Politics. Retrieved from http://www.cbc.ca/.

Fine, S. and J. Wingrove. "Retired Supreme Court justice Arbour slams practice of solitary confinement." (2014, December 16). *The Globe and Mail.*

Saywell, J.T. (2002). *The Lawmakers: Judicial Power and the Shaping of Canadian Federalism.* Toronto: University of Toronto Press.

Sharpe, R.J., and Roach, K. (2003). *Brian Dickson: A Judge's Journey.* Toronto: University of Toronto Press.

Verdun-Jones, S.N. (2015). *Criminal Law in Canada: Cases, Questions, and the Code*, 6th ed. Toronto: Nelson Education.

World Justice Project. (2015). Rule of Law Index. http://data.worldjusticeproject.org/#.

Pioneers of Canadian Policing: A Gallery

Major-Gen. Sir Sam Steele (page 246)

Clifford Shearing (page 253)

Robert Ratner (page 255)

John McMullan (page 255)

Chris Murphy (page 256)

Rick Linden (page 256)

SEVENTEEN
Pioneers of Canadian Policing

Joshua Murphy and Curt Taylor Griffiths

Introduction

Policing in Canada has evolved from an informal community responsibility to a complex, highly visible enterprise that presents challenges and opportunities for communities, governments, and police services. As policing in Canada has evolved, research that documents this relatively mysterious profession becomes ever more important. Yet historically Canada has produced little police research in comparison with to other jurisdictions, including the United States and the United Kingdom. However, since the 1970s, a number of highly influential voices have emerged, helping among other things to influence Canadian policing policy at the municipal, provincial, and federal levels.

This chapter identifies and discusses the pioneers of policing scholarship in Canada, from the earliest authors to the new generation of researchers. A brief overview of policing in Canada, its historical roots and development, and the current state of Canadian policing in the twenty-first century will begin our discussion.

Policing in Canada: An Overview

Policing in Canada is arguably the most high-profile, visible, dynamic, and—periodically—controversial branch of the Canadian criminal justice system (Griffiths 2016). Police officers are the ones who are called upon to respond to criminal offences, disorder, and conflict in the community. Police response to these many demands can have a profound impact on individual citizens and their neighbourhoods and communities, as well as officers and the police services within which they work (Griffiths 2016). Indeed, the most frequent contact citizens have with representatives of the criminal justice system will usually be the police. The police are embedded in the very fabric of Canadian culture in the form of the Royal Canadian Mounted Police—possibly the most widely recognized symbol of Canada throughout the world. Few other countries in the world have a police force that is so closely intertwined with national culture as the Mounties; this has had interesting implications throughout this nation's history.[28]

Unlike other agents of the Canadian criminal justice system, the police work in constantly changing environments, as well as evolving social, political, and cultural contexts. Indeed, in Canada the police operate in large, heavily populated urban centres and also in remote, sparsely populated communities. Moreover, advances in technology, such as the ubiquity of mobile phone cameras and the proliferation of social networking sites and online activism, have significantly increased the visibility of police actions and continue to have a profound impact on the way policing is viewed in the public sphere and how it is carried out by frontline officers.[29] The pervasiveness of the media and social media applications ensure that the actions and decisions of police receive in-depth coverage. This has helped to make the Canadian public more demanding and, at times, less forgiving of police misconduct.

The Historical Context

Canadian policing emerged in the nineteenth century. It has been shaped by a number of important events, mirroring to some degree the development of systems of punishment and corrections. For example, Canadian policing evolved through four major stages. Policing transitioned from relatively small standalone municipal police forces in Canada's earliest days to today's larger municipal (e.g., Toronto, Montreal, Vancouver, Winnipeg, Halifax, etc.), regional, provincial (i.e., Royal Newfoundland Constabulary, Ontario Provincial Police [OPP], and Sûreté du Québec [Quebec provincial police]), and federal (i.e., RCMP) police services. While the RCMP was initially created as the North-West Mounted Police (NWMP) in May 1873 by Prime Minister John A. Macdonald to police the expansive Rupert's Land (i.e., the area of Quebec and western Canada whose rivers drain into the Hudson Bay), the history of policing in Canada dates back much earlier to the 1600s, with the first police constables appointed in Quebec City around 1651 (Dickinson 1987). The first permanent NWMP base was established in 1874 in Fort Macleod, Alberta[30] (see Box 17.1). A three-part mandate generally guided these early municipal forces: 1) to police conflicts between ethnic groups and between labourers and their employers; 2) to maintain moral standards by enforcing laws against drunkenness, prostitution, and gambling; and 3) to apprehend criminals (Griffiths 2016). It is important to note that there was a reluctance of communities to establish policing systems unless confronted by serious disorder. Indeed, a key

[28] The police uniform of the Ertzaintza (Basque region of Spain) was inspired by the RCMP dress uniform—the red serge.

[29] The famous RCMP marching band and eventual parade of horses was introduced on May 24, 1876 at Swan River Barracks, near Pelly, Saskatchewan. The date commemorated Queen Victoria's birthday (Turner 1950:262).

[30] Today the fort is a museum and is the only Designated Historic Area in the province of Alberta.

theme in the emergence of formal policing in Canada, as in England, was a general hesitancy to create police forces that had authority over the populace.

Box 17.1. Major General Sir Sam Steele (1848-1919)

Sam Steele was the third officer sworn into the newly formed North-West Mounted Police (NWMP) in 1873 and was one of the officers to lead new recruits of the NWMP on the 1874 Long March west, a key moment in the federal government's vision of settlement of the Canadian West.

In October 1877 Steele was in the party of Commissioner J.F. MacLeod who went to Fort Walsh, Saskatchewan, to conduct negotiations between Sitting Bull and General Alfred Howe Terry of the United States Army. Steele played an important role: the duties of the NWMP began to change from a focus on the native population to the transcontinental railway. As the railway advanced west, Steele was put in charge of policing the line, establishing the NWMP in Regina. This eventually became the main headquarters of the force. During this time, Steele did much work as a magistrate, settling labour disputes and maintaining order among gamblers and whisky sellers. As construction of the railway reached Fort Calgary in 1883, Steele remained as commanding officer.

The discovery of gold in the Klondike presented a key challenge for the NWMP. Steele was a central figure during this time. To help control the hundreds of unruly and independent-minded—largely American—prospectors, Steele established a rule that no individual would be allowed to enter the Yukon without a ton of goods to support himself. This prevented the desperate and potentially volatile speculators from invading the territory (Macleod 1998). Indeed, Steele and his force made the Klondike Gold Rush one of the most orderly of its kind in history. The NWMP became famous around the world. Steele eventually commanded all NWMP in the Yukon area and was a member of the territorial council (Macleod 1998).

Steele's impact on the expansion and settlement of the Canadian west, particularly with the building of the railway, is extensive. Throughout his career, Steele helped to develop law enforcement in western and northern Canada, drawing much favourable publicity to the NWMP (Macleod 1998).

In fact, in 1896 Prime Minister Sir Wilfrid Laurier did not support the NWMP, reducing the number of sworn officers and planning to eventually disband the force. With the Klondike Gold Rush between 1896 and 1899, however, came a new need to maintain law and order; this helped to ensure the NWMP's continued existence. While municipal governments in the 1800s took a more proactive approach to creating crime control systems, including police forces, those early municipal forces were mostly ineffective at maintaining high moral standards or catching criminals. Many were notoriously corrupt.

The vast distances and sparse population of western Canada meant that local police forces did not emerge there until the mid- to late 1800s, with the first organized police force created in what is now British Columbia (Griffiths 2016). Before the evolution of police forces, most communities in western Canada policed themselves. As settlements grew they began to appoint constables to carry out peacekeeping duties and controlling disorder. The Hudson's Bay Company (HBC) played a unique role in policing in the Canadian West. For example, as late as 1861, the presiding judicial officer of the HBC served also as coroner, jailer, sheriff, and chief medical officer.

The emergence of provincial police forces following Confederation was tied to the establishment and growth of what is now the RCMP (Griffiths 2016). The Constitution Act provided that upon entry into Confederation, each province would enact legislation to create a provincial police force. All regions that eventually joined Confederation had police forces; however, these forces were beset by difficulties, notably poor leadership and a dearth of qualified officers. Eventually, Alberta and Saskatchewan signed agreements with the federal government for the services of the Royal North-West Mounted Police (RNWMP) that would see it serve as the provincial police force under a cost-sharing agreement between the provinces and Ottawa (Griffiths 2016). By the 1920s the provincial police forces on the Prairies had been replaced by the RCMP and between 1917 and 1950, the RCMP assumed provincial policing responsibilities in all provinces except Quebec and Ontario, which, along with Newfoundland and Labrador, continue to be policed by their own independent provincial police forces (Griffiths 2016).

The North-West Mounted Police, as noted above, was created in 1873 to police Rupert's Land, and was a military-style force modelled after the Royal Irish Constabulary. The force was a representative of the federal government and its officers were accountable only to their commanding officers, and not to local public or political authority (Murphy and McKenna 2007). Lieutenant-Colonel Frederick White was appointed the first Comptroller of the Force; over his 24 years of service he played an instrumental role in the gradual professionalization of the Force. George A. French became the NWMP's first Commissioner (1873–1876) (Turner 1950). In 1904 the name was changed to the Royal North-West Mounted police and in 1920 to the Royal Canadian Mounted Police (RCMP). While it was anticipated that the urbanization of Canada would lead policing to shift to local communities, this did not often happen.

The motives behind the establishment of the RCMP have been the subject of debate among scholars. There is some suggestion that the force was established to preserve peace in the Canadian West and protect Indigenous peoples from whisky traders and over-aggressive settlers. The relationship between the NWMP and Aboriginal peoples, however, was constantly undermined by Ottawa, which ignored the commitments it had made in treaties. Moreover, a number of Canadian scholars contend that the NWMP played a similar role to the Canadian Pacific Railway, namely, to establish political and economic sovereignty over the farthest points of the country (Morton 1977). This included settling Indigenous lands in an orderly manner and guarding against perceived threats of American expansion. While scholars continue to debate the early history of the RCMP, there is no doubt that it is now deeply woven into Canadian culture, both for better and for worse.

The complicated history and evolution of policing in Canada laid the groundwork for the policing arrangements that are found throughout the country today. Furthermore, the historical record demonstrates that, as in England, early efforts to develop formal police forces were met with resistance from communities that were unwilling to give a particular group power and authority. The mandate of police since those early days has evolved tremendously, with the role of police in the twenty-first century being more multifaceted than ever.

Canadian Policing in the Early Twenty-First Century

The landscape—geographical, jurisdictional, legislative, and political—of Canadian policing in the twenty-first century is markedly different from other countries (Murphy and Griffiths 2015). First, public policing is carried out at multiple levels: federal, provincial, municipal, and First Nations. This leads to complex and often confusing arrangements for the delivery of police services. Moreover, with the exception of Australia, there are major differences in the geographical contexts within which police services are delivered. That is, Canadian police services vary greatly in size and in terms of the areas for which they are responsible. At one end of the spectrum, there are three-officer RCMP detachments in many remote northern communities; at the other end are thousands of officers in the urban centres of Toronto and Montreal. Policing in remote and northern communities presents challenges to police services not seen elsewhere. In urban contexts, police must work in increasingly diverse communities that present unique challenges and opportunities (see Box 17.2). Such diverse environments subject Canadian police to more extensive internal and external review than any other component of the criminal justice/social service system. Indeed, perhaps more than other agencies, the police must justify their actions and often counter the initial impressions and accounts of events that may circulate on social media; they are also held accountable to political bodies, including municipal councils, provincial/federal governments and, in some instances, First Nations governments.

Policing in Canada in the early twenty-first century is significantly different than in previous eras. The role of the police has evolved. Many factors, including legislation and policy, have led to an expansion of the role of the police. Community policing, "downloading" of costs from provincial to municipal governments and a variety of initiatives designed to address the needs of vulnerable and at-risk groups are other factors leading to expanding police roles. Police services have become proactive, establishing collaborative relationships with agencies and communities to address issues of crime and disorder. Policing in Canada is evolving against the backdrop of the economics of policing; here, the public and government are questioning the cost of police services, asking police to "do more with less," and considering a devolution of some police responsibilities to non-sworn personnel in tiered-policing arrangements.

Driven in part by the current economic climate, Canadian police services have acknowledged the need to be more effective and efficient. This has led to

Box 17.2. Early Women in Policing: Laying the Foundations for Diversity

A key feature of Canada is its diversity. This includes visible minorities, newcomers, Indigenous peoples, religious groups, and people of different sexual orientations among others (Griffiths 2016). To address this, police services are making efforts to increase their diversity. However, this has not always been a priority, and historically police services lacked diversity, particularly in terms of gender.

The first woman joined the Toronto Police Department in 1888 as a matron to supervise women and children who were brought to the police station. The Vancouver Police Department hired Canada's first two women police constables on July 8, 1912 (Griffiths 2016). They acted as matrons in the jail, escorted women prisoners, and made regular patrols of pool halls, cabarets, dances, and other places where young people congregated. Winnipeg hired its first female police constables in 1916; they were "issued a badge, a whistle, a call box key and the Book of Rules and Regulations" (Templeman 1992). The women constables rarely left the police station and were always accompanied by a male officer when they did.

Women officers were paid less than their male counterparts until the mid-1960s and it was not until 1987 that a woman officer was promoted to the position of sergeant. The RCMP did not swear in its first female officers until 1974, the same year that women joined the uniformed ranks of the OPP (Griffiths 2016). It has been argued that the first women RCMP offices were seen in highly gendered terms and that their presence challenged the historical and cultural depictions of maleness and masculinity inherent in policing (Weaver 1995).

In recent decades, women have begun to ascend to executive positions in policing. Christine Silverberg became the first female police chief of a major Canadian city in Calgary in 1995, the first of only 13 women to hold such a post in Canadian history. While still underrepresented, the number of women in leadership positions is growing. Jennifer Evans is head of the OPP, one of Canada's largest police forces. It is no longer a rarity to see women as sergeants and inspectors. Police forces are now more aware of the importance of women in operational patrol and criminal investigation roles.

the adoption of private sector practices and innovative strategies including "best practices," strategic planning, the development of metrics to assess the outcomes of initiatives, strategic deployment of officers based on data analysis, new crime response and attack strategies meant to address the underlying causes of crime, the use of "real-time" data analysis to ensure intelligence-led operations, partnerships with academics to conduct applied research, collaborative relationships with social service and community agencies, and proactivity in highlighting the plight of high-risk and vulnerable populations, including the homeless and mentally ill.

In addition to these innovations, the twenty-first century has witnessed increasing use of technology in Canadian policing. This offers a number of potential benefits, but also raises issues, including the impact and cost-effectiveness of technology in regard to crime prevention and case investigation, not to mention its effect on citizens' rights and perceptions of safety (Griffiths 2016). The most notable examples of the encroachment of technology into policing include the expanding use of drones by police services in the absence of guidelines for their use and the deployment of Tasers to police officers in the absence of a clear policy. Another debate surrounds the growing use of body-worn cameras in the absence of national research on their impact on police-citizen encounters (issues include privacy concerns, the costs of the equipment, storage and retrieval, and the massive amount of digital media evidence that will be created).

Canadian policing today also faces increasing concerns with terrorism, both from abroad and within. Fighting terrorism is a resource-intensive effort, and the overall impact on police budgets and expenditures remains to be seen. How successful these efforts will be is another question. Moreover, Canadian police services are in a position where they must balance the need to engage in community-based policing with concerns over security and risk. Indeed, Canadian policing academic Chris Murphy (2005) has discussed what he calls the "securitization" of community policing; here the community is seen more as a strategic resource than a collaborative partner or key stakeholder. The impact of terrorism on the costs of policing will be important going forward; the same is true of community policing.

Given the increasing demands of the ever-more complex role of policing in Canada—consider cybercrime, transnational crime, cross-border organized crime, international terrorism, to name a few—high-quality research on policing has never been more important. However, policing research in Canada has traditionally received less attention than the disciplines of criminology and sociology. The existing research literature, while growing, is limited in comparison to other jurisdictions. That said, a small group of highly influential scholars have produced meaningful research on policing in Canada. We turn to this next.

The Evolution of Policing Research in Canada

As noted above, policing in the twenty-first century is a complex enterprise that presents challenges and opportunities for communities, governments, and police services. Research and evaluation are core components of the effort to assess and improve the effectiveness and efficiency of the police. Yet in spite of the importance of research and scholarship, policing research in Canada has been limited, in large part by the absence of funding, collaboration, and avenues for the dissemination of research (Murphy and Griffiths 2015). This lack of capacity has been evident in Canadian universities, where historically there have been few streams for police studies at the graduate level. The Canadian academic research community is small, with a limited (but growing) number of individuals producing the bulk of policing research (Murphy and Griffiths 2015). Across the country there are several university programs that include a focus on policing: the School of Criminology at Simon Fraser University, the Justice Studies Program at the University of Regina, the Centre of Criminology at the University of Toronto, and the International Centre for Comparative Criminology at the University of Montreal. Research conducted at other universities is generally specific to the interests of individual faculty members.

Early Pioneers and Policing Historians

First, it is important to acknowledge **Denis Szabo** (see Chapter 2 in this book) who established Canada's first School of Criminology at the Université de Montréal in 1960, as well as **John Edwards,** who established the Centre of Criminology at the University of Toronto. This early generation of criminologists laid the groundwork for the emergence of the research pioneers discussed here.

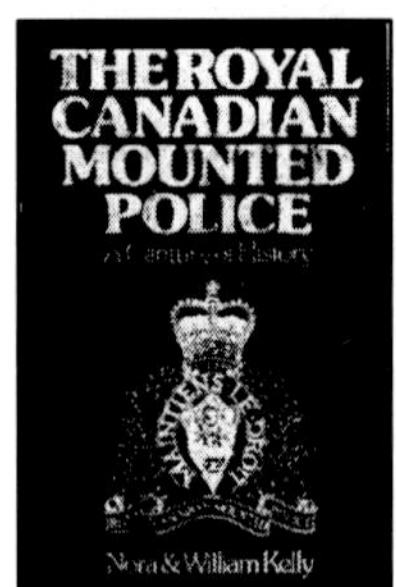

Before the 1970s the scholarship on Canadian policing was limited. There was no definitive textbook on Canadian policing. For example, the co-author of this chapter notes that when he first learned that he would be taking a position at a Canadian university in the early 1980s, he went to the library at the University of Montana to look for books on the topic of Canadian law enforcement. The only book he found was *Policing in Canada* (1975) by **William and Nora Kelly**, two of the earliest scholars of Canadian policing. Their textbook provides an early attempt at a comprehensive (though basic) overview of Canadian policing—its development, recruitment and training, the powers of police, and the processes and techniques of criminal investigation. In addition, the Kellys produced early works on the history of the RCMP, including *The Royal Canadian Mounted Police: A Century of History, 1873–1973* (1973), which Steve Hewitt (2006) refers to as the only comprehensive history of the

Mounties. While it contains dated interpretations and lacks critical distance (Hewitt 2006), it still constitutes the only work of its kind (see Box 17.3).

Within this early generation of policing scholars and historians, it is important to also mention the contributions of the following scholars: **R.C. MacLeod**, who formerly taught in the Department of History at the University of Alberta; **William Morrison**, a professor of history and director of the Centre for Northern Studies at Lakehead University in Thunder Bay; and **Daniel Koenig**, a former professor at the University of Victoria. In 1976 R.C. MacLeod produced an impressive historical analysis of the North-West Mounted Police, *The North-West Mounted Police and Law Enforcement.* MacLeod's examination of the history of the NWMP is a seminal study in the field (Perry 2003). Like McLeod, Morrison is a policing historian whose analysis of the RCMP continues to be an important source. Morrison's *Showing the Flag: The Mounted Police and Canadian Sovereignty in the North, 1894–1925* (1985) is likewise one of the few historical works that examines the role of the RCMP in policing the North.

Like R.C. MacLeod and William Morrison, Daniel Koenig is another member of this early generation of policing research pioneers; however, he was not a policing historian. Koenig is also important because he became a key policing scholar in British Columbia and was a prominent voice in policing on the West Coast. Koenig arrived at the University of Victoria in 1973 and remained there for his entire career as a professor of criminology. Koenig's ability to combine theoretical approaches to policing with practical applications resulted in his role as a regular consultant to the Victoria Police and the RCMP regarding police methods (Lowe, 2016), an example of an early police-academic research partnership. Koenig was also an editor of the International Police Executive Symposium and co-edited the book *International Police Cooperation: A World Perspective* (2001),

Box 17.3. Chronicling Pioneer Policing

In addition to William and Nora Kelly's overview of Canadian policing, there were a number of other notable books on this topic:

R.B. MacBeth (1921). *Policing the Plains: Being the Real-Life Record of the Famous Royal North-West Mounted Police.* London: Hodder and Stoughton. A book rich with anecdotal accounts of NWMP police officers dealing with crime and earning the respect of the Indigenous people.

Cecil Edward Denny (1939). *The Law Marches West.* Toronto: J.M. Dent.

Louis Charles Douthwaite (1939). *The Royal Canadian Mounted Police.* London: Blackie.

John Peter Turner (1950). *The North West Mounted Police, 1873–1893*, 2 vols. Ottawa: Edmond Cloutier.

John Sewell (1985). *The Real Story: Police in Canada.* Toronto: James Lorimer & Co.

which incorporated work from both academics and practitioners in policing at the international level (Lowe 2016).

Clifford Shearing (see Box 17.4), **Richard Ericson**, and **Jean-Paul Brodeur** emerged in the late 1970s and early 1990s in Ontario and Quebec. Ericson helped to develop the University of Toronto's Centre of Criminology. As Wood (2014) notes, Shearing's large-scale study of Toronto police calls for service, *Dial-a-Cop: A Study of Police Mobilization* (1984), and his study *Reconsidering the Police Role: A Challenge to a Challenge of Popular Conception* (1977) were important works that provided a more comprehensive understanding of police culture. Shearing's work with Ericson, *Culture as Figurative Action* (1991), illustrates the importance of story-telling in the transmission of the police culture as well as examining the police culture in general. Shearing also worked with **Philip Stenning**; both scholars were highly impactful in contributing empirical knowledge to the emerging area of private policing. Shearing also played an important role as a contributor to the development of policing strategy with the Canadian Law Commission.

Philip Stenning is another important scholar. Stenning was a long-standing and key member of the Centre of Criminology in Toronto from 1968 to 2002,

Box 17.4. Clifford Shearing: Policing Research Pioneer

Shearing's work in policing began as a student and early career scholar at the Centre of Criminology at the University of Toronto. At this time, the Centre was relatively small and lacked a distinct emphasis on police studies. Shearing's research served to contribute to the body of knowledge on what had been a neglected aspect of Canadian criminal justice. Shearing was also innovative in his perspective on policing. Whereas other theorists viewed police as operating with an "us vs. them" mentality, and as representatives of social elites, Shearing's work in the 1970s revealed a more "nuanced understanding of how police saw their roles, and the ways in which these perceptions were shaped by distinctions they made between various types of 'publics'" (Wood 2014:521).

Along with Philip Stenning, Shearing explored the expanding role of private policing (Wood 2014), helping to expand criminology to include the study of practices of social ordering beyond formal representatives of government (Shearing 2006). This research remains of particular importance given the fact that policing has become increasingly "decoupled" from government (Murphy and Clarke 2005) and because of the trend towards pluralization of policing (Bayley and Shearing 1996).

Shearing has also contributed to the development of a policing strategy for the Law Commission of Canada, in 2006 playing a key role (with Stenning) in drafting its report, *In Search of Security: The Future of Policing in Canada.* Shearing went on to play a critical role in policing internationally, working in South Africa, Australia, Argentina, and Northern Ireland.

as well as serving as a consultant and adviser to many government departments and commissions of inquiry in Canada and across the world. Stenning's work has explored a number of key areas of Canadian policing including the country's increasing multicultural society on police strategies. Stenning has also undertaken important work on police governance and accountability, applying an international perspective to the Canadian context.

Richard Ericson became director of the Centre of Criminology at the University of Toronto. Ericson produced important theoretical work on policing, including his book (with Kevin D. Haggerty), *Policing the Risk Society* (1997), as well as *Reproducing Order: A Study of Police Patrol Work* (1982) and *Making Crime: A Study of Detective Work* (1993). These last two books employed field observations and qualitative interviews. Ericson's work examined law enforcement through a critical lens, a new approach from much of the early

Box 17.5. Richard Ericson: Key Contributor to Policing Research

Richard Ericson (see Chapter 12) was a major player in policing research in Canada. He was instrumental in the growth of the Centre of Criminology, and with co-author Kevin Haggerty produced *Policing the Risk Society*, a reconceptualization of work carried out by the police. It became, according to Jerome Skolnick, "the most significant theoretical work on the police since Egon Bittner" (Garland 2007:xv). Furthermore, Ericson's books *Reproducing Order: A Study of Police Patrol Work* and *Making Crime: A Study of Detective Work* used field observations and qualitative interviews to study police patrol work from the viewpoint of line-level officers and detectives. This provided unique and valuable insight into the world of frontline and investigative policing. Ericson's scholarship was unique and ground-breaking in its critical view of frontline policing, highlighting the largely reactive and sedentary nature of this work. This unflattering view of the police drew criticism from the policing community. Ericson advocated for new ways to effectively manage and utilize police resources, a position echoed today in calls for evidence-led deployment and management of police resources. Ericson's work with Clifford Shearing on police culture and the transmission of values was also key. *Culture as Figurative Action* explores how culture operates as a "figurative logic" through stories and pieces of advice that police officers share; such stories influence how officers make situational judgements on how to act. This work laid the basis for our understanding of police culture.

work on Canadian policing. To this end, *Reproducing Order* should be regarded as a definitive publication in the study of policing in Canada (see Box 17.5).

An earlier chapter in this book discusses in detail the work of Jean-Paul Brodeur. Brodeur served as the director of the International Centre of Comparative Criminology at the University of Montreal and was a leading figure in francophone criminology. His primary field of interest was policing and his contributions to the literature have significantly expanded the body of knowledge of police and police work. Brodeur's seminal piece is the article "High policing and low policing: Remarks about the policing of political activities" (1983), which introduced the term "high policing" into the English language police studies lexicon. Brodeur's 2007 update of the paper in response to the events of 9/11 now seems prescient following the 2015 attacks on Parliament Hill and in Paris. In addition to these works, Brodeur wrote on a broad spectrum of other policing topics, including police deviance, undercover police work, and the police use of force. Furthermore, Brodeur was a significant voice in the development of policing policy in Canadian Indigenous communities. Brodeur's final publication, *The Policing Web* (2010), is another seminal contribution to the study of policing (see Box 17.6).

Early Critical Criminologists

Two names worth mentioning here are **Robert Ratner**, a scholar at the University of British Columbia (UBC) in Vancouver, and **John McMullan**, a scholar at St. Mary's University in Halifax. McMullan has authored a number of government reports, served on government commissions, councils, and boards and is a Commissioner of the Law Reform Commission of Nova Scotia, and Ratner's work on critical criminology in the 1970s and '80s in Western Canada represented an important scholarly contribution.

Ratner and McMullan's introduction of the critical framework to Canada is important here, providing some new perspectives for the study of Canadian policing. As noted earlier, much of the early research on Canadian police was largely descriptive in nature and lacked a critical lens. A more critical study of criminology influenced on how the police were observed, allowing a more balanced view of Canadian law enforcement.

> **Box 17.6. Jean-Paul Brodeur: A French Canadian Policing Pioneer**
>
> Brodeur's first major published criminological work was a study of the history of commissions of inquiry into the police in Canada from 1895 to 1970; this remains a key source on the politics of policing in Canada. It should be noted that in addition to his scholarship on commissions of police inquiry, Brodeur also served as research director for many of Canada's most high-profile and important commissions, including the Keable and Duchaine Inquiries into the FLQ crisis (Stenning and Roberts 2011).

The Next Phase of Canadian Research Pioneers

Shearing and Ericson eventually left Canada for institutions abroad; however, a number of new Canadian police scholars began to produce important work from the late 1980s continuing until today. Ongoing research is important, particularly in the current economics of policing environment and the push for more evidence-based policing practices. This group includes the following scholars: **Chris Murphy** at Dalhousie University (see Box 17.7); **Paul McKenna**, an adjunct professor at Dalhousie University; **Rick Linden** of the Department of Sociology at the University of Manitoba, who also serves as the Chair of the Manitoba Police Commission; **Curt T. Griffiths** at Simon Fraser University; **Steve Hewitt**, who spent time at the University of Saskatchewan before moving to the University of Birmingham in England; and **Margaret E. Beare** at York University in Toronto.

In addition to serving as the first director of the Nathanson Centre for the Study of Organized Crime and Corruption at Osgoode Hall Law School (1996–2006), **Margaret Beare** is an important figure in police research for a number of reasons. Not only is Beare is one of the few female scholars in the field; she also has spent considerable time with the Department of the Solicitor General Canada. During the 1980s the Ministry of the Solicitor General operated a well-staffed and highly qualified Police Research Unit, of which Margaret Beare served as director. This unit was a focal point for collaboration with university-based scholars (Murphy and Griffiths 2015). As a scholar, Beare has

Box 17.7. Chris Murphy: Exploring Policing in the Security State

Chris Murphy is a key voice in policing from the Maritimes. Murphy has produced important work on a wide spectrum of topics, including small-town policing, community and problem-oriented policing, Aboriginal policing, private policing, police resources, police culture, police research, police investigating police, and post-9/11 policing, and security developments. Murphy's book, *Securitizing Canadian Policing: A New Policing Paradigm for the Post 9/11 Security State?* (2007), considers the impact of increased security concerns on community policing strategy. Murphy's influence also lies in his collaborations with a number of police services, government policy bodies, and provincial and federal commissions of inquiry. One example is Murphy's contribution to the Law Commission of Canada report entitled *In Search of Security: The Future of Policing in Canada* (2006). Such contributions are important because most academic research conducted in Canada is published in professional journals and is inaccessible to police services (Bradley and Nixon 2009).

Paul McKenna, a lecturer at the School of Information Management at Dalhousie, is another important scholar. Like Murphy, McKenna collaborates with the public sector on projects involving public safety and policing initiatives in addition to his scholarly work. He has made important contributions on the economics of policing as well as the need for police services to engage in more evidence-led practices through partnerships with academics. Since 1997 he has been president of Public Safety Innovation, Inc., which provides a range of professional consultation services on policing and public security. McKenna and Murphy's analysis of police accountability and police investigating police is one of the few reports of its kind in Canada.

been involved in policing research for more than twenty years and has produced important publications on organized crime, corruption, and policing. Her recent co-edited book, *Putting the State on Trial: The Policing of Protest During the G20 Summit* (2015), is her latest contribution.

Anthony Doob, O.C., is one of the most well-known and influential criminologists in Canada (see Chapter 11). He has been largely responsible for the growth of the Centre of Criminology at the University of Toronto, serving as director or acting director longer than any other faculty member. Though policing is not his primary area of interest, he has produced work on policing and continues to be a key voice in discussions of policing policy moving forward. The Centre of Criminology has become as a major centre for policing research during his time as director.

Rick Linden and **Steve Hewitt** are also influential policing scholars. Steve Hewitt worked at the University of Saskatchewan, writing about the history of Canadian policing, specifically the RCMP. He has also written on the history of state surveillance in Canada, in particular spying by the RCMP at Canadian universities. Hewitt has also written about the history and evolution of the RCMP in Alberta and Saskatchewan with his own unique critical lens. Rick Linden has become a key criminologist and police researcher in Manitoba, authoring an influential review of women in Canadian policing. Linden has also collaborated with police services in Canada, including the Winnipeg Police Service. Linden played a key role in the development and implementation of the Winnipeg Auto Theft Suppression Strategy (WATSS; see www.winnipeg.ca/police/TakeAction/auto_theft.stm).

Curt Griffiths is another important policing scholar, both in British Columbia and nationally. His *Canadian Police Work* is a definitive text in police studies. Griffiths has also published many studies on a range of policing topics. He has contributed greatly to the Police Studies Centre in the School of Criminology at Simon Fraser University, a growing centre of policing research in Canada, as well as making considerable progress in bridging the gap between police services and academics, conducting applied research that has informed the policy of a number of police services across Canada. Griffiths has also written a study of the RCMP in the Eastern Arctic, a patrol deployment study of the Vancouver Police Department, an operational review of the Winnipeg Police Service, and a study of police and racial profiling in Toronto. In this respect, Griffiths has been a pioneer in both academic and applied research in Canada. He has collaborated on a number of operational reviews of police services and produced reports in the following areas: the factors associated with police inefficiencies; the current and potential role of private security; and the issues associated with police officer mental health.

Most recently he has been exploring the potential for research on the use of body-worn cameras in British Columbia and across Canada.

Moving Forward: Glimmers of Hope and a New Generation

In recent years, initiatives in Canadian policing research include the creation of a web-based repository for police-related research under the auspices of Public Safety Canada; the development of collaborative relationships between police services, unions, and academics; the increasing involvement of police associations as a sponsor of research; funding support for police research from Public Safety Canada; and Public Safety Canada's Policy Development Contribution Program (see, for example, http://www.publicsafety.gc.ca/cnt/cntrng-crm/plcng/index-en.aspx). Facilitated by police-academic partnerships and sponsorship from police unions/associations, policing scholars are producing applied research that has the dual function of contributing to the body of knowledge of policing in Canada, while also giving police organizations valuable data that can be used to inform policy, influence methods of deployment, shape training curricula, and improve police effectiveness and efficiency (Murphy and Griffiths 2015).

Canadian police research has been driven, in part, by the emergence of several centres for policing research across the country, including the Police Studies Research Centre in the School of Criminology at Simon Fraser University, the Police Studies Program in the Department of Justice Studies at the University of Regina, the Centre for Criminology and Sociolegal Studies at the University of Toronto, the International Centre for Comparative Criminology at the Université de Montréal, and the Police Research Lab in the Department of Psychology at Carleton University in Ottawa. These policing research centres along with other institutions are home to the latest generation of police scholars. This is a group of relatively young (30 to 50 years of age), geographically diverse individuals with a variety of research interests and focus areas under the policing umbrella. Additionally, these researchers are also cultivating collaborative partnerships with police services at the municipal, provincial, and federal levels. Individuals in this group include **Nick Jones** and **Rick Ruddell** at the University of Regina; **George Rigakos** at Carleton University; **Samuel Tanner** at the Université de Montréal; **Sara Thompson** at Ryerson University in Toronto; **Rick Parent** at Simon Fraser University; **Scot Wortley** at the University of Toronto; **Laura Huey** at the University of Western Ontario; and **Rose Ricciardelli** at Memorial University in Newfoundland and Labrador. It is interesting to note here that a growing number of the current voices in the field of policing research are women.

This current generation of police scholars is bridging the gap between academics of an earlier generation such as Chris Murphy, Paul McKenna, Rick Linden, Curt Griffiths, and Anthony Doob, and the next generation. As new partnerships and collaborations are forming, voices are bringing forward research from unique perspectives.

Conclusion

The bulk of Canadian scholarship on policing has been produced for the most part by a relatively small number of scholars over the last 40-odd years. These individuals are the pioneers of Canadian policing scholarship. Their work has had and continues to have a profound impact on our understanding of policing and the development of police policy and practice. This groundwork has encouraged a new generation of police researchers who aim to improve the state of Canadian police research in the twenty-first century.

References

Bayley, D., and Shearing, C. (1996). The future of policing. *Law & Society Review*, 30, 585-606.

Dickinson, J.A. (1987). Réflexions sur la police en Nouvelle-France. *McGill Law Journal*, 32, 497–522.

Garland, D. (2007). Richard Ericson: An appreciation. *The Canadian Journal of Sociology*, 32(4), xi–xviii.

Griffiths, C.T. (2016). *Canadian Police Work*, 4th end. Toronto: Nelson Education.

Hewitt, S. (2006). *Riding to the Rescue: The Transformation of the RCMP in Alberta and Saskatchewan, 1914–1939*. Ontario: University of Toronto Press.

Lowe, D. (2016). *Policing Terrorism: Research Studies into Police Counterterrorism Investigations.* Florida: Taylor & Francis Group.

Macleod, R.C. (1998). Steele, Sir Samuel Benfield. *Dictionary of Canadian Biography*, 14. University of Toronto/ Université Laval. http://www.biographi.ca/en/bio/steele_samuel_benfield_14E.html.

Morton, D. (1977). Calvary or police: Keeping the peace on two adjacent frontiers, 1870– 1900. *Journal of Canadian Studies*, 12, 27–37.

Murphy, J.J., and Griffiths, C.T. (2015). Back from the abyss: Glimmers of hope and the state of police research in Canada. Unpublished.

Murphy, C. (2005). *Securitizing Canadian Policing: A New Policing Paradigm for the Post 9/11 Security State?* Canada. metropolis.net/pdfs/cmurphy%20security%20policing %20article.pdf.

Murphy, C., and McKenna, P.F. (2007). *Rethinking Police Governance, Culture and Management.* Ottawa: Public Safety Canada.

Shearing, C. (2011). Re-considering the field of policing: A review of the policing web. *Canadian Journal of Criminology and Criminal Justice*, 53(3), 325–341.

Stenning, P.C., and Roberts, J.V. (2011). The scholarship of Jean-Paul Brodeur. *Canadian Journal of Criminology and Criminal Justice*, 53(3), 267–272.

Templeman, J. (1992). Women in policing: History 1916–1992. Retrieved from http://www.winnipeg.ca/police/abou/history/index.html

Weaver, J.C. (1995). *Crimes, Constables and Courts.* Montreal and Kingston: McGill-Queen's University Press.

Wood, J.D. (2014). Pioneers in policing: Clifford Shearing. *Police Practice and Research*, 15(6), 519–532.

Selected Bibliography

Brodeur, J.P. (1983). High policing and low policing: Remarks about the policing of political activities. *Social Problems*, 30(5), 507–520.

Brodeur, J.P. (2007). High and low policing in post 9/11 times. *Policing: A Journal of Policy and Practice*, 1(1), 25–37.

Brodeur, J.P. (2010). *The Policing Web.* New York: Oxford University Press.

Doob, A. (1993). The police, policing, and the allocation of resources to each: A report of a workshop." In A.N. Doob (ed.). *Thinking About Police Resources*. Toronto: University of Toronto Press.

Ericson, R.V. (1982). *Reproducing Order: A Study of Police Patrol Work.* Toronto: University of Toronto Press.

Ericson, R.V. (1981). *Making Crime: A Study of Detective Work.* Toronto: University of Toronto Press.

Ericson, R.V., and Haggerty, K.D. (1997). *Policing the Risk Society.* Oxford: Clarendon Press.

Griffiths, C.T. (2016). *Canadian Police Work*, 4th edn. Toronto: Nelson Education.

Hewitt, S. (2002). *Spying 101: The RCMP's Secret Activities at Canadian Universities, 1917–1997.* Ontario: University of Toronto Press.

Hewitt, S. (2006). *Riding to the Rescue: The Transformation of the RCMP in Alberta and Saskatchewan, 1914–1939.* Ontario: University of Toronto Press.

Huey, L. (2007). *Negotiating Demands: The Politics of Skid Row Policing in Edinburgh, San Francisco, and Vancouver.* Toronto: University of Toronto Press.

Kelly, W., and Kelly, N. (1976). *Policing in Canada.* Toronto: Macmillan.

Law Commission of Canada. (2006). *In Search of Security: The Future of Policing in Canada.* Ottawa: Minister of Public Works and Government Services. Retrieved from http://www.policecouncil.ca/reports/LCC2006.pdf

Linden, R., and Minch, C. (1984). *Women in Policing: A Review.* Canada: Solicitor General.

Macleod, R.C. (1978). *The North-West Mounted Police, 1873–1919.* The Canadian Historical Association.

Macleod, R.C. (1994). The RCMP and the evolution of provincial policing. In R.C Macleod and D. Schneiderman (eds.), *Police Powers in Canada: The Evolution and Practice of Authority.* Toronto: University of Toronto Press.

Morrison, W.R. (1985). *Showing the Flag: The Mounted Police and Canadian Sovereignty in the North 1894–1925.* Vancouver: The University of British Columbia Press.

Murphy, C. (2005). *Securitizing Canadian Policing: A New Policing Paradigm for the Post 9/11 Security State?* Canada.metropolis.net/pdfs/cmurphy%20security%20policing %20article.pdf

Murphy, C., and McKenna, P.F. (2010). *Police Investigating Police: A Critical Analysis of the Literature.* Ottawa: Commission for Public Complaints against the RCMP.

Murphy, C., and McKenna, P.F. (2007). *Rethinking Police Governance, Culture and Management.* Ottawa: Public Safety Canada.

Shearing, C.D., and Ericson, R.V. (1991). Culture as figurative action. *The British Journal of Sociology*, 42(4), 481–506.

Shearing, C.D., and Leon, J.S. (1977). Reconsidering the police role: A challenge to a challenge of a popular conception. *Canadian Journal of Criminology and Corrections*, 19(4), 331–345.

Shearing, C.D., and Stenning, P.C. (1987). *Private Policing.* California: Sage.

Shearing, C.D. (1984). *Dial-A-Cop: A Study of Police Mobilization.* Canada: University of Toronto Centre of Criminology.

Shearing, C.D. (1992). The relation between public and private policing. *Crime and Justice*, 15, 399–434.

Stenning, P.C., and Shearing, C. (1980). The quiet revolution: The nature, development and general legal implications of private security in Canada. *Criminal Law Quarterly*, 22, 220–248.

Stenning, P.C. (1981). *Legal Status of the Police.* Ottawa: Law Reform Commission of Canada.

Turner, J.P. (1950). *The North-West Mounted Police*, Vol. 1. Ottawa, ON: King's Printer and Controller of Stationery.

Canadian Corrections: A Gallery

William Lyon Mackenzie (page 265)

George Brown (page 266)

William John Hanna (page 268)

J. Dinnage Hobden (page 268)

Kingston Penitentiary, 1901 (page 269)

EIGHTEEN
Pioneers in Canadian Corrections

Rick Ruddell

Introduction

Canada is recognized as a world leader in the development, implementation, and delivery of correctional services (Correctional Service of Canada 2014a). These interventions are related to Canada's distinctive history as well as the efforts of a number of individuals who influenced correctional operations for both good and bad. Like correctional systems in other nations, Canadian practices have been shaped by a series of crises, scandals, and reforms. Correctional practitioners, stakeholders, prisoner advocates, and social scientists over the past two centuries have attempted to make correctional operations safer and work toward reducing offender recidivism. Not all of these efforts have been successful. Misguided or corrupt officials and political appointees with very little knowledge of corrections were responsible for the brutal treatment of prisoners, unnecessary suffering, and treatment that damaged rather than reformed offenders. Both groups are worthy of attention; however, one of the challenges in telling the full story is that much of what occurred in local corrections has been lost to time. As a result, the primary focus of this chapter is after 1835, the year Kingston Penitentiary was established.

Canada's system of short-term provincial incarceration and long-term federal imprisonment (two years and over) is somewhat different than correctional practices in the United States or other Commonwealth nations. In some respects, those differences are a result of Canada's distinctive "geography, political history, and government arrangements of the country as well as by economics, religion, and philosophical movements" (Ekstedt and Griffiths 1988:15). The correctional practices that evolved were also the product of the efforts of pioneers, policymakers, and politicians who grappled with question of how best to address problems of delinquency and crime. These pioneers were an eclectic mix of members of the clergy, politicians, and public servants.

Jones (2005) reminds us of the importance of acknowledging the efforts of these pioneers, as well as evaluating both their strengths and shortcomings. Often these individuals were required to respond to high rates of offender recidivism, correctional violence, escapes, riots, and wrongdoing on the part of correctional staff; this is particularly true in the early days of these fledgling systems. Other pioneers recognized the help that prisoners and ex-prisoners required and reached out to them, treating them with compassion and friendship. Taken together, these individuals helped shape the delivery of correctional services in Canada.

A Short History of Local/Provincial Corrections

The colonists who settled in the lands that became Canada imported the justice practices of their respective homelands, Britain and France. Living conditions in the colony were harsh for everybody and even minor offences were punished severely. Individuals accused of committing crimes were held in local gaols (pronounced "jails") until they had their day in court, although short-term incarceration was also used. Writing about Montreal between 1765 and 1799, Fyson (2006:259) reports more than three-fifths (61%) of individuals were fined and 23% were released on their recognizance. Imprisonment was imposed on 8% and corporal punishments on the remaining 7% of those found guilty. Physical punishments ranged from branding and flogging (i.e., whipping) to execution. Even the reliance on fines and corporal punishments did not reduce the overcrowding in local gaols. Punishments in Upper Canada, however, may have been more severe and between 1792 and 1830 there were 737 convictions in Circuit Courts (that dealt with more serious offences); 22% were sent to a gaol, 15% were condemned to death, 15% received corporal punishments and incarceration, 18% were sentenced to a fine and a gaol sentence, 9% were fined, 11% were banished and 7% were required to stand in the stocks (Nickerson 2010:87).

Prior to the 1830s, the primary role of gaols was the temporary detention of persons accused of committing crimes while awaiting court appearances. Because these facilities were only intended to hold persons for short periods, they had few comforts. Males and females were held together, as were children (a separate youth justice system was not developed until 1908). As today, most of the individuals held in these facilities were impoverished, suffering from poor physical or mental health, or from substance abuse. Some were incarcerated because of their inability to pay their debts. Many of these early gaols were makeshift facilities—spaces in public buildings that were converted into correctional facilities or attached to a township's courthouse. In smaller settlements there might have only been two or three cells and even in the 1970s some Nova Scotia towns did not have police lockups or cells to take arrestees (Thomson, Clairmont, and Clairmont 2003). American research has showed us that as the size of the town or city rises, the number of jail beds, staff professionalism, and sophistication of the facility also increases (Applegate and Sitren 2008). Waves of immigration led to population increases in Lower and Upper Canada. Temporary or makeshift facilities became obsolete as the need to hold persons accused of crime increased and more permanent structures were required. By the 1830s short-term periods of incarceration (a week to a month) were commonly imposed on offenders if a facility was available in the jurisdiction (Nickerson 2010).

Executions were also a relatively common punishment in the early days of the colony. One of the first recorded hangings in Canada was a teenage girl from Quebec found guilty of theft in 1649. Leyton-Brown (2010) observes that most executions took place at local gaols close to where the crimes that the offender(s) had committed. Between 1859 and 1967, there were at least 710 executions. Leyton-Brown (2010:vii) points out that "hanging occupied an important place—in some senses a central place—in Canada's criminal justice." The one consistent factor underlying capital punishment is that suspects were first held in the local gaol and, once convicted, most were executed there as well.

Pioneers: Advocates for Improved Conditions

We have very little knowledge of the identities of the people who ran these early local facilities; their names have generally been lost to history. Prior to Confederation, most temporary detention facilities were locally operated, not part of provincial systems. They suffered from the same plight as small-town police services that were led by officials with very little formal knowledge of the justice system (Thomson et al. 2003). In addition, prior to Confederation there was little accountability or oversight of gaol operations except for grand juries that were tasked with reporting on gaol conditions (Wetherell 1979), although after 1867 most provinces had gaol inspectors. In the paragraphs that follow seven advocates and reformers are identified. This list represents only a fraction of these correctional pioneers.

William Lyon Mackenzie (1795–1861): Prisoner Advocate

Born and raised in Dundee, Scotland, William Lyon Mackenzie emigrated to Canada (then Upper Canada) in 1820 to work as a journalist and then as a politician. Mackenzie became the first mayor of Toronto, and a vocal critic of the conditions in Ontario jails. In 1830 he wrote a report in response to prisoner complaints about the York gaol. This facility was notorious for harsh conditions for debtors (who did not receive food from the jailors), the mixing together of all prisoners (debtors and criminals, adults and children, and the mentally ill with the other prisoners), not to mention crowding, insufficient food, and overall of lack of sanitary conditions. While Mackenzie's report was not seen favourably by the city magistrates (who felt that his advocacy was an intrusion on their oversight of the jail), his work drew the attention of the province's lieutenant-governor. Oliver (1998) calls Mackenzie a "radical reformer." Mackenzie's grandson, William Lyon Mackenzie King, became the tenth prime minister of Canada, and Toronto's William Lyon Mackenzie Collegiate Institute is named after him.

George Brown (1818–1880): Investigating Prison Abuse

Born in Alloa, Clackmannanshire, Scotland, George Brown and his family emigrated to New York in 1837 where they began publishing newspapers. In 1843 they moved to Toronto to continue their publishing business. With his father's backing, he founded and became the first editor of Toronto's *The Globe* newspaper and a future father of Confederation. In 1849 he was appointed to head a commission investigating conditions at Kingston Penitentiary (KP). Brown's report chronicled incidents of "graft, corruption, cruelty and sinister politics" (Edmison 1953:245). McCoy (2012) reports how Brown identified eight key shortcomings of Warden Henry Smith's prison regime including starved prisoners, the sexual abuse of women offenders, flogging persons with mental illness, and the "silent system" (rules prohibiting inmates from talking to other inmates or the prison staff) that was driving some youngsters to insanity (see Box 19.1). The use of corporal punishments was of concern to the public; McCoy (2012:47) writes that in 1846 there were 6,063 punishments for 262 prisoners. There was also concern that Warden Smith's son abused both prisoners and keepers, and that he was involved in financial corruption (Curtis, Graham, Kelly, and Patterson 1985). Brown recommended that Smith be relieved of his job as warden and Smith subsequently resigned. These abuses led Brown to call for the closure of KP although throughout the prison's history other prisoner advocates would also argue for its closure.

Joseph Uldaric Leclerc (1836–?): Chaplain and Prisoner's Advocate

Father Leclerc was a chaplain in provincial and federal institutions in Quebec. After working in the community as a priest he started his career as a prison chaplain in the School of Reform for Lower Canada. In 1873 he started working at the federal government's newly constructed St. Vince de Paul penitentiary in Laval, Quebec, where he remained for ten years (Rose 1888). During his time with the federal corrections service it was said that he "dedicated his life to the humane treatment of prisoners" (Commissioner of Penitentiaries 1968:8) and in recognition of his efforts he is the only chaplain to have a prison named after him. In keeping with the rehabilitative nature of Father Leclerc's chaplaincy, the Commissioner of Penitentiaries (1961) notes the institution was

> a prison without walls and armed guards, [and that] Leclerc Institution embodies many of the ideas which were considered radical when Father Leclerc formulated them 100 years ago. Improved training of prison guards, in-prison education and employment, supervi-

> sion of paroled prisoners—all these were preached by Father Leclerc without appreciable results during his lifetime (11).

Although Leclerc was not around to see the outcomes of his advocacy, his efforts, and those of other pioneers, continue to bear fruit decades after their personal efforts ended.

John Beverley Robinson (1861–1896): Prisoner Advocate and Civil Servant

Born in Berthier, Lower Canada (now known as Quebec), John Robinson became a prominent Upper Canada lawyer and served as Attorney General (1818–1829) and Chief Justice (1829–1862). Robinson was critical of conditions for gaol inmates, including a lack of classification (e.g. mixing debtors, criminals, both genders, and adults and youth) and inadequate "heating, ventilation, clothing, bedding and medical attention" (Oliver 1998:70). Robinson as Chief Justice of Ontario became an advocate for improving conditions of confinement. He encouraged a grand jury investigating gaols to provide a full and accurate accounting of their often-inhumane conditions. Oliver (1998) reports Robinson's advocacy was not popular; most citizens wanted their taxes used to help more "deserving" persons.

Mary Jane O'Reilly (née: Redmond) (1840–?), Superintendent

The Andrew Mercer Ontario Reformatory for Females was Canada's first women-only institution. Established in Toronto in 1880 its rehabilitative nature differed from other provincial institutions; it more closely resembled a college than a prison (Ontario Ministry of Correctional Services, 2012; see also Brown 1975 for a detailed description of the reformatory). Born and raised in Ontario, Mary Jane O'Reilly was appointed as the first superintendent in 1880 and held that job until her retirement in 1901. Strange (1983:22) describes her as a middle-aged widow who was untrained in corrections, but she did tour women's institutions in Massachusetts and Indiana prior to her appointment.

As in other women's institutions of the Victorian era, most inmates had committed relatively minor crimes and were required to work in roles preparing them for domestic labour jobs and to receive religious instruction. Unlike male correctional facilities, there were few rules and O'Reilly attempted to cultivate a "home-like" atmosphere; this sometimes made the institution a frustrating place to work. Although sentences in the reformatory were relatively short, O'Reilly attempted to find work for all the inmates who were released. Oliver (1994:545) observes that "Under her leadership there were no scandals, riots, charges of brutality, or other incidents characteristic of punitive prisoners everywhere." Yet over time the institution's operations came under criticism and the facility was closed in 1969.

William John Hanna (1862–1919): Provincial Reformer

Born in Adelaide Township, a little east of Sarnia, Ontario, William Hanna became a lawyer and was elected to the provincial legislature in 1902. He was instrumental in carrying out a review of Ontario's provincial correctional centres, psychiatric facilities, and child welfare agencies. An advocate of correctional rehabilitation, Hanna founded the Ontario Reformatory in 1910, a prison farm that was constructed in Guelph (largely by inmate labour). Hanna's desire was to return inmates to the community in better physical and mental health than they were admitted (Comeau 1998). Although the reformatory (later named the Guelph Correctional Centre) closed in 2002, it still represents Hanna's hope of better outcomes for provincial prisoners.

In addition to being instrumental in prison reforms, he also served as an advisor to Canada's eighth prime minister, Robert Laird Borden (1911–1920), and in 1916 he was instrumental in introducing the Ontario Temperance Act, which prohibited the sale of alcohol (medical uses were excepted). This measure remained in effect for the duration of World War I.

J. Dinnage Hobden (1884–1978): Founder of the John Howard Society

There were a number of prisoner aid associations that emerged throughout the country about the time of Confederation. Volunteers from these agencies provided spiritual and emotional support to prisoners, as well as friendship and assistance in helping them return to the community. Over the next half century the number and activities of these groups waxed and waned; however, an important turning point was the establishment of the first John Howard Society in 1931 in British Columbia by Reverend J. Dinnage Hobden. Hobden named the organization after John Howard, a British prison reformer who died in 1790.

A Short History of Canadian Penitentiaries

The penitentiary is a relatively new innovation in human history and Eastern State Penitentiary (ESP), which was founded in 1829 in Philadelphia, is regarded as the first prison. ESP has been described as a "big house" prison as it is an imposing castle-like structure surrounded with a high stone wall. The design of ESP, which was one of the most expensive buildings in the U.S. when constructed, was intended to send a strong deterrent message to those considering crimes. Inside the walls, prisoners were expected to abide by the "silent system." The silence, combined with thoughtful reflection, was thought to lead to a prisoner's reformation, although the isolation and lack of interaction with others contributed to mental health problems. ESP became the prototypical prison, and quickly attracted the attention of policymakers, philosophers, authors such as Charles Dickens, and others interested in corrections.

Officials from Upper Canada also visited Eastern State Penitentiary, which served as a model for the provincial prison in the village of Portsmouth (later to become Kingston). Kingston Penitentiary (KP), Canada's first penitentiary, accepted its initial six prisoners in 1835, although the facility was still under construction (Correctional Service of Canada 2014c). During its first decades, KP admitted youngsters under ten years of age and accepted both male and female offenders. As in the local gaols of the 1830s, conditions of confinement were harsh. Practices such as solitary confinement, "a strict rule of silence," strict discipline and "constant collective employment" to "keep the convicts busy" were the norm (John Howard Society of Alberta 1988).

Box 18.1. Warden Smith of Kingston Penitentiary

While other pioneers described in this chapter were known for their work toward reform, Henry Smith, first warden of Kingston Penitentiary, is known for cruelty and corruption. Before becoming warden, Smith was a magistrate and businessman from the Kingston area who had some involvement in the construction of the facility (McCoy 2012). Smith became a controversial figure for the treatment of prisoners: many of the keepers (correctional officers) were illiterate and were encouraged to punish the prisoners harshly. Prisoners were whipped for minor violations of rules, such as smiling, laughing, or winking (Edmison 1953). According to McCoy (2012), other than placing prisoners on bread-and-water diets for minor rule violations, flogging was the only punishment that was meted out until 1847. Even pre-teenagers and persons with mental illness were whipped. An 11-year-old boy was flogged for speaking French while a 12-year-old girl was flogged on six different occasions (Edmison 1953). After 1847, prisoners were sometimes immobilized in a standing position for up to eight hours in a coffin-like "box."

By the mid-1840s Smith was a very powerful bureaucrat, and he was influential in the revision of the Penitentiary Act in 1846, although some of his motivations were questionable: he managed to increase his salary at the expense of other senior prison officials, whose salaries were reduced (Curtis et al. 1985). Smith's abuse of power allegedly extended to prisoner treatment; there were a number of complaints of abuse from inmates in addition to ever increasing allegations of corruption. A commission of inquiry was established to investigate KP. The 1849 Brown report led to Smith's resignation and the dismissal of other officials.

Unlike other fledgling penal institutions, KP was controversial from its founding until its closure in 2010. Its early days were defined by the abusive treatment of prisoners; the institution itself was designed to be an intimidating place called the "fortress of fear" (Kennedy 2013). The facility was home to every imaginable form of prison misconduct, from escapes and murders of staff and prisoners to riots, including major disturbances in 1932, 1954, and 1971 (Curtis et al. 1985). By 1978 it had been converted into a protective custody prison holding "the worst of the worst: sexual deviants, child murderers, sadists, reviled figures such as shoeshine boy killer Saul Betesh, Clifford Olson, Paul Bernardo, Russell Williams, the Shafias and Michael Briere, who sexually assaulted and strangled a 14-year-old girl and dismembered her body. None would have lasted a nanosecond in [the] general [prison] population" (Kennedy 2013) (see Box 18.1).

Provincial prisons were also established in Saint John, New Brunswick (1842) and Halifax, Nova Scotia (1844). When the British North America Act was signed in 1867 all three of these facilities became a responsibility of the federal government. The growing population and higher crime rates led to the expansion of Canada's prison system. Before the 1920s, facilities were constructed in St. Vincent de Paul (Quebec), Stony Mountain (Manitoba), New Westminster (British Columbia) Dorchester (New Brunswick), and Prince Albert (Saskatchewan) (Correctional Service of Canada 2014c).

Pioneers in Federal Corrections

The following individuals played a role in shaping the delivery of federal corrections after Canada became a dominion in 1867. These individuals are from a diverse range of backgrounds, ranging from academic researchers to members of the clergy and public servants. Moreover, these pioneers followed different priorities. Some focused on inmate rehabilitation while others helped to support the offender's transition back into the community. Although their backgrounds and priorities varied, they shared a common goal: to increase public safety by rehabilitating offenders.

Walter Palmer Archibald (1860–1922): Establishing Parole

The Salvation Army has always played a role in correctional reform and members of that organization have advocated on behalf of prisoners and their families. Brigadier Walter Archibald, who worked with the Salvation Army's Prison Gate program in Toronto—a program that helped ex-prisoners re-enter the community—was instrumental in formalizing parole in the early 1900s. Parole, as introduced with the Ticket of Leave Act in 1899, allowed prisoners to be released prior to the end of their prison sentence. As there was no system of parole supervision in the country, parolees were required to report to their local police on a regular basis.

According to the Parole Board of Canada (2015) Archibald traveled across the country—as a volunteer—to meet with offenders who were near their release dates, helping to determine their potential for early release. Archibald was appointed the first Dominion Parole Officer in 1905 and played a leadership role in formalizing parole. He began working with the federal correctional system in 1919. In addition to his role in evaluating prisoners for their potential for parole, Archibald advocated for ex-prisoners returning to the community, helping them find to jobs and re-establish themselves (Murray 2003). Archibald was passionate about his work and delivered many public presentations to community groups about the importance of helping prisoners live crime-free lives.

Justice Joseph Archambault (1879–1964): Royal Commission on Prisons

A Royal Commission headed by Canadian-born Justice Joseph Archambault was formed in 1936 to investigate problems within the federal prison system, including overcrowding, and funding shortfalls during the Great Depression. A series of 16 riots occurred between 1932 and 1937 (Correctional Service of Canada 2014b). Archambault's inquiry, the third in Canadian history (others had been held in 1914 and 1919), lasted two years. One of the challenges facing the federal correctional system of the 1930s was that little had changed in terms of correctional philosophies or orientation since the system had been established in 1867: the philosophy was based on punishment, deterrence, incapacitation, and retribution, with much less emphasis on helping offenders making positive changes that would reduce recidivism.

Archambault rejected prison practices such as the silent system of the 1800s and instead recommended prisoner rehabilitation based on employment, education, and utilizing professionals such as psychologists and teachers. Kidman (1938) notes the commission came up with four recommendations for the correctional system based on (a) protection of society; (b) safe custody of inmates; (c) strict but humane discipline; and (d) reformation and rehabilitation of prisoners. Although these recommendations were made in 1938 they were not put into effect until 1945. What is striking about that list—made 80 years ago—is that it is equally relevant today. Archambault was ahead of his time.

Agnes Macphail (1890–1954): Prison Reformer and Politician

Born in 1921 in Proton Township, Grey County, Ontario, Agnes Macphail was the first woman to become a member of parliament and for her entire career as a federal politician she was an advocate for prison reform. Macphail was also critical of the prison system's focus on incapacitation and punishment (including the use of corporal punishments). She was concerned that little had changed in the goals of corrections since the federal prison system was founded in 1867. Although the shortcomings of the prison system had been identified in reports released in 1914 and 1920, these were not acted upon because of World War I and public and political apathy for change (Crowley 1990).

Macphail had a number of interests, including placing correctional professionals in leadership roles rather than the traditional practice of appointing military officers or political cronies—who knew little about penology—into the top positions in prison systems (see Box 18.2). She was also a passionate advocate for rehabilitation so that once released, ex-prisoners could live productive lives (Crowley 1990:130). According to Macphail, one of the cornerstones of correctional rehabilitation was allowing prisoners to work, although there was political resistance when prisoners manufactured items competing with products made by community businesses. In an effort to reduce the possibility of unfair competition with public firms, prisoners were put to work to make prisons self-supporting (e.g., on prison farms) and to

Box 18.2. Elizabeth Fry and John Howard Societies

Since the 1960s the Elizabeth Fry and John Howard societies have played an increasingly important role in prisoner advocacy. Two of the pioneers profiled in this chapter—Dinnage Hobden and Agnes Macphail—were instrumental in founding these agencies. The John Howard Society of Victoria (2012) describes the history of the organization: "In 1946 the Citizens Service Association in Ontario changed its name and became the John Howard Society of Ontario. Most other provinces formed John Howard Societies between 1947 and 1960. In February of 1962 the John Howard Society of Canada was formed when all provinces, except for Quebec, ratified a constitution. Quebec joined the John Howard Society in 1980. The Northwest Territories joined in 1994."

The John Howard Society has grown into an influential national organization, providing services to provincial and federal inmates and ex-prisoners. In addition to playing an important role in assisting ex-prisoners, the John Howard Society acts as an advocacy organization on behalf of prisoners and their families.

In 1939 Agnes Macphail was instrumental in establishing the first Elizabeth Fry Society in Vancouver, which was named after the British prison reformer (born in 1780) who devoted her life to bettering the conditions for women and children in jails and prisons. Between 1939 and the 1960s the number of Elizabeth Fry Societies expanded throughout the country and a national organization (the Canadian Association of Elizabeth Fry Societies) was formed in 1969 and incorporated in 1978 (Canadian Association of Elizabeth Fry Societies 2015).

make items such as furniture for the federal government (which was the precursor to today's CORCAN correctional industries). Although Macphail was successful in expanding prison industries she also softened public opinion about the need to impose harsh punishments on prisoners.

T. Neil Libby (1930–1978): Community Re-entry

Members of the clergy have always played a role in supporting prisoners during their sentence behind bars and after their release. Before becoming a priest, Father Libby spent the early part of his working career working at the Ford Motor Company. In the early 1950s, he entered Trinity College in

Toronto and studied theology. He later attended Huron College in London where he earned a Licentiate in Theology in 1959. In 1962, Father Libby, an Anglican priest, was instrumental in founding Windsor House, one of the first halfway houses in Canada (where former prisoners live after their release from prison and prior to independent living). Father Libby based his approach on a Chicago halfway house named after St. Leonard, the patron saint of prisoners. The name of Windsor House was later changed to St. Leonard's, and there are now 16 St. Leonard's homes throughout Canada. These homes contract with the Correctional Service of Canada to house parolees. As these halfway homes are often in residential neighbourhoods, Libby and his colleagues had to overcome community resistance to their presence, especially when some of these facilities specialized in housing "lifers" (persons sentenced to terms of life imprisonment) (see Bolton 1982).

Father Libby passed away while attending a meeting of the International Halfway House Association (now known as the International Community Corrections Association), which he founded. A richer accounting of his work can be found in a book Libby co-authored with Archdeacon Bolton, *Halfway Home: The St. Leonard's Society of Canada* (Lone Pine Publications, 1982).

Michael Jackson (1943–): Prisoner Advocacy

Michael Jackson, professor emeritus at the University of British Columbia, has advocated for prisoner and Aboriginal rights since the 1970s. The Correctional Service of Canada (2014) reports that Jackson was instrumental in reforming the disciplinary process in federal prisons by recommending in 1971 that independent disciplinary tribunals be established in order to reduce bias. This was a significant change to the system. The tribunals were implemented in 1980. In addition to teaching law students about prisoner's rights and penal policy, Jackson published two books about Canadian corrections: *Prisoners of Isolation: Solitary Confinement in Canada* (1983) and *Justice Behind the Walls: Human Rights in Canadian Prisons* (2002) (see below).

Jackson earned a number of honours, including the Bora Laskin National Fellowship in Human Rights Research and the Ed McIsaac Human Rights in Corrections Award in 2009, given to individuals "who have demonstrated a lifelong commitment to improving Corrections and protecting the human rights of the incarcerated" (Office of the Correctional Investigator 2014). Jackson's advocacy continues. In 2014 he acted as intervenor in two Supreme Court of Canada cases that ruled that correctional practices abolishing accelerated parole and tougher parole eligibility rules were unconstitutional (Peter A. Allard School of Law 2014) (see Box 18.3).

Donald Andrews (1941–2010): Correctional Scholar

Donald Andrews was an internationally respected leader in the development of correctional interventions, including the Risk, Needs, and Responsivity (RNR) approach to reducing offender recidivism (Andrews and Bonta 2010). That model has been adopted by correctional services across the globe. In keeping with his focus on individual level factors, Andrews and his collaborator James Bonta were instrumental in the creation of a number of psychological tests that predict recidivism. Examples include the Level of Service Inventory-Revised (LSI-R). In addition to tailoring interventions to the unmet needs of the offender, Andrews also believed that correctional staff play a key role in the delivery of effective programs. These efforts centred on the notion that prison programs could respond to the unmet needs of these offenders, thereby reducing the risks that they posed. Andrew's accomplishments were recog-

Box 18.3. The Relationship between Corrections and the Military

One of the challenges in the early days of corrections, both in Canada and abroad, was the practice of appointing military leaders who had little knowledge of corrections to prison administration positions. Agnes Macphail was critical of the fact that senior leadership positions in corrections were given to political appointees or military officers with little expertise, arguing that those positions should be filled by competent individuals with training in penology (Crowley 1990). In the early days of the federal correctional system, there was a close relationship between the military and prisons. Crowley (1990:134) observes that many correctional officers in the 1920s and 1930s had prior military service; he describes them as "petty tyrants."

Putting military leaders in prison administration roles could be frustrating to inmates and staff. For example, in 1932 General D.M. Ormond was made Superintendent of Penitentiaries. According to the Parole Board of Canada (2015), "Between 1932 and 1934, the number of regulations increased from 194 to 724. By the end of his regime in 1938, there would be 1,500 regulations, covering every possible aspect of prison life, even dictating how a guard should tie his shoes!"

Military officers continued to be appointed to correctional leadership positions after World War II. Major-General R.B. Gibson was the first Prison Commissioner of the federal system. Unlike many of his military predecessors, Gibson was committed to reforming the prison system based on the contemporary knowledge of corrections (Correctional Service of Canada 2014).

There was a similar history of politicians appointing their supporters as wardens, superintendents, and to other leadership positions. The problem was that these individuals typically had little expert knowledge of corrections. The field did not advance and opportunities to encourage a more positive attitude to corrections were lost. Yesterday's practices of nepotism and cronyism, however, are now gone; today's correctional leaders are experienced correctional professionals (see Box 18.4).

nized by the American Society of Criminology, the American Probation and Parole Association, the Canadian Psychological Association, the Correctional Service of Canada, and the International Community Corrections Association. In 2012, Frances Cullen of the University of Cincinnati published an article in the journal *Punishment & Society* (14[1]: 94–114) in which he discussed the importance of rehabilitation. The article and issue were dedicated to the work Andrews had done in this field of study.

James Bonta (1949–): Correctional Scholar

Some of Jim Bonta's most noteworthy contributions that have increased our understanding of corrections were the product of partnerships with Donald Andrews. These scholars together introduced several practices that were controversial at the time, including relying upon the least restrictive correctional interventions and prioritizing treatment for medium- and high-risk offenders while not delivering any interventions for those offenders assessed as low risk. Jim Bonta also undertook a large number of initiatives on his own. Bonta, who served as director of the Corrections Research Unit with Public Safety Canada, examined correctional interventions for federally sentenced

Box 18.4. Canadian Correctional Scholarship

Canada has produced several influential correctional scholars and while much of their work emerged in the 1980s and 1990s, their influence continues to grow.

Jean-Claude Bernheim teaches at Laval University and advocates on behalf of prisoners. He has published extensively about their treatment behind bars, including their risk of suicide. In 2008 he was awarded the Ed McIsaac Human Rights in Corrections Award in recognition of his work on behalf of Canadian prisoners.

Donald Andrews, who taught at Carlton University, was instrumental in changing correctional practices after the 1994 publication of *The Psychology of Criminal Conduct* (co-authored by James Bonta). That work, now in its sixth edition, is one of the most highly cited correctional texts.

Paul Gendreau, professor emeritus of psychology at the University of New Brunswick, has also published extensively about corrections. In particular, he has carried out a number of meta-analyses that examined the effectiveness of correctional treatment and rehabilitation. Gendreau's work emphasizes the importance of correctional practices driven by research rather than fads or political agendas. In recognition of his contributions he was appointed to the Order of Canada in 2007.

Stephen Wormith serves as director of the Centre for Forensic Behavioural Science and Justice Studies at the University of Saskatchewan. Wormith has published extensively on offender rehabilitation and the factors associated with the successful transition from prison to the community. In addition, his work on risk assessment with adult and youthful offenders is highly cited and well regarded.

offenders and was also instrumental in developing strategies that increased the effectiveness of provincial probation officers, such as the strategic training initiative in community supervision (STICS). An idea that underlies all Bonta's work was the application of research in the development of community and custodial strategies intended to reduce recidivism and enhance public safety.

Howard Sapers (1957–): The Prisoner's Ombudsman

The Office of the Correctional Investigator (OCI) was created in 1973 after an investigation into a 1971 riot at Kingston Penitentiary recommended that an independent body be formed to respond to prisoner concerns (Office of the Correctional Investigator 2013). The Correctional Investigator acts as a federal

> **Box 18.5. Contributions by Scholars in the Correctional System**
>
> In addition to traditional academic scholarship, the federal government has provided considerable support for correctional research within Public Safety Canada, the Correctional Service of Canada, and the Parole Board of Canada, and all three of these agencies have research divisions. A number of notable researchers came from these agencies.
>
> **James Bonta** spent most of his career with Public Safety Canada, and although much of his recognition comes from the work he did with Donald Andrews, he is also well-regarded for his work on risk assessment and studies focusing on offenders being supervised in the community.
>
> **Mary Campbell** worked with Public Safety Canada in a number of roles prior to her retirement in 2013. Although she was a productive scholar, she is best known for her work as director general of the Corrections and Criminal Justice Division, and she still advocates for criminal justice practices that are driven by what the research demonstrates as effective, rather than "tough-on-crime" political agendas.
>
> **Karl Hanson** has carried out research on sex offenders for over two decades and his research is highly cited. Much of Hanson's current scholarship focuses on the development and examination of different instruments to predict sex offender recidivism.
>
> Other government researchers are less well known, but have played an important role in advancing correctional research. They include Frank Proporino, Larry Motiuk, and Brian Grant, who all served as director general of the Research Branch with the Correctional Service of Canada. Today Frank Proporino is heavily involved with the International Corrections and Prison Association (ICPA) and chairs the research and development expert group as well as serving as editor of the association's peer-reviewed journal.

ombudsman and is empowered to take complaints from federal prisoners about their treatment, investigate those complaints (as well as other relevant correctional operations), and make recommendations about the delivery of federal correctional services to the Solicitor General.

Howard Sapers is a former member of the Alberta Legislative Assembly (1997–2001), with extensive experience in public service. This includes holding senior positions with the Parole Board of Canada as vice-chair and serving as executive director of the John Howard Society of Alberta (1982–1993), as well as working for the National Crime Prevention Centre (2001–2003). He was also vice-chairperson of the National Parole Board—Prairies Region (2003–2004).

Sapers served as Correctional Investigator between 2004 and 2016. His role was significant. He led the OCI at a time of growth in prisoner numbers but also reductions in federal funding. Other (often related) problems included overcrowding, more prisoners suffering from mental illness, higher rates of inmate self-harm and suicide as well as deaths in custody, and greater numbers of Aboriginal and black offenders in the system (see Box 18.6).

Box 18.6. Correctional Service of Canada Commissioners

The Commissioner of the Correctional Service of Canada (CSC) leads nearly 18,000 employees working within 43 institutions, 92 parole offices, 15 community correctional centres, and the national headquarters (Correctional Service of Canada 2013; Public Safety Canada 2015). Commissioners play a key role in ensuring these employees are working together toward a common purpose: increasing public safety. According to the Correctional Service of Canada (2014d) the following individuals have served as Commissioners since 1977: Don Head (2008 to present); Keith Coulter (2005–2008); Lucie McClung (2000–2005); Ole Ingstrup (1996–2000 and 1988–1992); John Edwards (1993– 1996); Rheal J. Leblanc (1985–1988); and Don Yeomans (1977–1985)

The pathway to the Commissioner's office typically takes decades with considerable experience gained as correctional or parole officers, program specialists, and wardens prior to working in administrative positions in the national headquarters. These administrative experiences usually include appointments that expose these individuals to policy development, human resource management, the financial knowledge to operate an organization with a budget approaching $3 billion, and a comprehensive understanding of offender programming.

Each of these Commissioners has influenced the CSC by advancing a vision of an effective correctional system. For example, Ole Ingstrup was instrumental in carrying out the reforms recommended by the Task Force on Federally Sentenced Women (Moffat 1991). The current Commissioner, Don Head, has overseen the CSC during a time when the prison population has undergone a significant change in terms of demographic characteristics (e.g., there are more Aboriginal and black offenders), the incidence of mental health problems, as well as an upswing in prison gang membership (Correctional Service of Canada 2010).

Rev. Harry Nigh: Founder, Circles of Support and Accountability

Circles of Support and Accountability (CoSA) is a volunteer-based community re-entry program for high-risk sexual offenders. CoSA was formed in 1994 after a high-risk sexual offender named Charles Taylor was released from prison at the end of his sentence, but had nowhere to go and no community resources (Wilson et al. 2007). Correctional officials contacted Nigh, a pastor at a Mennonite church in Ontario, to help Taylor make a transition to the community. Nigh had worked with ex-offenders since 1973. He was able to gather a small group of volunteers together in what they called a "circle" to support Taylor's re-entry to the community. The volunteers met with Taylor and provided encouragement, friendship, mentoring and support in tasks such as finding a residence—support that few ex-offenders enjoy. Charlie Taylor died in 2006 after remaining crime-free for the entire 12 years following his release. Harry Nigh continues to work with ex-offenders as a chaplain (Tubb 2015).

CoSA is based on the notion that ex-prisoners benefit from support, both in managing everyday problems (such as getting to medical appointments, finding a safe place to live, or obtaining a job) and by having the support of other people who care about them. The CoSA concept was formalized in 1996 and there are now 18 sites across Canada providing support to ex-prisoners. The CoSA approach has also been exported to other nations and research has showed that it is an effective method of reducing sex-offender recidivism (Chouinard and Riddick 2015).

Conclusions

The innovation and practices that made Canada a world leader in the delivery of correctional programs focusing on offender rehabilitation were shaped by a number of pioneers over the past two centuries. The roles these individuals played were diverse, ranging from advocacy to scholarship. In addition, the importance of the clergy in working toward positive change in Canadian corrections cannot be underestimated. It would be impossible to determine which of these individuals played the most significant role, but there are a number of attributes that all shared, including advocacy, risk-taking, and compassion for offenders. It is important to acknowledge the risks that many of these individuals took in their steps to develop more effective ways of treating society's wrongdoers.

In this chapter the efforts of a number of pioneers were briefly described. Many other Canadians have made significant contributions to improving the lives of prisoners within institutions and helping them re-enter society, but their efforts have gone unpublished. The impact of their advocacy and hard work persists, however, because it enabled correctional officials, reformers, and other stakeholders to advocate for interventions based on just and humane rehabilitative models. As a result, Canadian correctional systems have resisted the worst aspects of the tough-on-crime policies adopted in the United States.

It is difficult to predict how the future of corrections in Canada will be shaped by today's pioneers and trailblazers. In the past, correctional reform has been driven primarily by individuals with a passion for social justice and the fair and humane treatment of offenders. In most cases the biggest contributions have been made by individuals from outside the formal correctional or political systems. The nature of corrections, however, has changed over time, becoming more professional and inclusive. Also, women and Aboriginal persons are playing a more significant role. The appointment of **Lucie McClung** as the first female commissioner of the CSC in 2000 represented a significant step forward for the field of corrections, and the contributions of women such as Mary Campbell have helped establish Canada as a world leader in corrections. Only time will tell the long-term impact of these individuals on offender rehabilitation and correctional management.

References

Links

Canadian Association of Elizabeth Fry Societies, http://www.caefs.ca/
Correctional Service of Canada, http://www.csc-scc.gc.ca/index-eng.shtml
John Howard Society of Canada, http://www.johnhoward.ca/
Office of the Correctional Investigator, http://www.oci-bec.gc.ca/index-eng.aspx

References

Andrews, D.A., and Bonta, J. (2010). *Psychology of Criminal Conduct*. London: Routledge.

Applegate, B.K., and Sitren, A.H. (2008). The jail and the community: Comparing jails in rural and urban contexts. *The Prison Journal* 88(2):252–269.

Bolton, K. (1982). *Halfway Home: St. Leonard's Society*. Edmonton: Lone Pine Publishing.

Brown, J.M. (1975). Influences affecting the treatment of women prisoners in Toronto, 1880–1890. Waterloo, ON: Wilfrid Laurier University, MA Thesis.

Canadian Association of Elizabeth Fry Societies. (2015). *About Us*. Retrieved from http://www.caefs.ca/about-us/

Chouinard, J.A., and Riddick, C. (2015). *An Evaluation of the Circles of Support and Accountability Demonstration Project*. Ottawa: Author.

Comeau, G.M. (1998). Hanna, William John. *Dictionary of Canadian Biography*. Retrieved from http://www.biographi.ca/en/bio/hanna_william_john_14E.html.

Commissioner of Penitentiaries. (1961). Leclerc institution opened by Minister of Justice. *Federal Corrections* 1(2):10–11.

Commissioner of Penitentiaries. (1968). Penitentiary complex in Quebec region offers variety of training. *Federal Corrections* 7(3):7–8.

Correctional Service of Canada. (2010). *Profile of a Canadian Offender*. Ottawa: Author.

Correctional Service of Canada. (2013). *CSC Statistics: Key Facts and Figures*. Retrieved from http://www.csc-scc.gc.ca/publications/005007-3024-eng.shtml.

Correctional Service of Canada. (2014a). *Correctional Programs*. Retrieved from http://www.csc-scc.gc.ca/correctional-process/002001-2001-eng.shtml

Correctional Service of Canada. (2014b). *1920–1939: Through Adversity*. Retrieved from http://www.csc-scc.gc.ca/about-us/006-2002-eng.shtml.

Correctional Service of Canada. (2014c). *Pre-1920: From Punishment to Penance*. Retrieved from http://www.csc-scc.gc.ca/about-us/006-2001-eng.shtml.

Correctional Service of Canada. (2014d). *CSC Commissioners (1977–2014)*. Retrieved from http://www.csc-scc.gc.ca/about-us/006-2007-eng.shtml.

Correctional Services Program. (2015). *Adult Correctional Statistics in Canada, 2013/2014*. Ottawa: Canadian Centre for Justice Statistics.

Crowley, T. (1990). *Agnes Macphail and the Politics of Equality*. Toronto: James Lorimer & Company.

Curtis, D., Graham, A., Kelly, L., and Patterson, A. (1985). *Kingston Penitentiary: The First Hundred and Fifty Years*. Ottawa: Correctional Service of Canada.

Edmison, J.A. (1953). The eternal problem of crime and criminals. *Queen's Quarterly* 60(3): 243–252.

Ekstedt, J.W., and Griffiths, C.T. (1988). *Corrections in Canada: Policy and Practice*, 2nd ed. Toronto: Butterworths.

Fyson, D. (2006). *Magistrates, Police, and People: Everyday Criminal Justice in Quebec and Lower Canada, 1764–1837*. Toronto: University of Toronto Press.

John Howard Society of Alberta. (1988). *Inmate Rights and Grievance Options*. Edmonton: Author.

John Howard Society of Victoria. (2012). *Our History*. Retrieved from http://www.johnhoward.victoria.bc.ca/history.html.

Jones, M. (2005). *Criminal Justice Pioneers in U.S. History*. Boston: Allyn and Bacon.

Kennedy, P. (2013). Icon of evil: 178 years of mistrust, loathing and fear at Kingston Pen. *Toronto Sun*. Retrieved from http://www.torontosun.com/2013/09/26/icon-of-evil-178-years-of-mistrust-loathing-and-fear-at-kingston-pen.

Kidman, J. (1938). Prison reform in Canada: The report on the Royal Commission on penal system. *Howard Journal of Criminal Justice* 5(2): 112–115.

Leyton-Brown, K. (2010). *The Practice of Execution in Canada*. Vancouver: UBC Press.

McCoy, T. (2012). *Hard Time: Reforming the Penitentiary in Nineteenth-Century Canada*. Edmonton: Athabasca Press.

Moffat, K.H. (1991). Creating choices or repeating history: Canadian female offenders and correctional reform. *Social Justice* 18(3): 184–203.

Murray, D.R. (2003). *Archibald, Walter Palmer*. Retrieved from http://www.biographi.ca/en/bio/archibald_walter_palmer_15E.html.

Nickerson, J. (2010). *Crime and Punishment in Upper Canada: A Researcher's Guide*. Toronto: Dundurn Press.

Office of the Correctional Investigator. (2013). *FAQ's*. Retrieved from http://www.oci-bec.gc.ca/cnt/faq-eng.aspx.

Office of the Correctional Investigator. (2014). *Professor Michael Jackson of the University of British Columbia receives the inaugural Ed McIsaac Human Rights in Corrections Award*. Retrieved from http://www.oci-bec.gc.ca/cnt/comm/press/press20090901-eng.aspx.

Oliver, P. (1994). "To govern by kindness": The first two decades of the Mercer reformatory for women. In J. Phillips, T. Loo, and Lewthwaite, S. (Eds.) *Crime and Criminal Justice* (pp. 516–572). Toronto: Osgoode Society and University of Toronto Press.

Oliver, P. (1998). *Terror to Evil-doers: Prisons and Punishments in Nineteenth-Century Ontario*. Toronto: University of Toronto Press.

Ontario Ministry of Correctional Services. (2012). A history of corrections. *Trillium* 13(3): 12.

Parole Board of Canada. (2015). *History of parole in Canada*. Retrieved from http://pbc-clcc.gc.ca/about/hist-eng.shtml.

Peter A. Allard School of Law. (2014). *Supreme Court Victory for Professor Michael Jackson*. Retrieved from http://www.allard.ubc.ca/news-events/ubc-law-news/supreme-court-victory-professor-michael-jackson.

Public Safety Canada. (2015). *Corrections and Conditional Release: Statistical Review*. Ottawa: Author.

Rose, G.M. (1888). *A Cyclopaedia of Canadian Biography: Being Chiefly Men of the*

Time. Toronto: Rose Publishing Company.

Strange, C. (1983). *The Velvet Glove: Maternalistic Reform at the Andrew Mercer Ontario Reformatory for Females 1874–1927*. Unpublished thesis: University of Ottawa.

Thomson, A., Clairmont, D., and Clairmont L. (2003). *Policing the Valley: Small Town and Rural Policing in Nova* Scotia. Halifax, NS: Dalhousie University, Atlantic Institute of Criminology.

Tubb, E. (2015). Chaplains keep up work with parolees—even without a paycheque. *The Star*. Retrieved from http://www.thestar.com/news/canada/2015/01/23/chaplains-keep-up-work-with-parolees-even-without-a-paycheque.htm.

Wetherell, D.B. (1979). To discipline and train: Adult rehabilitation programmes in Ontario prisons, 1874- 1900. *Social History* 12(23): 145–165.

Wilson, R.J., McWhinnie, A., Picheca, J.E., Prinzo, M., and Cortoni, F. (2007). Circles of support and accountability: Engaging community volunteers in the management of high-risk sexual offenders. *The Howard Journal* 46(1): 1–15.

Closing Thoughts

When I started to work on this book, I had no clear sense of how it would turn out. But, as I noted in the Introduction, it was an initiative that I had long wanted to undertake. At the outset, I probably had a narrower interpretation of what I meant by "pioneers"; however, the input and feedback I received from various colleagues across the country helped to broaden the book's scope. Yet, as also noted in the Introduction, some of my aspirations for this book had to be compromised for various reasons. Therefore, while I am genuinely touched by everyone who agreed to participate, I remain somewhat disappointed that I wasn't able to include other eminent pioneers and/or scholars. Another volume may well be in order to rectify any omissions or oversights.

For example, many students of pioneers covered in this book (along with students trained by other scholars prominent in the field) have already made their own mark on the discipline. Although **Julian V. Roberts** (formerly of the University of Ottawa) hasn't taught in Canada for some years now, an article surveying the most cited scholars in the *British Journal of Criminology* between 2006 and 2010 ranked Roberts ranked 34.5 of the top 50, with 33 citations in the journal. Meanwhile, **Richard V. Ericson** (see chapter 12) was ranked tenth with 57 citations. In terms of the *CJC* (*Canadian Journal of Criminology and Criminal Justice*), the top three were **Julian Roberts** (33 citations), **Anthony Doob** (32 citations; see chapter 11), and **Richard V. Ericson** (30 citations). Some of the younger pioneers not covered in this book but who also made the Top 50 list include **Kevin Haggerty** (University of Alberta, 16 citations), **Peter Carrington** (University of Waterloo, 15 citations), **Pierre Bourdieu** (14 citations), **Scot Wortley** (University of Toronto, 14 citations), **Jennifer Schulenberg** (University of Waterloo, 13 citations), and, from "the field," correctional investigator and adjunct professor at Carlton University **Ivan Zinger** (10 citations) (Cohn and Iratzoqui 2016).

As impressive as it is to be ranked among the most cited scholars in the field, it should also be noted that some scholars make their contributions in other ways. Some, for example, publish across a wide array of international journals, while others have published numerous books and/or government reports. Still others have not only generated a considerable body of research themselves but have supervised numerous students who have gone on to make their own mark in the field. Some of the entries in this book reflect the fact that many of the "new" pioneers are linked in some fashion to earlier scholars. For example, the entries for Szabo, Ericson, and Brodeaur were all prepared by former students who themselves have established very respectable careers. In other words, the criminology/criminal justice community is not only small but closely linked and intertwined.

In the spirit of ethnographic field study and narrative inquiry, I chose not to impose constraints on the entries prepared by the pioneers themselves. As the esteemed American sociologist David Matza (1969) observed, and I paraphrase, I approached this project as one who wanted to try to capture the nuances of the pioneers, appreciating their stories, rather than trying to "correct" them. As Kim (2016) points out, stories "always have something to tell us about stories themselves: They always involve self-reflexive and metafictional dimensions" (p. 9). Inevitably, then, there is considerable variation in how different pioneers recounted their careers and contributions to the field. On the other hand, most of the entries I prepared myself, as well as the final three chapters in the book, follow a more conventional narrative structure. In any event, I hope this work will inspire others to be aware of the history of our discipline and perhaps investigate that history themselves. Should a follow-up volume eventually be published, no doubt some of the pioneers included in it will have left their mark in areas virtually unknown to the very earliest pioneers, including forensic science, cyber-research, the links between mental health and crime, intimate partner violence, transnational crimes, and so on.

Now that more than half a century has passed since the first criminology and criminal justice programs were established in Canada, the names of some of the field's pioneers have begun to fade from prominence. Fortunately, several awards and distinctions ensure their legacy remains "alive" in some manner. When I first visited the University of Amsterdam, which has a small criminology program, I noted that its building, the Bonger Institute, was named after arguably their most famous criminologist, Willem A. Bonger (1876–1940) (a critical criminologist; see Bemmelen 1955). Similarly, in England, the Institute of Criminology at the University of Cambridge named their library the Radzinowicz Library after Sir Leon Radzinowicz, the first director of the Institute (1952–72). Similar examples can be found across Canada. The documentation centre at the International Centre for Comparative Criminology at the Université de Montréal was called the Denis Szabo Centre until it unfortunately was closed in 2012. The university still offers the Prix Denis Szabo recognizing the best scholarly articles published in French, as well as the Prix Jean-Paul Brodeur, established in 2011, which is awarded to an outstanding student whose work bridges theory and practice. Its first recipient (2009–10) was also the first Indigenous woman in Canada to receive a Ph.D. in criminology, **Lisa Monchalin** (now at Kwantlen University in British Columbia). Similarly, the criminology program at the University of Ottawa offers an award in honour of Tadeusz Grygier (the Tadeusz Grygier Founder's Graduate/Undergraduate Prize).

Some final thoughts. I set out several basic goals when I first pitched the idea for this book to the publisher. First and foremost, I wanted to prepare a dynamically structured resource that would offer a fair and reasonably comprehensive accounting of some of the key actors in Canadian criminology and criminal justice, and to share some of their most important ideas, research, and published work. I also hoped that I would be able to capture the spirit of what it takes to be a "pioneer." Another objective was to document the evolution of criminology and criminal justice programs in Canada, as well as to provide a descriptive overview of some of significant figures in the areas of law enforcement, the legal system, and corrections.

Finally, as with any published work, much as I have managed to accomplish in this book, there no doubt remain some hopes that are unfulfilled. That said, I trust that I have not misrepresented the contributions of those profiled in this volume, nor, I hope, would the limited coverage I was able to afford others be taken as a sign of disrespect. While I accept responsibility for any of the book's limitations or omissions, my hope is that the reader will look beyond any shortcomings and value the book for the reasons it was compiled in the first place. If I have accomplished this, then the exercise has indeed been rewarding on a number of levels.

JOHN WINTERDYK

References

Bemmelen, van J.M. (1955). Pioneers in criminology VIII: Willem Adriaan Bonger (1876–1940). *Journal of Criminal Law and Criminology* 46(3):293–302.

Cohn, E.G., and Iratziqui, A. (2016). The most cited scholars in five international criminology journals, 2006–10. *British Journal of Criminology* 56(3):602–623.

Kim, J-H. (2016). *Understanding Narrative Inquiry*. Los Angeles: Sage.

Matza, D. (1969). *Becoming Deviant.* Englewood Cliffs, NJ: Prentice Hall.

Index of Names